NEGLIGENCE AND ILLEGALITY

This book examines claims in negligence arising from illegal conduct of the claimant. An array of public policy and other grounds have been advanced for resolving these claims, resulting in an area that is characterised by confusing and contradictory case law. The book analyses the various explanations put forward as the basis for illegality doctrine within a framework of corrective justice theory. Illegality law poses particular challenges for the corrective justice explanation of negligence law, as many illegality tests are based on public policy considerations external to the relationship of the parties. The book argues that the only circumstance where illegality doctrine should be applied to deny a claim is where this is necessary to preserve the coherence of the legal system. It develops the work of Weinribian corrective justice theorists to explain how the principle of legal coherence fits within the framework of corrective justice theory, and why legal coherence is the only valid conceptual basis for a doctrine of illegality. It also contains a detailed study on the scope of the coherence rationale and the principles that will determine its application.

Volume 20 in the series Hart Studies in Private Law

Negligence and Illegality

Sharon Erbacher

HART PUBLISHING
OXFORD AND PORTLAND, OREGON
2017

Hart Publishing
An imprint of Bloomsbury Publishing Plc

Hart Publishing Ltd
Kemp House
Chawley Park
Cumnor Hill
Oxford OX2 9PH
UK

Bloomsbury Publishing Plc
50 Bedford Square
London
WC1B 3DP
UK

www.hartpub.co.uk
www.bloomsbury.com

Published in North America (US and Canada) by
Hart Publishing
c/o International Specialized Book Services
920 NE 58th Avenue, Suite 300
Portland, OR 97213-3786
USA

www.isbs.com

First published 2017

British Library Cataloguing-in-Publication Data
A catalogue record for this book is available from the British Library.

ISBN: HB: 978-1-50990-666-6
ePDF: 978-1-50990-668-0
ePub: 978-1-50990-667-3

Library of Congress Cataloging-in-Publication Data

Names: Erbacher, Sharon, author.

Title: Negligence and illegality / Sharon Erbacher.

Description: Oxford ; Portland, Oregon : Hart Publishing, an imprint of Bloomsbury Publishing Plc, 2017. | Series: Hart studies in private law ; volume 20 | Based on author's thesis (doctoral - Deakin University, Australia, 2015) issued under title: Negligence and the wrongdoing plaintiff : a corrective justice analysis. | Includes bibliographical references and index.

Identifiers: LCCN 2016037918 (print) | LCCN 2016038125 (ebook) | ISBN 9781509906666 (hardback : alk. paper) | ISBN 9781509906673 (Epub)

Subjects: LCSH: Liability (Law) | Illegality. | Restorative justice. | Torts—English-speaking countries.

Classification: LCC K923 .E73 2017 (print) | LCC K923 (ebook) | DDC 346.03/2—dc23

LC record available at https://lccn.loc.gov/2016037918

Typeset by Compuscript Ltd, Shannon
Printed and bound in Great Britain by Lightning Source UK Ltd

PREFACE

The law of illegality is still in turmoil nearly a quarter of a millennium after Lord Mansfield's sweeping pronouncement in *Holman v Johnson* that a court should not enforce a claim based on illegal conduct.[1] In the United Kingdom in particular, the proper basis of illegality doctrine continues to be vigorously debated. The UK Supreme Court now appears to have abandoned attempts to identify a principled basis for illegality doctrine, retreating in *Patel v Mirza* to a discretionary approach where context-specific policy considerations are weighed together with the proportionality of refusing relief.[2] As *Patel v Mirza* was handed down after the manuscript of this book had been submitted, it has not been possible to include a detailed analysis of that decision and its possible implications for negligence actions. I have, however, included some brief observations about it in Chapter 4, and my general criticisms of a policy and discretionary approach in that chapter apply equally to *Patel v Mirza* as to earlier decisions advocating a flexible approach.

I have argued that a policy approach is conceptually incoherent and inimical to the stability of private law illegality doctrine. Instead I have sought to establish that legal coherence is the only valid conceptual basis for a doctrine of illegality in negligence law, relying on reasoning of corrective justice to support this conclusion. While corrective justice theory has its critics, I seek to demonstrate that it provides a valid framework for resolving negligence claims connected to illegal conduct. The objective of the book is not only to develop the law relating to illegality, but also to develop an understanding of the application of principled reasoning of corrective justice to negligence claims.

I owe a particular debt to Allan Beever and his ground-breaking work, *Rediscovering the Law of Negligence*. This work not only influenced the direction of my own thoughts regarding the subject matter of this book, but helped to clarify my views about the theoretical structure of negligence law more generally. I am also very grateful to Professor Beever for his detailed feedback on my doctoral thesis on which this book is based, as well as to the other examiners for their constructive comments. A huge thanks also to my doctoral supervisors, Mirko Bagaric and Danuta Mendelson, for their assistance throughout the thesis writing process and for encouraging me to develop the work into a book.

1 *Holman v Johnson* [1775] 1 Cowp 342 [98 ER 1120].
2 *Patel v Mirza* [2016] UKSC 42.

The review and production process was conducted professionally and efficiently from beginning to end: thank you to all those at Hart Publishing and elsewhere who were involved.

The completion of a major research project extending over a number of years inevitably impacts on personal relationships. Many thanks to Damir for his support and patience during the writing process. Special thanks also to my parents Des and Glenda for their continual support and encouragement.

This book is based on the law as at 1 May 2016, other than the inclusion of commentary on *Patel v Mirza* at the proof stage.

Sharon Erbacher

CONTENTS

TABLE OF CASES

Australia

Canada

Singapore

United Kingdom

United States

TABLE OF LEGISLATION

Australia

1

Introduction

I. The Disordered State of Illegality Doctrine

Illegality doctrine 'skulks furtively' behind the maxim *ex turpi causa non oritur actio* ('an action arises not from a base cause').[1] This maxim is embodied in Lord Mansfield's famous declaration in 1775 in *Holman v Johnson* that 'No court will lend its aid to a man who founds his cause of action upon an immoral or an illegal act'.[2] Such statements are a reflection of the fundamental tenet of jurisprudence that a person should not profit from his or her wrong.[3]

In contemporary times the *ex turpi causa* maxim is considered 'too extreme and inflexible to represent sound legal policy',[4] and an unreliable guide to determining claims arising from an illegality. Modern courts have recognised that the maxim 'begs many questions',[5] and cannot 'provide a simple measuring rod for determining the boundaries of the principle'.[6] It does not establish a rationale or test for a principle of illegality, or explain why the court will not lend its aid to a claim founded on an illegal act.[7]

It is now accepted that there is no inflexible principle that a person who commits an illegal act is denied the right to recover compensation in negligence: 'no person becomes a *caput lupinum*, or an outlaw, in the eyes of the civil law merely because that person was engaged in some unlawful act'.[8]

[1] *Hall v Hebert* [1993] 2 SCR 159, 208–09 (Cory J).

[2] *Holman v Johnson* [1775] 1 Cowp 341, 343 [98 ER 1120, 1121].

[3] *Riggs v Palmer* (1889) 115 NY 506, 22 NE 188; *Cleaver v Mutual Reserve Fund Life Association* [1892] 1 QB 147; *Hall v Hebert* (n 1) 172–75 (McLachlin J, La Forest, L'Heureux-Dubé and Iacobucci JJ agreeing); *R (on the application of Best) v The Chief Land Registrar* [2015] EWCA Civ 17, [2016] QB 23 [43] (Sales LJ, McCombe LJ agreeing); *Edwards v State Trustees Limited* [2016] VSCA 28.

[4] *Nelson v Nelson* (1995) 184 CLR 538, 611 (McHugh J).

[5] *Bilta (UK) Ltd (in liquidation) v Nazir (No 2)* [2015] UKSC 23, [2016] AC 1 [60] (Lord Sumption). See also RA Buckley, *Illegality and Public Policy*, 2nd edn (London, Thomson Reuters, 2009) 1.

[6] *Les Laboratoires Servier v Apotex Inc* [2015] AC 430, [2014] UKSC 55 [57] (Lord Toulson). The High Court of Australia in *Miller v Miller* has also commented that the maxim is unhelpful due to its generality: [2011] HCA 9, (2011) 242 CLR 446, 454 [13] (French CJ, Gummow, Hayne, Crennan, Kiefel and Bell JJ).

[7] *Les Laboratoires Servier v Apotex Inc* [2012] EWCA Civ 593 [65] (Etherton LJ, Kitchin LJ and Laws LJ agreeing) (*Servier* CA).

[8] *Hall v Hebert* (n 1) 183 (McLachlin J, La Forest, L'Heureux-Dubé and Iacobucci JJ agreeing). See also *Miller v Miller* (n 6) [11] (French CJ, Gummow, Hayne, Crennan, Kiefel and Bell JJ).

A person who has broken the law enjoys rights 'not only in theory but enforceable in practice'.[9]

Nevertheless, there is widespread judicial acceptance that the public interest requires that there are some cases where a court should refuse an award of damages to a claimant where the loss is connected to an illegal act.[10] The problem is that the conceptual basis for illegality doctrine has proved elusive, and as a result courts have struggled to identify a single formula or comprehensive test to identify those cases where illegality doctrine should apply.[11] It is an area of law that is 'notoriously untidy',[12] and where there is a broad spectrum of views, all strongly held. The lack of a clear conceptual framework for the application of a principle of illegality has resulted in anomalous results and contradictory decisions,[13] and to unpredictable and inconsistent application of rules of public policy. Lord Sumption has observed that this area of law is characterised by 'a large body of inconsistent authority, which rarely arises to the level of general principle'.[14] Lord Hughes, likewise, has commented on the difficulty of identifying in the authorities 'a generalised statement of the conceptual basis for the doctrine under which illegality may bar a civil claim'.[15]

Lord Sumption has observed that the main reason for the chaotic state of the law is that courts have a distaste for applying their own rules because of the potential for the application of illegality doctrine to produce disproportionately harsh outcomes.[16] Judges have striven to reach a just outcome in the case before them, but this has been at the expense of the coherence and stability of principle.[17] This has led to a voluminous body of confusing and contradictory case law.

Before providing a brief overview of the different approaches advanced for resolving this type of claim, it is helpful to first explain the taxonomy of this area in the negligence context.

II. Taxonomy of Illegality Claims in Negligence Law

A. Categories of Claims Arising from an Illegality

There are three main contexts in which a defendant might raise the claimant's illegality as an answer to a claim in negligence. The first is where the claimant claims

[9] *Cross v Kirkby* [2000] EWCA Civ 426, [94] (Judge LJ).

[10] *Les Laboratoires Servier v Apotex Inc* (n 6) [23] (Lord Sumption, Lords Neuberger and Clarke agreeing); *Bilta (UK) Ltd (in liquidation) v Nazir (No 2)* (n 5) [60] (Lord Sumption).

[11] *Hounga v Allen* [2014] UKSC 47 [54] (Lord Hughes, Lord Carnwath agreeing).

[12] *Les Laboratoires Servier v Apotex Inc* (n 6) [57] (Lord Toulson).

[13] *Servier* CA (n 7) [63] (Etherton LJ, Kitchin and Laws LJJ agreeing).

[14] *Les Laboratoires Servier v Apotex Inc* (n 6) [14] (Lord Sumption, Lords Neuberger and Clarke agreeing).

[15] *Hounga v Allen* (n 11) Lord Hughes, (Lord Carnwath agreeing).

[16] Lord Sumption, 'Reflections on the Law of Illegality' (2012) *Restitution Law Review* 1, 2.

[17] ibid 3.

compensation for injuries sustained during the course of committing an illegal act. The illegal act might be committed in the course of a joint illegal venture with the defendant (joint illegality cases) or by the claimant acting alone (unilateral illegality cases). The archetypal joint illegality case involves a claim by a passenger in a motor vehicle for injuries negligently inflicted by the driver in circumstances where the parties at the time were jointly engaged in an illegal activity. That illegal activity might involve, for example, the unlawful taking and use of a motor vehicle;[18] reckless and dangerous driving;[19] attempting to flee the scene of a crime or to avoid a police pursuit,[20] or the transportation of illegal or stolen property.[21] Claims arising from a joint illegality have generally been rejected at least where the offence was of a serious nature.[22] A typical claim arising from an unilateral act of illegality is where a trespasser suffers injuries in the course of the trespass due to the negligence of an occupier; for example, where the claimant suffers injuries as a result of an electric shock received while attempting to remove electrical wires from overhead power lines to sell as scrap metal.[23] These claims have succeeded at common law,[24] though in Australia now fall to be determined (other than in Victoria) under statutory defences.[25]

The second context where a plea of illegality might be raised to defend a negligence claim is where the claimant is claiming for losses that are causally related to an illegal act committed by the claimant in circumstances where the defendant negligently caused (or failed to prevent) the claimant from engaging in that act. The most important claim of this type is the 'sanction-shifting' claim—so called because the claimant seeks to deflect the consequences of a criminal sanction onto the individual whose negligence was responsible for the imposition of the sanction. The claim might involve compensation for a statutory penalty,[26] or for other losses resulting from the claimant's conviction and detention for the illegal act. The case of *Gray v Thames Trains Ltd* provides an example.[27] The claimant suffered post-traumatic stress disorder arising out of a rail collision caused by the defendant's negligence. While under the effects of this disorder, the claimant stabbed a man to death and was sentenced to a period of detention in a psychiatric hospital. The claimant claimed damages from the defendant for, inter alia, loss

[18] *Smith v Jenkins* [1970] HCA 2, (1970) 119 CLR 397; *Gala v Preston* [1991] HCA 18, (1991) 172 CLR 243; *Miller v Miller* (n 6).

[19] *Pitts v Hunt* [1991] 2 QB 24 (CA).

[20] *Fabre v Arenales* (1992) 27 NSWLR 437; *Ashton v Turner* [1981] QB 137; *Joyce v O'Brien* [2014] EWCA Civ 546, [2014] 1 WLR 70.

[21] *Godbolt v Fittock* [1963] SR (NSW) 617; *Delaney v Pickett* [2011] EWCA Civ 1532, [2012] 1 WLR 2149.

[22] See, for example, *Smith v Jenkins* (n 18), *Gala v Preston* (n 18), *Joyce v O'Brien* (n 20).

[23] *Austin v The Electricity Networks Corporation* [2014] WASCA 89.

[24] See, for example, *Henwood v Municipal Tramways Trust (South Australia)* [1938] HCA 35, (1938) 60 CLR 438, *Revill v Newbery* [1996] QB 567 (CA). However, the English Courts have generally taken a stricter approach to unilateral illegality claims than their Australian counterparts: see, eg, *Vellino v Chief Constable of the Greater Manchester Police* [2001] EWCA Civ 1249, [2002] 1 WLR 218.

[25] See the legislation in n 84.

[26] *Colburn v Patmore* (1834) 149 ER 999; *Safeway Stores Ltd v Twigger* [2010] EWCA Civ 1472, [2011] 2 All ER 841.

[27] *Gray v Thames Trains Ltd* [2009] UKHL33, [2009] 1 AC 1339.

of earning capacity from the date of the manslaughter, non-pecuniary damages for the loss of reputation and for the feelings of guilt and remorse suffered, and an indemnity against civil claims by the dependants of his victim. The House of Lords refused to award compensation for any of these losses, an outcome consistent with the approach taken by courts in Australia and Canada.[28] While these claims can include a claim for compensation for losses that are not the result of the imposition of a legal sanction (such as non-pecuniary damages for the claimant's feelings of guilt and remorse for the crime), it will be convenient to refer to claims of this type as 'sanction-shifting and related claims'.

The third context in which the claimant's illegality might become relevant is where the defendant's negligence prevents a claimant from earning an income or deriving a profit from an illegal activity; for example, a claimant injured through the defendant's negligence seeks to recover damages for loss of earning capacity resulting from the inability to continue pursuing a criminal occupation.[29] Claims of this kind will be referred to as 'claims for illegal profits and earnings'. These claims are generally rejected on the ground that recovery of compensation would permit claimants to profit from their wrongdoing.[30]

B. Review of the Current Law

In this section I will briefly review the case law in Australia, England and Canada as it applies to the three categories of claim identified in the preceding section. My purpose in conducting this review is to identify the deficiencies of the prevailing law and the areas where further development is needed.

i. The Physical Injury Cases

The High Court of Australia has, over time, advanced a number of different rationales for denying compensation for injuries sustained during the course of participation in a joint illegal venture,[31] but has permitted claims arising out of an act of unilateral illegality unless incompatible with the purpose of the statute prohibiting the conduct.[32] However, in *Miller v Miller* the High Court identified the central policy concern at stake in both joint and unilateral illegality cases as the need to preserve coherence between negligence law and the area of law proscribing the

[28] *State Rail Authority of New South Wales v Wiegold* (1991) 25 NSWLR 500 (NSWCA); *British Columbia v Zastowny* [2008] 1 SCR 27.

[29] See, eg, *Burns v Edman* [1970] 2 QB 541.

[30] ibid. See also *Meadows v Ferguson* [1961] VR 594.

[31] The most influential of these was that it was not possible or feasible to set a standard of care: *Jackson v Harrison* [1978] HCA 17, (1978) 138 CLR 438; *Progress and Properties Ltd v Craft* [1976] HCA 59, (1976) 135 CLR 651; *Gala v Preston* (n 18). This now discredited approach will be discussed in ch 10.

[32] *Henwood v Municipal Tramways Trust (South Australia)* (n 24).

conduct.[33] This decision continues a major theme in contemporary High Court decisions that legal coherence is a fundamental legal value underlying Australian law.[34] The Court in *Miller v Miller* recognised that an incoherence in the law will arise if the claim is incompatible with the purpose of the legislation against which the claimant has offended (the statutory purpose explanation).[35] The focus on legal coherence is justified; although, as will be demonstrated in Chapter 7, the statutory purpose explanation will be of limited practical application in individual cases. Perhaps it is for this reason that it has not been adopted in other jurisdictions as the test, at least not as the primary or exclusive test, for resolving claims connected to an illegality. Further, the statutory purpose explanation can distract the court from its true task of undertaking a relational analysis of the rights and duties of the parties.

The law of illegality in the United Kingdom has rightly been criticised for its 'complexity, capriciousness and injustice'.[36] There remains considerable dissent and disagreement in that jurisdiction about the correct approach to illegality doctrine. The Supreme Court of the United Kingdom has examined the application of illegality doctrine in a range of private law contexts on four occasions, but has been unable to achieve consensus on the overarching test by which claims based on illegality might be determined.[37] The leading approach to the physical injury cases is currently the causation test, which requires denial of the claim where the illegality is the 'real' or 'effective' cause of the injuries.[38] The status of this test is, however, uncertain following *Hounga v Allen*, where a majority of the Supreme Court condemned the test for its inherent subjectivity.[39] The situation is complicated by the large array of other approaches that have gained judicial acceptance at different times. These include: whether the claim is 'inextricably bound up and linked with' or has a 'sufficient connection with' the illegal act;[40] whether the claim would create an inconsistency in the law;[41] whether the claim would be

[33] *Miller v Miller* (n 6) [15] (French CJ, Gummow, Hayne, Crennan, Kiefel and Bell JJ) [108] (Heydon J).

[34] *Sullivan v Moody* [2001] HCA 59, (2001) 207 CLR 562; *CAL No 14 Pty Ltd v Motor Accidents Insurance Board* [2009] HCA 47, (2009) 239 CLR 390; *Tame v New South Wales* [2002] HCA 35, (2002) 211 CLR 317; *Equuscorp Pty Ltd v Haxton* [2012] HCA 7, (2012) 246 CLR 498; *Hunter and New England Local Health District v McKenna* [2014] HCA 44, (2014) 253 CLR 270.

[35] *Miller v Miller* (n 6) [74] (French CJ, Gummow, Hayne, Crennan, Kiefel and Bell JJ) [103] (Heydon J).

[36] Lord Sumption (n 16) 12.

[37] *Hounga v Allen* (n 11); *Les Laboratoires Servier v Apotex Inc* (n 6); *Bilta (UK) Ltd (in liquidation) v Nazir (No 2)* (n 5); *Patel v Mirza* [2016] UKSC 42.

[38] *Gray v Thames Trains Ltd* (n 27). This approach was explicitly rejected in *Miller v Miller* (n 6) [11] (French CJ, Gummow, Hayne, Crennan, Kiefel and Bell JJ).

[39] *Hounga v Allen* (n 11) [37].

[40] *Cross v Kirkby* (n 9); *Vellino v Chief Constable of the Greater Manchester Police* (n 24).

[41] *Hounga v Allen* (n 11) [57] (Lord Hughes, Lord Carnwath agreeing) (in respect of claims arising out of the commission of a joint criminal enterprise); *Patel v Mirza* (n 37) [192] (Lord Mance), [214] (Lord Clarke), [230]-[232] (Lord Sumption) (in respect of claims for restitution of money paid for an illegal purpose).

incompatible with the purpose of the law proscribing the act,[42] and whether the claimant must rely on the illegal act in order to establish the claim.[43] The Supreme Court decisions reveal a schism between those judges who prefer a flexible policy-balancing approach and those who favour a rule-based approach. A majority of the Court in *Hounga v Allen* favoured an approach that focuses on whether the relevant public policies in the individual case merit the application of illegality doctrine.[44] A few months later, in *Les Laboratoires Servier v Apotex Inc*, a majority of the Supreme Court rejected a discretionary approach, and emphasised that the binding authority of *Tinsley v Milligan* requires that the focus must be on the connection between the illegality and the claim.[45] Despite this, there was still significant support for a policy approach in a third decision by that Court, *Bilta (UK) Ltd (in liquidation) v Nazir (No 2)*.[46] A flexible policy approach ultimately triumphed in *Patel v Mirza* where a majority have embraced a judicial discretion that is responsive to the underlying purpose of the area of law proscribing the conduct, other underlying public policies and the proportionality of refusing relief.[47] However, there were powerful dissents in that case from Lord Mance, Lord Clarke and Lord Sumption, who preferred to approach the matter as one of legal consistency. The amount and rapidity of change in this area prompted James Goudkamp to observe that, 'Each time a test for the application of the illegality doctrine is killed off, the law, Hydra-like, sprouts multiple additional tests to take its place'.[48]

The law in Canada is more settled, and also the narrowest in scope. Following the decision of *Hall v Hebert*, a defence of illegality is no longer available for claims for injuries sustained during the commission of an illegal act.[49] In that jurisdiction, the courts instead deal with the claimant's illegal conduct as a matter of apportionment for contributory negligence.[50] The Supreme Court of Canada has established that legal coherence is the sole justification for an illegality defence, and that an illegality defence is to be applied only where it would permit

[42] *Hounga v Allen* ibid [55] (Lord Hughes, Lord Carnwath agreeing); *Patel v Mirza* ibid [101] (Lord Toulson, Lady Hale and Lords Kerr, Wilson and Hodge agreeing).

[43] *Tinsley v Milligan* [1994] 1 AC 340; *Stone & Rolls Ltd (in liq) v Moore Stephens (a firm)* [2009] 1 AC 1391, [97] (Lord Scott), [129]–[131] (Lord Walker); *Patel v Mirza* [2014] EWCA Civ 1047 [2015] Ch 271 [22] (Rimer LJ), [103] (Vos LJ).

[44] *Hounga v Allen* (n 11) (Lord Wilson, Lady Hale and Lord Kerr agreeing). Lord Hughes (Lord Carnwath agreeing) favoured a narrower judicial discretion involving balancing various policies underlying the illegality doctrine, such as the degree of connection between the illegality and the claim and the requirement that the law must act consistently: see at [55] in particular.

[45] *Les Laboratoires Servier v Apotex Inc* (n 6) [13]–[20] (Lord Sumption, Lords Neuberger and Clarke agreeing); *Tinsley v Milligan* (n 42).

[46] *Bilta (UK) Ltd (in liquidation) v Nazir (No 2)* (n 5) (see generally the judgment by Lord Toulson and Lord Hodge).

[47] *Patel v Mirza* (n 37) [101] (Lord Toulson, Lady Kerr and Lords Kerr, Wilson and Hodge agreeing). Lord Neuberger also endorsed Lord Toulson's policy framework: [174], [186].

[48] J Goudkamp, 'The Doctrine of Illegality: A Private Law Hydra' (2015) 6 *The UK Supreme Court Handbook* 254, 274–75.

[49] *Hall v Hebert* (n 1).

[50] For a recent application of the principles from *Hall v Hebert* see *Pecheco v Degife* [2014] BCSC 1570.

the claimant to evade a criminal sanction or to profit from wrongdoing.[51] It is worth noting that, although the High Court of Australia and the Supreme Court of Canada have both identified legal coherence as the central policy consideration in issue, these courts have reached very different views about the consequences of this policy in respect of claims for injuries sustained by a claimant in the execution of a crime committed jointly with the defendant. In Canada it is thought that the joint illegality cases do not raise issues of legal coherence, whereas in Australia concerns about legal coherence are thought to be central to the resolution of these cases.[52]

ii. Sanction-shifting and Related Claims

There is largely a convergence of views across the jurisdictions in respect of sanction-shifting claims. In Canada and the United Kingdom, these actions are rejected based on the need to preserve the coherence of the legal system,[53] and such limited authority that exists in Australia likewise supports that approach.[54] There are, however, fundamental questions that remain unanswered in respect of claims of this kind, such as the extent to which their resolution is dependent upon the claimant's criminal culpability for the illegal act, and the precise circumstances in which an incoherence with the criminal law will arise if compensation is awarded. The position is also unclear in respect of other claims that are related to the consequences of an illegal act but that do not involve shifting responsibility for a sanction. Lord Hoffman in *Gray v Thames Trains Ltd* (who wrote the leading judgment) advanced a broad policy-based causation test to resolve this type of claim;[55] however, there is no support in other jurisdictions for a causation test.[56]

iii. Illegal Profits and Earnings

Claims that fall into the third category—claims for illegal profits and earnings—are generally rejected.[57] This area is notably under-developed, and it is generally assumed, without close analysis, that all claims for illegal profits and earnings must be rejected based on a generalised assumption that allowing such claims would amount to a wrongful profiting.[58] A sound conceptual basis for resolving these claims must be identified.

[51] *Hall v Hebert* (n 1); *British Columbia v Zastowny* (n 28).

[52] *Hall v Hebert* ibid; *Miller v Miller* (n 6).

[53] See, eg, *Gray v Thames Trains Ltd* (n 27); *Hall v Hebert* ibid; *British Columbia v Zastowny* (n 28).

[54] *State Rail Authority of New South Wales v Wiegold* (n 28). There is also authority in the United States for rejecting sanction-shifting actions: see the cases discussed in R Perry, 'The Role of Retributive Justice in the Common Law of Torts: A Descriptive Theory' (2006) *Tennessee Law Review* 177, 215–219.

[55] *Gray v Thames Trains Ltd* (n 27) [50]–[55].

[56] *Miller v Miller* (n 6) [11] (French CJ, Gummow, Hayne, Crennan, Kiefel and Bell JJ).

[57] *Meadows v Ferguson* (n 30); *Burns v Edman* (n 29); *Hewison v Meridian Shipping Services Pty Ltd* [2002] EWCA Civ 1821, [2003] ICR 766.

[58] J Goudkamp, 'A Revival of the Doctrine of Attainder? The Statutory Illegality Defences to Liability in Tort' (2007) 29(3) *Sydney Law Review* 445, 459.

C. Academic Commentary

Torts scholars writing in this area have also advanced different views about the true rationale for an illegality principle. Some commentators argue that a defence of illegality should not apply to claims for personal injury damages and that in that context the claimant's illegal conduct should merely be assessed as contributory negligence.[59] There is, however, a range of other views.[60] There have been calls in the extra-curial writings of two justices of the Supreme Court of the United Kingdom for a multifactorial statutory judicial discretion to deal with all claims that are connected to an act of illegality on the basis that it is impossible to identify one single encompassing principle capable of resolving these claims.[61] In this book I argue that, to the contrary, it is possible to identify a single criterion capable of resolving claims arising from an illegality: that criterion is legal coherence. The only relevant consideration is the coherence of the claim within the whole body of law governing the parties' relationship. I will explain this further now.

III. Book Purpose

Virgo has observed that fundamental questions about illegality doctrine are 'under-examined and under-theorised'.[62] The purpose of this book is to address these fundamental questions by a detailed examination of illegality doctrine within a corrective justice framework, with the intention of securing conceptual and doctrinal clarity in this 'knotty' area.[63] My adoption of a corrective justice framework is significant as contemporary approaches to illegality have been shaped by the contributions of proponents of this theory. The views of prominent corrective

[59] See, for example, C Debattista, 'Ex Turpi Causa Returns to the English Law of Torts: Taking Advantage of Wrong Way Out' (1984) 15 *Anglo-American Law Review* 15; B MacDougall, '*Ex Turpi Causa:* Should a Defence Arise from a Base Cause?' (1991) 55 *Sasketchewan Law Review* 1; R Glofcheski, 'Claimant's Illegality as a Bar to Recovery of Personal Injury Damages' (1999) 19 *Legal Studies* 6; J Goudkamp, 'The Defence of Joint Illegal Enterprise' (2010) 34 *Melbourne University Law Review* 425.

[60] Among the contemporary theorists who take a different approach are Graham Virgo and Paul S Davies: G Virgo, 'Illegality's Role in the Law of Torts' in M Dyson (ed), *Unravelling Tort and Crime* (Cambridge, Cambridge University Press, 2014), ch 7; G Virgo, 'The Defence of Illegality in Unjust Enrichment' in A Dyson, J Goudkamp and F Wilmot-Smith, *Defences in Unjust Enrichment* (London, Bloomsbury Publishing, 2016); PS Davies, 'The Illegality Defence–Two Steps Forward, One Step Back?' (2009) 73(3) *The Conveyancer and Property Lawyer* 182. Graham Virgo advocates for a test based on comparative responsibility of the parties. Paul Davies prefers a structured discretion where a variety of factors are balanced to determine the claim.

[61] Sumption (n 16); J Mance, '*Ex Turpi Causa*–When Latin Avoids Liability' (2014) 18(2) *The Edinburgh Law Review* 175. See also Davies ibid 46.

[62] Virgo, 'The Defence of Illegality in Unjust Enrichment' (n 60) 165. Virgo was there referring specifically to the role of illegality doctrine in unjust enrichment, though these observations are equally applicable to its role in negligence.

[63] *Parkingeye Ltd v Somerfield Stores Ltd* [2012] EWCA Civ 1338, [2013] QB 840 [28] (Jacob LJ); see also Toulson LJ at [43].

justice theorist Ernest Weinrib in his seminal 1976 article 'Illegality as a Tort Defence', which were adopted in the majority judgment of McLachlin J (as she then was) in *Hall v Hebert*, have had a significant influence on the development of illegality doctrine.[64] Accordingly, corrective justice principles help to explain the reasoning underlying the development of key aspects of illegality doctrine. At the same time, corrective justice theory exposes the unfairness and incoherence of the various public policy explanations put forward for denying compensation to the wrongdoing claimant. A failure by the courts to adhere to principled reasoning, and widespread reliance on public policy to decide cases, has resulted in doctrine that is capricious and unprincipled. Corrective justice theory provides a principled framework for deciding future cases in a consistent and systematic manner.

My particular aim is to verify the claim by corrective justice theorists that legal coherence is the only sound and persuasive rationale for an illegality principle. The notion that legal coherence (encompassing the related notion that a claimant must not profit from wrongdoing) provides the only justification for an illegality principle in negligence law is no longer novel or, in Australia or Canada, controversial. The principle of legal coherence was recognised by the High Court of Australia in *Miller v Miller* as the only justification for rejecting a claim connected to an act of illegality.[65] The Court was influenced in this respect by the decision of McLachlin J in *Hall v Hebert*, who, as mentioned, had adopted the views of Weinrib in his illegality article. Weinribian corrective justice proponents[66] have argued for some time that the only role of a principle of illegality is to prevent an incoherence in the law. They explain that the principle comes into play only when it is needed to maintain the integrity of the legal system by preventing an inconsistency arising between two or more areas of law.[67] Other commentators in this area who are not adherents of corrective justice have likewise identified legal coherence as a legitimate rationale for a principle of illegality, though not necessarily as the only rationale.[68]

My objective is to develop these views and consolidate coherence as the only legitimate rationale for an illegality principle. My further aim is to identify more precisely the relationship between corrective justice and legal coherence. Weinrib's

[64] EJ Weinrib, 'Illegality as a Tort Defence' (1976) 26 *University of Toronto Law Journal* 28; *Hall v Hebert* (n 1). The main themes of Weinrib's arguments were also adopted by Murphy J in *Jackson v Harrison* (n 31) 464–66.

[65] *Miller v Miller* (n 6) [15] (French CJ, Gummow, Hayne, Crennan, Kiefel and Bell JJ), [108] (Heydon J).

[66] I am using this term to refer collectively to scholars who have written in this area and who are proponents of Weinrib's theory of corrective justice—in this context Weinrib himself, as well as McLachlin CJ and Allan Beever. This is not to suggest that there might not be significant areas of disagreement between these scholars, or that they are the only scholars who support Weinrib's theory.

[67] Weinrib, 'Illegality as a Tort Defence' (n 64); A Beever, *Rediscovering the Law of Negligence* (Oxford, Hart Publishing, 2007) 380; *Hall v Hebert* (n 1).

[68] James Goudkamp has put forward convincing arguments for a coherence rationale: Goudkamp, 'A Revival of the Doctrine of Attainder?' (n 58) 451–55; Goudkamp, 'The Defence of Joint Illegal Enterprise' (n 59) 441–46. However, while Goudkamp believes legal coherence has an important role to play in this area (see Goudkamp, 'A Private Law Hydra' (n 48) 269) he is yet to be convinced that

illegality article pre-dated his work on corrective justice, and he is yet (to my knowledge) to provide a detailed account of illegality doctrine and its relationship with corrective justice theory. The law of illegality poses a significant challenge to the corrective justice claim that tort law is bilaterally structured because most formulations of illegality doctrine involve reference to external policy considerations or focus one-sidedly on the claimant's illegal conduct. In his breakthrough work on corrective justice, *The Idea of Private Law*, Weinrib acknowledges that challenge, but has not yet attempted to answer it.[69] Allan Beever's discussion of illegality in *Rediscovering the Law of Negligence* is illuminating, but relatively brief due to the book's objective of addressing all aspects of negligence law.[70] Other contemporary rights-based theorists operating in the Australian–Anglo sphere have not dealt with the defence in a substantive way. There is a need for a thorough contemporary exposition of illegality doctrine and its place within a corrective justice conception of negligence law.[71] This book will meet that need and fulfil the further need for a detailed study on the scope of the coherence rationale and the principles that will determine its application. A lack of understanding as to the scope of the coherence rationale has provided an opportunity for judges with a predisposition to decide the claim on public policy grounds to manipulate a coherence rationale to achieve the desired outcome.[72] Accordingly, it is an important aim of this book to identify precisely the ambit of the coherence rationale, and to carefully delineate the circumstances where an award of compensation to a wrongdoing claimant would introduce an incoherence between the law of negligence and the area of law against which the claimant has offended.

The law of illegality is overlaid by public policy concerns about whether a court should provide assistance to a wrongdoing claimant, as well as concerns about broader societal issues, such as the deterrence of criminal conduct. Moreover, it stands at the juncture of tort law and criminal law, and raises questions about the extent to which the law of negligence should reinforce the goals of the criminal law. To address this area of law it is therefore necessary to address fundamental

consistency should provide the sole rationale for illegality doctrine: J Goudkamp, 'A Long, Hard Look at Gray v Thames Trains Ltd' in PS Davies and J Pita (eds), *Jurisprudence of Lord Hoffmann: A Festschrift in Honour of Lord Leonard Hoffmann* (London, Bloomsbury Publishing, 2015) 54; J Goudkamp and L Mayr, 'The Doctrine of Illegality and Interference with Chattels' in A Dyson, J Goudkamp and F Wilmot-Smith (eds), *Defences in Torts* (Oxford, Hart Publishing, 2015) 243.

[69] EJ Weinrib, *The Idea of Private Law* (Cambridge, Mass, Harvard University Press, 1995) 169 fn 53(3).

[70] See Beever (n 67) 372–83.

[71] For an important discussion of the relationship between corrective justice, legal coherence and illegality doctrine see B McLachlin, 'Weaving the Law's Seamless Web: Reflections on the Illegality Defence in Tort Law' in A Dyson, J Goudkamp and F Wilmot-Smith (eds), *Defences in Torts* (Oxford, Hart Publishing, 2015).

[72] *cf* RW Kostal, 'Currents in the Counter-reformation: Illegality and Duty of Care in Canada and Australia' (1995) *Tort Law Review* 100, 115. The majority in *Hounga* (n 11) wrongly use the principle of coherence as a vehicle for taking into account public policy factors. This will be discussed further in ch 6, section VI, Other Misappropriations of the Coherence Rationale.

questions about the role of policy in tort law and the extent to which tort law can pursue concerns or goals that are independent of the relationship of the parties. I will explain that reasoning by reference to external policy concerns or goals (ie, that are external to the relationship of the parties) is inconsistent with a corrective justice model of torts law. A principle of illegality that is based on public policy, or that allows the rectificatory function of tort law to be subordinated to goals of the criminal law, is not a principle of corrective justice.

I will seek to demonstrate that the various explanations advanced for an illegality principle (other than legal coherence) are conceptually incoherent for the reason that they are based on policy concerns that are external to the parties' relationship (including the concerns of the criminal law); are based on the moral culpability of the claimant or the nature of the act; and/or focus singularly on the claimant's conduct rather than relationally on both parties. I will argue that the only valid conceptual basis for an illegality principle is legal coherence (what I term 'the principle of coherence' or 'coherence rationale'). A claim should be rejected because of the claimant's illegality only where recognition of that claim would create an inconsistency between negligence law and the area of law proscribing the conduct. The specific argument I advance in this book is that a claim based on an illegal act must be rejected where negligence and the area of law proscribing the conduct intersect so as to negate an essential requirement for establishing the claim to damages. This will be the case where:

(a) an element of the claim is incompatible with the purpose of the statute proscribing the conduct (the statutory purpose explanation), or
(b) the loss or damage suffered by the claimant is not loss or damage recognised by the law because it resulted from the application of the legal process (the no loss or damage explanation).

The statutory purpose explanation as developed in *Miller v Miller* has fundamentally altered the landscape of Australian law in this area, and I undertake a detailed and critical study of the implications of this new approach for all illegality claims in negligence. I will explain that the statutory purpose explanation is justifiable on the basis of legal coherence, but that courts should adopt this explanation to disallow a claim only where recognition of the claim would clearly be incompatible with the purpose of the statute governing the conduct. This explanation is unlikely to be of practical importance in many cases.

The 'no loss or damage' explanation (which focuses on whether a right has been infringed and the valuation of that right) is advanced by Beever in *Rediscovering the Law of Negligence*.[73] I will seek to build upon that explanation and demonstrate its potential application to some (but not all) heads of loss in the sanction-shifting and related claims, and to certain claims for illegal profits and earnings. In doing

[73] Beever (n 67) 379–83.

so I have sought to promote an explanation that is consistent both with rights-based and loss-based conceptions of negligence law.[74]

There is one further circumstance (apart from the need to preserve the coherence of the legal system) where the illegality of the claimant will be a relevant factor. Where the claim is for injuries sustained in the commission of a joint illegal venture between the parties, it will be necessary to closely examine the features of that relationship to determine whether the claimant could reasonably expect the defendant to exercise the ordinary standard of care. It will not be reasonable to expect the defendant to act with normal care and competence if the careless act was inherent in the execution of the joint venture as contemplated by the parties. The rationale for these principles is that they are required to preserve legal coherence—in this situation, the internal coherence of the negligence action. These principles are not based per se on the illegal conduct of the claimant, but rather on the features of the parties' relationship. For this reason, these principles are not principles of illegality, although the joint illegal venture forms the relational features that justify the rejection of the claim.

IV. Scope and Terminology

I focus exclusively in this book on the application of illegality doctrine to claims in the tort of negligence. I am not concerned with the operation of illegality principles in other areas of tort law; for example, in respect of torts of trespass to the person or interference with chattels.[75] Nor am I am concerned with cases where the issue is whether the force used to defend against an attack was reasonable.[76] As Lord Sumption has pointed out, those cases can be adequately determined by normal self-defence principles and it is not necessary to engage illegality principles to resolve them.[77] As my focus is exclusively on negligence law, any conclusions that I draw might have limited relevance to the application of illegality doctrine to other areas of private law, such as contract, trusts and restitution. Those other areas might require different approaches; this is not a matter on which I attempt to comment.

There have been two complex decisions in the United Kingdom that have turned, at least in part, on the issue of attribution to a corporation of illegal conduct by director-shareholders: *Stone & Rolls Ltd (in Liq) v Moore Stephens (a firm)*

[74] By the term 'loss-based conceptions of negligence' I am referring to theories that view compensation for loss as the primary objective of negligence law.

[75] For an interesting discussion of this latter area see Goudkamp and Mayr, 'The Doctrine of Illegality and Interference with Chattels' (n 68).

[76] See, eg, *Cross v Kirkby* (n 9).

[77] Sumption 'Reflections on the Law of Illegality' (n 16) 6; *cf Flint v Tittensor* [2015] EWHC 466 (QB).

and *Bilta (UK) Ltd (in liquidation) v Nazir (No 2)*.[78] The corporate law doctrine of attribution is outside the scope of this book. Issues of attribution become largely irrelevant in any event when the proper basis of the law of illegality is recognised correctly to be the coherence of the law. Whether the corporation should be denied a claim due to the illegality of its directors or shareholders will depend solely on the coherence of the claim with the statutory scheme or legal doctrine that has been violated.[79] Thus, these cases will be discussed to the extent they discuss the basis of illegality doctrine, but those aspects of them relating to attribution will not be addressed.[80]

I concentrate primarily on claims that have a connection with a breach of public law (criminal law or statute law), as these represent the typical case that has come before the courts. The Supreme Court of the United Kingdom has suggested that the doctrine of illegality could extend to 'misconduct', such as prostitution, which, while not criminal, is contrary to public policy and involves criminal acts by secondary parties.[81] I argue in this book that the illegality doctrine turns only on whether permitting the claim for compensation would prevent the legal system from operating as a coherent, unified whole. As no legal incoherence arises where the conduct was not illegal, but merely morally reprehensible; such forms of 'misconduct' cannot attract the operation of illegality principles, and will not be considered further.

While it is commonplace in this area to speak of a 'defence' of illegality, throughout this book I adopt the neutral terminology of a 'principle of illegality', 'illegality principles' or 'illegality doctrine', unless discussing a particular case or article where the defence terminology is used. The claimant's illegal conduct is sometimes used as the foundation of a defence, but at other times is used to negate an element of the claim, such as duty of care, breach of duty or causation.[82] At other times it is described as neither a defence nor as negating a particular element of the claim, but as a 'rule of judicial abstention', where the court withholds relief in the public interest.[83] The adopted terms are intended to encompass all situations where the claimant's claim is denied by reason of the illegality of the claimant's conduct.

[78] *Stone & Rolls Ltd (in Liq) v Moore Stephens (a firm)* (n 43); *Bilta (UK) Ltd (in liquidation) v Nazir (No 2)* (n 5). See also *Safeway Stores Ltd v Twigger* (n 26).

[79] See the discussion in ch 8, section VIII, Corporate Responsibility.

[80] For academic commentary on attribution principles as they apply in the illegality context see, eg, P Watts, 'Corrupt Company Controllers, Their Companies, and their Companies' Creditors—Dealing with Pleas of *Ex Turpi Causa*' (2014) 2 *Journal of Business Law* 161; I Fletcher, 'Fraudulent Trading, Ex Turpi Causa, and the Directors' Duties: the Supreme Court Rulings in Bilta (UK) Ltd (in Liquidation) v Nazir (No 2)' (2016) 29 *Insolvency Intelligence* 12.

[81] *Les Laboratoires Servier v Apotex Inc* (n 6) [25] (Lord Sumption, Lords Neuberger and Clarke agreeing), [34] (Lord Mance).

[82] See, eg, *Miller v Miller* (n 6) where the High Court of Australia considered that when the claim is denied on the basis it would incompatible with the purpose of the statute proscribing the conduct it is because no duty of care arises on the facts.

[83] *Les Laboratoires Servier v Apotex Inc* (n 6) [23] (Lord Sumption, Lords Neuberger and Clarke agreeing); *Bilta (UK) Ltd (in liquidation) v Nazir (No 2)* (n 5) [60] (Lord Sumption).

V. Structure

The chapters of this book can be divided into three main groupings: Chapters 1–3 (conceptual foundations); Chapters 4–5 (incoherent policy and connection approaches); and Chapters 6–10 (coherent explanations for resolving illegality claims based on the principle of legal coherence).

In Chapters 2 and 3, I introduce key illegality principles and lay down the concepts that will inform later chapters. In Chapter 2, I explain the key features of corrective justice, and address my reasons for, and the key implications of, adopting a corrective justice framework for claims connected to illegal conduct. In Chapter 3, I examine the relationship between tort law and criminal law and explain that an award of compensation to a wrongdoing claimant will not usually create the potential for an incoherence to arise between these bodies of law.

In Chapters 4 and 5, I focus on the current approaches of the Supreme Court of the United Kingdom to illegality claims. In Chapter 4, I examine the role of policy and discretion in illegality claims. In Chapter 5, I address the common law causation approach, which is currently the leading test in the United Kingdom in negligence cases, as well as related tests that focus on the connection between the claim and the illegality. These are the 'reliance', 'close connection' and 'inextricable link' tests. I explain that the current policy and connection approaches adopted by the UK Supreme Court are conceptually incoherent, and accordingly do not provide a sound basis for the application of an illegality principle. I also discuss briefly in Chapter 5 the statutory causation tests, as enacted in legislation in most Australian jurisdictions.

In Chapters 6–10, I elaborate on the circumstances where a claim must be rejected so as to preserve the coherence of the legal system. In Chapter 6, I provide an overview of the circumstances and types of claims where issues of legal coherence might arise. In Chapters 7–9, I apply the general principles formulated in chapter six to specific contexts, and examine the two explanations for denying a claim on the ground of legal coherence: the statutory purpose explanation and the no loss or damage explanation. In Chapter 7, I apply the statutory purpose explanation to the physical injury cases, where the claimant is acting illegally at the time of the injury. In Chapters 8 and 9, I apply the 'no loss or damage' explanation to the sanction-shifting (and related) claims, and to claims for illegal profits and earnings respectively. In Chapter 10, I focus on the joint illegality cases. I reject previous explanations advanced for resolving these claims and develop a new relational explanation designed to preserve the internal cohesion of the negligence action.

I conclude in Chapter 11 with some brief remarks.

VI. Focus on the Common Law

This book focuses on common law principles of illegality. An important objective of the book is to make a substantial contribution to the law of illegality in England and Canada; in particular to the former, where the law is in a chaotic state. In these jurisdictions the law of illegality is still largely based on the common law.

The situation in Australia is different as there are statutory illegality provisions in each Australian jurisdiction other than Victoria.[84] Nevertheless, it is still relevant in Australia to address common law principles. There are three main reasons why common law principles of illegality in Australia have not been rendered obsolete by the introduction of the statutory provisions. First, with the possible exception of the New South Wales legislation, the statutory exclusions will not apply to sanction-shifting claims, nor to claims for illegal profits and earnings. The target of the provisions are claims for injuries sustained at the time the claimant was acting illegally; however, even in respect of that category of claim the statutory provisions do not evince an intention to 'cover the field'.[85] The statutory provisions operate as a defence to a claim, and are enlivened only once the claimant has established the elements of the claim by reference to general law principles.[86] A court should thus logically determine whether the elements of the claim are satisfied before considering the operation of the statutory defences.[87]

Second, there are exclusions and gaps in the statutory defences so that not all claims for injuries sustained at the time of committing a criminal act will fall within the scope of the provisions. The most significant exclusion[88] is that the New South Wales legislation has no application to claims for injuries sustained in the course of a joint criminal enterprise. Thus, in this significant jurisdiction (and also in Victoria), these claims will still fall to be determined exclusively according to the common law.[89] Nor (with the exception of New South Wales and Western Australia) will the statutory defences apply where the injuries were sustained

[84] Civil Law (Wrongs) Act 2002 (ACT), s 94; Civil Liability Act 2002 (NSW), ss 54, 54A; Personal Injuries (Liabilities and Damages) Act 2003 (NT), s 10; Civil Liability Act 2003 (Qld), s 45; Civil Liability Act 1936 (SA), s 43; Civil Liability Act 2002 (Tas), s 6(1); Offenders (Legal Action) Act 2000 (WA), s 5.

[85] The legislation in several jurisdictions has express savings provisions: Civil Liability Act 2002 (NSW), s 3A(1); Civil Liability Act 2003 (Qld), s 7(2); Civil Liability Act 2002 (Tas), s 3A(2); Civil Liability Act 1936 (SA), s 43(4)(c) (preserves the common law relating to joint illegal enterprises only).

[86] See, eg, *Presidential Security Services of Australia Pty Ltd v Brilley* (2008) Aust Torts Reports 81, 968 (NSWCA); *Miles v Williams* [2013] QSC 162.

[87] See, eg, *Quine v Keerasawat* [2014] WADC 150.

[88] Also, the defences in each jurisdiction are limited to indictable or 'serious' offences and as such, will not apply to regulatory or summary offences; for example, of the kind enacted in road safety legislation.

[89] Civil Liability Act 2002 (NSW), s 54(2).

following the completion of the crime; for example, where a burglar is injured while fleeing the scene of the crime.[90]

Third, and most importantly, these statutory defences undermine corrective justice, and it is questionable whether they have a legitimate role to play within a coherent system of compensation for the victims of negligence. The legislatures should reassess whether the policy objectives they are seeking to achieve outweigh the loss of corrective justice entitlements.[91] It is submitted that these defences should be repealed, and that Australian courts should be free to determine illegality claims in accordance with the principles formulated in this book.

[90] As in *Joyce v O'Brien* (n 20).

[91] See ch 5, section V, A Statutory Causation Test.

2

Theoretical Perspectives

I. Introduction

This chapter, together with Chapter 3, provides the conceptual basis for the book. Claims arising from illegality raise questions about the proper function of the law of negligence, and about the use of policy-based reasoning in negligence cases. In this chapter I outline the key features of corrective justice theory as it applies to the law of negligence, and explain my reasons for adopting a corrective justice framework for analysing claims connected to an illegal act. I then explain the key implications of using corrective justice as the theoretical construct, and in the course of doing so canvass theoretical and pragmatic objections to public-policy-based reasoning.

II. Debates about the Proper Basis of Tort Law

The vigorous and ongoing debate as to the proper theoretical foundation of tort law—particularly between corrective justice theorists and instrumentalists—is well known. Corrective justice[1] theory regards tort law as a rights-based instrument of corrective justice designed to rectify wrongs committed by one party against the other in a relationship. Corrective justice theory emphasises tort law's autonomy both institutionally and substantively. Instrumentalist theories regard tort law as functionalist (consequentialist) in nature and a vehicle for promoting wide social or economic goals such as loss-spreading, deterrence and retribution.[2] Also noteworthy is the emerging intermediate view that tort law is *primarily* concerned with interpersonal justice, but that it is appropriate for courts

[1] I note that Allan Beever now prefers the term 'commutative justice' to corrective justice on the basis that too much misunderstanding has developed around the latter term: A Beever, *Forgotten Justice: The Forms of Justice in the History of Legal and Political Theory* (Oxford, Oxford University Press, 2013) 79–80.

[2] Central among these have been the law and economic theorists but it also includes legal realists, such as Jane Stapleton and John Fleming (see the works cited in n 6 below).

to make reference to broader policy considerations in limited circumstances and under strict constraints.[3]

In the past, the debate about the proper foundation of tort law has tended to be more muted in Australia and the United Kingdom than in North America.[4] In Australia the dominant theory has been legal realism due to the influence of distinguished scholars such as John Fleming and Jane Stapleton.[5] According to Fleming and Stapleton, policy is instrumental to torts decisions, and insistence on principle is a cloak for undisclosed and unidentified policy reasoning.[6] Nevertheless, in recent years there has been a resurgence of discussion and debate in both Australia and the United Kingdom about the proper function of the law of torts.[7] This has included discussion and debate about corrective justice theory, impelled by corrective justice or rights-based accounts of tort law by contemporary theorists Ernest Weinrib, Allan Beever and Robert Stevens.[8] There are many points on which these theorists would disagree.[9] Nevertheless, these theorists advocate in common an explanation of tort law based on the rights we have against each other, and the notion of correlative rights and duties arising out of an interaction.[10] Throughout the book, I will adopt the terminology of 'corrective justice theory'. I mean this term to encompass theories that view corrective justice as the justificatory structure of tort law as well as emerging rights-based theories of tort law.[11] My primary focus, however, will be on Weinrib's account of corrective justice and Beever's development and application of that theory to negligence law.

[3] See the works of Andrew Robertson and Christian Witting in particular: A Robertson, 'Constraints on Policy-Based Reasoning in Private Law' in A Robertson and T Hang Wu (eds), *The Goals of Private Law*, (Oxford, Hart Publishing, 2009) ch 11; A Robertson, 'On the Function of the Law of Negligence' (2013) 33(1) *Oxford Journal of Legal Studies* 31; C Witting, 'Tort Law, Policy and the High Court of Australia' (2007) 31 *Melbourne University Law Review* 569; C Witting, 'The House that Dr Beever Built: Corrective Justice, Principle and the Law of Negligence' (2008) 71(4) *Modern Law Review* 621.

[4] D Priel, 'Torts, Rights and Right-wing Ideology' (2011) *Torts Law Journal* 1, 1–2.

[5] A Beever, *Rediscovering the Law of Negligence* (Oxford, Hart Publishing, 2007) 8–11.

[6] J Stapleton, 'Duty of Care Factors: A Selection from the Judicial Menus' in P Cane and J Stapleton (eds), *The Law of Obligations: Essays in Celebration of John Fleming* (Oxford, Clarendon Press, 1998) 62; J Stapleton, 'The Golden Thread at the Heart of Tort Law: Protection of the Vulnerable' (2003) 24 *Australian Bar Review* 135, 136, 138; JG Fleming, *The Law of Torts*, 9th edn (Sydney, LBC Information Services, 1998) 153–56.

[7] R Stevens, *Torts and Rights* (Oxford, Oxford University Press, 2007) 311–12.

[8] EJ Weinrib, *The Idea of Private Law* (Cambridge, Mass, Harvard University Press, 1995); Beever, *Rediscovering* (n 5); Stevens ibid.

[9] For example, Stevens' rights-based account of tort law rejects the weak conception of corrective justice, where it is uncoupled with a system of rights, as 'trite': ibid 327. Stevens is unconvinced by corrective justice accounts of tort law on the basis that corrective justice cannot explain the primary rights that we have: ibid 326–28. Compare the views of Allan Beever in: A Beever, 'Our Most Fundamental Rights' in D Nolan and A Roberston (eds), *Rights and Private Law* (Oxford, Hart Publishing, 2012) ch 3; Beever, *Forgotten Justice* (n 1), 106–14.

[10] For discussion of the core features of corrective justice theory, see J Coleman, 'The Practice of Corrective Justice' in DG Owen, *Philosophical Foundations of Tort Law* (Oxford, Oxford University Press, 1995) 66–67; D Nolan and A Robertson, 'Rights and Private Law' in D Nolan and A Roberston (eds), *Rights and Private Law* (Oxford, Hart Publishing, 2012) ch 1.

[11] This terminology has also been adopted by other commentators: see, for example, D Nolan, 'Causation and the Goals of Tort Law' in A Robertson and T Hang Wu (eds), *The Goals of Private Law* (Oxford, Hart Publishing, 2009) 166.

III. Main Features of Corrective Justice Theory

I will provide only a relatively brief overview of the primary themes of corrective justice as relevant to this book. Where a more detailed discussion of a particular aspect of corrective justice theory is required for the purpose of discussing a specific topic I deal with it at that point.

Corrective justice theorists advocate that private law is an expression of Aristotle's idea of corrective justice pursuant to which liability rectifies the injustice inflicted by one person on another.[12] Weinrib summarises the key features of corrective justice:

> Corrective justice is the term given to the relational structure of reasoning in private law. This term has a venerable history, having first been formulated by Aristotle and then continuously discussed and refined in the two and half millennia since. It conceptualizes the parties as the active and passive poles of the same injustice (as the doer and the sufferer of injury in Aristotle's account). It directs us, accordingly, to normative considerations that pertain not to either (or even to each) of the poles taken on its own, but to the relationship as such.[13]

As an instrument of corrective justice, tort law is thus concerned solely with the bilateral relationship and interaction between the parties to the dispute. A corrective justice account of tort law treats the relationship of the parties as a 'bipolar unit in which each party's normative position is intelligible only in the light of the other's'.[14] Weinrib couples corrective justice with the Kantian concept of rights, arguing that Kantian right embodies a specific form of correlativity, namely that of right and duty.[15]

Weinrib claims that corrective justice is a theoretical framework that is both immanent and critical. It is immanent in that it captures the correlative structure of the parties' relationship as 'the most pervasive and distinctive feature of private law'; it is critical in that it insists this feature 'must inform the justifications for particular doctrines and institutions'.[16] A particular principle or decision will reflect corrective justice (and hence, the law's internal coherence) where it reflects the morality of correlativity: 'tort law reflects the morality distinctive to the relationship of doing and suffering harm'.[17] Thus, tort law has its own 'special morality'; it does not express 'morality at large' but has a 'special moral nature …

[12] EJ Weinrib, 'Corrective Justice in a Nutshell' (2002) 52 *University of Toronto Law Journal* 349, 349.

[13] EJ Weinrib, *Corrective Justice* (Oxford, Oxford University Press, 2012) 2 (citation omitted).

[14] ibid.

[15] Weinrib, *The Idea of Private Law* (n 8) 122–23. There is no necessary agreement between rights theorists as to the system of rights underlying torts law: see the discussion in Nolan and Robertson (n 10) 7–10.

[16] EJ Weinrib, 'Punishment and Disgorgement as Contract Remedies' (2003) 78 *Chicago-Kent Law Review* 55, 59. See also Weinrib, *The Idea of Private Law* (n 8) 146.

[17] EJ Weinrib, 'The Special Morality of Tort Law' (1989) 34 (3) *McGill Law Journal* 403, 403.

as a medium for the vindication of the claimant's rights against the defendant'.[18] Beever explains that for corrective (or commutative) justice:

> The investigation is into the relationship between two people. It examines their interaction and it takes those two people as a unit. It does not seek to compare their positions to those of others, external to the interaction. It is an interpersonal justice.[19]

Beever explains that an interpersonal *in*justice occurs in negligence law 'when one person wrongs another or, which is the same, when one person interferes with the rights of another'.[20] Corrective justice rectifies this injustice by the provision of a remedy aimed at restoring the equality of the parties to the interaction.[21]

If corrective justice theory is accepted as the explanation for tort liability, when deciding torts cases judges should aim only to provide a remedy for a wrong done to one of the parties.[22] Judges should be focused only on factors that pertain to the relationship between the parties as doer and sufferer of the same harm, and should not impose on the relationship an independent policy of their own choice:[23] 'Tort law is not public law in disguise.'[24] The rejection of a claim on public policy grounds amounts to a 'judicial confiscation' of what is due to the claimant in order to subsidise external policy objectives.[25] Corrective justice theory is thus non-instrumental and formalist in nature,[26] and one of Beever's aims in *Rediscovering the Law of Negligence* is to demonstrate that negligence law can be understood 'in a principled way without appeal to policy'.[27]

In summary, in corrective justice there is a 'unity of doing and suffering': that is, a correlation of the doing of, and the suffering of, harm. The claimant's right and the defendant's duty not to interfere with that right are correlative, and the reasons for imposing liability on the defendant must correlate with the reasons for the claimant's right.

It is now necessary to explain how the corrective justice notion of correlativity applies to negligence law. In order for liability in negligence to arise, the harm suffered by the claimant must be to a right, such as the right to bodily integrity or a proprietary interest, and the defendant must have breached a duty correlative with that right (that is, the scope of the duty must include abstaining from infringing a right of that kind).[28] The various elements of negligence liability and the principles

[18] ibid 405.

[19] Beever, *Forgotten Justice* (n 1) 80. See also Beever, *Rediscovering the Law of Negligence* (n 5) 42–44.

[20] Beever, *Rediscovering the Law of Negligence* ibid 45.

[21] Weinrib, *Corrective Justice* (n 13) 16.

[22] Weinrib, 'The Special Morality of Tort Law' (n 17) 409; Weinrib, 'Punishment and Disgorgement' (n 16) 59–62.

[23] Weinrib, 'The Special Morality of Tort Law' ibid 408–410; Weinrib, *The Idea of Private Law* (n 8) 144.

[24] Weinrib, 'The Special Morality of Tort Law' ibid 410. See also Stevens, *Torts and Rights* (n 7) 324: 'The law of torts is not a proxy for the achievement of [social] goals'.

[25] cf EJ Weinrib, 'Does Tort Law Have a Future?' (2000) 34 *Valparaiso University Law Review* 561, 566. See also Beever, *Rediscovering the Law of Negligence* (n 5) 176–77.

[26] Weinrib, *The Idea of Private Law* (n 8) ch 2.

[27] Beever, *Rediscovering the Law of Negligence* (n 5) 71.

[28] Weinrib, *The Idea of Private Law* (n 8) 134–35; Weinrib, *Corrective Justice* (n 13) 19–20.

and concepts underlying them express the *normative* correlativity between right and duty.[29] In other words, it is the concepts and principles of negligence liability that express the conditions under which the defendant's conduct is a wrongful infringement of the claimant's right.[30] The elements of negligence liability and the legal doctrines underlying them should be expressive of the correlativity of the claimant–defendant relationship.[31] Liability in negligence arises where a defendant breaches a duty correlative with the claimant's right by creating an unreasonable risk of harm to a class of persons that includes the claimant.[32] Central to the negligence analysis then are the questions whether the defendant's conduct created an unreasonable risk of harm that caused the claimant's injury (breach of duty and factual causation), and whether the claimant's injury is within the risk that rendered the defendant's conduct unreasonable (duty of care and proximate causation).[33] Where negligence liability, and thus a wrongful infringement of a right, is established, the normal remedy given is an award of compensatory damages. This is because the claimant's right encompasses not only the substantive right, but also the remedial right to be compensated by an award of monetary damages from a person who wrongfully infringes that right.[34] The damages available for infringement of the right to physical integrity include non-pecuniary and pecuniary damages.[35]

IV. Reasons for Adopting a Corrective Justice Framework

In this section I explain further my reasons for adopting corrective justice as the theoretical framework for understanding and analysing claims connected to an illegal act by the claimant. On one previous occasion I indicated sympathy with an instrumentalist view of negligence law in the context of causation.[36] Having since read Weinrib's and Beever's writings on illegality and on corrective justice more generally, I am persuaded of the explanatory power of corrective justice theory for

[29] Weinrib, *The Idea of Private Law* ibid 145–46.
[30] Weinrib, 'Corrective Justice in a Nutshell' (n 12) 353.
[31] Weinrib, *The Idea of Private Law* (n 8) 146.
[32] EJ Weinrib, 'The Passing of *Palsgraf*' (2001) 54 *Vanderbilt Law Review* 803, 808.
[33] See generally Weinrib, *The Idea of Private Law* (n 8) ch 6; Weinrib, 'Does tort law have a future?' (n 25) 562–65. Beever argues that these elements can be collapsed into one single question: 'Did the defendant create an unreasonable risk of the claimant's injury?' See Beever, *Rediscovering the Law of Negligence* (n 5) 37.
[34] EJ Weinrib, 'Causal Uncertainty' (2016) 36 *Oxford Journal of Legal Studies* 135.
[35] Stevens, *Torts and Rights* (n 7) 25, ch 4; Weinrib, *Corrective Justice* (n 13) 95–96. See also Beever, *Rediscovering the Law of Negligence* (n 5) 246–50.
[36] M Bagaric and S Erbacher, 'Causation in Negligence: From Anti-jurisprudence to Principle—Individual Responsibility as the Cornerstone for the Attribution of Liability' (2011) 18 *Journal of Law and Medicine* 1.

the resolution of claims under consideration here; that is, claims arising from an illegality. My view is that reliance on public policy in this area has led to uncertain and unsatisfactory illegality doctrine, which in turn has resulted in the distortion of ordinary negligence principles relating to (in particular) duty of care and causation. Doctrinal clarity can be achieved in this area only through a singular focus on considerations of interpersonal justice to the exclusion of external public policy considerations. These are of course the main tenets of corrective justice theory. The emphasis of corrective justice theorists on the principle of coherence as the only legitimate rationale for illegality doctrine has also influenced my decision to adopt a corrective justice model. It would be possible to justify the coherence rationale without reliance on corrective justice.[37] Nevertheless, corrective justice principles support and inform (and provide theoretical justification for) my own views regarding the appropriate basis for illegality doctrine.

It is not my intention to provide a defence of corrective justice theory as an explanation of negligence law; that is not the objective of this book and in any event, it is not possible to do this in the confines of this book. I reserve my judgment as to the explanatory power of corrective justice theory for other areas of negligence law where the theory has proved especially contentious, such as the special duty categories. This is not because I am hostile to the claim that corrective justice provides the only sound structural principle for the whole of negligence law, but because I would need to do further studies in those other areas before I could confidently express an opinion about them. The main criticisms of corrective justice theory include: that it provides no criteria for choosing one liability rule over another in particular cases;[38] that it is wrong (even absurd) to suggest that torts law does not or should not, pursue external goals;[39] that it is overly dogmatic and fails to account adequately for the need for pragmatism, flexibility and discretion in negligence law;[40] and that it is an ideologically right-wing explanation of torts law.[41] Contemporary corrective justice theorists are criticised for 're-writing or re-engineering the case law'.[42]

[37] J Goudkamp and L Mayr, 'The Doctrine of Illegality and Interference with Chattels' in A Dyson, J Goudkamp and F Wilmot-Smith (eds), *Defences in Torts* (Oxford, Hart Publishing, 2015) 242–43.

[38] P Cane, 'Corrective Justice and Correlativity in Private Law' (1996) *Oxford Journal of Legal Studies* 471, 478–80. For a response see Beever, *Rediscovering the Law of Negligence* (n 5) 46–50.

[39] Cane ibid 483–84; Robertson, 'Constraints on Policy-Based Reasoning in Private Law' (n 3) ch 11; S Hedley, 'Courts as Public Authorities, Private Law as Instrument of Government' in K Barker and D Jensen, *Private Law: Key Encounters with Public Law* (Cambridge, Cambridge University Press, 2013) 92. For a response see Beever, *Rediscovering the Law of Neligence* (n 5) ch 1.

[40] J Dietrich, 'What is "Lawyering"? The Challenge of Taxonomy' (2006) 55(3) *Cambridge Law Journal* 549. Dietrich also argues that the objection to the use of policy is in itself a policy decision external to the logic of corrective justice theory: at 566. For a response see A Beever, 'Policy in Private Law: An Admission of Failure' (2006) 25(2) *The University of Queensland Law Journal* 287, 297–99, 304–05.

[41] Priel 'Torts, Rights and Right-wing Ideology' (n 4). For a response see Beever, *Rediscovering the Law of Negligence* (n 5) 52–55.

[42] T Kaye, 'Rights Gone Wrong: The Failure of Fundamentalist Tort Theory' (2010) 79 *Mississippi Law Journal* 931, 934–35, see also 959–66.

Corrective justice theorists such as Beever have responded to these criticisms,[43] and it is not my intention to re-canvass these debates here. Whatever one's views might be regarding the persuasiveness of these criticisms, theories based on corrective justice have recently assumed a prominence in contemporary theoretical debates regarding the proper functioning of tort law.[44] Accordingly, it is a worthwhile exercise in itself to test illegality doctrine against the main precepts of this enduring and influential theory. Moreover, I have already mentioned an additional reason for adopting a corrective justice framework for analysing illegality doctrine. This is that the contributions of corrective justice proponents Weinrib and McLachlin CJ have influenced significantly the development of this doctrine, in particular their view that the only proper basis for an illegality defence is the preservation of the coherence of the legal system. Commentators have recognised the need for a contemporary, detailed exposition of illegality doctrine and its place within a corrective justice framework, as well as the need for a detailed justification of the coherence rationale.[45] This book meets those needs.

Accordingly, my objective is modest and limited to demonstrating that an emphasis on relational reasoning[46] and the correlative structure of negligence liability provides a principled framework for understanding illegality doctrine as it applies to negligence law. The current reliance on public policy and singular focus on the claimant's conduct rather than the contribution of both parties to the harm has hindered the development of satisfactory doctrine in this area. It is only through a singular focus on the relationship of the parties, and the coherence of the claim within the whole body of law governing that relationship, that it is possible to find a coherent path for resolving these claims. It is not my aim to formulate explanations that are dependent on an analysis of rights violations (although I incorporate such analyses into my reasoning in Chapter 8). Rather, one of my aims is to put forward explanations that are consistent with the main precepts of corrective justice and rights-based theories, but that could apply equally to a loss-based approach to negligence law (ie, an approach that is oriented to compensation for harm). Thus, it is not my aim, or even possible given the limitations of this book, to explain and justify the system of rights that forms the basis of the law of negligence, or to choose between competing conceptions of rights. This is largely unnecessary anyway for the purposes of this book as I am almost exclusively concerned with claims arising from personal injury. Any of the competing systems or

[43] See the references in nn 38–41.

[44] There have been two contemporary edited books of contributions that focus on discussing and debating the merit of corrective justice and rights-based theories: Robertson and Hang Wu (eds), *The Goals of Private Law* (Oxford, Hart Publishing, 2009); Nolan and Roberston (eds), *Rights and Private Law* (Oxford, Hart Publishing, 2012).

[45] James Goudkamp (a prolific contributor to this area) and John Murphy have identified the need for a detailed study into corrective justice theory and illegality doctrine: J Goudkamp and J Murphy, 'Tort Statutes and Tort Theories' (2015) 131 *Law Quarterly Review* 133, 153. See also Goudkamp, 'A Long, Hard Look at Gray v Thames Trains Ltd' in PS Davies and J Pita (eds), *Jurisprudence of Lord Hoffmann: A Festschrift in Honour of Lord Leonard Hoffmann* (London, Bloomsbury Publishing, 2015) 51–54.

[46] This term is used in Weinrib, *Corrective Justice* (n 13) 79.

conceptions of rights would recognise the right to bodily safety and the availability of compensation for the value of the infringed right.[47]

V. Key Implications of Adopting a Corrective Justice Framework

Before discussing the normative implications that flow from adopting a corrective justice analysis of claims connected to illegal conduct, it is necessary to address the issue of whether corrective justice theory has a normative agenda at all. The primary function of corrective justice theory is to provide a conceptual framework for understanding and analysing private law, rather than to state prescriptively what the law *should* be.[48] While the explanatory power claimed for corrective justice is considerable, the claim is not that *all* established tort principles and *all* decided tort cases can be explained by corrective justice. Weinrib recognises that particular principles and decisions, even those of longstanding pedigree that have been extensively followed, may be erroneous to the extent that they fail to reflect adequately the internal corrective justice framework of the law.[49] Beever is similarly cautious in terms of his claims about the explanatory power of corrective justice for decided cases. He accepts that not every negligence case will fit with corrective justice theory, but nevertheless argues that the central cases and most 'standard' (non-controversial) cases will instantiate corrective justice.[50]

The argument is that the law will always *tend to* corrective justice.[51] Weinrib argues that through a process of 'incremental transformation or reinterpretation or even the repudiation of specific decisions', private law will work towards internal coherence, informed by corrective justice.[52] Corrective justice theory assists the law in these efforts to 'work itself pure'[53] by putting forward accounts of the law that are *interpretive* rather than purely *descriptive*.[54] That is, corrective justice theory seeks not merely to describe the law as it is, but to put forward an interpretation of the law that, in Beever's words, is the most 'coherent and meaningful'.[55]

[47] ibid 53; Beever, *Rediscovering the Law of Negligence* (n 5) 63; Stevens, *Torts and Rights* (n 7) 7. Other rights that are clearly protected that are of possible relevance to this book are the right to freedom of movement (liberty) (Stevens, at 7) and the right to reputation: Stevens, at 8.

[48] Beever, Rediscovering the Law of Negligence (n 5) 21.

[49] Weinrib, *The Idea of Private Law* (n 8) 13; Weinrib, *Corrective Justice* (n 13) 8.

[50] Beever, *Rediscovering the Law of Negligence* (n 5) 28–34.

[51] ibid 509.

[52] Weinrib, The Idea of Private Law (n 8) 13.

[53] Weinrib, 'Corrective Justice in a Nutshell' (n 12) 356.

[54] Beever, *Rediscovering the Law of Negligence* (n 5) 21–28; Nolan and Robertson, 'Rights and Private Law' (n 10) 4–6.

[55] Beever, *Rediscovering the Law of Negligence* ibid 21, see also 28–34. For a discussion of the interpretivist function of rights-based theories see Nolan and Robertson, 'Rights and Private Law' ibid 5–6.

Departures from corrective justice are criticised as 'unprincipled and chaotic'.[56] Weinrib emphasises that corrective justice provides the internal standard for criticising norms that are not consonant with the corrective justice structure of private law. That is, corrective justice fulfils the 'theoretical function of providing the internal standpoint for identifying unfair or incoherent doctrine'.[57] If a legal norm—such as a particular formulation of an illegality principle—is inconsistent with corrective justice, then it is exposed as unfair or incoherent. Beever similarly argues that a principled corrective justice approach will help us to understand why some cases are rightly or wrongly decided.[58] Corrective justice provides the structure for working out the principles, concepts and rules that are suitable to the relationship of the parties, and therefore 'indicates the distinct kind of practical reasoning that supports fair and coherent determinations of liability'.[59] Accordingly, corrective justice theory is normative to the extent that it seeks to identify and criticise legal norms that do not conform to the 'justificatory framework'[60] of the private law and to eliminate those anomalous norms in the future development of the law.[61]

Donal Nolan and Andrew Robertson recognise that it would be a mistake to regard rights-based theories as having no normative or prescriptive function.[62] As a corollary to identifying principles that are inconsistent with the correlative structure of corrective justice, corrective justice theory fulfils a normative function via its insistence that claims must be assessed according to its justificatory structure rather than external policy considerations or social goals.[63] Challenges to the use of policy in torts decisions are thus a feature of rights-based theories.[64] The rejection of policy is such a significant implication of a corrective justice analysis of claims based on an illegality that I will discuss developments in the United Kingdom toward an explicit public policy approach to illegality claims as a separate chapter (Chapter 4). At this point I will briefly discuss three other main implications of the adoption of a corrective justice framework that will inform my analysis throughout this book.

[56] Beever, *Rediscovering the Law of Negligence* ibid 507.

[57] Weinrib, *Corrective Justice* (n 13) 97; see also 3–4, 7–8, 13–14, 35–37. See also Weinrib, *The Idea of Private Law* (n 8) 42; EJ Weinrib, 'Civil Recourse and Corrective Justice' (2011) *Florida Statute University Law Review* 273, 291.

[58] Beever, *Rediscovering the Law of Negligence* (n 5) 31–32.

[59] Weinrib, *Corrective Justice* (n 13) 7; see also 97.

[60] Weinrib, *The Idea of Private Law* (n 8) 19.

[61] Beever, *Rediscovering the Law of Negligence* (n 5) 507–08.

[62] Nolan and Robertson,' Rights and Private Law' (n 10) 10–13. In these passages, the authors discuss the normative implications of rights-based theories.

[63] ibid 11–12. Nolan and Robertson identify a third normative implication of rights-based theories (not currently relevant) as being that some corrective justice theorists place limits on what can amount to a private law right: at 12–13.

[64] Beever, *Rediscovering the Law of Negligence* (n 5) ch 1; Beever, 'Policy in Private Law: An Admission of Failure' (n 40); Stevens, *Torts and Rights* (n 7) ch 18.

The first implication flows from the requirement that the focus must be on considerations that are relevant to *both parties* to the interaction. Weinrib explains this as follows:

> [T]he only normative considerations that are significant are those that apply correlatively to both parties. Normative considerations that reflect the correlative situation of the two parties set terms for their interaction that take account of their mutual relationship and therefore are fair to both parties.[65]

It is inconsistent with the correlative structure of corrective justice to decide liability and entitlements by reference to considerations that focus solely on the conduct of one party—in this context, the claimant's illegal conduct. A singular focus on the claimant's conduct privileges the defendant at the expense of the claimant.[66] The liability regime must not operate as 'a hodgepodge of factors separately relevant only to one or the other of the parties'.[67] A principle that turns on the one-sided consideration of the illegality of the claimant's conduct cannot be regarded as a manifestation of corrective justice.[68] As Weinrib has put it, 'This defense [of illegality] is inconsistent with corrective justice, because illegality as such is not relevant to the direct interaction of doer and sufferer'.[69] Beever explains that 'The fact that the claimant acted illegally may explain our lack of sympathy with the claimant, but it does not in itself affect the relationship between the claimant and the defendant'.[70] Approaches that focus on the connection between the claim and the illegal act (see Chapter 5) are contrary to reasoning of corrective justice in that they focus unilaterally on the claimant's conduct rather than relationally on both parties.

The second implication is that, for essentially the same reasons, a principle of illegality should not be used as a vehicle for 'punishment' or to support other goals of the criminal law. The promotion of criminal law purposes in the law of tort is inconsistent with the corrective justice account of tort law.[71] Criminal law goals such as retribution and deterrence are concerns that focus unilaterally on the conduct of one of the parties, or on the effect of the claim on third persons who are not parties to the claim, rather than relationally on the parties to the interaction.[72] Corrective justice theory demonstrates that objections to the adoption of punitive

[65] Weinrib, 'The Passing of *Palsgraf*' (n 32) 805–06.

[66] Weinrib, 'Corrective Justice in a Nutshell' (n 12) 351, 355.

[67] Weinrib, 'The Passing of *Palsgraf*' (n 32) 806; see also Weinrib, 'Does Tort Law Have a Future?' (n 25) 561–72.

[68] R Perry, 'The Role of Retributive Justice in the Common Law of Torts: A Descriptive Theory' (2006) *Tennessee Law Review* 177, 208–209.

[69] Weinrib, *The Idea of Private Law* (n 8) 169 fn 53.

[70] Beever, *Rediscovering the Law of Negligence* (n 5) 379.

[71] Weinrib, 'Punishment and Disgorgement as Contract Remedies' (n 16); Weinrib, *Corrective Justice* (n 13) 97, 171.

[72] *cf* Weinrib, *Corrective Justice* (n 13) 97; See also Weinrib, 'Punishment and Disgorgement as Contract Remedies' (n 16) 86–93. The essentially one-sided focus of the inquiry whether to award punitive damages has been noted by the High Court of Australia: *Gray v Motor Accident Commission* [1998] HCA 70, (1998) 196 CLR 1, 7 (Gleeson CJ, McHugh, Gummow and Hayne JJ).

and deterrence measures in tort law (such as punitive damages) are valid because such measures are fundamentally inconsistent with its structure.[73] Consequently, illegality doctrine is inconsistent with the bipolar structure of tort law where used as an additional 'punishment' of the claimant,[74] or as a means of deterring others from engaging in similar conduct.[75]

A third implication of the adoption of corrective justice theory is that a claimant's entitlements should not be based on his or her moral culpability or blameworthiness. The 'special morality' of tort law—namely that of 'interpersonal morality'—has been described above. One manifestation of this peculiar form of morality is that tort law should not resolve claims according to the moral culpability of the parties. In the same way that the *defendant's* moral culpability or character does not affect liability,[76] the *claimant's* moral culpability or character likewise should not affect entitlements.[77] As McLachlin J recognised in *Hall v Hebert*, tort law does not require the claimant to be of a particular moral character in order to bring a claim.[78] An illegality principle that turns on the culpability of the claimant is inconsistent with corrective justice reasoning and therefore incoherent.[79] Accordingly, questions about whether the illegal act constitutes 'turpitude' that engages the public interest[80] are irrelevant on a corrective justice account of tort law. Likewise, approaches that compare the respective culpability or moral blameworthiness of the parties[81] are inconsistent with a principled approach to negligence law.[82]

[73] A Beever, 'The Structure of Aggravated and Exemplary Damages' (2003) 23 *Oxford Journal of Legal Studies* 87, particularly 107–09. Beever argues that the belief that punishment has a role to play in tort law stems from a misunderstanding that it is based on a mix of retributive and distributive justice: A Beever, 'Justice and Punishment in Tort: A Comparative Theoretical Analysis' in C Rickett (ed), *Justifying Private Law Remedies* (Oxford, Hart Publishing, 2008) ch 11.

[74] I am here using the term 'punishment' in a generic sense to mean 'a hardship or deprivation: the taking away of something of value for a wrong': M Bagaric, *Punishment & Sentencing: A Rational Approach* (London, Cavendish Publishing Ltd, 2001) 38.

[75] Contrast PS Davies, 'The Illegality Defence—Two Steps Forward, One Step Back?' (2009) 73(3) *The Conveyancer and Property Lawyer* 182, 186–88, where the author argues that the illegality defence should be used as a means of punishing the claimant in circumstances where the claimant's culpability 'outweighs' that of the defendant.

[76] Weinrib, 'The Special Morality of Tort Law' (n 17) 406; Weinrib, *The Idea of Private Law* (n 8) 54, 155–56; J Coleman, *Risks and Wrongs* (Oxford, Oxford University Press, 1992) 333–35. Compare J Goudkamp, 'The Spurious Relationship between Moral Blameworthiness and Liability for Negligence' (2004) 28 *Melbourne University Law Review* 343.

[77] EJ Weinrib, 'Illegality as a Tort Defence' (1976) *University of Toronto Law Journal* 28, 37.

[78] *Hall v Hebert* [1993] 2 SCR 159, 182.

[79] The culpability of the claimant is also irrelevant once the proper basis of illegality doctrine is understood to be the principle of coherence: ch 6, section VIII, Conclusion.

[80] See *Les Laboratoires Servier v Apotex Inc* [2014] UKSC 55, [2015] AC 430 [25]–[30] (Lord Sumption, Lords Neuberger and Clarke agreeing), [34] (Lord Mance). For a detailed discussion of the scope of 'turpitude' see G Virgo, 'The Defence of Illegality in Unjust Enrichment' in A Dyson, J Goudkamp and F Wilmot-Smith, *Defences in Unjust Enrichment* (London, Bloomsbury Publishing, 2016) 177–80.

[81] In *Patel v Mirza* [2016] UKSC 42 a majority of the Supreme Court of the United Kingdom held that a relevant factor will be whether there is a marked disparity in the parties' respective culpability.

[82] The main contemporary academic advocate of a test based on the comparative responsibility of the parties is Graham Virgo: G Virgo, 'Illegality's Role in the Law of Torts' in M Dyson (ed), *Unravelling Tort and Crime* (Cambridge, Cambridge University Press, 2014), ch 7.

In sum, a principle of illegality that focuses on factors relating to culpability or one-sidedly on the claimant's illegal conduct, or that seeks to reinforce the external goals of the criminal law, has no place in the law of negligence if viewed as a manifestation of corrective justice.

VI. Public Policy and Corrective Justice

A. Terminology

The illegality principle directly raises questions about the role of policy in the law of negligence. A variety of 'public' and 'legal' policy justifications have been put forward to deny compensation where the claimant's injuries are causally related to illegal conduct. The distinction between 'principles' and 'policies', and then further between 'public policies' and 'legal policies', is notoriously difficult to draw.[83] For example, the goal of promoting the coherence of the legal system is sometimes described as a 'public policy',[84] sometimes as a 'legal' or 'judicial' policy,[85] and at other times as a 'principle'.[86] To avoid the potential for confusion, in this book I have adopted the approach of Ernest Weinrib, who distinguishes between 'relational' policy considerations and 'extra-relational' policy considerations. Relational 'policy' considerations refer to factors that arise out of and evaluate the nature of the relationship between the parties to the dispute, such as evaluating the effect of recognising a duty of care on other legal obligations (legal coherence).[87] Relational 'policy' considerations conform to corrective justice reasoning. Extra-relational policy considerations—the pursuit of a collective community goal, such as deterrence—represent concerns that are independent of or external to the relationship of the parties. These concerns are contrary to corrective justice.[88] Accordingly, in this book I will refer to external (extra-relational) policy considerations as 'public policy' considerations.[89]

[83] K Barker et al, *The Law of Torts in Australia*, 5th edn (Melbourne, Oxford University Press, 2012) 459; Witting, 'Tort Law, Policy and the High Court of Australia' (n 3) 572–73. Jane Stapleton has suggested that it would be preferable to avoid that terminology altogether and instead refer to 'concerns' or 'factors': Stapleton, 'The Golden Thread' (n 6) 136.

[84] *Gray v Thames Trains Ltd* [2009] UKHL 33, [2009] 1 AC 1339 [7] (Lord Phillips), [24], [29] (Lord Hoffmann).

[85] ibid [74], [77] (Lord Rodger); *British Columbia v Zastowny* [2008] 1 SCR 27, [23], [30] (Rothstein J); *HL v Attorney General of Canada* [2005] SCR 401 [143] (Fish J).

[86] Lord Sumption, 'Reflections on the Law of Illegality' [2012] *Restitution Law Review* 1, 9; J Mance '*Ex Turpi Causa*—When Latin Avoids Liability' (2014) 18(2) *The Edinburgh Law Review* 175, 191.

[87] Weinrib, *Corrective Justice* (n 13) 66–67, 76, fn 95.

[88] ibid.

[89] Ronald Dworkin adopts a similar definition of 'policy'. He states that arguments of principle attempt to justify a decision by showing that the person has a right to the benefit claimed, whereas arguments of policy attempt to justify a decision by showing that it will increase aggregate social welfare. For a succinct summary of Dworkin's theory in this respect see J Bell, *Policy Arguments in Judicial Decisions* (Oxford, Clarendon Press, 1983) 14–17.

What is important is that Weinrib has clarified that not *all* concerns that might be classified as 'policy' are objectionable from a corrective justice perspective; only *extra-relational* public policy concerns must be excluded from the negligence analysis. It is quite legitimate to take into account *relational* 'policy' concerns when determining negligence entitlements.

B. Extra-relational Public Policy

At the centre of the debate about the proper function of tort law is whether judges should decide torts cases with a view only to rectifying wrongs and restoring justice in the relationship between the parties, or whether judges, at least in some circumstances, can take into account broader social, economic and political factors so as to maximise the benefit to society as a whole.[90]

Questions about the role of policy in the law of negligence feature centrally in the illegality cases. This area is characterised by an overlay of policy concerns that courts should not 'demean' themselves by providing assistance to a wrongdoing claimant. These policy concerns are reflected in illegality principles that are based on the 'affront to public conscience' of awarding a remedy to the wrongdoing claimant;[91] the need to maintain the dignity of the court;[92] the inappropriateness of a court regulating the rights of parties to an illegal enterprise;[93] or the need to avoid an appearance of condoning the criminal conduct.[94] There has also been an overlay of concerns about the broader societal consequences of decisions, reflected in the development of doctrine designed to combat the 'offensiveness' to public notions of the fair distribution of resources that a claimant should be compensated for the consequences of his or her own criminal conduct,[95] or the need for the court to avoid actually condoning the criminal conduct by lessening the normative effect of the criminal law.[96] Many of the tests adopted by the courts, while

[90] For a representative range of views about the legitimacy of using public policy, see, eg, J Bell, *Policy Arguments in Judicial Decisions* ibid 14–17; M Kirby, *Judicial Activism: Authority, Principle and Policy in the Judicial Method* The Hamlyn Lectures (London, Sweet & Maxwell, 2004); D Heydon, 'Judicial Activism and the Death of the Rule of Law' [2004] *Otago Law Review* 2; Dietrich, 'What is "Lawyering"?' (n 40); H Luntz, 'The Use of Policy in Negligence Cases in the High Court of Australia' in M Bryan (ed), *Private Law in Theory and Practice* (Abingdon, Routledge-Cavendish, 2007); Witting, 'Tort Law, Policy and the High Court of Australia' (n 3); A Robertson, 'Policy-based reasoning in duty of care cases' (2013) 33(1) *Legal Studies* 119.

[91] *Thackwell v Barclays Bank plc* [1986] 1 All ER 676 (QBD); *Kirkham v Chief Constable of Greater Manchester Police* [1990] 2 QB 283 (CA), 291 (Lloyd LJ); *Euro-Diam v Bathurst Ltd* [1990] 1 QB 1 (CA), 35 (Kerr LJ, Russell LJ and Sir Denys Buckley agreeing). This test was later abandoned in *Tinsley v Milligan* [1994] 1 AC 340.

[92] *Parkinson v College of Ambulance Ltd* [1925] 2 KB 1, 13 (Lush J).

[93] See the judgments of Jacobs J in *Progress and Properties Ltd v Craft* (1976) 135 CLR 651 and *Jackson v Harrison* (1978) 138 CLR 438.

[94] *Cross v Kirkby* [2000] EWCA Civ 426 (CA), [76] (Beldam LJ); *Gray v Thames Trains Ltd* [2008] EWCA Civ 713, [2009] 1 AC 1339 (CA) [20] (the Court).

[95] *Gray v Thames Trains Ltd* (n 84) [51] (Lord Hoffmann).

[96] *Gala v Preston* [1991] HCA 18, (1991) 172 CLR 243, 270–73 (Brennan J).

ostensibly based on legal principle, are no more than a cloak for policy decisions regarding whether it is appropriate in all the circumstances to allow the claim, and can in effect amount to a public conscience test in disguise.[97] There is recent authority in England for openly balancing public policy considerations for and against the application of illegality doctrine.[98]

Public policy reasoning is inconsistent with the correlative structure of negligence liability. Public policy concerns are external to negligence law, as they are external to the parties' relationship: policies ignore one or both parties.[99] Policy considerations that are 'uncontrolled by the relationship of the parties' can have no normative relevance to the position of the claimant.[100] Thus, corrective justice theorists argue that an appeal to policy is not only not *needed*, it is *impermissible.*[101] Policy concerns 'fragment the relationship between the parties and transform the law's concern from the wrong done and suffered to the choice of social goals'.[102] Accordingly, the denial of a claim on public policy grounds because of the claimant's illegality—whether by way of a freestanding defence or through the negation of an element of the claim such as duty of care or causation—is inconsistent with corrective justice because the focus is no longer on the relationship of the parties.

In Chapter 4 I will discuss in detail the public policy-balancing approach as advocated by the Supreme Court of the United Kingdom.[103] I will explain that deciding illegality claims according to whether the public policy in the individual case justifies its application is not only theoretically incoherent, it will have a further destabilising effect on the law in this area due to the inherent instability of policy reasoning.

C. Relational 'Policy' of Legal Coherence

The High Court of Australia in *Sullivan v Moody* held that there are various 'legal policies' or 'policies of the law' at work that can be identified and applied to novel cases, including the policy of legal coherence.[104] Weinrib also recognises that there

[97] R Glofcheski, 'Plaintiff's Illegality as a Bar to Recovery of Personal Injury Damages' (1999) 19 *Legal Studies* 6, 12; see also 13–14 (referring to the standard of care explanation); M McInnes, 'Advancement, Illegality and Restitution' (1997) 5 *Australian Property Law Journal* 1, 16 (referring to the statutory purpose explanation). See also generally ch 5, where I explain that the connection tests are also a proxy for public policy.

[98] *Hounga v Allen* [2014] UKSC 47, [2014] 1 WLR 2889 (Lord Wilson, Lady Hale and Lord Kerr agreeing); *Les Laboratoires Servier v Apotex Inc* (n 80) (Lord Toulson); *Bilta (UK) Ltd (in liquidation) v Nazir (No 2)* [2015] UKSC 23, [2016] AC 1 (Lords Toulson and Hodge); *Patel v Mirza* (n 81) [101] (Lord Toulson, Lady Kerr and Lords Kerr, Wilson and Hodge agreeing).

[99] Weinrib, *The Idea of Private Law* (n 8) 210–14; Beever, *Rediscovering the Law of Negligence* (n 5) 176.

[100] Weinrib, *Corrective Justice* (n 13) 60.

[101] Beever, *Rediscovering the Law of Negligence* (n 5) 29–30.

[102] Weinrib, 'Does Tort Law Have a Future?' (n 25) 571; see also Weinrib, *Corrective Justice* (n 13) 61.

[103] See the cases in n 98.

[104] *Sullivan v Moody* [2001] HCA 59, (2001) 207 CLR 562, 579 [49] (the Court). See also *Cattanach v Melchior* [2003] HCA 38, (2003) 215 CLR 1, 34 [70]–[74] (McHugh and Gummow JJ). 'Policies of the

are important legal policies that derive from the operation of the entire system of law, and endorses the statements in *Sullivan v Moody* of the importance of the law operating as a coherent, unified institution.[105] Legal coherence is a major theme of Weinrib's corrective justice works,[106] and, as I will explain further in Chapter 6, considerations of legal coherence are relational considerations and hence, unlike public policy considerations, are consistent with the correlative structure of negligence liability.[107]

It is important, however, that there is a clear understanding as to the precise circumstances when an award of compensation to a wrongdoing claimant will create an incoherence with the area of law proscribing the conduct. A lack of clarity about the basis of the coherence rationale can leave it open to manipulation by judges pursuing a public policy agenda.[108] There is a need to clearly delineate the ambit of the coherence rationale to guard against its use as a vehicle for public policy decision-making. This book undertakes that task.

VII. Conclusion

I have explained in this chapter my reasons for adopting corrective justice theory as the analytical framework for considering claims by wrongdoing claimants, as well as my caveats on the adoption of that theory. I have also discussed the key implications of adopting corrective justice theory, including that the pursuit of public policy objectives though the application of illegality doctrine is impermissible as being incompatible with the bipolar structure of negligence law. Moreover, a 'one-sided' principle of illegality that focuses only on the claimant's illegal conduct is inconsistent with corrective justice because it is not reflective of the correlative structure of negligence liability.[109] Nor can a principle of illegality, consistently with corrective justice, be founded on the claimant's moral culpability or be designed so as to reinforce external goals, such as the goals of the criminal law. In Chapter 3 I will expand on this last point, by exploring further the relationship between tort law and criminal law.

law' have been described as 'abstract legal propositions that explain or rationalize relatively less abstract legal propositions': P Cane, 'Taking Disagreement Seriously: Courts, Legislatures and the Reform of Tort Law' in M Bryan (ed), *Private Law in Theory and Practice* (Abingdon, Routledge-Cavendish, 2007) 32.

105 Weinrib, *Corrective Justice* (n 13) 76.

106 Though admittedly Weinrib is concerned primarily with the internal coherence of private law actions.

107 See ch 6, section III, Concerns About Legal Coherence are Relational Concerns.

108 For an example, see the majority judgment in *Hounga v Allen* (n 98) [44].

109 Weinrib, *The Idea of Private Law* (n 8) 169.

3

The Tort–Crime Interface

I. Introduction

This chapter examines the tort–crime interface as it applies to illegality doctrine. The principles discussed here—together with those from Chapter 2—provide the conceptual foundation for the remainder of the book.

Illegality doctrine is not confined to conduct that is criminal; however, most cases that have come before the courts have involved a criminal offence. This area therefore raises fundamental questions about the relationship between criminal law and tort law and the extent to which an award of compensation to the claimant for the consequences of his or her illegal conduct would create a conflict with that area of the criminal law that proscribes and punishes that conduct. The intersection between tort law and criminal law is only recently receiving attention from the courts and commentators. Graham Virgo has observed that it is a 'frontier for legal analysis which has not received the attention it deserves' and further identifies a tendency among members of the judiciary and commentators to assume that there is no benefit to investigating how parallel concepts and principles operate across the legal boundaries.[1] Virgo identifies claims arising from an illegality, in particular the sanction-shifting claims, as raising fundamental issues about the boundary between tort and crime and the extent to which it is desirable to ensure consistency between these bodies of law.[2]

In this chapter I argue that coherence between tort law and criminal law is undeniably an important value of the legal system. However, I also argue that it should not be assumed that an award of damages for harm caused by criminal conduct will necessarily create an incoherence with the criminal law. Given the divergent functions of these bodies of law, the actual potential for a conflict arising between them because of an award of compensation to a wrongdoing claimant is minimal. My further argument is that a principle of illegality should not be used to support the goals of the criminal law—not only would this be contrary to the corrective justice basis of tort law, but a principle of illegality is simply not an effective vehicle

[1] G Virgo, 'We Do This in the Criminal Law and That in the Law of Tort: A New Fusion Debate' in SGA Pitel, JW Neyers, E Chamberlain (eds), *Tort Law: Challenging Orthodoxy* (Oxford, Hart Publishing, 2013) 117.

[2] ibid 103–110.

for supporting the aims of the criminal law. I return to the interaction of tort law and criminal law in chapter 8 where I argue that rules from the criminal law that establish criminal responsibility should not determine the question of who bears civil responsibility for the harm resulting from the criminal act.

II. Consistency between Tort Law and Criminal Law an Important Value of the Legal System

There is no consensus about the correct model for the relationship between tort law and criminal law. One model, dubbed the 'orthodoxy of partition' by Matthew Dyson, is that the two bodies of law are entirely separate and there is no benefit to seeking to achieve consistency of interpretation and approach.[3] Adherents to this view tend to emphasise the divergent objectives of tort law and criminal law as a justification for variances in the application of parallel substantive rules. To support this view they might point to the statement by Hayne J in *Harriton v Stephens* that the chief focus of tort law is compensation for harm, whereas the chief focus of the criminal law is the infliction of punishment by the State for conduct that contravenes stipulated standards.[4] Corrective justice theorists would undoubtedly prefer the similar, though rights-oriented, observations of Lord Scott in *Ashley v Chief Constable of Sussex Police*, made in the context of self-defence:

> In my opinion … this plea for consistency between the criminal law and the civil law [rules of self-defence] lacks cogency for the ends to be served by the two systems are very different. One of the main functions of the criminal law is to identify, and provide punitive sanctions for, behaviour that is categorised as criminal because it is damaging to the good order of society. … The function of the civil law of tort is different. Its main function is to identify and protect the rights that every person is entitled to assert against, and require to be respected by, others. The rights of one person, however, often run counter to the rights of others and the civil law, in particular the law of tort, must then strike a balance between the conflicting rights.[5]

Lord Scott here provides a clear statement of the different aims of criminal and tort law. Nevertheless, the adoption of a rigid position that the two bodies of law are completely separate and that there is no reason to seek consistency of approach between them would be at odds with the recent emphasis by the High Court of Australia on the importance of the legal system operating as a cohesive unit.[6]

[3] M Dyson, 'Challenging the Orthodoxy of Crime's Precedence over Tort: Suspending a Tort Claim Where a Crime May Exist' in Pitel et al, *Tort Law: Challenging Orthodoxy* (Oxford, Hart Publishing, 2013) 121–25. See also Virgo, 'We Do This in the Criminal Law' (n 1) 98–99.

[4] *Harriton v Stephens* [2006] HCA 15, (2006) 226 CLR 52 [164].

[5] *Ashley v Chief Constable of Sussex Police* [2008] UKHL 25, [2008] AC 962 [17]–[18]; see also [76] (Lord Carswell).

[6] For discussion of relevant authorities and the importance of legal coherence see Michael Gillooly, 'Legal Coherence in the High Court: String theory for Lawyers' (2013) *Australian Law Journal* 33.

A major theme of recent High Court decisions has been that a duty of care does not arise where it would disrupt a statutory scheme governing the relationship of the parties or where it would subvert established liability rules.[7] In *Miller v Miller*, the High Court turned its 'cohesion spotlight' onto the law relating to joint criminal enterprises, stressing the need to ensure that the imposition of negligence liability is compatible with the purpose of the criminal legislation proscribing the claimant's conduct. The importance of promoting coherence between tort law and the criminal law when determining the application of illegality principles has also been emphasised by the Supreme Court of Canada and the House of Lords.[8] The need to preserve legal coherence is also an important theme of Weinribian corrective justice theories.[9]

Coherence between tort law and criminal law is thus an important aspiration of the legal system. The courts should seek to interpret the rules in both tort and crime in such a way as to ensure that they operate harmoniously. This does not necessarily mean, however, that the goals of tort law should cede to those of the criminal law. Matthew Dyson refers to the view that tort law should always cede to the criminal law as the 'orthodoxy of priority'.[10] The main judicial proponent of the 'orthodoxy of priority' in Australia is Brennan J, who has argued that the criminal law is the primary means by which societal order is achieved, and that civil law principles should not be allowed to trespass upon the operation of the criminal law.[11] The view that tort law is automatically subservient to the criminal law should be rejected. It has been pointed out that there are many torts that are more harmful and that have more deleterious consequences to society than many crimes—compare a negligent act causing a major train derailment with a minor theft—and thus it can be doubted whether criminal law should be seen as necessarily discharging a more important social function than tort law.[12] Applied in particular to illegality claims, the negligence that has caused the injury might be much more serious in terms of 'social consequences' than the offence committed by the claimant. Thus, the objective of providing rectification of a wrong might be just as important a legal value (or more important) than the policies underlying

[7] *Sullivan v Moody* [2001] HCA 59, (2001) 207 CLR 562 [42], [53]–[55] (the Court); *Tame v New South Wales* [2002] HCA 35, (2002) 211 CLR 317 [28] (Gleeson CJ), [58] (Gaudron J) [123] (McHugh J) [323] (Callinan J); *C.A.L. No 14 Pty Ltd v Motor Accidents Insurance Board* [2009] HCA 47, (2009) 239 CLR 390 [39]–[42] (Gummow, Heydon and Crennan JJ). See also *Hunter and New England Local Health District v McKenna* [2014] HCA 44, (2014) 253 CLR 270.

[8] *Hall v Hebert* [1993] 2 SCR 159; *Gray v Thames Trains Ltd* [2008] EWCA Civ 713, [2009] 1 AC 1339.

[9] *Hall v Hebert* ibid 181–2 (McLachlin J); Ernest J Weinrib, *Corrective Justice* (Oxford, Oxford University Press, 2012) 76; A Beever, *Rediscovering the Law of Negligence* (Oxford, Hart Publishing, 2007) 379–83.

[10] Dyson 'Challenging the Orthodoxy' (n 3) 125–26.

[11] *Gala v Preston* [1991] HCA 18, (1991) 172 CLR 243, 272; see also 271.

[12] *cf* J Goudkamp, 'Can Tort Law be used to Deflect the Impact of Criminal Sanctions? The Role of the Illegality Defence' (2006) 14 *Torts Law Journal* 20, 44; J Hall, 'Interrelations of Criminal Law and Torts II' (1943) 43 *Columbia Law Review* 967, 972–73.

the rule that criminalised the claimant's act.[13] For this reason, criminal law policies should not be enshrined as necessarily dominant,[14] and claims arising from an illegality should not be rejected merely on the ground that this is needed to promote the more 'important' goals or policies of the criminal law.

In any event, it is important to keep in mind in this context that consistency does not mean sameness. Difference does not necessarily mean disharmony, and courts should not assume that because the principles in tort law produce a different outcome to criminal law that a conflict has arisen that must be resolved: 'Coherence does not necessarily require symmetry or even tidiness'.[15] Graham Virgo has pointed out that it is not always necessary to remove differences between tort law and criminal law, though it is necessary for those differences to be acknowledged and justified by reference to underlying principles.[16] Differences in the operation of concepts or principles will commonly arise between the criminal law and tort law, and those difference will sometimes be justified due to the divergent functions of the two areas of law.[17] For example, for reasons I develop elsewhere, it is not desirable to seek to achieve symmetry between principles of criminal and civil responsibility for the purpose of allocating responsibility for harm resulting from the claimant's illegal act.[18]

Thus, the objective should not be to achieve absolute consistency at the expense of intelligible law. However, there will be areas where the two areas of law will intersect, and where the principles of both branches of the law should be developed as a coherent whole. Illegality doctrine sits at one point of intersection between tort and crime, and provides an example where negligence and criminal law principles need to be melded so as to develop a unified law across the two branches. The Chief Justice of Canada, Beverley McLachlin, has explained this point with characteristic eloquence. After referring to the need for coherence between tort law and criminal law, her Honour continued:

> This does not mean, however, that the principles of the criminal law necessarily trump those of tort law or even that the principles of the two domains will be relevant to one another in a large number of cases. Criminal and tort law have different objectives and their internal logic often works according to different principles. There are often good reasons for not applying the same principles across these domains, as recognised by Lord Scott [in *Ashley v Chief Constable of Sussex Police*]. But there are some situations where it may be useful to consider the principles of both domains as a coherent whole, provided

[13] *Jackson v Harrison* [1978] HCA 17, (1978) 138 CLR 438, 465 (Murphy J); NH Crago, 'The Defence of Illegality in Negligence Actions' (1964) 4 *Melbourne University Law Review* 534, 547; EJ Weinrib, 'Illegality as a Tort Defence' (1976) 26 *University of Toronto Law Journal* 28, 44.

[14] Weinrib, 'Illegality as a Tort Defence' ibid 43; J Goudkamp, 'A Long, Hard Look at Gray v Thames Trains Ltd' in PS Davies and J Pita (eds), *Jurisprudence of Lord Hoffmann: A Festschrift in Honour of Lord Leonard Hoffmann* (London, Bloomsbury Publishing, 2015) 52.

[15] (Lord) R Toulson, 'Foreword' in M Dyson (ed), *Unravelling Tort and Crime* (Cambridge, Cambridge University Press, 2014).

[16] Virgo, 'We Do This in the Criminal Law' (n 1) 117.

[17] ibid.

[18] See ch 8, section III, The Consistency Rule.

> this can be done in a way that respects the principles of each domain. The illegality defence is one such situation.[19] (footnote omitted)

This recognises two points: (a) due to the quite distinct functions of tort law and criminal law, there is only a limited potential for a genuine conflict between them to arise, but (b) where a conflict does arise the aim should be to develop the principles of both areas so as to resolve this conflict. I will elaborate on point (a) in the next section, where I will explain that claims arising from an illegality will not usually create the potential for an incoherence with the criminal law. This is because an award of compensation for injuries sustained as a result of illegal conduct does not generally permit the claimant to profit from his or her crime, nor undermine or stultify the punitive or normative effect of the criminal law.[20] I will elaborate on point (b) in Chapters 6–9, where I will examine the circumstances where the principles of tort law and criminal law will operate cohesively to prevent a claim arising from an illegality. For present purposes, it suffices to concede that the result of striving for legal coherence between these two areas of the law when formulating a doctrine of illegality for negligence law will be that the principles of negligence law will be shaped so as to recognise the impact of the principles of the criminal law (not the other way around).[21] However, that is quite different to an argument that the negligence law must cede to the *policies* or *goals* of the criminal law. Moreover, it is the inevitable result of the fact that, in this specific context, negligence law is responding to the prohibition on the claimant's conduct by the criminal law.

III. An Award of Compensation is not 'Profit'

It is commonplace in this area to point out that compensation for harm does not result in a profit to the claimant. Focusing for now on claims for injuries sustained while in the course of committing an illegal act (joint and unilateral illegality cases), an award of compensation does not create an inconsistency in the law by permitting the claimant to profit from the wrongdoing because receiving compensation for an injury is not a profit. The claimant in these cases is not seeking compensation that would enable the claimant to escape the consequences of a criminal sanction, nor the profits or earnings from illegal conduct. Rather, the compensation is for the injury suffered: 'it provides the value of an injury inflicted

[19] B McLachlin, 'Weaving the Law's Seamless Web: Reflections on the Illegality Defence in Tort Law' in A Dyson, J Goudkamp and F Wilmot-Smith (eds), *Defences in Torts* (Oxford, Hart Publishing, Oxford, 2015) 220.

[20] Graham Virgo makes the same point in the context of unjust enrichment claims: G Virgo, 'The Defence of Illegality in Unjust Enrichment' in Dyson et al, *Defences in Unjust Enrichment* (London, Bloomsbury Publishing, 2016) 173–74.

[21] *cf* K Burns et al, 'Australia: A Land of Plenty (of Legislative Regimes), in M Dyson (ed), *Comparing Tort and Crime: Learning From Across and Within Legal Systems* (Cambridge, Cambridge University Press, 2015) 408.

by another'.[22] Beever explains that an award of compensation for injuries sustained while acting illegally does not permit a rebate or evasion of the criminal sanction:

> Were the claimant [injured through the negligent driving of a criminal accomplice] able to recover in tort, he would be placed in the position in which he would have been had the defendant not driven negligently. This means that the Court would seek to place the claimant in the position in which he would have been had he not been *physically injured*. But this does not mean that the claimant would be compensated for the criminal sanction imposed in accordance with [the criminal legislation proscribing the taking and unlawful use of a motor vehicle]. In the end, the claimant's position would be that of a person uninjured *but punished*.[23]

Beever recognises that allowing the claimant to recover damages in negligence for injuries sustained while acting illegally does not result in the claimant escaping the consequences of the criminal law. The claimant is punished but (as far as money can do) uninjured.[24] Accordingly, it is quite consistent to punish the claimant through the criminal courts yet compensate the claimant for his or her injuries through the civil courts; the one does not undermine or cancel out the other.

In fact, for this category of claim the converse is true; it is not the *allowance* of a claim that disrupts the punitive function of the criminal law, but the *denial* of a claim that has this effect. It is widely acknowledged by writers in this area that denial of compensation inflicts an additional sanction on the claimant to that imposed by the criminal courts.[25] (I am here using the term 'sanction' in a generic sense to mean 'a hardship or deprivation; the taking away of something of value for a wrong.')[26] The imposition of an additional sanction on the claimant potentially distorts the proportional aims of criminal sentencing.[27] The principle of proportionality in sentencing is one that is widely accepted by lawyers and philosophers.[28] The sentence imposed should be commensurate with the gravity of the offence and the culpability of the wrongdoer. Where the claimant's conduct has been dealt with by the criminal justice system (including where a decision has been made not to prosecute the claimant), the denial of a claim in tort will

[22] M McInnes, 'Ex Turpi Causa and Tort—A Canadian Perspective' [1993] *Cambridge Law Journal* 379, 381. See also Beever, *Rediscovering the Law of Negligence* (n 9) 374; J Goudkamp, 'The Illegality Defence in the Law of Negligence after Miller v Miller' (2011) 7(10) *Australian Civil Liability* 130, 131.

[23] Beever, *Rediscovering the Law of Negligence* ibid 374.

[24] ibid.

[25] Goudkamp, 'Can Tort Law be used to Deflect the Impact of Criminal Sanctions?' (n 12) 36–7; J Goudkamp, 'The Defence of Joint Illegal Enterprise' (2010) 34 *Melbourne University Law Review* 425, 442; Beever, *Rediscovering the Law of Negligence* (n 9) 374. See also *Jackson v Harrison* (n 13) 464 (Murphy J).

[26] M Bagaric, *Punishment & Sentencing: A Rational Approach* (London, Cavendish Publishing Ltd, 2001) 38.

[27] Crago 'The Defence of Illegality in Negligence Actions' (n 13) 547; Weinrib, 'Illegality as a Tort Defence' (n 13) 45; Goudkamp, 'Can Tort Law be used to Deflect the Impact of Criminal Sanctions?' (n 12) 37. For the same argument in the context of unjust enrichment refer to Virgo, 'The Defence of Illegality in Unjust Enrichment' (n 20) 175.

[28] Bagaric, *Punishment & Sentencing* (n 26) 163–64.

result in a punishment not envisaged by the criminal system.[29] The imposition of the civil sanction amounts to a 'surcharge'[30] and thus distorts the attempts of the criminal law to determine in advance a proportional sanction.

Further, the punishment that denial of a tort action inflicts is measured, not by reference to the seriousness of the offence and the culpability of the claimant, but rather by the fortuitous amount of the loss.[31] It has been pointed out that 'tortious actions are often a blunt and ineffective means to punish wrongdoers' as the punishment will usually bear no relationship to the crime committed.[32] In the main context in which it is recognised (contrary to corrective justice) that negligence law can fulfil a punitive function, namely in the context of punitive damages, the High Court of Australia has introduced safeguards to ensure that offenders are not disproportionately punished by the imposition of the civil sanction in addition to the criminal sanction.[33] No such safeguards against disproportion exist, however, where the courts are considering refusing compensation to a wrongdoing claimant.

Weinrib sums up the problems as follows: 'What is at stake here is a variation on the well-known cleavage between tort law, which reacts to fortuitous losses, and criminal law, which pre-announces measured penalties to anticipated undesirable conduct.'[34] Weinrib then goes on to point out that the refusal of the negligence claim frustrates both branches of the law. Tort law cannot fulfil its function of rectifying wrongs, and criminal law is prevented from fulfilling its function of providing proportional and predetermined punishments for wrongful conduct.[35] Further, unless there is a clear intention by the legislature to inflict punishment by way of a denial of a civil claim, the increased punishment is unauthorised by statute.[36] This offends the fundamental principle of the law that punishment should be limited to that which the legislature has stipulated.[37] A separate concern is that it is a punishment imposed without the usual procedural safeguards that apply to a criminal conviction (such as proof beyond reasonable doubt).[38] For these

[29] Weinrib, 'Illegality as a Tort Defence' (n 13) 45; J Goudkamp, 'Self-defence and Illegality under the Civil Liability Act 2002 (NSW)' (2009)18 *Torts Law Journal* 61, 85.

[30] Weinrib, 'Illegality as a Tort Defence' ibid 51.

[31] ibid 46–47. See also RA Prentice, 'Of Tort Reform and Millionaire Muggers: Should an Obscure Equitable Doctrine Be Revived to Dent the Litigation Crisis? (1995) 32 *San Diego Law Review* 53, 115–119; Goudkamp, 'Self-defence and Illegality' (n 29) 67–68; Goudkamp, 'Can Tort Law be used to Deflect the Impact of Criminal Sanctions?' (n 12) 37; Goudkamp, 'The Defence of Joint Illegal Enterprise' (n 25) 44; J Goudkamp and L Mayr, 'The Doctrine of Illegality Interference with Chattels' in A Dyson, J Goudkamp and F Wilmot-Smith (eds), (Hart Publishing, Oxford, 2015) 239–40.

[32] M Bagaric, P Faris and R Carter, *Torts: Compensation for Harm* (Melbourne, Palgrave MacMillan, 2011) 12.

[33] *Gray v Motor Accident Commission* [1998] HCA 70, (1998) 196 CLR 1, 14–17 (Gleeson CJ, McHugh, Gummow and Hayne JJ).

[34] Weinrib, 'Illegality as a Tort Defence' (n 13) 45–46.

[35] ibid.

[36] Beever, *Rediscovering the Law of Negligence* (n 9) 380.

[37] This fundamental principle is recognised by R Dworkin, *Taking Rights Seriously* (London, Duckworth, 1977) 26.

[38] Prentice 'Of Tort Reform and Millionaire Muggers' (n 31) 116.

reasons, it is not the award of compensation, but rather the refusal of compensation, which potentially creates a discordance with the criminal law in respect of claims for injuries sustained while the claimant was committing a criminal act.

The sanction-shifting claims and claims for illegal profits and earnings raise different considerations. In these cases an award of compensation can create an inconsistency in the law either because it allows the claimant to escape the consequences of a lawfully imposed sanction or to profit from illegal conduct. Even in this context, however, courts need to be conscious of the risk of double punishment.[39] Thus, Kirby P (as he then was) in *State Rail Authority of New South Wales v Wiegold* suggested that double punishment can result where a claimant is denied a claim for loss of earning capacity resulting from conviction and detention on top of punishment by way of imprisonment.[40] I will return to discuss claims of this kind in more detail in Chapter 8, where I will argue that an award of compensation for loss of earning capacity consequential upon conviction and detention does not create an incongruity with the criminal law, and hence this head of loss should be recoverable.[41] However, an award of compensation for non-economic losses resulting from detention would create an incongruity with the criminal law and hence this head of loss should be irrecoverable.

In summary, with the exception of some sanction-shifting claims and claims for illegal profits and earnings, an award of compensation to the wrongdoing claimant does not create an inconsistency with the criminal law. There is an important qualification to this statement, which is that an incoherence will arise where it is part of the purpose of the statute proscribing the conduct to deprive the claimant of the benefit of a civil action. I will defer discussion of this important point to Chapter 7.

IV. Illegality Doctrine Does Not Support the Criminal Law in a Conceptually Coherent or Rational Way

It is sometimes suggested that illegality doctrine should be applied so as to further the goals of the criminal law.[42] The clearest statement of this in Australia is in the judgment of Brennan J in *Gala v Preston*, where his Honour argued that a claim by a wrongdoing claimant should be denied where it would undermine the normative effect of the criminal law.[43] Before discussing Brennan J's approach,

[39] K Roach, 'Blaming the Victim: Canadian Law, Causation and Residential Schools' (2014) 64 *University of Toronto Law Journal* 566, 582–83.

[40] *State Rail Authority of New South Wales v Wiegold* (1991) 25 NSWLR 500, 505.

[41] See ch 8, section VI, Loss or Damage That Is Recoverable.

[42] See, eg, PS Davies, 'The Illegality Defence—Two Steps Forward, One Step Back?' (2009) 73(3) *The Conveyancer and Property Lawyer* 182, 186–88. Davies argues that punishment is an appropriate objective of an illegality defence.

[43] *Gala v Preston* (n 11) 270–73.

I will first address the point that an aspiration towards coherence does not provide a reason for using a principle of illegality as a means of supporting and furthering the goals of the criminal law. I will argue, in reliance in part on Weinrib's writings in this area, that reinforcement of the goals of the criminal law are not legitimate or rational aims of a coherent system of negligence law.

Contemporary theories of crime and punishment emphasise that the key goals of crime and punishment are proportional sentencing and general deterrence.[44] There are both theoretical and pragmatic objections to the use of illegality doctrine as a vehicle to promote these goals of the criminal law. From a theoretical perspective, the promotion of criminal law goals in the law of negligence is inconsistent with the bipolar structure of negligence law. Punishment is a one-sided consideration that focuses unilaterally on the conduct of one of the parties (normally the defendant, but in this case the claimant).[45] Further, a goal of general deterrence is inconsistent with the correlative structure of liability because it focuses only on the conduct of one of the parties (in this context, the claimant) without reference to the relationship between them, and seeks to promote goals independent of the relationship of the parties. In this respect, the Chief Justice of Canada, Beverley McLachlin, has observed that the policy goal of deterrence is not consistent with a corrective justice account of tort law because it 'fails to embrace both parties'.[46] Consequently, an illegality principle that has the express purpose of furthering the goals of the criminal law is inconsistent with the justificatory structure of negligence law.

There are also pragmatic objections to the suggestion that the law of torts through the proxy of illegality doctrine can pursue the goals of the criminal law. Illegality doctrine is incapable of supporting the goals of the criminal law in a rational and effective way. Application of illegality doctrine to deny a claim for compensation has a distortive effect on the overall pattern of regulation for that conduct.[47] Moreover, as argued in section III above, illegality doctrine distorts proportional sentencing and undermines the fundamental principle that punishment must be authorised by Parliament. Thus, a principle of illegality is poorly equipped to support the goal of the criminal law to impose proportional punishments.

[44] I Freckelton QC (title ed), *The Laws of Australia*, Title 12 'Criminal Sentencing' (Lawbook Co) [12.1.240]–[12.1.250] (current as at 14 November 2014) [accessed 20 April 2016]; See section 12.1.3 'Proportionality' (current updating author: D Andrewartha). This represents the retributivist view of criminal liability, though it is noted that utilitarian theorists likewise identify these as to the two key goals of the criminal law: Bagaric, *Punishment & Sentencing* (n 26) chs 6, 7, 273–75; M Bagaric and T Alexander, '(Marginal) General Deterrence Doesn't Work—And What it Means for Sentencing' (2011) 35 *Criminal Law Journal* 269, 280–82.

[45] EJ Weinrib, 'Punishment and Disgorgement as Contract Remedies' (2003) 78 *Chicago-Kent Law Review* 55, 86–93. The essentially one-sided focus of the inquiry whether to award punitive damages was recognised by the High Court of Australia in *Gray v Motor Accident Commission* (n 33) 7 (Gleeson CJ, McHugh, Gummow and Hayne JJ).

[46] McLachlin 'Weaving the Law's Seamless Web' (n 19) 221, citing EJ Weinrib 'The Special Morality of Tort Law' (1989) 34 (3) *McGill Law Journal* 403, 409.

[47] Weinrib in 'Illegality as a Tort Defence' (n 13) 44–46.

Nor is the application of an illegality bar effective as a mechanism of deterrence. Despite the suggestions of Brennan J in *Gala v Preston* to the contrary,[48] the denial of a civil claim is unlikely to reinforce the deterrent effect of the criminal legislation proscribing the conduct. Brennan J held that a duty of care is not owed by one participant in a joint illegal enterprise to another participant where the recognition of a duty of care would condone a breach of the law creating the offence.[49] Recognition of a duty of care in these circumstances would, his Honour said, be contrary to public policy.[50] Brennan J held that admission of a duty of care will condone a breach of the criminal law where it would destroy the normative influence of the criminal offence taking into account matters such as: the gravity of the offence; the threat to public order or safety, and the impact that recognition of a duty of care would have on the effectiveness of criminal penalties designed to secure obedience to the law.[51]

This analysis is deeply problematic and the High Court in *Miller v Miller* was correct to reject it.[52] It is doubtful that it is possible to gauge the extent to which allowing a civil remedy might impair or destroy the normative (especially the deterrent) effect of the criminal law, and Brennan J gives no guidance as to the way in which this effect could be measured.[53] His Honour in fact accepted that the principle could not be expressed in a manner that was 'self-executing', and that ultimately a decision that the normative effect of a particular offence would be destroyed by permitting the claim must be a determination of policy.[54] The highly subjective nature of the exercise envisaged by Brennan J has been remarked upon with disfavour by commentators in this area.[55]

Additionally, Brennan J's analysis is flawed to the extent that it is premised on the notion that tort law remedies can influence behaviour. It is widely acknowledged that tort law is unlikely to have a significant normative effect on people's conduct, and that any normative effect would be inconsequential when compared with the impact of the threat of criminal sanctions.[56] There is scant empirical research into

[48] *Gala v Preston* (n 11) 270–273.

[49] ibid.

[50] ibid 271.

[51] ibid 270–73.

[52] *Miller v Miller* [2011] HCA 9, (2011) 242 CLR 446, [66]–[67].

[53] ibid [66]; *Gala v Preston* (n 11) 278 (Dawson J). For other criticisms of Brennan's 'non-condonation' approach, see Beever, *Rediscovering the Law of Negligence* (n 9) 372–75.

[54] *Gala v Preston* (n 11) 273.

[55] RW Kostal, 'Currents in the Counter-reformation: Illegality and Duty of Care in Canada and Australia' (1995) *Tort Law Review* 100, 107–108; R Glofcheski, 'Claimant's Illegality as a Bar to Recovery of Personal Injury Damages' (1999) 19(6) *Legal Studies* 6, 15.

[56] Prentice 'Of Tort Reform and Millionaire Muggers' (n 31) 110–15; Goudkamp, 'The Defence of Joint Illegal Enterprise' (n 25) 441; G Virgo, 'Illegality's Role in the Law of Torts', in M Dyson (ed), *Unravelling Tort and Crime* (Cambridge, Cambridge University Press, 2014) 187; Goudkamp and Mayr 'The Doctrine of Illegality Interference with Chattels' (n 31) 240. See also R Stevens, *Torts and Rights*, (Oxford, Oxford University Press, 2007) 322–23; J Mance, '*Ex Turpi Causa*—When Latin Avoids Liability' (2014) 18(2) *The Edinburgh Law Review* 175, 182–83; G Virgo, 'The Defence of Illegality in Unjust Enrichment' (n 20) 174.

the effect of private law on real world behaviour.[57] Nevertheless, there is a strong basis for assuming that tort law will not affect the incidence of crime. The weight of empirical studies suggests that even the harshest criminal sanctions do not reduce crime.[58] It is highly unlikely then that the denial of tortious remedies would have this effect. The Chief Justice of the Supreme Court of Canada, Beverley McLachlin, observes that the argument that the application of an obscure body of law would deter criminal behaviour when the criminal law has failed to do so 'may give too much credit to wrongdoers as informed, rational actors, coolly calculating the potential consequences of their actions before engaging in wrongdoing'.[59]

In sum, there is much to commend Weinrib's argument that 'The denial of a tort claim as a means of providing auxiliary support to the criminal law is … completely devoid of justification'.[60]

V. Conclusion

In this chapter, I have argued that a principle of illegality should not be used to support the aims of the criminal law. It is undeniably an important value of the legal system that tort law and criminal law should work in a coherent fashion. However, careful analysis reveals that it is possible to overstate the potential for a conflict to arise between tort law and criminal law through an award of compensation to a wrongdoing claimant. Due to the divergent aims of tort and crime, and the fact that an award of compensation does not generally undermine the punitive or deterrent effects of the criminal law sanction, the potential for a genuine inconsistency to arise will be small.

I will argue in Chapters 6–9 that there will only be two situations where a claim by a wrongdoing claimant should be denied based on the need to preserve coherence between tort law and the area of the law proscribing the conduct. Even then, this is not because tort law gives way to the criminal law, but rather because the two areas of law work *in combination* to prevent the claim. These two situations are: where an award of compensation would stultify or undermine the purpose of the statute that the claimant contravened (the statutory purpose explanation), and where the loss or damage suffered by the claimant as a result of the illegal conduct is not one that has a legal value (the no loss or damage explanation). I will introduce these two situations in Chapter 6, and will then discuss the statutory purpose explanation and the no loss or damage explanation thoroughly in Chapters 7–9.

[57] J Morgan, 'Reforming Punitive Damages in English law' in L Meurkens and E Nordin (eds), *The Power of Punitive Damages—Is Europe Missing Out?* (Cambridge, Intersentia, 2012), 191–92. See also H Luntz, 'The Australian Picture' (2004) 35 *Victoria University of Wellington Law Review* 879, 902.

[58] The relevant studies are reviewed in: Bagaric and Alexander, '(Marginal) General Deterrence Doesn't Work' (n 44). See also Law Commission, *The Illegality Defence* (Law Comm No 189, 2009) para 7.9.

[59] Beverley McLachlin 'Weaving the Law's Seamless Web' (n 19) 213.

[60] Weinrib, 'Illegality as a Tort Defence' (n 13) 46.

4

Policy and Discretion

I. Overview

There is ongoing debate and disagreement among members of the Supreme Court of the United Kingdom about the correct approach to claims founded on illegal conduct, and, in particular, about the role of discretion and public policy in resolving these claims. The majorities in *Hounga v Allen* (*Hounga*) and *Les Laboratoires Servier v Apotex Inc* (*Servier*)—decided only a few months apart—expressed opposing views about the relevance of policy and discretion in illegality claims.[1] These contrasting views persisted into *Bilta (UK) Ltd (in liquidation) v Nazir (No 2)* (*Bilta*)[2] and *Patel v Mirza* (*Patel*),[3] where the Court again split on the merit of a context-specific, policy-sensitive illegality doctrine. These decisions demonstrate a tension between, on the one hand, an approach which encourages explicit evaluation and weighing of competing public policy considerations and, on the other hand, a more orthodox rule-based approach.

The majorities in *Hounga* and *Patel* adopted a flexible policy-balancing approach where there is open discussion and consideration of the competing public polices for and against application of illegality doctrine in a particular case.[4] In comparison, Lord Sumption, who wrote for the majority in *Servier*, opposes judicial attempts to introduce a policy-based or discretionary approach to illegality doctrine.[5] Lord Mance and Lord Clarke likewise oppose a public policy-based discretionary approach.[6] However, despite the efforts of these justices (in particular Lord Sumption) to resist a broad discretionary approach based on considerations

[1] *Hounga v Allen* [2014] UKSC 47, [2014] 1 WLR 2889; *Les Laboratoires Servier v Apotex Inc* [2014] UKSC 5, [2015] AC 4305.

[2] *Bilta (UK) Ltd (in liquidation) v Nazir (No 2)* [2015] UKSC 23, [2016] AC 1 [98]–[101] (Lord Sumption), [166]–[174] (Lords Toulson and Hodge);

[3] *Patel v Mirza* [2016] UKSC 42.

[4] See *Hounga* (n 1) [42] (Lord Wilson, Lady Hale and Lord Kerr agreeing); *Patel* (n 3) [101] (Lord Toulson, Lady Hale and Lords Kerr, Wilson and Hodge agreeing).

[5] *Servier* (n 1) [13]–[21]. See also his judgments in *Bilta*: (n 2) [98]–[101] and *Patel v Mirza* (n 3) [261]–[265] (Lord Clarke agreeing).

[6] *Patel v Mirza* (n 3) [204]–[208] (Lord Mance); [216]–[219] (Lord Clarke).

of public policy and the merits of the claim, this is now the leading approach in the United Kingdom.[7]

These decisions of the Supreme Court were not negligence cases, and it is unclear whether the now favoured policy-balancing approach has replaced pre-existing tests applied by UK courts in negligence cases, such as the causation and inextricable link tests. However, the majority in *Hounga* was critical of these tests,[8] and there is an implicit preference in the majority judgment in that case and in *Patel* for a public policy framework to be applied in all private law illegality claims. The public policy framework adopted in these cases is thus likely to be applied by lower courts to negligence claims,[9] and to further entrench public policy as the basis for the law of illegality in the UK, including for negligence claims.

In this chapter my focus is on public policy reasoning as it has been applied to illegality across the private law. I explain the divergent views taken by members of the UK Supreme Court to the role of policy and discretion in illegality claims, before assessing whether policy and discretionary approaches can bring the necessary clarity and conceptual coherence to the law of illegality. My conclusion is that public policy and discretionary approaches are unstable and will have a detrimental effect on the coherence of private law illegality doctrine. In addition, these approaches are conceptually incoherent for the reason that they are incompatible with the immanent bilateralism of tort law. This discussion provides the background to my assessment in subsequent chapters of a number of specific public policy-based tests that have been developed to resolve negligence claims, including the mentioned causation and inextricable link tests.

II. Defining Public Policy

In this book I have adopted the distinction drawn by Ernest Weinrib between 'relational' policy considerations and 'extra-relational' policy considerations.[10] Relational policy considerations that arise out of and evaluate the nature of the relationship between the parties to the dispute (such as the principle of coherence),[11] are not external to the relationship of the parties, and hence are consistent with

[7] *Patel v Mirza* decides the issue. In that case, six out of nine justices adopted a broad policy discretion: see [101] (Lord Toulson, Lady Hale, Lords Wilson and Hodge agreeing), [122] (Lord Kerr), [174], [186] (Lord Neuberger).

[8] *Hounga* (n 1) [37]–[38] (Lord Wilson, Lady Hale and Lord Kerr agreeing).

[9] In *AB v Chief Constable of X Constabulary* [2015] EWHC 13 (QB) Males J adopted Lord Wilson's policy framework from *Hounga*; contrast *McCracken v Smith* [2015] EWCA Civ 380, where the Court of Appeal ignored *Hounga*, preferring Lord Sumption's approach in *Servier*.

[10] See ch 2, section VI, Public Policy and Corrective Justice.

[11] EJ Weinrib, *Corrective Justice* (Oxford, Oxford University Press, 2012), 66–67, 76, fn 95. I will explain further in ch 6 the reasons why legal coherence is a relational, not an extra-relational, factor, and hence cannot properly be characterised as public policy: see ch 6, section III, Concerns About Legal Coherence Are Relational Concerns.

a corrective justice model of tort law. Extra-relational policy considerations—the pursuit of a collective community goal—represent concerns that are independent of, or external to, the relationship of the parties. These concerns are contrary to corrective justice.[12] Accordingly, a reference in this chapter to 'public policy' considerations is a reference to external (extra-relational) policy considerations.

III. Public Policy Out in the Open

There are a number of putative 'doctrines' of illegality that are in fact no more than a foil for the application of public-policy-based reasoning.[13] The new policy approach of the UK Supreme Court encourages judges to openly decide cases according to whether public policy considerations warrant the application of an illegality bar. This view was adopted by a majority of the Supreme Court of the United Kingdom in *Hounga* where Lord Wilson (Lady Hale and Lord Kerr agreeing) explicitly balanced the competing policies for and against the application of illegality doctrine to the facts of the case. *Hounga* involved a claim for damages against an employer in the statutory tort of discrimination. The claimant and her employers were complicit in arranging for the former to enter the country in breach of immigration controls so she could work illegally as an *au pair* for the employer's family. The Supreme Court held unanimously that the claim was not defeated by virtue of the fact the claimant was an illegal immigrant and the contract of employment that formed the basis of the discrimination complaint was an illegal contract. In the leading judgment Lord Wilson explicitly balanced public policy considerations to determine whether the claimant's illegality should defeat the claim. His Lordship appeared to consider himself bound by *Tinsley v Milligan* to apply the reliance test, pursuant to which the claim will fail if the claimant needs to plead or rely on the illegality in order to found it. However, Lord Wilson agreed with Lord Phillips in *Stone & Rolls Ltd (in Liq) v Moore Stephens (a firm)*[14] that because of the arbitrary nature of the reliance test it cannot be applied as a 'rule of thumb', and must be 'softened' by considering underlying policies.[15] His Lordship emphasises the view that illegality doctrine is founded upon public policy, and states that it is necessary to ask two questions: first, 'what is the aspect of public policy which founds the defence?'; and second, 'is there another aspect of public policy to which application of the defence would run counter?'[16]

Lord Wilson held (correctly) that that aspect of policy that founds the illegality doctrine is the need to preserve the integrity of the legal system. His Lordship cited

[12] ibid.

[13] See, in particular, the connection approaches in ch 5 generally, as well as the discussion of the standard of care approach in ch 10, section III, Background: The Standard of Care Approach.

[14] *Stone & Rolls Ltd (in Liq) v Moore Stephens (a firm)* [2009] UKHL 39, [2009] AC 1391 [25].

[15] *Hounga* (n 1) [30].

[16] ibid [42].

McLachlin J's judgment in *Hall v Hebert*, where (adopting the views of Ernest Weinrib)[17] her Honour recognised that there will be two situations where a claim must be rejected so as to preserve the integrity of the legal system: where a claim would allow a person to evade or obtain a rebate of a penalty prescribed by the criminal law, and where it would allow a person to profit from the illegal conduct.[18] His Lordship conceded that an award of compensation to the claimant in that case (*Hounga*) would not permit her to evade a criminal penalty, nor would it permit her to profit from her wrongful conduct in entering into the illegal contract.[19] That conclusion should by itself have disposed of the case: the claim should be allowed because an award of damages to the claimant in this situation does not undermine the coherence of the law. However, Lord Wilson considered that these two situations 'may best be taken as an example of [the concern about the integrity of the legal system] rather than as the only conceivable instance of it'.[20] He considered that an enquiry into the impact of the claim on the integrity of the legal system could encompass an examination of the impact of the claim on wider public policies or goals relevant in the individual case.

One public policy factor his Lordship considered relevant in that case was the impact that the application or disallowance of illegality doctrine would have on the entry into illegal contracts of employment. His Lordship held that the integrity of the legal system would not be compromised as an award of damages for unlawful dismissal would not encourage immigrants to enter into illegal employment contracts, while failing to award damages might encourage *employers* to enter into illegal employment contracts in the belief they could discriminate against their employees with impunity.[21] Lord Wilson thus concluded that the policy arguments that supported the application of an illegality bar were not strong. His Lordship then turned to the second question posed; namely, whether there is a policy that would run counter to the application of illegality doctrine. Lord Wilson held that there was a relevant countervailing public policy that applied in this case—this was the public policy against human trafficking and forced labour.[22] His Lordship argued that the employer's conduct was akin to trafficking, and that the more important public goal of combatting trafficking outweighed the public policies in support of illegality doctrine in this case.[23] His Lordship apparently thought that an award of compensation to the claimant would go some way to counteracting the mistreatment the claimant had endured, which he considered was 'close' to trafficking.[24]

[17] EJ Weinrib, 'Illegality as a Tort Defence' (1976) 26 *University of Toronto Law Journal* 28.
[18] *Hall v Hebert* [1993] 2 SCR 159, 174–6, 179–80.
[19] *Hounga* (n 1) [44].
[20] ibid.
[21] ibid.
[22] This public policy derived from a European Convention to which the United Kingdom was a party and other international instruments: ibid [47]–[51].
[23] ibid [52].
[24] ibid [49]–[5]. Lord Wilson stopped short of finding that the employer's conduct amounted to human trafficking, but said 'it was so close to it that the distinction will not matter for the purpose of' determining the claim: at [49].

This review of Lord Wilson's judgment demonstrates that, while his Lordship claimed to be deferring to the precedential force of the reliance test, his reasons for rejecting the application of illegality doctrine on the facts of the case were almost exclusively grounded on public policy considerations. His Honour utilised the reliance test as a vehicle for public policy-based reasoning, directly contrary to the rejection of discretionary reasoning in *Tinsley*.[25] Moreover, even when purporting to apply the principle of coherence (which is not a public policy consideration), his Lordship was concerned primarily with preserving the operation of relevant public policies operating in that area rather than with preserving the coherent operation of the different branches of the legal system. As I explain further in Chapter 6, Lord Wilson demonstrated a flawed understanding of the principles of legal coherence that he was purportedly relying on from *Hall v Hebert*, resulting in a distortion of those principles.[26]

Lord Wilson's approach thus lacked both precedential authority and conceptual coherence. Nonetheless, Lord Toulson and Lord Hodge endorsed Lord Wilson's policy framework in *Bilta*.[27] The facts of *Bilta* were that its directors caused it to be involved in a VAT fraud, resulting in a liability to the tax and customs authority (HRMC) in excess of £38 million. Bilta was wound up by HRMC and the liquidators commenced proceedings against the company's directors for breach of fiduciary duty and against third parties for dishonestly assisting the directors in their breach of duty. The defendants sought to strike out the claim on the ground that Bilta was prevented from recovering losses caused by its own illegal actions in committing the fraud. The case turned predominantly on the question whether knowledge of illegality by the directors was to be attributed to the corporation. The Court, for various reasons, held that attribution should not take place and that the claim against the directors could proceed.[28] The main basis on which Lord Toulson and Lord Hodge decided the case was that the illegality doctrine was not to be applied to defeat the claim against the directors because of the countervailing public interest in ensuring that directors of insolvent or potentially insolvent companies have regard to the interests of creditors.[29]

[25] For a contrary view see E Lim, *Attribution and the Illegality Defence* (2016) 79 *Modern Law Review* 468, 485–86. Lim argues that *Tinsley* does not prevent a consideration of policies underlying illegality doctrine, only the consequences for the parties of applying it.

[26] Ch 6, section VI, Other Misappropriations of the Coherence Rationale.

[27] *Bilta* (n 2) [167]–[174]. See also Lord Toulson in *Servier* (n 1) [63].

[28] For academic commentary on this aspect of the case, see S Griffin, 'Attribution Rules and Issues Around the Illegality Defence' (2015) *Company Law Newsletter* 1; I Fletcher, 'Fraudulent Trading, Ex Turpi Causa, and the Directors' Duties: the Supreme Court Rulings in Bilta (UK) Ltd (in Liquidation) v Nazir (No 2)' (2016) 29 *Insolvency Intelligence* 12.

[29] *Bilta* (n 2) [125]–[127]. Lords Toulson and Hodge claimed to have based their decision in that case on 'statutory policy': [174]. However, their Lordships did not in substance apply a statutory purpose approach; nor, it would seem, were they purporting to do so. Their Lordships made no attempt to apply general principles of statutory construction to either the legislation containing the directors' duties or the tax legislation against which *Bilta* offended to identify whether it was a purpose of either piece of legislation to allow a claim against directors for a breach of duty even if the illegal acts of the directors could be attributed to the company. This was a matter, presumably, on which the legislation was silent. Thus, their Lordship's used 'statutory policy' as a proxy for public policy decision making.

Subsequently, *in Patel v Mirza* (involving a claim in unjust enrichment) six members of a nine-member panel endorsed a flexible discretionary approach, which involves balancing policies for and against the application of illegality doctrine and determining whether it would be disproportionate to refuse relief. Lord Toulson, who wrote the leading judgment, adopted a tripartite test for determining illegality claims, requiring a court to consider: (a) the underlying purpose of the prohibition that has been transgressed, and (b) any competing public policies, and (c) the need for a proportional response.[30] Lord Toulson ostensibly based this approach on the need to maintain the coherence of the legal system, but was in fact laying down a broad policy-balancing approach that ultimately provides courts with a discretion to decide the case according to where the public interest lies and the respective merits of the parties.[31] As I will demonstrate in Chapter 4, this approach shares no common conceptual foundations with a principle of legal coherence.

In *Patel*, the claimant was seeking repayment of £620,000 paid to the defendant pursuant to an agreement to invest it in shares based on insider information, where that information never eventuated and the money was never invested. Lord Toulson held that the claim should be allowed. There was no public policy reason why the claimant should be required to forfeit the monies paid in the circumstances where the purpose for which the monies were paid was never carried out, nor would forfeiture be and just a proportionate response to the illegality in those circumstances.[32]

IV. Lord Sumption's Stance Against Public Policy Reasoning

In *Servier* (a patent case) Lord Sumption in his leading judgment stressed that illegality doctrine is a rule of law, and not a discretionary power to decide the case on the perceived balance of the merits of the parties to the dispute.[33] Lord Sumption was insistent that the basis of illegality doctrine remains that formulated in by the House of Lord in *Tinsley v Milligan*. On this approach, illegality doctrine is not discretionary, nor dependent on a 'judicial value judgment' about the balance of equities in each case, but applies wherever a sufficient connection exists between

[30] *Patel v Mirza* (n 3) [101] (Lord Toulson, Lady Hale, Lords Wilson and Hodge agreeing). Lord Kerr wrote a concurring judgment. Lord Neuberger also (with seeming reluctance) endorsed Lord Toulson's policy framework for reaching an outcome in particular cases: (n 3), in particular [174], [186]. Lord Mance pointed out the slender authority relied upon by Lord Toulson for his policy approach: [207].

[31] See the summary by Lord Mance of Lord Toulson's approach: ibid [206].

[32] ibid [115]. Lord Toulson endorsed the conclusions of Gloster LJ in the Court of Appeal in this respect.

[33] *Servier* (n 1) [13].

the illegality and the claim.[34] Lord Sumption's statements in *Servier* about the nature of illegality doctrine were directed at rejecting the approach adopted by the Court of Appeal below, which he characterised as being based largely on subjective judgments about the seriousness of the illegality and the merits of the claim.[35] His Lordship did not explicitly address Lord Wilson's policy approach in the earlier decision in *Hounga*,[36] though it is implicit in his judgment that he rejected a policy-based discretionary approach of any kind.[37] In his subsequent judgments in *Bilta* and *Patel* Lord Sumption does expressly reject a policy-balancing approach. His Lordship in *Bilta* again reiterates that illegality doctrine is not based upon a discretionary value judgment, and observes that arguments based on policy 'can easily degenerate into the kind of discretionary weighing of the equities rejected in [*Tinsley* and *Servier*]'.[38] His Lordship makes the important point that:

> The fact that the illegality defence is based on policy does not entitle a court to reassess the value or relevance of that policy on a case-by-case basis. In a broad sense, any rule of law which imposes civil liability in respect of a wrong may be described as a reflection of legal policy. It does not follow that the courts may apply the illegality defence or not according to the relative importance which they attach to the policy underlying it by comparison with desirability of allowing an otherwise sound claim to succeed.[39]

He later points out that:

> Courts normally examine the policy rationale of a rule of law in order to discover what the rule is, not in order to decide whether they approve of its application in a particular case. The scope for conflict between competing public policies is therefore limited.[40]

Lord Sumption thus rejected the argument that a court can evaluate competing public policies in order to determine the application of illegality doctrine.

In *Patel v Mirza*, Lord Sumption repeated his objections to a policy-balancing discretionary exercise, pointing out that it:

> converts a legal principle into an exercise of judicial discretion, in the process exhibiting all the vices of 'complexity, uncertainty, arbitrariness and lack of transparency…'.[41]

[34] ibid [13]–[20] (Lord Sumption, Lord Neuberger and Lord Clarke agreeing). See also *Bilta* (n 2) [60]–[64] (Lord Sumption).

[35] ibid [21].

[36] James Goudkamp has explained that one reason for the lack of engagement by the court in *Servier* with the judgment in *Hounga* were that the arguments in *Servier* were heard before *Hounga* was handed down: J Goudkamp, 'The Doctrine of Illegality: A Private Law Hydra' (2015) 6 *The UK Supreme Court Yearbook* 254, 258, 265.

[37] His Lordship was critical of the suggestion by the Law Commission of England and Wales that illegality cases should be decided by reference to underlying polices: *Servier* (n 1) [20]. Ernest Lim argues that there is nothing in Lord Sumption's majority judgment in *Servier* that precludes a public policy-balancing approach: E Lim, *Attribution and the Illegality Defence* (2016) 79 *Modern Law Review* 468, 484–86.

[38] *Bilta* (n 2) [99].

[39] ibid.

[40] ibid [101].

[41] *Patel v Mirza* (n 3) [265].

Lord Sumption together with Lord Mance and Lord Clarke (who also rejected the majority's policy approach), preferred to decide the case on the basis that there is no inconsistency in the law in permitting repayment of money where this would simply restore the parties to the status quo ante and would not give effect to the illegal act or any right derived under it.[42] I submit that these judges were correct to reject the policy framework laid down by the majority in favour of an approach that focuses on questions of legal coherence. My objections to a public policy approach are set out in the next section.

V. Evaluation of a Public Policy Approach

Dissatisfied with the rigidity of the *Tinsley* reliance test and related connection tests, lower courts had been applying a flexible, discretionary approach prior to *Hounga* and *Patel*.[43] It is therefore not surprising that they appear to be embracing a flexible public policy framework.[44] But is it the right solution? The reliance test and the connection variants are clearly unsatisfactory (see generally Chapter 5), but the 'bigger question' is whether it is appropriate to substitute an approach where the operation of illegality doctrine is dependent on the balance of public policy.[45] Theoretical and pragmatic objections can be made to this kind of policy reasoning.

The fundamental objection of corrective justice theorists to reasoning motivated by public policy is that it renders negligence law incoherent. The pursuit of public policy goals in negligence is inconsistent with an interpersonal (corrective) justice conception of tort law.[46] Considerations of public policy are external to the parties' relationship because they ignore one or both parties.[47] Weinrib explains that public policies 'fragment the relationship between the parties and transform the law's concern from the wrong done and suffered to the choice of social goals'.[48] Denial of a claim on public policy grounds is thus a denial of the immanent bilateralism of tort law.

[42] ibid, see in particular [197]–[199] (Lord Mance), [210] (Lord Clarke), [250]–[253], [268] (Lord Sumption).

[43] *Les Laboratoires Servier v Apotex Inc* [2013] RPC 21, [2012] EWCA Civ 593 (*Servier* CA); *Parkingeye Ltd v Somerfield Stores Ltd* [2012] EWCA Civ 1338.

[44] See *AB v Chief Constable of X Constabulary* (n 9); *R (on the application of Best) v The Chief Land Registrar* [2015] EWCA Civ 17, [2016] QB 23 [51] (Sales LJ, McCombe LJ agreeing). Arden LJ in the latter case expressed some reservations about whether *Hounga* formulates an approach of general application: at [111]. Her Honour preferred to resolve the case by a statutory purpose approach.

[45] *cf Hounga* (n 1) [41].

[46] See ch 2, section VI, Public Policy and Corrective Justice.

[47] EJ Weinrib, *The Idea of Private Law* (Cambridge Mass., Harvard University Press, 1995) 210–14; A Beever, *Rediscovering the Law of Negligence* (Oxford, Hart Publishing, 2007) 176.

[48] EJ Weinrib, 'Does Tort Law Have a Future?' (2000) 34 *Valparaiso University Law Review* 561, 571; see also Weinrib, *Corrective Justice* (n 11) 61.

These theoretical objections tend to be the main focus of challenges by corrective justice proponents to the use of policy.[49] However, collateral attacks are also made on the unsatisfactory legal outcomes that result from public policy reasoning. There are two distinct, though related, practical objections raised to policy reasoning: (a) policy reasoning is unstable and leads to uncertain and unpredictable outcomes; and (b) policy reasoning involves weighing values and goals that are incommensurable.[50]

A. The Destabilising Effect of Public Policy Reasoning on the Law of Illegality

Allan Beever and Robert Stevens argue that judges lack the technical competence to identify and weigh disparate, and potentially conflicting, policy considerations.[51] This problem is exacerbated by insufficient evidence about the policies in question, some of which might be incapable of adequate assessment.[52] Beever says that reference to policy in negligence cases 'in practice reflects little more than someone's intuitions and prejudices in particular circumstances'.[53] Stevens points out that when judges in negligence cases have sought to weigh conflicting policy considerations they seem to rely on their 'instincts as to which policy has greater force' rather than empirical evidence.[54] The dissatisfaction with policy reasoning is not limited to those who advocate a corrective justice account of negligence liability. Other commentators writing about policy-based exceptions to negligence liability recognise similarly that policy choices in negligence cases tend to be based on speculation, unproven hypotheses and assertions about the effects of

[49] A Beever, 'Policy in Private Law: An Admission of Failure' (2006) 25(2) *The University of Queensland Law Journal* 287, 297.

[50] These are not the only objections. For example, Robert Stevens argues that judges do not have the political legitimacy to develop public policy: R Stevens, *Torts and Rights* (Oxford, Oxford University Press, 2007) 308–09. Stevens argues that if judges are to engage in policy reasoning they must be subject to an election process and scrutiny of their political and social views: at 312–14.

[51] Stevens ibid 308–10; Beever, *Rediscovering the Law of Negligence* (n 47) 172–73. See also Weinrib, *Corrective Justice* (n 11) 60; D Jensen, 'Theories, Principles, Policies and Common Law Adjudication' (2011) 36 *Australian Journal of Legal Philosophy* 34, 53–4; C Witting, 'The House that Dr Beever Built': Corrective Justice, Principle and the Law of Negligence' (2008) 71(4) *Modern Law Review* 621, 638.

[52] Stevens, *Torts and Rights* ibid 225, 234, 310; Beever, *Rediscovering the Law of Negligence* ibid 172–73. See also Witting, 'The House that Dr Beever Built' ibid 638; K Burns, 'It's Not Just Policy: The Role of Social Facts in Judicial Reasoning in Negligence Cases' (2013) 21 *Torts Law Journal* 73, 84–92. Lord Phillips has conceded that issues of policy are not always readily resolved by the courts: *Van Colle v Chief Constable of the Hertfordshire Police* [2008] UKHL 50, [2009] 1 AC 225 [102]. Even former Justice of the High Court, Michael Kirby, who strongly advocates for open consideration of policies, concedes that evidence will often not be available to the court about the political, social or economic consequences of imposing liability: *Pyrenees Shire Council v Day* [1998] HCA 3, (1998) 192 CLR 330 [253].

[53] Beever, *Rediscovering the Law of Negligence* ibid 54.

[54] Stevens (n 50) 309–10; see also 233–35.

imposing liability, with no empirical foundation supporting those choices.[55] Policy reasoning has been said to rely 'too heavily on hyperbole and exaggeration as a substitute for empirical evidence'.[56] Policy-based exceptions in negligence law have been criticised on the ground that they lack coherence and certainty in scope and application.[57]

In a series of writings, Christian Witting (who is not a proponent of corrective justice) persuasively argues against over-reliance on policy reasoning. Witting draws attention to the fact that courts are much better equipped to conduct the backward-looking exercise of resolving particular claims in dispute than the forward-looking exercise of developing policies in the public interest.[58] He argues that where the concern of the court is with the effect of a holding on a diverse group of persons not parties to the proceedings who do, or who might in the future, occupy similar positions to the plaintiff and defendant, the policy reasoning involves much prediction, guesswork and associated risk of error.[59] The need to make predictive assessments—when combined with the fact that policy perspectives are contestable and that reasonable people might take different views as to the best policy course of action—makes policy reasoning 'unstable' and incapable of consistent application or offering definite guidance for decision-making.[60] Witting warns that courts should be suitably wary about placing reliance on 'contentious and contestable policy perspectives'.[61]

The decision in *Hounga* is instructive in demonstrating these identified deficiencies of policy decision-making. It will be recalled that Lord Wilson balanced

[55] J Morgan, 'Policy Reasoning in Tort Law: the Courts, the Law Commission and the Critics' (2009) 125 *Law Quarterly Review* 215, 217–220; DPJ Walsh, 'Police Liability for a Negligent Failure to Prevent Crime: Enhancing Accountability by Clearing the Public Policy Fog' (2011) 22 *King's Law Journal* 27, 42; Z Jamil, 'Police Liability for Negligent Investigations: Unravelling the Blanket of Immunity' (2013) 1 *Birkbeck Law Review* 303, 316–319. These commentators were writing about the liability of police for negligent investigation and suppression of crime and make the point that there is an absence of empirical evidence underlying the assertions that imposition of liability will result in defensive policing. I am not suggesting, however, that these commentators reject the use of policy altogether in negligence claims. For example, Jonathan Morgan does not argue that courts should never consider policy, just that any policy argument should be carefully scrutinised: at 221.

[56] Walsh ibid 40. Walsh was there commenting specifically on the defensive policing policy exception. Note that Walsh argues convincingly that the policing cases can be decided more effectively by reference to established negligence principles, such as indeterminacy of liability and standard of care, and that policy arguments merely add unnecessary confusion to this area: see at 46–51 in particular.

[57] Walsh ibid 40–44. Walsh is here discussing the uncertain scope of the policy exception in negligence for police authorities investigating and suppressing crime. See also C Witting, 'Tort Law, Policy and the High Court of Australia' (2007) 31 *Melbourne University Law Review* 569, 589, who argues that reliance on policy in the wrongful birth and wrongful life cases has been detrimental to decisiveness in legal reasoning.

[58] Witting, 'Tort Law, Policy and the High Court of Australia' ibid 570, 577.

[59] ibid; see also Witting, 'The House that Dr Beever Built' (n 51) 633.

[60] C Witting, 'Duty of Care: An Analytical Approach' (2005) 25(1) *Oxford Journal of Legal Studies* 33, 38–42; Witting, 'Tort Law, Policy and the High Court of Australia' ibid 570, 577; Witting, 'The House that Dr Beever Built' ibid 633–35, 638. See also JCP Goldberg and BC Zipursky, 'The *Restatement (Third)* and the Place of Duty in Negligence Law' (2001) 54 *Vanderbilt Law Review* 657, 723.

[61] Witting, 'Tort Law, Policy and the High Court of Australia' ibid 590. See also Goldberg and Zipursky ibid.

the public policy consideration of whether permitting the claim would encourage illegal immigrants to enter into illegal contracts of employment (he considered this suggestion to be fanciful) against the public policy consideration of whether denying the claim would encourage employers to enter into illegal contracts in the belief they could discriminate against employees with impunity (he considered this suggestion to have merit).[62] Lord Wilson refers to no evidence to support his conclusions on these policy matters, sustaining the argument that judges are disposed to making policy assessments on the basis of instinct or 'guesswork' rather than evidence.[63] Decisions about the social impact of the claim should be left to the legislature, which has access to the necessary information to predict that likely impact.[64] In addition, any claim that tort liability has any influence on real-world behaviours should be treated with considerable scepticism. This is because there is very little basis for concluding that tort law has a significant normative effect on people's conduct.[65]

Lord Wilson's reliance in *Hounga* on the public policies directed to combating human trafficking and forced labour illustrates the related point that policy reasoning is unstable because of the divergent opinions likely to be taken about what policy requires in a particular case. Lord Wilson argued that any policy in support of denying the claim should give way to the more important public policy against human trafficking as reflected in international instruments to which the United Kingdom was a party.[66] International human rights were therefore central to Lord Wilson's public policy analysis; on those facts it was the fundamental right not to be forced into slavery or servitude that was central to his decision not to apply illegality doctrine.[67] However, Lord Hughes held that the public policies against human trafficking (and associated human rights protection) did not require the imposition of civil liability in that case. The international instruments relating to trafficking do not automatically absolve a trafficked person who commits a criminal offence.[68] Moreover, the statutory tort of discrimination is not co-extensive with trafficking and hence there was no obligation under international instruments to provide compensation to the claimant as a (putative) victim of trafficking.[69] Lord Hughes concluded that it was therefore not possible 'to read across from the law of human trafficking to provide a separate or additional reason' for permitting the claim.[70]

[62] *Hounga* (n 1) [44].
[63] Stevens (n 50) 309–10.
[64] RA Buckley, *Illegality and Public Policy*, 2nd edn (London, Thomson Reuters, 2009) 90.
[65] Refer to the discussion of this point in ch 3, text to nn 56–59.
[66] *Hounga* (n 1) [52].
[67] A Bogg and S Green, 'Rights Are Not Just For the Virtuous: What *Hounga* Means for the Illegality Defence in the Discrimination Torts' (2015) 44 *Industrial Law Journal* 101, 115. See also V Umeukeje, '*Hounga*: The Position of Illegal Migrant Workers and the Legal Process' (2015) 20 *Coventry Law Journal* 29, 33.
[68] *Hounga* (n 1) [63].
[69] ibid [65].
[70] ibid [67].

There will be considerable uncertainty following *Hounga* as to whether international human rights potentially can defeat the operation of the law of illegality and, if so, the range of human rights that can have this effect. Alan Bogg and Sarah Green have applauded Lord Wilson's judgment for its 'radical revision' of illegality doctrine and its 'potential to bring international human rights law in to the very heart of the English common law'.[71] However, as James Fisher has pointed out, private lawyers concerned with the stability and prospective certainty of the law would not agree with Bogg and Green that the destabilising effect of *Hounga* is a welcome development in illegality doctrine.[72]

The difficulty of securing consistency in decision-making from public policy-based reasoning is also demonstrated by *Bilta*. Lord Toulson and Lord Hodge considered as a matter of policy that the protection given to creditors through the medium of directors' duties would be emptied of content if illegality doctrine prevented the enforcement of those duties.[73] Lord Sumption, however, doubted that this public policy required the non-application of illegality doctrine. Lord Sumption identified other statutory remedies available to liquidators against malfeasant directors in order to cast doubt on the proposition that the duties owed by directors to companies would be of no effect if a civil claim was denied for the claimant's illegality.[74] It is submitted that the judgment on whether *the public interest* requires[75] that a company in liquidation should have a claim against a director for breach of duty notwithstanding the company's illegality is one that should be made by the legislature, taking into consideration all relevant policy considerations.

This is not to suggest that the outcomes in *Hounga* and *Bilta* were incorrect. The decisions in those cases not to apply illegality doctrine so as to bar the claims were right, for reasons that I will return to later.[76] My objection is to the 'public interest' reasoning that was used to reach that result.

B. Incommensurability

The second main objection that has been raised to policy reasoning on practical grounds is that public policies are diverse and competing and will often pull in opposite directions in terms of the outcomes they demand.[77] Policy reasoning will

[71] Bogg and Green (n 67) 122.

[72] JC Fisher, 'The *Ex Turpi Causa* Principle in *Hounga* and *Servier* (2015) 78 *The Modern Law Review* 854, 862. Moreover, it must be questioned whether courts have the political legitimacy to make decisions to embed international human rights jurisprudence into the common law. The extent to which the common law should incorporate international human rights arguably is a matter for the legislature, which should itself determine the relevance of international instruments for UK domestic law: Stevens (n 50) 308–309; Jensen (n 51) 53–54.

[73] *Bilta* (n 2) [125]–[127].

[74] ibid [104].

[75] As opposed to whether the coherence of the law requires this.

[76] See below, section VIII, Concluding Remarks on Policy.

[77] A point acknowledged by Toulson LJ (as he then was) in *Parkingeye Ltd v Somerfield Stores Ltd* (n 43) [44].

often require judges to balance disparate public goals that are incommensurable,[78] in the sense that they lack an underlying conceptual basis or a 'common measure'.[79] Where there is no common standard or yardstick by which these conflicting goals can be measured, the view of the judge as to where the balance should be struck will be based purely on intuition as to what is best for societal well-being.[80] *Hounga* is again indicative. Lord Wilson's approach requires concerns about legal coherence to be balanced against a range of public policy concerns which have no relationship to the question of whether principles in one area of the law will undermine or conflict with already established legal principle in another area of the law. In the case itself, this involved balancing legal coherence concerns against public policy concerns regarding the impact of civil liability on the incidence of illegal employment contracts, and the fight against human trafficking. Legal policies designed to ensure that the different branches of the legal system operate coherently are normatively different to public policies designed to combat illegal immigration and the exploitation and abuse of illegal immigrants. These policy goals 'lack a common measure in the sense of not having a sufficient overlap in concepts', making it difficult to weigh them in a rational manner.[81] There is no underlying concept common to these goals that could legitimately be used as the basis for trading off one against the other.[82] Lord Wilson's policy-balancing framework (and the policy framework adopted by the Court in *Patel*) is objectionable because it invariably will require courts to balance plural policy criteria that have conflicting and competing demands, giving rise to problems of incommensurability. To adapt the words of Weinrib, a policy-balancing approach 'puts into circulation … different normative currencies between which no rate of exchange exists'.[83]

The case of *R (on the application of Best) v The Chief Land Registrar* demonstrates these concerns about incommensurability.[84] The question before the Court was whether a person claiming to have established title to a residential property by virtue of adverse possession could rely on periods of possession that constituted the criminal offence of trespass. Sales LJ identified that to resolve this issue it was necessary to weigh two competing public interests: on the one hand, the public

[78] Witting, 'Tort Law, Policy and the High Court of Australia' (n 57) 577–78; Witting, 'The House that Dr Beever Built' (n 51) 634; Beever, *Rediscovering the Law of Negligence* (n 47) 173; Stevens (n 50) 310; EJ Weinrib, 'The Disintegration of Duty' in MS Madden (ed), *Exploring Tort Law* (Cambridge, Cambridge University Press, 2005) 149, 167.

[79] For general discussion of the notion of incommensurability see R Chang, 'Incommensurability (and Incomparability)' in H LaFollette (ed), *The International Encyclopedia of Ethics* (Chichester, Wiley-Blackwell, 2013) 2591 and B Chapman 'Law, Incommensurability, and Conceptually Sequenced Argument' (1998) 146 *University of Pennsylvania Law Review* 1487, 1487–88.

[80] Reference to monistic 'supervalues', such as the well-being of the society, are ultimately unhelpful as views will differ as to what will best promote well-being: Chang ibid 2593.

[81] ibid 2591.

[82] Chapman (n 79) 1488.

[83] EJ Weinrib, 'The Disintegration of Duty' (n 78) 168. Weinrib was there referring to the incommensurability of corrective justice and public policy in the context of the *Anns* test of duty of care. However, the same argument applies in the current context.

[84] *R (on the application of Best) v The Chief Land Registrar* [2015] EWCA Civ 17, [2016] QB 23.

interest in encouraging use of and investment in land and, on the other, the public interest in ensuring that persons do not benefit from their criminal occupation of residential premises.[85] These policies demand different outcomes: the first policy demands that the claim for adverse possession should be successful; the second that it should not be. The broad policy framework adopted in *Hounga* and *Patel* offers no guidance as to how a court is to determine whether, and in what circumstances, the policy that a criminal should not profit from their wrong is outweighed by the broader policy goals of the possessory title regime. Fortunately, the members of the court (Arden LJ writing a separate judgment) were able to decide the correct balance by reference to legislative intent and a purposive construction of the criminal trespass statute.[86] Their Honours inferred from extrinsic materials and from the terms, provisions and operation of the criminal statute that it was not one of the purposes of that statute to interfere with established laws governing acquisition of title by adverse possession.[87] If the offence had not been statutory in nature, or had the statute provided no guidance about the effect commission of an offence has on a claim for adverse possession—the Court would have been left with a 'stark choice'[88] between the two conflicting policy goals and no yardstick to determine which of them to prioritise. As Stevens observes, where public goals compete, the correct outcome of a case becomes more, not less, difficult for a judge to identify.[89]

The open-ended nature of the policy discretion compounds the identified shortcomings of public policy-based reasoning. Their Lordships do not limit the range of public policy considerations that are potentially relevant, and hence a large number of heterogeneous policy considerations possibly come into play on the facts of any particular case. Judges are free to choose from a mélange of possible policy considerations, exacerbating the risk of incommensurability and uncertainty in outcomes. As Graham Virgo has observed, a broad discretion to determine illegality claims has the potential to 'collapse' into 'the exercise of an arbitrary choice'.[90] Beever condemns broad policy discretions as an invitation to judges to make open-ended political decisions and 'to pursue their personal visions of the good society'.[91] Beever would view a policy discretion as converting the test of illegality into

[85] ibid [45]–[46].

[86] Lady Justice Arden explicitly based her reasons on a statutory purposive interpretation, independently of balancing the conflicting public policies: ibid [101]. Sales LJ adopted Lord Wilson's approach from Hounga; however, the substance of his reasoning was to adopt a purposive construction of the criminal legislation. The criminal provision in question was Legal Aid, Sentencing and Punishment of Offenders Act 2012, s 144.

[87] ibid [70]–[71] (Sales LJ), [101]–[108] (Arden LJ) (MCombe LJ agreeing with both).

[88] ibid [103] (Arden LJ).

[89] Stevens (n 50) 310.

[90] G Virgo, 'The Defence of Illegality in Unjust Enrichment' in A Dyson, J Goudkamp and F Wilmot-Smith, *Defences in Unjust Enrichment* (London, Bloomsbury Publishing, 2016) 180, 192.

[91] Beever, *Rediscovering the Law of Negligence* (n 47) 172. Beever was there talking about the *Anns* formulation of duty of care; however, the criticism is equally valid to a public policy-balancing approach.

'a tabula rasa that judges are called on to fill in however they see fit in individual cases'.[92] John Goldberg and Benjamin Zipursky similarly denounce 'all-things-considered' policy assessments, whereby judges are free to rely on whatever public policy they subjectively consider to be relevant.[93] Goldberg and Zipursky explain that broad policy discretions violate rule of law virtues of transparency, predictability and stability:

> As numerous scholars from across the jurisprudential and political spectrums have argued, all-considered policy judgments lack features that are critical to rule-of- law values. They do not engender predictability or stability. They undercut the capacity of the law to guide. They open up courts to various political pressures, both at an individual level and on a broader level. There is little distinction between decisions of this nature and decisions that are mere exercises of discretion by those who have power.[94]

Thus, they argue that large-scale policy judgments are not judgments that judges have the competence (or, for that matter, the political legitimacy) to make.[95]

VI. Public Policy in Negligence Claims

There was no suggestion in *Hounga* or *Patel* that the flexible policy approach advocated there was to be confined to the particular types of claims there under consideration (the statutory tort of discrimination and unjust enrichment based on a total failure of consideration). Following these cases there will be increased emphasis on public policy factors favouring and militating against application of illegality doctrine in all private law illegality cases, including in negligence. Precisely how a policy-balancing approach would be applied in the negligence context remains to be seen. There would presumably be more attention given to general policy concerns previously identified as relevant in the negligence context; polices such as deterrence,[96] the need to avoid an appearance of condoning the criminal conduct;[97] the need for the court to avoid actually condoning the criminal conduct by lessening the normative effect of the criminal law,[98] and the 'offensiveness' to public notions of the fair distribution of resources that a claimant should be compensated for the consequences of his or her own criminal conduct.[99]

[92] Beever ibid 171, again talking about the *Anns* formulation of duty of care.
[93] Goldberg and Zipursky (n 60) 722; see also at 723.
[94] ibid 722–23. See also generally Joseph Raz, *The Authority of Law: Essays on Law and Morality* (Oxford, Oxford University Press, 1979), ch 11 'Rule of Law and its Virtue'.
[95] Goldberg and Zipursky ibid 750.
[96] Law Commission, *The Illegality Defence* (Law Comm No 189, 2009) para 7.67 ('Law Commission No 189').
[97] *Cross v Kirkby* [2000] EWCA Civ 426 (CA) [76] (Beldam LJ); *Gray v Thames Trains Ltd* [2008] EWCA Civ 713, [2009] 1 AC 1339 (CA), 1350 [20] (the Court).
[98] *Gala v Preston* [1991] HCA 18, (1991) 172 CLR 243, 270–273 (Brennan J).
[99] *Gray v Thames Trains Ltd* [2009] UKHL33, [2009] 1 AC 1339 [51] (Lord Hoffmann).

Context-specific public policy considerations are also likely to become relevant. For example, if the claimant in *Hounga* was to bring a claim in negligence for compensation for physical injuries inflicted on her by the defendants, a court applying a policy framework would no longer focus on the causal link between the harm and the illegality (the current leading approach to illegality claims),[100] but rather would compare the same competing policy concerns identified as relevant in the statutory tort action. A common claim in the negligence context is for injuries arising out of a joint enterprise between the claimant and defendant to take a vehicle (often stolen) for a joy ride.[101] The policy approach invites courts when determining a claim of this kind to consider broad policy objectives such as the public interest in ensuring the security of private property interests, and of ensuring safe roads and deterring dangerous driving. However, this approach provides no guidance as to how these policy objectives should be weighed against other relevant policies underlying illegality doctrine, in particular the policy of legal coherence. This raises the problem of incommensurability. A policy-balancing approach requires issues relating to the coherence of the law (on the one hand) to be balanced against public policy factors of the kind identified. The decision as to how to resolve the claim might be relatively straightforward where all the factors point in the same direction, but becomes complex where they do not. It is not clear, for example, how a court would resolve a joy-riding claim where there are no issues of legal coherence, but the important public policy of deterring the theft of motor vehicles and the associated risk of dangerous driving applies. Policy-motivated reasoning makes hard negligence cases even harder to determine.[102]

The application of public policy reasoning would make the outcome of negligence cases uncertain and impossible to predict. The UK cases have held that a relevant policy factor in negligence cases will be the seriousness of the offence.[103] In *AB v Chief Constable of X Constabulary* a former undercover police officer brought proceedings against his former employer for damages for psychiatric injury in the form of an adjustment disorder.[104] The claimant argued that this disorder arose from negligence by the employer in failing to provide appropriate support to the claimant when he was deployed undercover to gather intelligence on a serious organised crime group. The claimant had misused cocaine during the period of his deployment undercover, and the defendant argued that the psychiatric injury was the result of the claimant's own misconduct in abusing cocaine and his dismissal from the police force when this was discovered. Mr Justice Males accepted

[100] The leading authority is *Gray v Thames Trains Ltd* ibid.

[101] See, for eg, *Miller v Miller* [2011] HCA 9, (2011) 242 CLR 446; *Gala v Preston* (n 98).

[102] Stevens (n 50) 310.

[103] The seriousness of the offence was considered by the UK courts to be a relevant consideration prior to *Hounga*: see, eg, *Joyce v O'Brien* [2014] 1 WLR 70, 84 [51] (Elias LJ, Rafferty and Ryder LJJ agreeing); *Gray v Thames Trains Ltd* (n 99) [83] (Lord Rodger); *Stone & Rolls Ltd v Moore Stephens (a firm)* (n 14) [24] (Lord Phillips), [219] (Lord Walker); *Servier* (n 1) [23]–[30].

[104] *AB v Chief Constable of X Constabulary* (n 9).

the defendant's argument and held, applying the public policy framework from *Hounga*, that the claimant's illegal conduct prevented him from bringing a claim. To allow the claim where it was caused by his own serious criminal conduct would be against public policy.[105]

In *AB v Chief Constable of X Constabulary* the misconduct was serious; in other cases, there will be disagreement about whether the illegality was sufficiently serious to justify refusal of the claim on public policy grounds. Judges are likely to take different stances about whether a particular offence is sufficiently serious to enliven the defence, and ultimately this will depend on their own personal views about the significance of the claimant's illegality. As Lord Grabiner has observed, 'questions over what is "turpitude" allow for wriggle room for the advocates and the judge to find the "right" answer, dressed up as principle'.[106] The inevitable outcome of a focus on the seriousness of the offence will be a lack of certainty and predictability in the outcomes of individual cases. Furthermore, while judges might claim that their views about the seriousness of the offence would reflect the views of the majority of people, they (judges) do not necessarily have the competence to gauge public opinion or community consensus on that topic. As Stevens has observed: 'The claim that a judge can act as a spokesman for society and its values is implausible'.[107] The risk is that judges will attribute their own personal values with no empirical evidence that those personal values are shared more widely in the community.[108]

The decision of Kirby P (as he then was) in *State Rail Authority of New South Wales v Wiegold* illustrates this point.[109] His Honour held that requiring an employer who negligently injured an employee to compensate that employee for the financial consequences of a term of imprisonment imposed when the impecunious claimant turned to growing marijuana would not be an affront to the community because many law-abiding citizens smoke marijuana.[110] Another judge, however, might view public opinion about the seriousness of the offence quite differently, based on his or her own moral or ethical predispositions. As Stevens has pointed out 'The law is not, and should not be, determined by the judge's best guess of majority public opinion.'[111]

[105] ibid [23].

[106] Lord Grabiner, 'Public Policy, Illegality and Contracts', The Annual Cambridge Allen & Overy Lecture 2015, Cambridge, 24 November 2015. See also *McCracken v Smith* [2015] EWCA Civ 380, [81]–[87] (Clarke LJ) (difficulty of determining whether road traffic offences are turpitude).

[107] Stevens (n 50) 311 (citation omitted). See also Weinrib, 'Does Tort Law have a Future?' (n 48) 566; Beever, *Rediscovering the Law of Negligence* (n 47) 172–3; Jensen (n 51) 53–54.

[108] *Neindorf v Junkovic* (2005) 80 ALJR 341, [9] (Gleeson CJ).

[109] *State Rail Authority of New South Wales v Wiegold* (1991) 25 NSWLR 500 (NSWCA).

[110] ibid 505. For a discussion of the use by courts of 'social facts' and an argument that corrective justice theory does not adequately account for this judicial practice, see Burns (n 52).

[111] Stevens (n 50) 311; contrast N Strauss, '*Ex Turpi Causa Oritur Actio?*' (2016) 132 *Law Quarterly Review* 236, 261. Strauss argues that a test that requires a judge to determine the matter from the viewpoint of ordinary and reasonable members of the public does require the application of an objective standard.

VII. Are These Objections to Public Policy Reasoning Overstated?

For advocates of a corrective justice model of negligence law, the theoretical objections to the use of public policy are insuperable. Others are more open to the use of policy, perhaps in a limited fashion. The debate among torts scholars about the use of policy reasoning in negligence is fierce and there are those who argue that it is legitimate for judges to rely on public policy when deciding negligence cases,[112] even if under strict constraints.[113] The arguments around policy are diverse; however, a common argument put forward by those who favour policy reasoning is that an open discussion of policy will enable judges to better explain the reasons for their decisions, and will make judicial reasoning more 'transparent'.[114] These same perceived merits of policy reasoning are also relied upon by those who advocate a policy-driven approach to illegality claims in particular.[115] The argument is that when deciding illegality cases courts often rely on covert, unexpressed, policy judgments, and that the advantage of a policy approach is that it encourages these policies to be expressed and acknowledged openly. However, Beever argues persuasively that due to the subjective and intuitive nature of policy reasoning, and the difficulty of measuring incommensurable values, policy detracts rather than enhances the ability of courts to give good reasons. Far from enabling judges to make clear the grounds of their decision, an appeal to policy 'in fact requires judges to make decisions of a kind that cannot be made in a public and open manner but must be made in an intuitive and private one'.[116] While policy reasoning 'appears to have the virtue of transparency', in reality it undermines the transparency of that area of the law and makes the outcome of future cases much harder to predict.[117]

Those who support the use of policy would no doubt claim that these objections can be overcome or are overstated. It might be argued that empirical evidence regarding the political or social consequences of a decision can be adduced so that judges are no longer required to rely on intuition or guesswork as to the impact

[112] See, eg, J Bell, *Policy Arguments in Judicial Decisions* (Oxford, Clarendon Press, 1983) ch III; M Kirby, *Judicial Activism: Authority, Principle and Policy in the Judicial Method* The Hamlyn Lectures (London, Sweet & Maxwell, 2004); J Stapleton, 'The Golden Thread at the Heart of Tort Law: Protection of the Vulnerable' (2003) 24 *Australian Bar Review* 135; J Dietrich, 'What is "Lawyering"? The Challenge of Taxonomy' (2006) 55(3) *Cambridge Law Journal* 549.; H Luntz, 'The Use of Policy in Negligence Cases in the High Court of Australia' in M Bryan (ed), *Private Law in Theory and Practice* (Abingdon, Routledge-Cavendish, 2007).

[113] A Robertson, 'Policy-based reasoning in duty of care cases' (2013) 33(1) *Legal Studies* 119.

[114] See, eg, Stapleton (n 112); Kirby (n 112) 84.

[115] See, eg, PS Davies, 'The Illegality Defence: Turning Back the Clock' [2010] 74(4) *The Conveyancer and Property Lawyer* 282; PS Davies, 'The Illegality Defence and Public Policy' (2009) 125 *Law Quarterly Review* 556.

[116] Beever, *Rediscovering the Law of Negligence* (n 47) 175.

[117] Stevens (n 50) 307.

of their decisions. However, it will not always be possible to assess adequately the societal consequences of a decision and, even if this were possible, there will often not be sufficient research available on which parties could rely.[118] The cost of commissioning the necessary research would be prohibitively expensive for most parties. Any evidence put before the judge is unlikely adequately to inform a decision how to resolve conflicting policies and to ascertain what course of action would best promote the overall welfare of society. In this respect Weinrib has argued that 'given the heterogeneity of possible policy considerations, a rigorous comparison would require the elaboration and application of some metric of social gains and losses—a task beyond judicial competence'.[119]

A further argument put forward by those who support a policy approach to illegality claims is that the objective of identifying one single comprehensive test of illegality that will bring certainty to this area is unattainable.[120] Nicholas Strauss argues that 'after nearly a quarter of a millennium of failing to achieve anything more definite, it is perhaps time to admit defeat' and to allow a degree of discretion, policy and value judgment in deciding these claims.[121] The argument essentially is that the current rules are so uncertain that a policy/discretionary approach cannot be much worse. However, my argument is that there is one single test that can provide future stability to illegality doctrine in negligence claims, and that is the test of legal coherence. This test does not have the same vices as a test of public policy. An appeal to legal coherence is not an appeal to considerations that are external to the parties' relationship because that relationship includes their juridical relationship and their rights and duties must be assessed within the legal system as a whole. A legal coherence test of illegality is thus consistent with corrective justice.[122] In addition, the pragmatic objections to the use of public policy do not apply to the 'policy' of legal coherence. Judges have the legal training and expertise to identify the potential for the imposition of negligence liability to cut across statute law and other doctrines and rules of responsibility established in other areas of the law, and this potential can be predicted in advance. Accordingly, the principle of coherence does not pose the same threat to rule of law values as public policy reasoning.

[118] Witting, 'Duty of Care: An Analytical Approach' (n 60) 39; Jensen (n 51) 52–53; Bell (n 112) 83. The relevant empirical evidence simply might not be available. To give an example from a different context, Dermot Walsh points out that the Law Commission of England and Wales surveyed the available research on the impact of tort liability on public authorities and concluded that it is impossible to predict that impact. Yet this is often given as a policy reason by courts to reject claims in negligence against public authorities: Walsh (n 55) 42.

[119] Weinrib, 'The Disintegration of Duty' (n 78) 167. See also Beever, *Rediscovering the Law of Negligence* (n 47) 173.

[120] *Patel* (n 3) [90] [113] (Lord Toulson, Lady Hale and Lords Wilson and Hodge agreeing); [137] (Lord Kerr); *Servier* CA (n 43) [63]–[75] (Etherton LJ, Kitchin and Laws LJJ agreeing). See also: Strauss (n 111) 256–57; Law Commission No 189 (n 96) para 7.67; Davies, 'Two Steps Forward, One Step Back?' (2009) 73(3) *The Conveyancer and Property Lawyer* 182, 185.

[121] Strauss ibid 265.

[122] See ch 6, section III, Concerns about Legal Coherence are Relational Concerns.

VIII. Concluding Remarks on Public Policy

The outcomes in *Hounga*, *Bilta* and *Patel* were the right ones. In none of these cases would an award of damages have created an incoherence in the legal system. In none of these cases would an award of damages have shifted responsibility for a loss that the criminal law ascribed to the claimant on to a third party, or permitted the claimant to profit from wrongdoing. Nor was it a purpose of the legislation that proscribed the conduct in these cases to deny an award of damages. It is the reliance on reasoning of public policy to reach these outcomes which is objectionable, and ultimately not needed when a more principled framework based on the principle of coherence is available.

Some commentators have welcomed a public policy-balancing test for its pragmatism and its engagement with the merits of the case, comparing it favourably against the technical and arbitrary reliance test.[123] I am not advocating for the perpetuation of the reliance test. This test and the other connection tests are doctrinally and conceptually unsatisfactory.[124] Where I differ from these commentators is on the question whether a policy-balancing approach is a legitimate substitution for these tests. A test that leaves the outcomes of cases dependent on an intuitive decision whether public policy merits its application will destabilise illegality doctrine, and do violence to rule of law values of transparency and predictability and to the bilateralism of tort law.[125]

IX. A Structured Discretion

Following a major review of illegality doctrine in private law over the course of a decade, the Law Commission of England and Wales ('the Commission') decided ultimately that it was not 'productive' to search for a single test that could govern all aspects of the law of illegality.[126] The Commission instead recommended that courts should adopt a discretionary approach, where in each individual case they consider whether the application of illegality doctrine can be justified on the basis of a range of policies underlying that doctrine. It identified a number of policy rationales underlying the law of illegality that had previously been identified in the case law, including: (a) furthering the purpose of the rule which the illegal conduct has infringed; (b) consistency; (c) preventing the claimant from profiting from his or her own wrong; (d) deterrence; and (e) maintaining the integrity of the legal

[123] RA Buckley, 'Illegality in the Supreme Court' (2015) 131 *Law Quarterly Review* 341. See also Goudkamp, 'A Private Law Hydra' (n 36) 262–63.

[124] See generally ch 5.

[125] *cf* Fisher (n 72) 862.

[126] Law Commission No 189 (n 96) para 7.67.

system.[127] These policies would need to be balanced against the relative merits of the parties and the proportionality of the claim and the loss, in order to ensure that the outcome reached is a 'just' one.[128] The Commission encouraged judges to '"bend" the rules' to give effect to these policies.[129]

The structured discretion promoted by the Commission was apparently intended to have a narrower compass than an 'all-things-considered' policy approach. A structured discretion does not by its nature invite a judge to consider the impact of applying illegality doctrine on broader political, social or economic goals relevant in that context. For example, a structured discretion would not, on the facts of a case such as *Hounga*, invite consideration of broader public policy concerns about the promotion of international human rights. Rather, consideration is restricted to the relevant policies identified in the case law as underlying illegality doctrine. The Law Commission sought to emphasise that this discretionary approach would involve only incremental change, as the different considerations are already found within the case law.[130] The objective of this section of the chapter is to consider the merit of introducing a discretion of this kind, either judicially or by legislation.

The focus of this discussion is not to criticise individual factors that are said to be relevant to the exercise of the discretion. A number of the factors suggested by the Commission or the courts—such as deterrence, knowledge of illegality and intention to commit a crime, degree of culpability, and connection between the claim and the illegality—have been criticised in other chapters.[131] These factors can be criticised on the basis of one or all of the following grounds: they are concerned with promoting goals such as punishment or deterrence which are not legitimate goals of tort law; they are 'one-sided' considerations that focus singly on the conduct of the claimant rather than relationally on both parties, and they are subjective and dependent on the view of the individual judge. It is not intended to repeat these arguments. Rather, the focus will be on the merits of the general conception of a discretion where a limited range of policies identified as justifying the application of the doctrine are evaluated and balanced to resolve individual cases. First I will discuss attempts by the judiciary to introduce a discretion of this nature. I will conclude that this discretionary approach, while narrower, shares the same failings as a policy-balancing approach. It involves a large degree of subjectivity, will result in uncertain outcomes, and requires judges to balance considerations that are incommensurable. I will then discuss whether a statutory structured discretion would be more palatable, and will again conclude that, while it would result in less uncertainty, it is not an appropriate solution as it still requires the weighing of incommensurables.

127 ibid, para 7.69.

128 ibid.

129 ibid, para 3.140.

130 Law Commission, *The Illegality Defence* (Law Comm No 320, 2010) para 3.37 (Law Commission No 320).

131 See generally chs 2, 3 and 5.

A. A Judicially Structured Discretion

There is significant judicial support in the United Kingdom for a structured discretion, where a claim founded on an illegality is resolved by reference to a range of factors perceived as justifying denial of the claim.[132] The authority for this approach is generally attributed to dictum by Lord Hoffmann in *Gray v Thames Trains Ltd*.[133] In *Gray*, Lord Hoffmann stated that illegality doctrine is not based on a single justification, but on a group of reasons that vary in different situations.[134] The Commission regarded this statement as an endorsement of a discretionary approach that involves examination of the policy rationales underlying illegality doctrine.[135] Lord Sumption has pointed out that Lord Hoffmann's statement cannot bear this weight.[136] Lord Hoffmann was not in that case advocating for a discretionary approach to resolving illegality claims. Rather, he identified two specific rules that will apply to determine the recoverability of particular heads of loss that are the consequence of an act of illegality.[137] Despite the dubious support provided by Lord Hoffmann's judgment for a discretionary approach, the English Court of Appeal has relied on it to justify just such an approach.[138] The nature of the proposed discretion was explained by Etherton LJ (Kitchin and Laws LJJ agreeing) in the Court of Appeal in *Servier* as one which permits 'an intense analysis of the particular facts and of the proper application of the various policy considerations underlying the illegality principle so as to produce a just and proportionate response to the illegality'.[139]

Lord Hughes in *Hounga* (Lord Carnwath agreeing) took a similar approach. His Lordship argued that there is no one comprehensive test of illegality, while apparently rejecting an uncontrolled policy discretion of the kind advocated by Lord Wilson in that case. Instead, Lord Hughes favoured a structured discretion encompassing a range of factors which potentially will be relevant in individual cases.[140] His Lordship identified two primary considerations: consistency in the law (legal coherence); and the closeness of the connection between the illegality and the claim made.[141] His Lordship accepted that in individual cases a court will also likely need to consider a broader range of factors, such as the purpose of the

[132] *Hounga* (n 1) (Lord Hughes, Lord Carnwath agreeing); *Servier* CA (n 43) (Etherton LJ, Kitchin and Laws LJJ agreeing).

[133] *Gray v Thames Trains Ltd* (n 99).

[134] ibid [30].

[135] Law Commission No 320 (n 130) in particular para 3.38.

[136] *Servier* (n 1) [19] (Lord Neuberger and Lord Clarke agreeing).

[137] See ch 8, section III, The Consistency Rule.

[138] *Servier* CA (n 43) [73] (Etherton LJ, Kitchin and Laws LJJ agreeing). Individual members of the Court of Appeal have also favoured using a structured discretion to resolve these claims: see Ward LJ in *Hewison v Meridian Shipping Services Pty Ltd* [2003] ICR 766, [2002] EWCA Civ 1821; Gloster LJ in *Patel v Mirza* [2014] EWCA Civ 1047 [2015] Ch 271.

[139] *Servier* CA (n 43) [75].

[140] *Hounga* (n 1) [55].

[141] ibid.

law that is infringed, the gravity of the illegality, the claimant's knowledge of the illegality and intention to commit a criminal offence, and the degree of culpability or 'blameworthiness' of the claimant.[142]

The majority in *Patel* also suggested that similar factors would be relevant to the exercise of the broad discretion laid down by them to determine illegality claims. The majority adopted a policy-balancing exercise of the kind critiqued above (including an evaluation of the purpose of the law that was infringed and competing public policies) and combined that with a multi-factorial discretion aimed at determining whether it would be disproportionate to refuse relief to the claimant. Lord Toulson writing for the majority stated that it was 'not helpful' to lay down a 'prescriptive or definitive list' of factors relevant to the assessment of proportionality, but indicated that potentially relevant factors would include 'the seriousness of the conduct, its centrality to the [claim], whether it was intentional and whether there was marked disparity in the parties' respective culpability'.[143]

Any attempt to introduce a discretionary multi-factorial analysis of illegality claims should be resisted. A discretion that is limited to the policies perceived to justify illegality doctrine (of the kind proposed by Lord Hughes in *Hounga*) appears more palatable than an uncontrolled discretion which allows judge *carte blanche* to take into account whatever matter of public policy or other consideration the court considers contextually relevant (of the kind proposed by the majorities in *Hounga* and *Patel*). However, ultimately the same theoretical and pragmatic objections identified in respect of a policy-balancing approach also apply to a structured discretion.

i. A Structured Discretion Introduces a Theoretical Incoherence into Negligence Law

A structured discretion introduces an incoherence into the corrective justice framework of negligence law by including factors that focus one-sidedly on the plaintiff's conduct or that pursue goals that are external to the relationship of the parties. These incoherent factors were identified above, namely: deterrence; knowledge of illegality and intention to commit a crime; degree of culpability; and connection between the claim and the illegality. These theoretical concerns are exacerbated by the potential that courts will use these factors as proxies for bringing into account wider matters of public interest. The Court of Appeal in *Servier*, when assessing the degree of culpability of the claimant, took into account the broader public interest in competitors taking a commercial risk to market products in breach of a patent which it reasonably and honestly believed to be invalid, even if this belief turns out to be ill-founded.[144] In this way, the Court used the structured discretion as a vehicle for taking into account broad matters of public interest.

[142] ibid [55], [58].
[143] *Patel* (n 3) [107].
[144] *Servier* CA (n 43) [82].

Other suggested factors included in the discretion—consistency of the law, furthering the purpose of the rule infringed by the claimant, preventing a defendant from benefiting from wrongdoing and maintaining the integrity of the legal system—are all aspects of the principle of coherence and are consistent with corrective justice. However, there is no need for a structured discretion to accommodate these considerations, and no need to weigh or balance these factors against each other as they do not conflict. These factors are all expressive of one general principle that an award of damages must be denied where it would create an incoherence in the juridical relationship of the parties, as situated within the legal system as a whole.

ii. A Structured Discretion Will Make Decisions More Difficult and Unpredictable

The Law Commission claimed that the law of illegality would be 'clearer, more transparent and easier to understand' if judges discussed the various policy rationales openly in relation to the facts of the case before them.[145] However, it is submitted that a discretionary approach will reduce transparency in this area, and will lead to unpredictable and uncertain outcomes. The courts have emphasised that the range of factors that can be considered when exercising the discretion is not closed.[146] The absence of authoritative guidance as to relevant factors will result in judges in similar cases employing different considerations to reach their conclusions.[147]

Even those commentators who support a discretionary approach recognise that coherence will be difficult to achieve through individual decisions in disparate fact situations.[148] The process of individual decision-marking would make it difficult for courts to reach a consensus on the relevant list of factors.[149] Lord Sumption in *Servier* strongly rejected a discretionary fact-centred process (at least, one developed by the courts).[150] His Lordship chastised the Court of Appeal below for adopting a discretionary assessment of the claim that involved value judgments about the significance of the illegality and the culpability of the claimant.[151] His Lordship characterised the approach of the Court of Appeal as one that depended 'on largely subjective judgments about how badly [the claimant] had behaved

[145] Law Commission No 320 (n 130) para 3.10. See also Law Commission No 189 (n 96) para 7.67.

[146] *Hounga* (n 1) [55] (Lord Hughes, Lord Carnwath agreeing); *Servier* CA (n 43) [73] (Etherton LJ, Kitchin and Laws LJJ agreeing).

[147] *cf* Paul S Davies, 'Two Steps Forward, One Step Back?' (n 120) 208.

[148] Davies, 'Turning Back the Clock' (n 115) 296, 298. Davies prefers a legislated discretion.

[149] *Servier* (n 1) [20].

[150] *Servier* ibid [13]–[21]; *Bilta* (n 2) [99]. In extra-curial writings Lord Sumption has expressed the view that a 'large element of judicial discretion' is required to resolve claims based on an illegality, though he would appear to prefer that this discretion is the subject of legislation rather than judicial development: Lord (Jonathan) Sumption, 'Reflections on the Law of Illegality' [2012] *Restitution Law Review* 112.

[151] *Servier* ibid.

and how much it mattered'.[152] He then went on to condemn this approach on the ground that it 'was a process, discretionary in all but name, whose outcome would have been exceptionally difficult for either party's advisers to predict in advance'.[153]

The unpredictability of outcomes to which Lord Sumption refers is compounded by the incommensurability of the factors that have been identified as relevant to the exercise of the discretion. Some of the nominated factors are expressive of the law's concern with ensuring that the whole legal system operates in a unified, coherent fashion. Other factors reflect completely different concerns. Factors that involve an assessment of the seriousness of the illegality, the claimant's knowledge and intention to commit an illegal act and the degree of culpability involved are concerned with promoting goals of retribution and deterrence, and perhaps with a concern that the courts should not be seen to be judicially condoning illegal conduct that is of a serious nature. These factors all go to turpitude, and are irrelevant to a determination whether allowing the claim would undermine coherence with the area of law proscribing the conduct. For example, allowing a claimant to use negligence law to deflect a penalty imposed for a strict liability offence will create an incoherence with the statutory regime that created that offence where that statute imposes responsibility for the relevant loss on the claimant personally, even though the claimant was not at fault.[154] James Fisher states perceptively that 'Acting inconsistently in the face of a minor wrong is no less an example of judicial inconsistency than acting inconsistently in the face of a grave wrong'.[155] The broader point is that there is no common conceptual basis or underlying rationale between matters that go to legal coherence and the other factors that go to turpitude that would provide a conceptually legitimate means of weighing them. If, hypothetically, the facts of a case give rise to issues of legal coherence, but the turpitude is relatively minor, how does a judge proceed to balance these competing concerns? How is the judge to determine logically which of these concerns to prioritise when, in the words of Weinrib already quoted, they 'are different normative currencies between which no rate of exchange exists'?[156]

In an important paper examining claims in restitution under illegal contracts, Peter Birks criticised proposals to introduce a discretion, noting that it does not fit comfortably in a pluralistic society where views will differ about whether the illegal conduct is deserving of moral condemnation:

> Discretion and pluralism sit awkwardly together. Discretion, structured or not, depends in large measure on moral intuition. It cannot thrive when no one morality commands

[152] ibid [21].
[153] ibid.
[154] This is discussed further in ch 8 Section VIII Culpability of the Claimant is Irrelevant.
[155] Fisher (n 72) 863.
[156] Weinrib, 'The Disintegration of Duty' (n 78) 168.

> the assent of the whole community. Transparent legal rationality is the cement of a society divided by moral pluralism. So, we should not rush to discretionary solutions but use discretion sparingly, as a last recourse.[157]

This recognises that different judges will take different views depending on their individual moral compass about how serious the illegality is and how much it matters, and that accordingly the exercise of the discretion largely becomes a matter of 'moral intuition'. Birks characterises a discretion, even a structured one, as involving 'an undesirable degree of fluidity'.[158] There are thus good reasons why English common law 'has generally set its face against discretion'.[159]

If a judicially structured discretion is not the answer, is a statutorily structured discretion? In the next section I discuss whether a discretion conferred by statute will provide the certainty and predictability in outcomes that a judicial discretion cannot.

B. A Statutorily Structured Discretion

The Commission initially recommended that legislation should be enacted to give courts a structured statutory discretion to decide the application of illegality doctrine on the facts of a particular case.[160] The proposed statutory discretion would require the court to determine whether the claim should be allowed or disallowed in light of individual factors specified in the legislation. The specified factors were essentially the same as those that the Commission encouraged courts to take into account in developing a judicial discretion.[161] The Commission later concluded that legislation was not needed in this area as the courts had already begun the process of developing a structured discretion to resolve torts claims founded on an illegality.[162]

The lack of a legislative response has been criticised by Lord Sumption and Lord Mance, who in extra-curial writings have urged the Commission to reconsider a statutory discretion. These Lordships believe that the problems with the law of illegality are so intractable that certainty can only be achieved in this area through a statutory discretionary regime.[163] In his judicial opinions Lord Sumption has strongly opposed the development by the courts of a judicial discretion. This has been primarily on the basis that a discretionary approach was precluded by

[157] P Birks, 'Recovering Value Transferred Under An Illegal Contract' (2000) 1 *Theoretical Inquiries in Law* 155, 160.

[158] ibid 156.

[159] Lord (Jonathan) Mance, '*Ex Turpi Causa*—When Latin Avoids Liability' (2014) 18(2) *The Edinburgh Law Review* 175, 192.

[160] Law Commission, *The Illegality Defence in Tort* (Law Comm No 160, 2001) para 7.16.

[161] Law Commission No 189 (n 96) para 7.69.

[162] Law Commission No 320 (n 130) in particular para 3.38.

[163] Sumption (n 150) 9; Mance (n 159) 191–92. See also J Goudkamp and M Zou, 'The Defence of Illegality in Tort Law: Beyond Judicial Redemption?' (2015) 74 *Cambridge Law Journal* 13, 16.

the authority of *Tinsley*,[164] but also on the basis that a discretion requires judges to make subjective value judgments about the significance of the illegality and the culpability of the claimant, making the outcome of cases difficult to predict in advance. Presumably, his Lordship believes that implementing the discretion by statute (rather than by judicial development) will cure these defects of a discretionary approach. That is probably optimistic. The specification of a limited number of factors in legislation—provided they are carefully delineated—would reduce the uncertainty that results from discretionary decision-making,[165] but would not completely eradicate it. Even advocates of a statutory discretion acknowledge that it will result in a degree of uncertainty because judges will still disagree as to the relevance or proper weighting of individual factors in a particular case.[166] The structured discretion as formulated by the Commission contains factors that are incommensurable, with the result that courts will be called upon to make value judgments about which factors should be given priority when they conflict. It might theoretically be possible for the legislature to adopt a lexical ordering system, where different criteria are ranked and conceptually sequenced.[167] However, there would be considerable controversy about the appropriate ordering of the different criteria,[168] and it is unlikely that agreement could be reached on this complicated matter.

Nor does a statutory discretion overcome the theoretical challenges posed by corrective justice theory. A number of the proposed individual factors are inconsistent with the relational structure of negligence law in that they focus one-sidedly on the plaintiff's illegal conduct and/or seek to reinforce the goals of the criminal law. This is not to suggest that corrective justice theory is intrinsically hostile to legislative reform that undercuts corrective justice. However, in deciding whether to implement a legislative scheme, it will be relevant to consider whether concerns that support the scheme are sufficient to outweigh the values that the scheme would undermine, including corrective justice[169] because a legislative scheme that does not realise corrective justice 'will have a disvalue'.[170] It is arguable that the policy objectives of the proposed statutory discretion do not outweigh the deleterious impact on corrective justice entitlements. The primary policy objective of enacting a discretion in legislation would be to bring clarity to the law of illegality because of the repeated failure of the courts to identify a single

164 *Servier* (n 1) [19]–[21] (Lords Neuberger and Clarke agreeing); *Bilta* (n 2) [62], [99] Tinsley has now been rejected by a majority of the UK Supreme Court in *Patel v Mirza* [2016] UKSC 42: see at [110] (Lord Toulson, Lady Hale, Lords Kerr, Wilson and Hodge agreeing).

165 J Goudkamp, 'A Private Law Hydra' (n 36) 269.

166 Law Commission No 189 (n 96) para 7.62; Davies, 'Two Steps Forward, One Step Back?' (n 120) 185–86. Davies argues (at 186) that where the outcome of a discretion is not clear-cut because the parties are equally blameworthy, those parties do not 'deserve a law that is uncertain'. However, as discussed in ch 2, the morality of the parties is an irrelevant consideration in negligence law: see ch 2, Section V, Key Implications of Adopting a Corrective Justice Framework.

167 See the explanation by Bruce Chapman of a lexical ordering system: Chapman (n 79) 1490.

168 ibid.

169 A Beever, 'Corrective Justice and Personal Responsibility in Tort Law' (2008) 28(3) *Oxford Journal of Legal Studies* 475, 499.

170 ibid.

formula for the application of illegality doctrine. However, a formula is available in the form of the principle of coherence. The policy need for a statutory discretion does not outweigh the disvaluing of corrective justice entitlements in the circumstance where there is a valid basis for illegality doctrine that is consistent with corrective justice. Moreover, because the potential for a claim to disrupt the coherence of the legal system can be predicted in advance by judges and legal advisers, a legal coherence test does not give rise to the same uncertainty as a statutory discretion.

X. Conclusion

The workload of judges and the manner in which counsel has presented the case means that courts often do not have the opportunity to assess the structure of the law of illegality as a whole.[171] Due to the complexity of this area, it is perhaps understandable then that courts have resorted to policy and discretion. Where courts are struggling to identify one convincing rationale for illegality doctrine, it is to be anticipated that they will resort to a multi-factorial approach where a range of public policy and other considerations are evaluated in order to resolve the particular claim before them. However, an approach constructed on policy and discretion will have a corrosive effect on the stability and coherence of the law of illegality.[172] The new approach advanced by Lord Toulson for the majority in *Patel* compounds this problem as it involves both an uncontrolled policy discretion and a structured discretion to determine proportionality, thus doubling the risk of uncertainty and unpredictability of decision making. Lord Mance legitimately criticised this approach for requiring courts:

> to make a value judgment, by reference to a widely spread mélange of ingredients, about the overall 'merits' or strengths, in a highly unspecific non-legal sense, of the respective claims of the public interest and of each of the parties.[173]

Lord Toulson acknowledged that his 'range of factors' approach is open to criticism for engendering uncertainty, but defended it in part on the ground that it would result in no greater uncertainty than current rule-based approaches which have failed to provide the necessary certainty and stability.[174] However, Peter Birks

[171] cf Law Commission, Illegal Transactions: The Effect of Illegality on Contracts and Trusts (Law Comm No 154, 1999), para 5.10.

[172] *cf* Charles Mitchell 'The Canadian Law of Unjust Enrichment and Restitution' (2015) 131 *Law Quarterly Review* 323, 324. Mitchell was there referring to the uncertain state of the law of illegality following the conflicting decisions in *Servier* and *Bilta*; however, the same sentiments apply to a discretionary approach to illegality.

[173] *Patel* (n 3) [206].

[174] ibid [90] [113] (Lord Toulson, Lady Hale and Lords Wilson and Hodge agreeing); see also [137] (Lord Kerr). Some academic commentators have also used this argument to defend a discretionary approach: see, eg, Davies, 'Two Steps Forward, One Step Back?' (n 120) 185; Strauss (n 111) 256–67, 265.

was more optimistic about the ability of the common law to settle itself and to move to an intelligible theory of illegality without the need to rely on discretion.[175] Birks rejected a discretionary approach, and argued that the trouble currently facing the law of illegality can be cured simply by focusing on the 'principle against self-stultification',[176] which is a negative form of expression of the principle of coherence.[177] Birks points out that an enquiry based on legal coherence 'can be answered analytically ... without setting sail on the sea of discretion'.[178] Moreover, it has the 'great advantage' that it is amoral, and divorced from judgments about the blameworthiness of the parties.[179]

In the next chapter I will examine the various 'connection' approaches put forward by English courts for resolving illegality claims. I will explain that these tests—which are ultimately founded on public policy—are incapable of providing the needed clarity and theoretical legitimacy to this area of the law. Then, in Chapter 6, I will explain why Peter Birks was correct in identifying the coherence principle as the correct basis for a principle of illegality.

[175] Birks (n 157) 158. Birks was there discussing claims in restitution for recovery of benefits conferred under an illegal contract. The High Court of Australia subsequently adopted this approach in *Equuscorp Pty Ltd v Haxton* (2012) 246 CLR 498.

[176] Birks ibid 160.

[177] *Equuscorp Pty Ltd v Haxton* (n 175) [38] (French CJ, Crennan and Kiefel J).

[178] Birks (n 157) 158.

[179] ibid 168.

5

The Connection Tests

I. Overview

The courts in the United Kingdom have devised a number of tests for resolving claims arising out of illegal conduct that scrutinise the closeness of the connection or relationship between the claim and the illegal conduct. Various formulae have been used to denote the requisite connection or relationship: 'reliance'; 'inextricable link'; 'close or sufficient connection'; and 'causation'. There has been considerable judicial support for three different connection tests: the reliance test; the inextricable link or sufficiency of connection test (these tests appear to be synonymous); and the causation test.[1] The reliance test, adopted by Lord Browne-Wilkinson for the majority in *Tinsley v Milligan*,[2] was the leading test in non-negligence claims until its rejection by a majority of the Supreme Court of the United Kingdom in *Patel v Mirza*.[3] While the reliance test was never adopted as the primary test for resolving negligence claims (in this context the causation test has been the preferred approach),[4] there has been significant support in the negligence cases for all three tests, including the reliance test.[5]

The reliance test is the narrowest of the tests, in that its focus is confined to the procedural connection between the claim and the illegality.[6] The other tests

[1] Lord Sumption has suggested that the connection tests are simply evidential tests which may assist in deciding whether the claim is or is not founded on the illegal act: Lord Sumption, 'Reflections on the Law of Illegality' [2012] *Restitution Law Review* 1, 10.

[2] *Tinsley v Milligan* [1994] 1 AC 340, 370, 375–76 (Lord Browne-Wilkinson, Lord Jauncey and Lord Lowry agreeing).

[3] In *Hounga v Allen* [2014] UKSC 47, [2014] 1 WLR 2889 [30] Lord Wilson (Lady Hale and Lord Kerr agreeing), described the reliance test as having 'maximum precedential authority'. However, a majority of the Supreme Court in *Patel v Mirza* [2016] UKSC 42 refused to follow *Tinsley v Milligan*, and rejected the reliance test: [110] (Lord Toulson, Lady Hale, Lords Kerr, Wilson and Hodge agreeing).

[4] *Gray v Thames Trains Ltd* [2009] UKHL33, [2009] 1 AC 1339.

[5] *Stone & Rolls Ltd (in Liq) v Moore Stephens (a firm)* [2009] UKHL 39, [2009] AC 1391 [129]–[131] (Lord Walker, Lord Brown agreeing) (reliance test); *Clunis and Islington Health Authority* [1998] QB 978 (CA) 990 (Beldam LJ, Otton and Judge LJJ agreeing) (reliance test); *Vellino v Chief Constable of the Greater Manchester Police* [2001] EWCA Civ 1249, [2002] 1 WLR 218 (inextricable link test); *Gray v Thames Trains Ltd* [2008] EWCA Civ 713, [2009] 1 AC 1339 [20] (the Court) (inextricable link test) (*Gray v Thames Trains Ltd* CA).

[6] *Bilta (UK) Ltd (in liquidation) v Nazir (No 2)* [2015] UKSC 23, [2016] AC 1 [102] (Lord Sumption); J Fisher, 'The *Ex Turpi Causa* Principle in *Hounga* and *Servier* (2015) 78 *The Modern Law Review* 854, 857; *cf Patel v Mirza* (n 3) [239], [262] (Lord Sumption).

focus more widely on the degree of factual connection between the loss and the illegality, and are intended to permit more flexibility than the reliance test.[7] These tests essentially seek to determine whether the illegality merely provided the occasion for, or background to, the loss that was sustained (in which case the claim will succeed), or was directly and closely connected to the loss (in which case the claim must fail). All three tests are intended to exclude from the realm of illegality doctrine losses resulting from illegal conduct that is merely collateral to the claim.[8]

The connection tests have never secured significant judicial support in Australia or Canada. The High Court of Australia in *Miller v Miller* specifically held that connection tests—at least when formulated in the language of causation—are incapable of providing a satisfactory explanation for claims for injuries sustained while the claimant is committing an illegal act.[9] It will be argued, for three main reasons, that the Australian and Canadian courts have been correct to eschew the connection tests in favour of a principle of coherence. First, all three tests (including the reliance test) require the making of subjective judgments as to whether the relevant relationship exists between the illegality and the claim. Secondly, the tests are merely a proxy for the application of public policy. In *R (on the application of Best) v The Chief Land Registrar*, Sales LJ highlighted the policy basis of connection tests when he commented that, when it is found that a sufficient connection does not exist, this is merely 'a way of saying that the public policy associated with the particular crime in issue is not centrally engaged and is outweighed by other general public policies inherent in the relevant civil law to be applied'.[10] Thirdly, all three tests are conceptually incoherent. They are inconsistent with the bilateralism of tort law in that they focus unilaterally on the claimant's illegal conduct and hence 'fail to embrace both parties'.[11]

This chapter will discuss all three connection tests; however, the focus is on the causation test. As mentioned, it is this test that is currently the dominant approach to resolving negligence claims in the United Kingdom, and also—by virtue of statute—in most Australian jurisdictions.[12]

[7] *cf* Fisher ibid 857.

[8] *cf Les Laboratoires Servier v Apotex Inc* [2014] UKSC 55, [2015] AC 430 [18] (Lord Sumption). Lord Sumption is there referring only to the reliance and close connection tests, though the same proposition applies to the causation test.

[9] *Miller v Miller* [2011] HCA 9, (2011) 242 CLR 446 [21], quoting Stallybrass (ed), *Salmond on Torts*, 9th edn (London, Sweet & Maxwell, 1936) 484.

[10] *R (on the application of Best) v The Chief Land Registrar* [2015] EWCA Civ 17, [2016] QB 23, [61].

[11] EJ Weinrib, 'The Special Morality of Tort Law' (1989) 34 (3) *McGill Law Journal* 403, 409.

[12] The common law causation test was formulated by Lord Hoffmann (who wrote the leading judgment) in *Gray v Thames Trains Ltd* (n 4). Most Australian jurisdictions have enacted statutory defences that have as their central criterion the causal link between the criminal conduct and the harm: see the legislation cited in n 205 below.

II. The Reliance Test

The reliance test was adopted by a majority of the House of Lords in *Tinsley v Milligan* in the context of a claim to an equitable interest in property.[13] Pursuant to this test, the claim must be rejected if the claimant is required to plead the illegal conduct or rely on it in evidence in order to establish the claim. The reliance test is the narrowest (and strictest) of the various connection tests. It focuses only on those matters that are required to formulate and establish the claim whereas the other tests are concerned more broadly with the factual connection between the illegality and the claim.[14]

The Australian and Canadian courts never embraced the reliance test,[15] but it lingered on in the United Kingdom.[16] It was not until 2016 in *Patel v Mirza* that the UK Supreme Court finally departed from *Tinsely v Milligan* and rejected the reliance test.[17] In any event, although there was some authority for applying the test to negligence claims,[18] the prevailing view was that it was not a useful test. In this context. In the leading negligence case of *Gray v Thames Trains Ltd* Lord Hoffmann (who wrote the main judgment) thought that the test has no application to negligence claims.[19]

The Supreme Court in *Patel v Mirza* was correct to banish the reliance test from the law of illegality.[20] The following discussion will briefly explain why.[21]

Tinsley v Milligan was controversial from the outset; Mitchell McInnes commented a few years after *Tinsley* that 'it is difficult to think of a House of Lords'

[13] The test derived from the decision of the Court of Appeal in *Bowmakers Ltd v Barnet Instruments Ltd* [1945] KB 65.

[14] *Bilta (UK) Ltd (in liquidation) v Nazir (No 2)* (n 6) [102] (Lord Sumption); *Patel v Mirza* (n 3) [239], [262] (Lord Sumption); Fisher (n 6) 857.

[15] It was specifically rejected by the High Court of Australian in *Nelson v Nelson* (1995) 184 CLR 538.

[16] *Stone & Rolls Ltd (in Liq) v Moore Stephens (a firm)* (n 5) [129]–[131] (Lord Walker, Lord Brown agreeing); *Hounga v Allen* (n 3) [30] (Lord Wilson, Lady Hale and Lord Kerr agreeing); *Hniazdzilau v Vajgel* [2016] EWHC 15 (Ch).

[17] *Patel v Mirza* (n 3) [110] (Lord Toulson, Lady Hale and Lords Kerr, Wilson and Hodge agreeing).

[18] *Stone & Rolls Ltd (in Liq) v Moore Stephens (a firm)* (n 5) [129]–[131] (Lord Walker, Lord Brown agreeing); *Clunis and Islington Health Authority* (n 5) 990 (Beldam LJ for the Court).

[19] *Gray v Thames Trains Ltd* (n 4) [30]–[31].

[20] Although Lords Mance, Clarke and Sumption did not abandon the reliance test completely, they in effect confined its operation to circumstances where reliance on the illegality would create an inconsistency in the law: *Patel v Mirza* (n 3), see in particular [197]–[199] (Lord Mance), [210] (Lord Clarke), [250]–[253], [268] (Lord Sumption).

[21] For other contemporary critiques of the test see the works by James Goudkamp, in particular J Goudkamp, 'A Long, Hard Look at Gray v Thames Trains Ltd' in PS Davies and J Pita (eds), *Jurisprudence of Lord Hoffmann: A Festschrift in Honour of Lord Leonard Hoffmann* (London, Bloomsbury Publishing, 2015) 37–39; J Goudkamp, 'The Doctrine of Illegality: A Private Law Hydra' (2015) 6 *The UK Supreme Court Yearbook* 254, 261–62.

judgment in recent years that has met with more derision and less enthusiasm'.[22] The test is indefensible by reason of its promotion of form over substance;[23] in the words of McInnes, it is a 'remarkable triumph of artificiality'.[24] As Nicholas Strauss has pointed out, it does not reflect well on the law that the outcome of a case should turn on arcane authorities relating to questions of onus of proof rather than on the facts of the case.[25] The test is insensitive to issues of coherence in the law, such as whether allowing the claim would be incompatible with the purpose of the statute against which the claimant has offended.[26] It is essentially a procedural test that is dependent solely on the adventitious[27] allocation of the onus of proof in a particular case, and whether the evidence that the claimant necessarily relies on is based on the illegality.[28] Even Lord Sumption, who has been most insistent that the basis of illegality doctrine remains that formulated in *Tinsley v Milligan*, views the reliance test in the procedural form adopted in that case as technical and capricious.[29] This recognises that the test can operate indiscriminately and lead to disproportionately harsh outcomes.[30] The courts have consistently failed to locate a conceptual basis or policy justification for the test,[31] or to articulate a convincing rationale why reliance on the illegal conduct should be the determining factor.[32]

A further criticism of the reliance test is that the concept of 'reliance' on the illegality can be difficult to apply in practice.[33] The courts have not always

[22] M McInnes, 'Advancement, Illegality and Restitution' (1997) 5 *Australian Property Law Journal* 1, 9.

[23] *Nelson v Nelson* (n 15) 558 (Deane and Gummow JJ), 609 (McHugh J).

[24] McInnes (n 22) 10.

[25] N Strauss, 'Ex Turpi Causa Oritur Actio?' (2016) 132 *Law Quarterly Review* 236, 254.

[26] *Nelson v Nelson* (n 15) 558 (Deane and Gummow JJ), 609 (McHugh J).

[27] *Tribe v Tribe* [1996] Ch 107, 134 (Millett LJ). James Goudkamp also makes the point that issues tend to be allocated to questions of liability or a defence at random, and hence it will often be a matter of luck as to whether or not the claimant must rely on the illegal conduct in order to establish the claim: Goudkamp, 'A Long, Hard Look at Gray v Thames Trains Ltd' (n 21) 38; J Goudkamp, 'The Doctrine of Illegality: A Private Law Hydra' (n 21) 261. See also G Virgo, 'The Defence of Illegality in Unjust Enrichment' in A Dyson, J Goudkamp and F Wilmot-Smith, *Defences in Unjust Enrichment* (London, Bloomsbury Publishing, 2016) 181–82.

[28] The Law Commission, *The Illegality Defence* (Law Comm No 320, 2010) para 2.13 (Law Comm No 320). See also *Hounga v Allen* (n 3) [30] (Lord Wilson, Lady Hale and Lord Kerr agreeing); *Moore Stephens (a Firm) v Stone & Rolls Ltd (In Liq)* [2008] EWCA Civ 644, [2008] 3 WLR 1146 [16] (Rimer LJ, Keene and Mummery LJJ agreeing.

[29] Lord Sumption, 'Reflections on the Law of Illegality' (n 1) 5. His Lordship now recognises that the fact of reliance on the illegality is relevant only insofar as it is reliance in order to enforce an illegal contract or otherwise for a purpose that would create an inconsistency in the law: [236]–[239] (Lord Clarke agreeing); see also [199] (Lord Mance).

[30] *Nelson v Nelson* (n 15) 558 (Deane and Gummow JJ); *Moore Stephens (a firm) v Stone & Rolls Ltd (in Liq)* (CA) (n 28) [16] (Rimer LJ, Keene and Mummery LJJ agreeing).

[31] *Nelson v Nelson* ibid 610 (McHugh J); *Tribe v Tribe* (n 27) 134 (Millett LJ).

[32] Goudkamp, 'A Long, Hard Look at Gray v Thames Trains Ltd' (n 21) 38; Goudkamp, 'A Private Law Hydra' (n 21) 261; Virgo, 'The Defence of Illegality in Unjust Enrichment' (n 27) 182.

[33] Law Comm No 320 (n 28) para 2.14. See also *Hounga v Allen* (n 3) [30] (Lord Wilson, Lady Hale and Lord Kerr agreeing); *Patel v Mirza* (n 3) [134] (Lord Kerr).

identified with precision which party bears the onus of proof on a given issue.[34] There are further difficulties with determining exactly which facts are essential and necessary for the claimant to establish the case.[35] To draw an example from Australian negligence law, in the joint illegal enterprise cases the issue is whether the illegality negates a duty of care that otherwise would be owed.[36] A common scenario that arises is that the claimant and defendant jointly steal a car and take it for a joyride. The defendant negligently causes an accident in which the claimant is injured. The claimant can establish that a duty of care was owed by relying on the ordinary relationship of driver and passenger, without relying on the illegality. Authority suggests that it is the defendant who bears the evidential onus of establishing that the illegal aspect of the parties' relationship transforms that relationship from that of ordinary driver and passenger into one in which no duty of care is owed.[37] It has also been suggested that the court can raise the illegality on its own motion in the public interest.[38] In these cases the illegality will be raised by the defendant (or the court) and the claimant does not need to plead or directly rely on the unlawful taking and use of the car in order to establish the claim. However, the facts led by the claimant to establish that the driving was negligent and that the negligence caused the injury arise out of the unlawful use, and is likely to disclose that illegality. Moreover, the claimant bears the overall legal onus of proving that a duty of care was owed. In these circumstances it is not clear whether the illegality 'of necessity' forms part of the claimant's case.[39] These kinds of difficulties prompted the Law Commission of England and Wales to comment that, of the tests proposed by the courts to resolve illegality claims, the application of the reliance test poses the most difficulties for negligence claims.[40]

This discussion demonstrates that, despite the ostensible objectivity of the test, in practice it will in some cases require subjective judgements as to whether the requisite reliance is present.[41] There can be a divergence of views on the facts of a given case as to whether the reliance test is satisfied.[42] Where there is some

[34] Goudkamp, 'A Long, Hard Look at Gray v Thames Trains Ltd' (n 21) 38; Goudkamp, 'A Private Law Hydra' (n 21) 261. For an example, refer to the discussion in the Court of Appeal in *Patel* v *Mirza* [2014] EWCA Civ 1047, [2015] Ch 271 (*Patel v Mirza* CA) of onus of proof questions in the context of a claim for repayment of money on the ground that the consideration had totally failed.

[35] Law Commission, *The Illegality Defence* (CR No 189, 2009) para 7.53 (Law Comm No 189).

[36] *Miller v Miller* (n 9).

[37] *Gala v Preston* [1991] HCA 18, (1991) 172 CLR 243, 253–54 (Mason CJ, Deane, Gaudron and McHugh JJ).

[38] *Les Laboratoires Servier v Apotex Inc* (n 8) [23] (Lord Sumption, Lords Neuberger and Clarke agreeing); *Bilta (UK) Ltd (in liquidation) v Nazir (No 2)* (n 6) [100] (Lord Sumption).

[39] *Tinsley v Milligan* (n 2) 376–77 (Lord Browne-Wilkinson, Lords Jancey and Lowry agreeing); *Patel v Mirza* CA (n 34) [78]–[79] (Gloster LJ).

[40] Law Comm No 189 (n 35) para 7.53.

[41] Fisher (n 6) 857.

[42] See, for example, the difference in view between Lord Sumption on the one hand, and Lord Toulson and Lord Hodge on the other, regarding whether the reliance test was satisfied in *Bilta (UK) Ltd (in liquidation) v Nazir (No 2)* (n 6) [63] (Lord Sumption); [167] (Lords Toulson and Hodge). See also the difference in views between Rimer LJ and Vos LJ on the one hand, and Gloster LJ on the other, in the Court of Appeal in *Patel v Mirza* about the application of the reliance test on the facts of that case: (n 34) [15]–[22] (Rimer LJ), [78]–[93] (Gloster LJ), [102]–[103] (Vos LJ).

uncertainty on onus and evidentiary issues, judges are able to manipulate the reliance test to dispose of the case in accordance with their subjective views about the merits and morality of the claim.[43] The result is that in cases where onus and evidentiary issues are straightforward the reliance test will operate arbitrarily and indiscriminately; in others, where there is uncertainty about the necessity for reliance, the test is too malleable to provide the needed certainty. This led Richard Buckley to observe that, far from promoting legal certainty and coherence, the test gives rise to legal uncertainties in application and arbitrariness in result.[44]

Even prior to *Patel v Mirza*, the UK Supreme Court had sought to temper the reliance test and introduce more flexible public policy decision-making. The genesis of this approach is dicta of Lord Phillips in *Stone & Rolls Ltd (in Liq) v Moore Stephens (a firm)* that *Tinsley v Milligan* was concerned with the effect of illegality on title, and did not lay down a universal rule that a court will never entertain a claim where the claimant must rely on illegal conduct to establish it.[45] His Lordship considered that the reliance test could not 'automatically be applied as a rule of thumb' and that the underlying policies had to be considered.[46] This approach was endorsed by Lord Wilson (for the majority) in *Hounga v Allen* and by Lord Toulson and Lord Hodge in *Bilta (UK) Ltd (in liquidation) v Nazir (No 2)*.[47] The view was that Lord Phillips was correct to 'soften' the reliance test by having regard to whether public policy requires the application of illegality doctrine.[48] The relationship between the reliance test and a public policy-based approach was not explored in these judgments[49] suggesting that the Supreme Court had merely been paying lip service to *Tinsley v Milligan*. Even Lord Sumption—who is yet to formally abandon the reliance test—has confined its application to circumstances where reliance on the illegality would create an incoherence in the law.[50] The decision by a majority of the Supreme Court to take the final step and formally reject the test will be widely welcomed by both judges and commentators.[51]

[43] Law Comm No 189 (n 35) para 7.53.

[44] RA Buckley, 'Illegality in the Supreme Court' (2015) 131 *Law Quarterly Review* 341, 343.

[45] *Stone & Rolls Ltd (in Liq) v Moore Stephens (a firm)* (n 5) [21]–[25].

[46] ibid [25].

[47] *Hounga v Allen* (n 3) [29]–[30]; *Bilta (UK) Ltd (in liquidation) v Nazir (No 2)* (n 6) [138]–[139], [167]–[174].

[48] ibid.

[49] Goudkamp, 'A Private Law Hydra' (n 21) 273. Lim has attempted to reconcile the two tests, arguing that *Tinsley v Milligan* does not prevent a consideration of policies underlying illegality doctrine, only the consequences for the parties of applying it: E Lim, *Attribution and the Illegality Defence* (2016) 79 *Modern Law Review* 468, 485–86.

[50] *Patel v Mirza* (n 3), [250]–[253], [268] (Lord Sumption); see also [197]–[199] (Lord Mance), [210] (Lord Clarke).

[51] As mentioned, the text was controversial from the outset, and the judicial and academic condemnation of it has been resounding.

III. The Inextricable Link (Sufficient Connection) Test

A further test developed by English courts that overlaps with the reliance test, but which focuses more widely on the factual connection between the loss or injury and the illegal conduct, is the inextricable link test. On this approach a claim must be rejected where the harm suffered is 'inextricably bound up and linked with' the illegal conduct.[52] The test examines whether there is a sufficiently close connection between the loss suffered and the illegal purpose, and excludes consequences of the illegality that are regarded as merely collateral or incidental to the claim.[53] Lord Hughes in *Hounga* explained that the question is whether the illegality is sufficiently closely connected to the harm, or whether it 'can properly be regarded as collateral, or as doing no more than providing the context for the relationship which gives rise to the claim'.[54]

The inextricable link test is attributed to *Cross v Kirkby*, where Beldam LJ (Otton LJ agreeing) and Judge LJ framed the issue as whether the claim is inextricably linked to the criminal activity.[55] In a much-quoted passage Beldam LJ formulated the principle as applying when the claim 'is so closely connected or inextricably bound up with his own criminal or illegal conduct that the court could not permit him to recover without appearing to condone that conduct.'[56] *Cross v Kirkby* involved a claim in tort for assault and battery; however, the inextricable link principle has been adopted as a test of general application,[57] including in negligence claims.[58] In *Vellino v Chief Constable of the Greater Manchester Police* the police visited the claimant's second floor apartment to serve an arrest warrant. The claimant, who had a history of evading arrest by jumping from his balcony, suffered injury when he jumped from a window.[59] In an influential judgment, Stuart-Smith LJ rejected a claim in negligence against the police authority on the ground that the escape from legal custody 'was integral to the claim'.[60]

Some judges such as Lord Hughes in *Hounga v Allen* prefer to frame the question in terms of whether there is a sufficiently close connection between the harm

[52] This test was formulated in *Cross v Kirkby* [2000] EWCA Civ 426.

[53] *Cross v Kirkby* ibid [102] (Judge LJ). See also *Les Laboratoires Servier v Apotex Inc* (n 8) [18] (Lord Sumption, Lords Neuberger and Clarke agreeing).

[54] *Hounga v Allen* (n 3) [58].

[55] *Cross v Kirkby* (n 52).

[56] ibid [76]. See also Judge LJ at [102]–[103].

[57] It has been applied, for example, in a number of statutory discrimination cases: *Hall v Woolston Hall Leisure Ltd* [2000] EWCA Civ 170, [2001] 1 WLR 225; *Vakante v Governing Body of Addey and Stanhope School (No 2)* [2004] EWCA Civ 1065, [2004] ICR 279; *Hounga v Allen* (n 3).

[58] *Vellino v Chief Constable of the Greater Manchester Police* (n 5); *Gray v Thames Trains Ltd* CA (n 5).

[59] *Vellino v Chief Constable of the Greater Manchester Police* ibid.

[60] ibid [71].

suffered and the illegal purpose.[61] Despite the difference in terminology, Lord Hughes appeared to view the sufficiency of connection test as synonymous with the inextricable link test.[62] The language of 'close connection' and 'inextricable link' have been used interchangeably in other cases,[63] supporting the view that the two tests are coterminous.

The inextricable link test has never taken hold in Australia or Canada. Early Australian authority had held that the relevant question was whether there was a sufficiency of connection between the injury and illegal purpose.[64] However, the High Court of Australia has been firm in its rejection of tests that are based on the degree of the connection between the illegality and the harm.[65] There is also considerable uncertainty about the future of the inextricable link test in the United Kingdom, at least as an exclusive or primary test for resolving illegality claims. Lord Hoffmann in *Gray* appeared to subsume it into the causation test.[66] Lord Wilson in *Hounga v Allen* disagreed, characterising the inextricable link test as an independent test,[67] but stated that the 'bigger question' is whether the inextricable link test is the proper legal basis for the application of illegality doctrine.[68] His Lordship unhelpfully failed to answer this question, however, it would appear that if he saw the inextricable link test as having a continuing role it would only be as a threshold test, followed by an evaluation of the public policy considerations for and against an evaluation of the claim.[69] The majority decision in *Patel v Mirza* also prefers a policy approach to an inextricable link test.[70]

For the reasons discussed in Chapter 4, the policy/discretionary approach proposed is inappropriate. However, the inextricable link test is not a suitable replacement, as it has significant shortcomings.[71] There are three main arguments for rejecting the test.

The first argument for rejecting the inextricable link test is that it is unprincipled in nature. It is unavoidably subjective, and as a result permits courts to

[61] *Hounga v Allen* (n 3) [55] (Lord Hughes, Lord Carnwath agreeing).

[62] In concluding that there was not a sufficiency of connection between the illegal activity and the claim in that case Lord Hughes indicated that he agreed with the reasons given by Lord Wilson, who had employed the inextricable link formula: ibid [59].

[63] *Cross v Kirkby* (n 52) [76] (Beldam LJ, Otton LJ agreeing); *Hall v Woolston Hall Leisure Ltd* (n 57) [42] (Peter Gibson LJ, Moore-Bick J agreeing); *Gray v Thames Trains Ltd* (n 4) [20].

[64] *Godbolt v Fittock* [1963] SR NSW 617. The relevant question according to Sugarman J in that case is 'one of the sufficiency of the connection [between the injuries suffered and the execution of the criminal purpose] to require a conclusion that it would be contrary to public policy that damages should be awarded for the injury or that the injury had its origin in a *turpis causa*': at 624.

[65] *Miller v Miller* (n 9) [21].

[66] *Gray v Thames Trains Ltd* (n 4) [54].

[67] *Hounga v Allen* (n 3) [36] (Lord Wilson, Lady Hale and Lord Kerr agreeing).

[68] ibid [41].

[69] See A Bogg and S Green, 'Rights Are Not Just for the Virtuous: What *Hounga* Means for the Illegality Defence in the Discrimination Torts' (2015) 44 *Industrial Law Journal* 101, 107.

[70] *Patel v Mirza* (n 3).

[71] J Goudkamp, 'A Long, Hard Look at Gray v Thames Trains Ltd' (n 21) 39.

decide the case based on their own individual notions about the merits of the claim. Lord Wilson in *Hounga v Allen* recognised that the inextricable link formula 'has a potential for inconsistent application driven by subjective considerations'.[72] He considered that the 'subjectivity inherent in the requisite value judgment [of determining an inextricable link]' was well demonstrated by the case before him.[73] This was a reference to the fact that the Court of Appeal had decided unanimously that an inextricable link existed, whereas both his Lordship and Lord Hughes were firmly of the opinion that it did not. In *Hounga v Allen* the claimant was subjected to acts of physical, verbal and emotional abuse perpetrated by her employers while working illegally for them as an *au pair*. The claimant eventually was evicted from the home and dismissed from the employment, and successfully recovered damages in the statutory tort of discrimination. Lord Wilson concluded (albeit with some consciousness of the inherent subjectivity of this conclusion) that the claim was not inextricably linked with the illegal employment contract because the contract provided no more than the context for the discrimination and dismissal. However, this conclusion perhaps does not sit well with the views expressed by Lord Wilson later in his judgment that it was credible that employers of illegal immigrants might be emboldened to commit acts of discrimination out of a belief that they can do so with impunity.[74] If this assumption is correct, it is arguable that there is a strong factual connection between the illegal employment and the discrimination,[75] yet Lord Wilson disapproved of the reliance by the Court of Appeal on the special vulnerability of the claimant to discrimination and maltreatment by virtue of her illegal status.[76] This is not to suggest that one view or the other is correct. The point is merely that different views will be taken as to the sufficiency of the connection.

Lord Rodger in the House of Lords in *Gray v Thames Trains Ltd* also criticised the inherent subjectivity of the inextricable test, observing that it is likely to give rise to conflicting responses as differing views are taken as to whether the inextricable link exists on the facts of a particular case.[77] His Lordship also referred to the divergent views in the case before him about whether the inextricable link test was established on the facts as evidence of the shortcomings of the test.[78] The facts of *Gray* were, relevantly, that the claimant stabbed a man to death and was sentenced to a period of detention in a psychiatric hospital for manslaughter. The claimant established that he had committed the manslaughter while under the

[72] *Hounga v Allen* (n 3) [37]. Lord Sumption in *Patel v Mirza* also rejects the inextricable link test on the ground that it 'degenerate[s] into a question of instinctive judicial preference for one party over another': (n 3) [240].

[73] ibid [38]

[74] ibid [44].

[75] See Nicholas Strauss (n 25) 252.

[76] *Hounga v Allen* (n 3) [39].

[77] *Gray v Thames Trains Ltd* (n 4) [74]. Lord Hoffmann also expressed reservations about the test: at [54].

[78] ibid.

effects of a post-traumatic stress disorder arising out of a rail collision caused by the defendant's negligence. The claimant claimed damages for, inter alia, loss of earning capacity from the date of the manslaughter, non-economic losses for loss of reputation and feelings of guilt and remorse, and an indemnity against civil claims by the dependants of his victim.

At first instance in *Gray*, Flaux J rejected the claim on the ground that to establish the claim the claimant had to rely on the manslaughter and establish that it was caused by the disorder (and ultimately the defendant's negligence). The claim for loss of earning capacity was so closely connected or inextricably bound up with the claimant's own criminal conduct that it could not be allowed.[79] Lord Hoffmann in the House of Lords confirmed (without discussion) that 'it is hard to think of a more inextricable link [between the claim and the manslaughter]'.[80] Yet the Court of Appeal held that the loss of earning capacity was not inextricably bound up with the manslaughter and that that part of the claim could succeed. This was on the basis that the claim for loss of earning capacity arose on the date of the rail collision, and thus pre-dated the manslaughter.[81] The divergence in views and failure to provide a convincing justification for the conclusions on the facts illustrates the problem being discussed; namely, that there is no rational basis for deciding whether or not there was an inextricable link between the claim and the crime. *Gray* demonstrates that the inextricable link test is 'too malleable' to be helpful in resolving the outcomes of particular cases.[82]

The underlying reason for the subjectivity of the inextricable link test is that ultimately it is based on considerations of policy[83]—such as whether the court should appear to condone the criminal conduct[84]—rather than legal principle. The policy basis of the test allows courts to manipulate it in order to determine cases according to their own value judgment about the merits of the claim and the seriousness of the illegality. Lord Sumption, writing extra-curially, refers to the 'unprincipled character' of the inextricable link test, and argues that the Court in *Cross v Kirkby* (where the test was first formulated) was in effect seeking to reinstate a 'public conscience' test, entailing a comparison of the respective degree of culpability of the parties.[85] His Lordship then expresses the view that in *Cross v Kirkby* the claimant's 'real problem was that the Court of Appeal did not like the cut of his jib'.[86] He cautioned that this 'may be understandable in human terms, but it is hardly a substitute for legal analysis'.[87] The same tendency of courts to use the

79 *Gray v Thames Trains Ltd* [2007] EWHC 1558 (QB), [30]–[32].
80 *Gray v Thames Trains Ltd* (n 4), [48].
81 *Gray v Thames Trains Ltd* CA (n 5) [22]–[24] (the Court).
82 PS Davies, 'The Illegality Defence and Public Policy' (2009) 125 *Law Quarterly Review* 556, 558.
83 *Vellino v Chief Constable of the Greater Manchester Police* (n 5) [70] (Stuart-Smith LJ).
84 *Cross v Kirkby* (n 52) [76]; *Gray v Thames Trains Ltd* CA (n 5) [24] (the Court).
85 Lord Sumption, 'Reflections on the Law of Illegality' (n 1) 6.
86 ibid.
87 ibid.

inextricable link test as a mechanism for denying a claim where they consider the claimant to be unworthy of relief has also been identified in the context of *Hounga v Allen* and the statutory tort of discrimination.[88] A more principled alternative must be found.

The second—though closely related—argument for rejecting the inextricable link test is that, due to the vagueness of the very notion of an 'inextricable' link,[89] the courts have been unable to identify rational criteria that could be used to determine its existence. When applying the test, the courts tend to take into account a range of criteria that have no logical connection to an analysis whether the claim and illegality are factually connected.[90] For example, in *Vellino v Chief Constable of the Greater Manchester Police* Stuart-Smith J held that the crime in question must be sufficiently serious to merit the application of the test, and excluded trivial offences from its ambit.[91] Yet the seriousness of the offence is not relevant as a matter of logic to the question whether it has a sufficient connection (however liberally that phrase is interpreted) with the claim.[92] A claim for a tripping injury sustained in the course of a criminal trespass is closely connected to the offence; the fact that the offence might have been trivial in the circumstances is of no importance. The excision from the test of claims that are closely connected with a minor offence betrays the reality that the test is no more than a proxy for public policy. Commentators in other contexts in which the test is applied, such as the statutory tort of discrimination, have also noted the tendency of courts to loosen the test by reference to factors such as the gravity of the illegality and the culpability of the claimant.[93] As Lord Wilson recognised in *Hounga v Allen* (a discrimination case), these are matters that are logically irrelevant to the application of the test.[94] For example, the fact the tripping trespasser is a child, and hence not particularly blameworthy, does not lessen the conclusion that the claim is connected to the illegal act of trespassing. The inclusion of extraneous considerations highlights the unprincipled nature of the test, and led Alan Bogg to observe that the application of the test by some judges has given it

[88] S Forshaw and M Pilgerstorfer, 'Illegally Formed Contracts of Employment and Equal Treatment at Work' (2005) 34 *Industrial Law Journal* 158, 171; Bogg and Green (n 69) 118. The authors of both papers made these comments in the course of discussing the decision in *Vakante v Governing Body of Addey and Stanhope School (No 2)* (n 57).

[89] Sumption 'Reflections on the Law of Illegality' (n 1) 6; Goudkamp, 'A Long, Hard Look at Gray v Thames Trains Ltd' (n 21) 40.

[90] Refer to Lord Wilson's discussion of *Vakante v Governing Body of Addey and Stanhope School (No 2)* (n 57) in *Hounga v Allen* (n 3) [35].

[91] *Vellino v Chief Constable of the Greater Manchester Police* (n 5) [70].

[92] *Hounga v Allen* (n 3) [35] (Lord Wilson, Lady Hale and Lord Kerr agreeing).

[93] See generally, AL Bogg, 'Race Discrimination and the Doctrine of Illegality' (2013) 129 *Law Quarterly Review* 12, discussing *Vakante v Governing Body of Addey and Stanhope School (No 2)* (n 57) and the Court of Appeal judgment in *Hounga v Allen* [2012] EWCA Civ 609, [2012] IRLR 685. See also Lord Hughes in *Hounga v Allen* who viewed the extent of the claimant's turpitude as relevant to the assessment whether there is a sufficiently close connection between the illegality and the claim: (n 3) [58] (Lord Carnwath agreeing).

[94] *Hounga v Allen* ibid [35].

'an accordion-like quality, allowing it to expand or contract its reach at the moral discretion of the court'.[95]

It is unlikely that a rational basis can in fact be identified for distinguishing between acts of illegality that are sufficiently connected to the injury and those that should be regarded as collateral, a point made by Ernest Weinrib in respect of an analogous test.[96] Similar criticisms have been made of 'connection' tests deployed in other contexts. The causation test entails a similar enquiry, namely whether the illegality was the cause of the harm or merely provided the opportunity or context for the harm to be suffered. The High Court of Australia in *Miller v Miller* held that attempts to make these distinctions draw the law into a 'logical and legal labyrinth'.[97] In the field of vicarious liability the leading test in the UK is whether there is a 'close connection' between the employee's tortious act and the employment. In *Various Claimants v Catholic Child Welfare Society* Lord Phillips (the other members of the Court agreeing) pointed out that a test of close connection 'tells one nothing about the nature of the connection [required]'.[98] In *Dubai Aluminium Co Ltd v Salaam* Lord Nicholls (Lord Slynn and Lord Hutton agreeing) conceded that the close connection test 'affords no guidance on the type or degree of connection which will normally be regarded as sufficiently close to prompt the legal conclusion [that vicarious liability should be imposed]'.[99] The inextricable link test suffers the same shortcomings; as James Goudkamp has observed, 'the inextricable link test tells us what we are searching for, but does not tell us how to find it'.[100]

The argument advanced so far is that the 'inextricable link' test is incapable of effecting consistency in decision-making due to its vague and unprincipled nature, and that this by itself is reason enough to discard it. However, there is an even more fundamental reason why the test is not appropriate as a basis for resolving illegality claims. The third argument for rejecting the inextricable link test is that it is inconsistent with the correlative structure of negligence liability because its focus is confined in a one-sided manner to the claimant's illegal conduct and whether it is sufficiently 'linked with' the harm. It fails to address the position of *both* parties in a relational manner, and hence is contrary to corrective justice. It is submitted that it should be cast off from the law along with the reliance test.

[95] Bogg (n 93) 14. In a separate article with Sarah Green, Alan Bogg proposed the retention of the inextricable link test as a factual threshold test, followed by a normative evaluation of policy factors: Bogg and Green, 'Rights Are Not Just for the Virtuous' (n 69). An approach that relies on policy factors was criticised and rejected in ch 4.

[96] EJ Weinrib in 'Illegality as a Tort Defence' (1976) 26 *University of Toronto Law Journal* 28, 37–38.

[97] *Miller v Miller* (n 9) [21], quoting Stallybrass (ed) (n 9) 484.

[98] *Various Claimants v Catholic Child Welfare* [2012] UKHL 56, [2013] 2 AC 1 [74].

[99] *Dubai Aluminium Co Ltd v Salaam* [2002] UKHL 48, [2003] 2 AC 366 [25].

[100] Goudkamp, 'A Long, Hard Look' (n 21) 40. See also Goudkamp, 'A Private Law Hydra' (n 21) 262; J Goudkamp and M Zou, 'The Defence of Illegality in Tort Law: Beyond Judicial Redemption?' (2015) 74 *Cambridge Law Journal* 13, 16.

IV. The Causation Test

A. Overview of the Causation Test

The leading approach in England at present to resolving negligence claims that arise out of illegal conduct is the causation test. This approach purports to allocate legal responsibility for harm arising from illegal conduct through the application of causation principles. The central question on this approach is whether the claimant's illegal conduct caused the injuries (in which case the claim is denied) or merely provided the occasion for the injuries to be sustained (in which case it is not).[101] This explanation draws upon earlier authorities to the effect that if a cause of the injuries (in this context, the claimant's illegal act) was merely a factor that formed part of the history or narrative of events that led to the injury, it can be ignored for the purposes of legal liability.[102] However, if the facts justify a conclusion that the illegal act is the 'real, substantial, direct or effective cause' of the harm, then sole responsibility for the harm will be allocated to the claimant.[103]

These principles have been said to provide the explanation for the 'Sunday observance' cases in the United States, where the claim was for physical injuries arising out of travel on a Sunday for secular purposes. The principle said to arise from those cases was that a distinction is to be drawn between the situation where the illegal act does no more than create a prior state of affairs upon which the defendant's negligence operates (in which case the illegality is to be ignored) and where it is the immediate, active cause of the injuries.[104]

Following Lord Hoffmann's judgment in *Gray v Thames Trains Ltd*, the causation test is currently the accepted explanation in England for resolving personal injury claims in negligence arising from an illegality.[105] This test has, however, been comprehensively rejected by the Australian High Court,[106] and has no support in Canada. The High Court in *Miller v Miller* held that 'causation alone' does not provide a satisfactory principle to determine when the claimant's participation in a joint criminal enterprise should preclude a claim.[107] The Court said that development of the law by reference only to notions of whether there

[101] *Gray v Thames Trains Ltd* (n 4) [54] (Lord Hoffmann, Lords Phillip, Scott and Rodgers agreeing).
[102] *Stapley v Gypsum Mines Ltd* [1953] AC 663, 687 (Lord Asquith).
[103] ibid.
[104] See the discussion of these cases and the explanation given in *Henwood v Municipal Tramways Trust (South Australia)* (1938) 60 CLR 438, 459 (Dixon and McTiernan JJ) and *Miller v Miller* (n 9) [19]–[20].
[105] For recent examples of the application of these principles to personal injury claims in negligence, see *McCracken v Smith* [2015] EWCA Civ 380; *AB v Chief Constable of X Constabulary* [2015] EWHC 13 (QB).
[106] *Miller v Miller* (n 9) [11], [21] (French CJ, Gummow, Hayne, Crennan, Kiefel and Bell JJ); *Henwood v Municipal Tramways Trust (South Australia)* (n 104) 459–60.
[107] *Miller v Miller* ibid [11].

was a connection between the illegal conduct and the harm suffered would inevitably lead the law into the 'logical and legal labyrinth' that characterised the common law defence of contributory negligence.[108] This is a reference to the approach taken when contributory negligence was a complete defence, when it was necessary for the courts to determine whether, for the purposes of attributing legal responsibility, the claimant's contributory conduct was the sole cause of the harm notwithstanding the causal contribution of the defendant's breach.[109]

The High Court was correct to reject the causation test. It is highly subjective, and subverts ordinary principles of causation that seek to allocate responsibility for the harm between the parties. If the test was to have an application it would have to be as a public policy defence. However, a public policy defence that focuses on the one-sided consideration of the claimant's illegal conduct is inconsistent with the bipolar structure of corrective justice. The causation test is thus both doctrinally and conceptually incoherent. Before elaborating on these points further I will explain by way of background the development of the test in the United Kingdom.

B. Development of the Causation Test in the United Kingdom

In his leading judgment in *Gray v Thames Trains Ltd*, Lord Hoffmann formulated a broad rule of public policy that prevents a claimant from recovering any damage that is causally linked to a criminal act.[110] Lord Hoffmann justified this broad exclusionary rule on the basis that 'it is offensive to public notions of the fair distribution of resources that a claimant should be compensated (usually out of public funds) for the consequences of his own criminal conduct'.[111] His Lordship stated that a distinction must be drawn between cases where the criminal act of the claimant caused the harm, and those where the criminal act merely provided the occasion for the defendant to negligently inflict the harm. His Lordship suggested that this issue could be resolved by established principles of causation: 'It is the same principle by which the law normally holds that even though damage would not have occurred but for a tortious act, the defendant is not liable if the immediate cause was the deliberate act of another individual.'[112] Thus, he says that the question is a simple one of causation:

> Can one say that, although the damage would not have happened but for the tortious conduct of the defendant, it was caused by the criminal act of the claimant? (*Vellino v Chief Constable of the Greater Manchester Police* [2002] 1 WLR 218). Or is the position

[108] ibid [21], quoting Stallybrass (ed) (n 9) 484.
[109] ibid.
[110] *Gray v Thames Trains Ltd* (n 4) [50]–[55] (Lord Hoffmann, Lord Phillips agreeing at [7], Lord Scott agreeing at [56], Lord Rodger agreeing at [87]). This wider rule is critiqued at length in J Goudkamp, 'The Defence of Illegality: *Gray v Thames Trains Ltd*' (2009) 17 *Torts Law Journal* 205.
[111] ibid [51].
[112] ibid [54].

> that although the damage would not have happened without the criminal act of the claimant, it was caused by the tortious act of the defendant? (*Revill v Newbery* [1996] QB 567).[113]

Lord Hoffmann preferred the direct application of this causation principle rather than other formulations adopted in earlier cases, such as the inextricable link test.[114] In fact, his Lordship appeared to view these other tests as a metaphor for establishing a causal connection. This was despite the fact that those earlier authorities made it clear that they were formulating tests of public policy rather than causation. In *Cross v Kirkby* Judge LJ stated that in formulating the inextricable link test he was intending a public policy formula that 'goes well beyond questions of causation in the general sense'.[115] Sir Murray Stuart-Smith in *Vellino v Chief Constable of the Greater Manchester Police* (who also adopted an 'inextricable link' test) also emphasised that the doctrine is one of public policy that only applies to criminal conduct that is sufficiently serious to merit the application of the principle.[116]

There are recent indications that in other contexts the Supreme Court of the United Kingdom has resiled from Lord Hoffman's causation test. The majority in *Hounga v Allen* criticised the test for its inherent subjectivity, and refused to apply it to a statutory tort context.[117] Nor was there any support for a causation test in the most recent decisions of the Supreme Court, *Bilta (UK) Ltd (in liquidation) v Nazir (No 2)* and *Patel v Mirza*, involving claims for breach of fiduciary duty and restitution respectively.[118] Nevertheless, *Gray* is still the leading authority on the application of illegality doctrine to personal injury claims in negligence, and the causation principles developed in that case continue to be applied by the lower courts.[119] Accordingly, despite its marginal status in other contexts, the causation test is still the governing test in England for resolving personal injury claims in negligence that have a connection with an illegal act by the claimant.[120]

The case of *Gray* was concerned with harm arising from an illegal act by the claimant that was said to have been the *consequence* of the defendant's negligence, not with harm suffered while the claimant was acting illegally. Nevertheless, in a

[113] ibid.

[114] ibid.

[115] *Cross v Kirkby* (n 52) [103].

[116] *Vellino v Chief Constable of the Greater Manchester Police* (n 5) [72]. His Honour thought that a crime punishable by imprisonment would be expected to qualify.

[117] *Hounga v Allen* (n 3) [37] (Lord Wilson, Lady Hale and Lord Kerr agreeing). Alan Bogg and Sarah Green argue persuasively that the causation test can have no application to statutory tort actions because questions of causation between the wrong and the damage are not integral to the statutory tort action in the same way they are in negligence actions: A Bogg and S Green, 'Rights Are Not Just For the Virtuous' (n 69) 104.

[118] *Bilta (UK) Ltd (in liquidation) v Nazir (No 2)* (n 6), *Patel v Mirza* (n 3).

[119] *McCracken v Smith* (n 105); *AB v Chief Constable of X Constabulary* (n 105).

[120] This test was not applied to a claim in negligence against auditors for the recovery of financial loss: *Stone & Rolls Ltd (in Liq) v Moore Stephens (a firm)* (n 5). However, the primary issue in that case was corporate attribution, and no clear majority emerged as to the legal basis of illegality law.

series of cases the English Court of Appeal has applied these principles to the latter type of claim, in particular to claims for physical injury arising out of a joint illegal enterprise. The relevant authorities are: *Delaney v Pickett*, *Joyce v O'Brien* and *McCracken v Smith*.[121]

In *Delaney v Pickett*, the claimant, Delaney, was a passenger in a motor vehicle driven by Pickett. The car collided with another vehicle due to the negligence of Pickett and the claimant suffered severe head injuries and brain damage. The claimant and Pickett were both found to be in possession of cannabis at the time of the accident. The trial judge found that the purpose of the car journey was to transport illegal drugs intended for resale and that the claimant and Pickett were acting in concert in a joint illegal enterprise for an illegal purpose. The Court of Appeal, acting on the basis that the trial judge's findings of fact regarding the purpose of the journey were correct,[122] held that the claimant was nevertheless entitled to compensation from Pickett. Ward LJ wrote the leading judgment on this aspect of the claim, concluding that the claimant's illegality did not prevent the claim. His Honour considered that the crucial question in these cases is whether the claimant's illegal activity merely gave the occasion for the commission of the negligent act, or whether it was the cause of the injury.[123] Applying this principle to the facts, His Honour held that the claimant's injury was not caused by the criminal activity, but by the negligent driving of Pickett; the illegal acts were merely incidental to the claim and the claimant was entitled to recover from Pickett.[124] The other members of the Court, Richards and Tomlinson LJJ, agreed with Ward LJ's conclusions on the facts,[125] with Tomlinson LJ observing that 'there was no relevant nexus between the illegality upon which the claimant was engaged and the tortious conduct of [Pickett] which gave rise to his injuries'.[126]

This case recognises that, in the motor vehicle accident cases, the direct and immediate cause of the injuries will be the negligent manner in which the defendant drove the car. Notwithstanding, in the subsequent case of *Joyce v O'Brien* the Court of Appeal held that the claim should be denied because the claimant's illegal conduct was the cause of the harm.[127] Even though the defendant's negligent driving had also contributed to the harm, this was to be ignored for the purpose of allocating legal responsibility. The claimant and defendant stole some ladders and were attempting to make a speedy escape with the ladders in the back of a

[121] *Delaney v Pickett* [2011] EWCA Civ 1532, [2012] 1 WLR 2149; *Joyce v O'Brien* [2014] EWCA Civ 546, [2014] 1 WLR 84; *McCracken v Smith* (n 105).

[122] Ward LJ would have preferred to treat the case as one of simple possession rather than possession with intent to supply, but proceeded based on the trial judge's findings: ibid [28].

[123] *Delaney v Pickett* (n 121) [37].

[124] ibid. His Honour thought the position would have been a fortiori if it had been a case of simple possession of the cannabis, as this 'could not possibly have any causative effect on the first defendant's driving': at [29].

[125] ibid [60], [64].

[126] ibid [73].

[127] *Joyce v O'Brien* (n 121).

van. The defendant drove the van dangerously and the claimant suffered injuries when he fell from the back of the vehicle. Lord Justice Elias (Rafferty and Ryder LJJ agreeing) states that the relevant question following *Gray v Thames Trains Ltd* is whether the claimant's injury should, as a matter of public policy, be treated as having been caused by the claimant's own criminal conduct, notwithstanding that the immediate cause was the act of a partner in crime.[128] His Honour continued:

> I would formulate the principle as follows: where the character of the joint criminal enterprise is such that it is foreseeable that a party or parties may be subject to unusual or increased risks of harm as a consequence of the activities of the parties in pursuance of their criminal objectives, and the risk materialises, the injury can properly be said to be caused by the criminal act of the claimant even if it results from the negligent or intentional act of another party to the illegal enterprise.[129]

His Honour later concluded that, although the damage may not have occurred but for the defendant's negligent driving, it was caused by the claimant's criminal activity because 'The injury resulted both from [the claimant's] personal conduct in placing himself in such a dangerous position; and because he took the heightened risk of dangerous driving by his uncle and that risk materialised'.[130]

It is obvious that Elias LJ would have preferred to analyse the case through the mechanism of duty of care with a focus on whether the claimant could reasonably expect the defendant to exercise the normal standard of care (see generally Chapter 10). However, his Honour felt constrained by *Gray* to force this principle into a causation framework.[131] In the subsequent case of *McCracken v Smith*, Richards LJ praised the 'brave attempt' by Elias LJ to reconcile the two approaches (duty of care and causation), but also expressed sympathy for the view that the joint illegal enterprise cases should be resolved through the mechanism of duty of care rather than through the straightjacket of causation.[132] His Lordship lamented that, given that *Gray* was concerned with a very different situation to a joint illegal enterprise scenario, the court in *Delaney v Pickett* (of which he was a member) might have 'seized too readily on the causation analysis as providing an obvious answer to the issue in that case'.[133] However, Richards LJ reluctantly considered that it was too late to backtrack and that he was obliged to apply the causation test.[134]

In *McCracken v Smith* the claimant was injured when the trials bike on which he was a passenger collided with a minibus. The driver of the bike was a 16-year-old boy who did not have a driving licence, and who, prior to the accident, was driving the bike dangerously in a cycling lane. The claimant successfully brought

[128] ibid [28].
[129] ibid [29].
[130] ibid [47].
[131] ibid [28].
[132] *McCracken v Smith* (n 105) [46]. Lord Justices Underhill and Christopher Clarke agreed with Lord Richards' judgment.
[133] ibid.
[134] ibid [47].

proceedings in negligence against the driver of the bike and the driver of the minibus. Mr Justice Keith at first instance rejected the argument that the claim against the driver of the bike was barred for illegality, and apportioned liability between both the driver of the bike and the driver of the minibus on the ground they were both negligent.[135] The driver of the minibus appealed, inter alia, on the ground that the trial judge was wrong to reject the illegality defence. The main judgment in the Court of Appeal was delivered by Richards LJ, who held that the illegality doctrine should have been applied to prevent a claim against the driver of the bike. The claimant was a participant in a joint illegal enterprise to ride the bike dangerously, and this participation was *the* cause of his injuries. His Lordship expressed his conclusion on this point as follows:

> Since there was a joint enterprise between [the claimant] and [the driver of the bike] to ride the bike dangerously, and the increased risk of harm as a consequence of such riding was plainly foreseeable, [the claimant's] injury can properly be said to have been caused by his own criminal conduct even though it resulted from the negligent act of [the driver of the bike].[136]

His Lordship then went on to consider whether illegality doctrine applied also to prevent a claim against the minibus driver. His Lordship recognised that the answer would be easy if the court had been at liberty to adopt a duty-of-care analysis: the dangerous riding of the bike clearly did not impact on the nature of the duty or standard of care reasonably to be expected of the minibus driver.[137] He found the causation analysis more problematic (unsurprisingly), but ultimately concluded that the accident had two causes—the negligent riding of the bike (for which the claimant was criminally responsible) and the negligent driving of the minibus. In that circumstance it would be wrong to single out one of them as the mere 'occasion' for the injury and the other as the 'true' cause.[138] Accordingly, Richards LJ considered that the correct approach was to 'give effect to both causes', by allowing the claimant to recover in negligence against the minibus driver, and to reduce damages for contributory negligence so as to reflect the claimant's own fault and responsibility for the accident.[139]

Thus, the Court applied different rules of causation to the claim against the driver of the bike on the one hand (where *the* cause of the harm was found to be the criminal conduct of the claimant) and against the minibus driver on the other hand (where both the criminal conduct of the claimant and the negligence of the minibus driver were both recognised as causes). This demonstrates the unprincipled character of the causation test, and the irreconcilability of this test with ordinary principles of causation. If this test is to be accepted as an explanation

[135] *McCracken v Smith* [2013] EWHC 3620 (QB). Liability was apportioned between the driver of the bike and the minibus driver in the ratio of 80% and 20% respectively.

[136] *McCracken v Smith* (n 105) [47] (Underhill and Christopher Clarke LJJ agreeing).

[137] ibid [50]

[138] ibid [51].

[139] ibid [52].

for rejecting claims by wrongdoing claimants, it must be on the basis that it is a rule of public policy that operates independently of the causation element. I will elaborate on these points in the next section.

C. The Doctrinal Incoherence of a Causation Test

i. No Valid Test for Identifying the Claimant's Illegal Conduct as the Effective Cause of the Harm

The unsatisfactory and complex nature of any enquiry into whether the claimant's conduct was *the* cause of the harm or merely part of a set of events that led to it has been well documented.[140] There is no logic to singling out one factual cause over another as being the single cause of the injury. As Windeyer J queried in *National Insurance Co of New Zealand Ltd v Espagne*, 'How can one factor be logically more efficacious than another in producing a result for which both must exist?'[141] In the context of illegality claims, where the defendant's negligence and the claimant's illegal conduct are concurrent causes (as in cases such as *Joyce v O'Brien* and *McCracken v Smith*), there is no logic to singling out one factual cause as being relatively more effective than another. There is no rational and principled test for distinguishing between the circumstances where the claimant's illegal conduct should be regarded as the sole cause the harm on the one hand, and circumstances where that conduct should merely be treated as comparative fault for the purpose of a contributory negligence assessment on the other.[142] In *Joyce v O'Brien*, Elias LJ suggested that the relevant test is whether the criminal conduct materially increased the risk of the harm.[143] However, this reasoning establishes nothing more than that the conduct contributed to the harm: that is, that it was a factual cause. It provides no guidance as to why that particular cause should be treated as the sole cause and why the defendant's negligent act, which is the direct and immediate cause of the harm, should be disregarded.[144]

140 WJ Ford, 'Tort and Illegality: The *Ex Turpi Causa* Defence in Negligence Law (Part One)' (1977) 11 *Melbourne University Law Review* 3, 41–44; RA Prentice, 'Of Tort Reform and Millionaire Muggers: Should an Obscure Equitable Doctrine Be Revived to Dent the Litigation Crisis?'(1995) 32 *San Diego Law Review* 53, 104–05.

141 *National Insurance Co of New Zealand Ltd v Espagne* [1961] HCA 15, (1961) 105 CLR 569, 593, quoted by McHugh J in *March v Stramare (E & MH) Pty Ltd* [1991] HCA 12, (1991) 171 CLR 506, 529.

142 Ford (n 140) 41–44; Prentice (n 140) 104–105.

143 *Joyce v O'Brien* (n 121) [29].

144 In a different context (the statutory defence of self-induced intoxication in s 50 of the Civil Liability Act 2002 (NSW)), Ipp JA held that identification of the single cause of the harm requires identification of the 'direct' or 'effective or dominant operative cause' of the harm: *Russell v Edwards* [2006] NSWCA 19 [40]–[41]. If Ipp JA's formulation was to be accepted, the plaintiff's illegal conduct in a case such as *Joyce v O'Brien* (where the injuries directly result from the defendant's negligence) cannot be considered to be the real cause of the harm, as the 'direct', 'effective or dominant' cause is the defendant's negligent act of driving the vehicle. The result in *Joyce v O'Brien* cannot be reconciled with the principle as formulated by Ipp JA.

The recent decision in *McCracken v Smith* provides a good illustration of the contradictions that result from courts attempting to isolate one of a number of concurrent causes as the 'true' or 'effective' cause.[145] The claimant suffered injuries while a passenger on a trials bike in an accident caused by the negligence of both the driver of the bike and the driver of the minibus with which the bike had collided. Richards LJ, who felt bound by authority to apply a causation analysis, held that in respect of the claim against the driver of the bike the claimant's injury was caused by his own criminal conduct, 'even though it resulted from the negligent act of [the driver of the bike]'.[146] The self-contradiction in this statement is evident. On the one hand, it recognises that the negligent driving and the contributory negligence of the claimant were both causes of the harm, but on the other it isolates only one of those causes as being *the* cause. The correct approach would have been to permit a claim against the driver of the bike, but reduce the claimant's damages for his contributory negligence. This was the approach taken to the 'innocent' defendant, the minibus driver. Lord Justice Richards recognised (correctly) that in that claim there *were* two separate causes—the dangerous driving of the bike (for which the claimant was criminally responsible) and the negligent driving of the minibus. *Both* causes had to be given effect, as it would be 'wrong' to single out one of them as being the 'true' cause of the injuries.[147] Thus, the claimant was permitted to recover from the minibus driver, subject to a reduction for contributory negligence to reflect the claimant's causal contribution to his injuries.[148]

There is no principled basis for drawing a distinction between the causation of the injuries in the claim against the driver of the bike on the one hand, and against the minibus driver on the other. In respect of both claims there were two concurrent causes which combined to bring about the loss: the negligence of the operator of the vehicle (the bike and the minibus respectively), and the claimant's own illegal conduct in participating in the dangerous driving of the bike. In the same way that there is no rational basis for treating the claimant's conduct as *the* cause of the injuries in respect of the claim against the minibus driver, there is no rational basis for doing so where the claim is against the driver of the bike. In both claims there are two concurrent 'but for' causes, both of which contributed to the harm. Richards LJ does not even attempt to provide a principled reason for drawing a distinction between the two claims; instead he justifies his decision as being in the 'public interest'.[149] This was because the approach enabled the claimant to recover for the negligence of the minibus driver, 'but not for [his] own criminal conduct'.[150] However, it is not clear how the public interest is advanced by allowing

[145] *McCracken v Smith* (n 105).
[146] ibid [47] (Underhill and Christopher Clarke LJJ agreeing).
[147] ibid [51].
[148] ibid [51]–[53].
[149] ibid [53].
[150] ibid.

a claim against the 'innocent' defendant in circumstances where that defendant will be unable to claim a contribution from the 'complicit' defendant who was found to also be responsible for the accident, but who is protected by an illegality defence.[151]

The decision at first instance in *McCracken v Smith* also illustrates the paradoxes that can result from the application of the causation test. Mr Justice Keith held that the claimant's illegal conduct did not prevent the claim as it was the negligent riding of the biking, not the illegal conduct, that was the cause of the injuries.[152] Yet his Honour later held that the claimant's damages had to be reduced for contributory negligence representing the very same conduct that constituted the illegal conduct.[153] On appeal Richards LJ recognised that this finding of contributory negligence did not sit comfortably with the judge's earlier finding that the illegal conduct was not the cause of the injuries, but His Honour did not offer a solution to the paradox.[154] This is because there is no satisfactory solution to be found, at least not one that is doctrinally sound. The approach of Keith J is a further illustration of the doctrinal irrationality of the causation test and its destructive effect on the coherence of principles of causation as they apply to personal injury claims.

Turning to sanction-shifting and related claims, formulating the issue as one of causation *ostensibly* provides a more convincing explanation for the denial of relief. This is because the claimant's illegal conduct will often be the most direct and immediate cause of the harm whereas the defendant's negligence is the more indirect cause. Upon closer examination, however, the causation test is no more helpful in this context. Briefly, in *Gray* the claimant committed manslaughter while under the effects of a post-traumatic stress disorder arising out of a rail collision caused by the defendant's negligence. The claimant claimed damages for, inter alia, non-economic losses for feelings of guilt and remorse, and an indemnity against civil claims by the dependants of his victim. Lord Hoffmann held that the claimant could not recover as the effective cause of these losses was the claimant's own illegal conduct. To treat the claimant's criminal conduct as *the* effective cause of the harm in *Gray* was illogical given the defendant's negligence was a continuing (partial) cause of the harm. Lord Sumption's observations about the case in extra-judicial writings are percipient. His Lordship points out that the negligence of the defendant rail authority was just as much an 'effective' cause of the harm as the act of killing by the claimant:

> In *Gray's* case itself, I rather doubt whether it was right to say that the homicidal tendencies brought about by the negligence of the Thames Trains did no more than create the

[151] As will be discussed in ch 10, when a duty-of-care analysis is applied there will be situations where the complicit defendant will be able to take advantage of an illegality bar, but the innocent defendant will not. This is the product of the application of principled reasoning of corrective justice, but it could not be argued that this result somehow advances a broader public interest (ie other than the interest in remedying an interpersonal injustice).

[152] *McCracken v Smith* (QB) (n 135) [47].

[153] ibid [83].

[154] *McCracken v Smith* (n 105) [26].

> occasion for him to commit homicide. It seems to me that it was an effective cause of his doing so, notwithstanding that another effective cause was necessary before his pre-existing propensity to kill actually resulted in a killing.[155]

Lord Sumption concluded that 'What barred the claim in *Gray's* case was not the relative causal efficacy of the negligence and the killing, *but the illegal character of the killing*.'[156] In other words, the claimant was prevented as a matter of policy, not causation, from recovering his losses.

Thus, there is no rational basis in either the physical injury cases or the sanction-shifting cases for singling out one factual cause as being more 'effective' than another. The causation test cannot therefore be regarded as a mechanism of factual causation. Nor, as I will discuss next, can the causation test be accommodated within a conception of legal ('scope of liability') causation.

ii. A Causation Test is Inconsistent with 'Scope of Liability' Causation

The question of whether the claimant's illegal conduct is to be viewed as the 'real' or 'effective' cause of the harm might in Australia be considered a problem of legal causation to be answered by reference to the statutory 'scope of liability' principle.[157] The argument would be that, even though the harm might not have occurred but for the negligent act of the defendant (that is, factual causation is present), the 'real' or 'effective' cause was the claimant's illegal conduct. Hence, it would not be appropriate to attribute legal responsibility for the harm to the negligent defendant.

The scope of liability aspect of causation involves a normative evaluation[158] of whether the connection that exists between the breach by the negligent defendant and the particular harm suffered by the claimant is sufficiently strong to justify the imposition of liability on the defendant.[159] It involves a consideration of whether the features of the connection between the breach and the consequence are such that, in the context of the relevant legal rule, the defendant should be held legally responsible for that consequence.[160]

Jane Stapleton (whose writings were pivotal to the introduction of the statutory scope of liability provisions) states that a consequence will be within the defendant's scope of liability where the 'risk of such a consequence was one of the risks that made the defendant's conduct careless'.[161] Interestingly, a similar principle

155 Lord Sumption, 'Reflections on the law of illegality' (n 1) 8.

156 ibid (emphasis added).

157 Commonwealth of Australia, *Review of the Law of Negligence: Final Report* (2002), 117 [7.49]. See, eg, Wrongs Act 1958 (Vic), s 51.

158 *Wallace v Kam* [2013] HCA 19, (2013) 250 CLR 375, 385 [22] (French CJ, Crennan, Kiefel, Gageler and Keane JJ).

159 D Nolan, 'Causation and the Goals of Tort Law' in A Robertson and HW Tang (eds), *The Goals of Private Law*, (Oxford, Hart Publishing, 2009) 165.

160 J Stapleton, 'Reflections on Common Sense Causation in Australia' in S Degeling, J Edelman, J Goudkamp (eds), *Torts in Commercial Law* (Sydney, Lawbook Co, 2011) 352.

161 ibid 354.

is formulated by Weinrib and Beever, who reject Stapleton's legal realist views. Weinrib's theory does not accommodate a principle of legal causation as a separate enquiry. Weinrib instead treats issues that would be considered in Australia as matter of legal (scope of liability) causation—such as intervening acts—as integral to remoteness.[162] Beever explicitly rejects that 'there is a special legal conception of causation',[163] (that is, that legal causation is a separate inquiry) and also regards legal causation issues as relevant to remoteness.[164] Weinrib and Beever both emphasise the need for a normative connection between the defendant's negligence and the injury suffered by the claimant. Thus, Weinrib has recognised that 'the claimant's injury [must be] within the risk that renders the defendant's act wrongful'.[165] Similarly, Beever states that the test for remoteness is whether the unreasonable risk created by the defendant (standard of care) 'was an unreasonable risk of the injury that the claimant suffered'.[166] In the current context, the particular 'legal causation' issue will be whether the harm resulting from the claimant's illegal conduct should, as a matter of law, be viewed as the sole cause of the harm because it was not unreasonable for the defendant to create that risk of harm.

It seems that, at least in this particular context, there will be little practical difference between the corrective justice viewpoint and the viewpoint of Stapleton—*provided* that policy considerations are excluded from the analysis and the focus is on the factors that link the defendant's negligence and the harm and the reasons why the defendant's conduct is wrongful (unreasonable). It is not necessary to explore this issue further, because the causation test cannot be reconciled with normative causation principles, no matter how they are formulated. In essence this is because in these cases, there is a clear normative connection between the negligence and the harm and therefore a causal link is established. It will be convenient to discuss claims for physical injuries sustained by the claimant in the course of committing an illegal act separately from sanction-shifting claims and claims for illegal profits and earnings. However, essentially the same arguments apply to all claims.

Turning first to claims for physical injuries, the central question is whether, where the claimant's injuries were negligently inflicted while the claimant was engaged in illegal conduct, the sole or 'effective' cause of the harm should be viewed (as a matter of law) as the claimant's own conduct so as to 'truncate'[167] the defendant's legal responsibility. As discussed previously, cases such as *Joyce*

162 See, eg, EJ Weinrib, *The Idea of Private Law* (Cambridge Mass, Harvard University Press, 1995) 219–21.

163 A Beever, *Rediscovering the Law of Negligence* (Oxford, Hart Publishing, 2007) 39.

164 ibid ch 4.

165 Weinrib, *The Idea of Private Law* (n 162) 160 (though noting there that he was referring to both requirements of duty of care and proximate causation (remoteness)). See also Beever, *Rediscovering the Law of Negligence* (n 163) 158.

166 Beever ibid 115.

167 J Stapleton, 'Factual Causation' (2010) 38 *Federal Law Review* 467, 467.

v O'Brien suggest that a claim by one participant in a joint illegal venture to another will be rejected where the claimant's criminal conduct is viewed as the 'real' cause of the harm. The approach in *Joyce v O'Brien* is, however, inconsistent with the approach of the Australian courts in analogous contexts, which treat the contribution of the claimant to the harm as a matter for contributory negligence rather than legal causation.[168] There are no issues of legal causation raised by these cases, as illustrated by the typical case where the claimant suffers personal injuries in a motor vehicle accident while engaged in a joint illegal enterprise with the driver of the vehicle. There is no reason in these cases to question the quality of the connection between the breach and the harm suffered. Both the content of the duty and the standard of care owed by the driver are directed to ensuring that physical injury of the kind suffered by the claimant did not occur. There is no intervening act or event that could break the chain of causation between the negligent driving and the harm, nor could the injuries suffered by the claimant be said to have been a 'coincidental consequence' of the negligent driving.[169] As Ward LJ recognises in *Delaney v Pickett*, in the case of a motor vehicle accident, the direct and immediate cause of the accident will be the negligent manner in which the defendant drove the vehicle.[170] To ignore this direct cause and to treat the claimant's conduct as having been the sole cause of the accident—as the courts did in *Joyce v O'Brien* and in *McCracken v Smith* (in respect of the driver of the bike)—operates unjustly on the claimant and is inconsistent with scope of liability principles.

Thus, as a general rule the normative connection between the breach and the harm will be clearly established in these cases. What makes the driver's act wrongful (unreasonable) is careless driving in light of the foreseeable risk of personal injury to other road users (including passengers) and the passenger has suffered injury of that foreseeable kind. In the words of Weinrib, 'the claimant's injury is within the risk that renders the defendant's act wrongful'.[171] While the claimant's conduct in participating in a risky joint illegal venture also contributed to the harm, any causal contribution by the claimant is a matter for apportionment through the mechanism of contributory negligence.[172]

Although I have concentrated here on the joint illegality cases, the same principles apply to unilateral illegality cases. For example, assume a thief suffers injuries from an electric shock while attempting to steal overhead power lines due to the negligence of the electricity authority in failing to disconnect the current to the power lines or to provide a warning that the lines were still active.[173] While most responsibility should be apportioned to the thief through the mechanism of contributory negligence, it is doctrinally incoherent to ignore the defendant's causal

168 See, eg, *Zanner v Zanner* [2010] NSWCA 343, (2010) 79 NSWLR 702.

169 This is because the negligent driving created or increased the risk of those injuries: *Chappel v Hart* [1998] HCA 55 (1998) 195 CLR 232, 244–5 [27] (McHugh J), 289–90 [146] (Hayne J).

170 *Delaney v Pickett* (n 121) [37].

171 Weinrib, *The Idea of Private Law* (n 162) 160.

172 *March v Stramare (E & MH) Pty Ltd* (n 141).

173 These are the facts of *Austin v The Electricity Networks Corporation* [2014] WASCA 89.

contribution to the harm altogether and to treat the claimant's criminal conduct as the *sole* cause of the injury. The same reasoning that dictates that reduction of 100 per cent for contributory negligence cannot be made also applies in this situation.[174] Once the defendant's negligence has been shown to contribute to the harm, it is illogical to ignore the defendant's causal contribution and attribute sole responsibility to the claimant.[175]

The same arguments apply to sanction-shifting and related claims and claims for illegal profits and earnings. I have pointed out the difficulties with singling out the claimant's illegal conduct as the effective cause of the harm even in respect of claims of the kind under consideration in *Gray*.[176] The defendant's causal contribution to the harm cannot be ignored or considered a less effective cause merely because it was not the most direct cause of the harm. When approached directly as a matter of legal causation, the question is whether there is a normative connection between the defendant's breach and the harm. Issues around legal causation—in particular whether the manslaughter broke the chain of causation between the negligence and the losses—do not appear to have been fully explored at trial in *Gray*. The Court of Appeal considered, without finally deciding, that the better view based on the authority of *Corr v IBC Vehicles Ltd*[177] was that there was no break in the chain of causation. The claimant committed the manslaughter while acting under the effects of the depression and post-traumatic stress disorder caused by the defendant's negligence, which severely impaired his capacity to make rational judgments and which led him to kill the victim.[178] Lord Hoffmann in *Gray*, also relying on *Corr v IBC Vehicles Ltd*, also acted on the basis that the manslaughter did not amount to a break in the chain of causation between the defendant's negligence and the loss suffered by the claimant.[179] His Lordship was of the view that the defendant's negligence was a continuing (partial) cause of the claimant's losses.[180] This view is in accordance with the existing law governing when an intervening act of the claimant will break the chain of causation. There is authority both in Australia and in England (including *Corr v IBC Vehicles Ltd*) that recognises that an act committed while under the influence of a mental

[174] A reduction by 100% is not possible at common law either in Australia or in the United Kingdom: *Wynbergen v Hoyts Corporation Pty Ltd* [1997] HCA 52, (1997) 149 ALR 25, 29; *Pitts v Hunt* [1991] 2 QB 24 (CA); *Anderson v Newham College Further Education* [2002] EWCA Civ 505, [2003] ICR 212. For discussion, see J Goudkamp, 'Rethinking Contributory Negligence' in SGA Pitel, JW Neyers, E Chamberlain (eds), *Tort Law: Challenging Orthodoxy* (Oxford, Hart Publishing, 2013) 344–46.

[175] *Wynbergen v Hoyts Corporation Pty Ltd* ibid.

[176] See text to nn 154–156.

[177] *Corr v IBC Vehicles Ltd* [2008] UKHL 13, [2008] AC 284. An employee injured by the employer's negligence committed suicide as result of the depression caused by the injuries. The suicide did not amount to a *novus actus* because the employer's negligence was a contributing cause of it: [14]–[17] (Lord Bingham), [29] (Lord Scott) [42] (Lord Walker), [45]–[46] (Lord Mance), [53] (Lord Neuberger).

[178] *Gray v Thames Trains Ltd* CA (n 5) [39]–[46].

[179] *Gray v Thames Trains Ltd* (n 4) [28]–[29], [45]–[46] (Lord Hoffmann). See also Lord Brown at [94]–[98].

[180] ibid.

disorder created by the defendant's negligence is not, in law, a truly voluntary act.[181] In those circumstances the claimant's conduct is not regarded as unreasonable conduct breaking the chain of causation, and hence the defendant's negligence is regarded as a contributing cause of the claimant's act.[182] These principles apply to *Gray*, and accordingly it was 'reasonable as between the claimant and the defendant'[183] that the scope of the defendant's liability should extend to the consequences of the manslaughter. A relevant normative connection was established between the negligence and the harm.

The application of principled reasoning of corrective justice might point to a different result. Beever explains that the central question is whether the defendant created an unreasonable risk of the act that is said to be intervening. An act by the claimant (in this case the manslaughter) will not intervene so as to break the chain of causation where the defendant created an unreasonable risk that it would occur.[184] The specific issue on this approach is whether the risk that the claimant would commit a violent crime while in the grip of the disorder was so small that the defendant was reasonably justified in ignoring it. There was a foreseeable risk that the claimant would suffer post-traumatic stress disorder as a result of a mass casualty accident, and there was evidence before the Court of Appeal that depressive symptoms, including uncontrollable rage and aggression, are prominent in sufferers of that disorder.[185] However, there was no evidence whether the risk that a victim of the train crash would kill another person was one that should have been appreciated by a reasonable train authority, such that the risk created by the defendant was an unreasonable (substantial) one.[186] Beever says that it helpful to approach such issues by asking: Would it have been sensible to have said to the defendant 'Be careful with your signalling because if you cause a crash one of the victims of the crash might kill a stranger?'[187] When reduced to such plain language, the intuitive answer might be 'no'. However, the answer will ultimately depend on what the defendant knew, or ought to have known, about the nature of psychiatric disorders that have been suffered in previous train accidents and the types of behaviour that has resulted from those disorders. Once that evidence is known, one might more comfortably give a different answer.

Even if the courts in *Gray* were wrong to act on the basis that the manslaughter was not an intervening event, that does not really matter for current purposes because the reality is that the court *did* act on this basis. Hence, an assessment

[181] *Haber v Walker* [1963] VR 339; *Medlin v State Government Insurance Commission* [1995] HCA 5, (1995) 182 CLR 1, 6–7 (Deane, Dawson, Toohey and Gaurdron JJ), 23 (McHugh J); *Corr v IBC Vehicles Ltd* (n 177).

[182] ibid.

[183] *Medlin v State Government Insurance Commission* (n 181) 13 (Deane, Dawson, Toohey and Gaurdron JJ). See also *Corr v IBC Vehicles Ltd* (n 177) [17] (Lord Bingham).

[184] Beever, *Rediscovering the Law of Negligence* (n 163) 156–62.

[185] *Gray v Thames Trains Ltd* CA (n 5), [53].

[186] See Beever, *Rediscovering the Law of Negligence* (n 163) 157.

[187] ibid 159.

of Lord Hoffmann's causation test must be made on the assumption that there was no intervening act in that case. On that assumption, it was illogical for Lord Hoffmann to treat the claimant's criminal conduct as the effective cause of the harm. This is because, in the absence of an intervening event, *both* the defendant's negligence and the claimant's illegal act must be treated as *concurrent* causes. Thus, despite suggestions to the contrary,[188] the claimant in *Gray* was refused compensation, not because of an absence of a causal link between the negligence and the harm, but because of the application of an independent rule of public policy based on the claimant's illegal act.

An even more compelling argument can be made that the causation test fails to provide a convincing explanation for denying claims for illegal profits and earnings. In these cases the direct and dominant cause of the inability to earn the income or acquire the profits is the negligent act of the defendant, not an act of the claimant and there is no reason to question the quality of the connection between the negligence and the loss (for example, no issue of a *novus actus interveniens* arises). In those circumstances it would be contrary to established principle to single out the claimant's illegal act as the effective cause of the loss.

D. The Conceptual Incoherence of the Causation Test

In the last section I demonstrated that it is impossible to reconcile the causation test with normal principles of causation that seek to allocate responsibility for the harm between the claimant and defendant in a relational manner. Despite the use of causation language, a decision to reject a claim is not truly based on the relative causal contributions of the negligence and the claimant's illegal conduct. There is an obvious explanation why Lord Hoffmann, who is a leading jurist on causation, deviated from general causation principles. The explanation is that his Lordship was not even purporting to apply normal principles of causation. He was not suggesting that the operation of the causation test would negate causation on ordinary principles; rather, he formulated his rule as a rule of public policy based on the illegal character of the conduct.[189] Accordingly, if this approach is to be justified, it must be as a public policy doctrine.

The public policy-based causation test is inconsistent with the correlative structure of negligence liability because it focuses in a one-sided manner on the conduct of the claimant and ignores the contribution of the defendant to the

[188] See Goudkamp, 'A Long, Hard Look at Gray v Thames Trains Ltd' (n 21) in particular 42–43; Bogg and Green, 'Rights Are Not Just for the Virtuous' (n 69) 103. But see J Goudkamp and L Mayr, 'The Doctrine of Illegality and Interference with Chattels' in A Dyson, J Goudkamp and F Wilmot-Smith (eds), *Defences in Torts* (Oxford, Hart Publishing, 2015) 235.

[189] Lord Sumption also interprets the rule as one of public policy rather than an application of ordinary causation principles: Lord Sumption, 'Reflections on the Law of Illegality' (n 1) 8. See also G Virgo, 'Illegality's Role in the Law of Torts' in M Dyson (ed), *Unravelling Tort and Crime* (Cambridge, Cambridge University Press, 2014), 197.

harm. Corrective justice excludes considerations relevant to one of the parties that do not encompass the correlative situation of both parties.[190] In the words of Weinrib, 'a justificatory consideration that fits into the normative structure of corrective justice cannot have a justificatory force that reaches only one of the parties.'[191]

This conclusion (that the causation test is a one-sided doctrine) requires elaboration and justification. The language adopted by Lord Hoffmann has echoes of the complete defence of contributory negligence at common law,[192] which Weinrib views as being consistent with the correlative structure of negligence liability on the basis that it involves looking at the fault of the claimant *relative to* the fault of the defendant in their interaction.[193] However, a doctrine of illegality, when based on a test of causation, does not *in substance* involve a weighing of the respective culpability and causal contributions of the parties to determine the effective cause of the harm. This point can be illustrated clearly by claims for personal injury caused by (for example) the defendant's negligent driving. If one were to compare the respective culpability and causal responsibility of the parties for the harm, the defendant's negligent driving must be viewed as the 'dominant', 'direct' or 'effective' cause of the harm, and yet in *Joyce v O'Brien*, the claimant's illegality was held to have this effect. Thus, despite employing similar language to that of the common law contributory negligence defence, the causation illegality principle is not *in substance* a doctrine designed to weigh the respective responsibility of both parties. Rather, it is a rule of public policy that operates to deny the claim where the claimant's illegal conduct had a sufficiently close connection with the harm. Unless the illegal conduct is incidental to the claim (as in *Delaney v Pickett*) it (the claim) must fail.

The same reasoning applies to the causation test as it is applied to sanction-shifting claims. It will be recalled that Lord Sumption observed that what really barred the claim in *Gray* 'was not the relative causal efficacy of the negligence and the killing, but the illegal character of the killing'.[194] This highlights that the courts are not engaged in a genuine attempt to balance the causal responsibility of the parties for the harm, but are making public policy decisions based singularly on the closeness of the connection between the claimant's illegal conduct and the harm.[195] The operation of the causation test in this way reflects its origins in the inextricable link test, which focuses on the connection between the illegal conduct and the crime. The cases that developed that test (and which were relied upon by

[190] EJ Weinrib, *Corrective Justice* (Oxford, Oxford University Press, 2012).

[191] Weinrib, *The Idea of Private Law* (n 162) 120.

[192] *Miller v Miller* (n 9) [21].

[193] Weinrib, *The Idea of Private Law* (n 162) 169 fn 53(1). Beever, views apportionment as a conceptually superior mechanism than a complete defence of contributory negligence because 'as both the negligence of the claimant and of the defendant materialised in the claimant's injury, both must always be relevant': Beever, *Rediscovering the Law of Negligence* (n 163) 342.

[194] Sumption, 'Reflections on the Law of Illegality' (n 1) 8.

[195] ibid.

Lord Hoffmann) recognised that it is not a principle of causation, but a special rule of public policy.[196]

Accordingly, the causation test focuses in a one-sided manner on the claimant's conduct, and is not in substance directed to weighing the relative fault or causal contributions of the parties to the interaction. It 'amounts to a judicial confiscation of what is rightly due to the claimant in order to subsidise policy objectives unilaterally favourable to the defendant'.[197] The conclusion that this explanation is inconsistent with corrective justice reasoning is predictable, given that Lord Hoffman justified it on concerns of *distributive justice*, namely the offence 'to public notions of the fair distribution of resources that a claimant should be compensated (usually out of public funds) for the consequences of his own criminal conduct'.[198] A decision about the proper distribution of resources is inherently political in nature, and is incompatible with the non-political nature of corrective justice.[199] The causation test demonstrates 'the incoherence of combining distributive and corrective considerations within a single relationship'.[200]

Moreover, the causation test is unsatisfactory because it involves inherently subjective value judgments, a characteristic which has not escaped the attention of the Supreme Court. In *Hounga* Lord Wilson (with whom Lady Hale and Lord Kerr agreed) observed that 'Every formulation of a requirement to identify the active or effective cause of an event … has a potential for inconsistent application driven by subjective considerations.[201] The causation test has a superficial attraction because it seems to lay down clear and principled criteria for the application of illegality law. However, when scrutinised more closely it is realised that it is not based in causation doctrine and that its application is subjective and a foil for public policy decision-making. As one commentator has observed: 'Although the test can be easily stated the answer will always be rather subjective'.[202] The causation test suffers from the same shortcomings of the inextricable link test, discussed in section III above. Because it is based on policy rather than legal principle, it is unavoidably subjective and can be manipulated to reach a desired outcome based on a judge's own conceptions of the merits of the claim. In this respect, Bruce MacDougall has suggested that 'causation is a convenient tool for judges to justify a desired result purely on the facts and personalities involved in the case'.[203]

[196] *Cross v Kirkby* (n 52) [103] (Judge LJ); *Vellino v Chief Constable of the Greater Manchester Police* (n 5) [70] (Stuart-Smith LJ).

[197] EJ Weinrib, 'Does Tort Law Have a Future?' (2000) 34 *Valparaiso University Law Review* 561, 566.

[198] *Gray v Thames Trains Ltd* (n 4) [51]. James Goudkamp has argued convincingly that notions of distributive justice fall short of justifying the causation rule: Goudkamp, 'The Defence of Illegality: *Gray v Thames Trains Ltd*' (n 110) 212; Goudkamp, 'A Long, Hard Look at Gray v Thames Trains Ltd' (n 21) 44–45.

[199] Weinrib, *The Idea of Private Law* (n 162) 210–11.

[200] ibid 163; see also 75.

[201] *Hounga v Allen* (n 3) [37].

[202] R Milligan, 'Illegality as a Complete Defence in Personal Injury Claims' (2015) 122 *Reparation Bulletin* 2, 4.

[203] B MacDougall '*Ex Turpi Causa*: Should a Defence Arise From a Base Cause?' (1991) 55 *Saskatchewan Law Review* 1, 30.

In sum, corrective justice analysis exposes the incoherence of the causation test. Reasoning of corrective justice requires that the contributions of *both* parties to the harm must be taken into account in a relational manner. The causation test fails to do this. Hence, it should be no surprise that the causation test is inconsistent with established principles of causation that seek to allocate responsibility between the parties to the interaction. Further, the causation approach is ultimately based on public policy, and hence, is inherently subjective and unstable. Lord Sumption has observed that to formulate the issue as one of causation is 'less helpful than it sounds' and 'is not so much an answer as a restatement of the question'.[204] The comprehensive rejection of the causation test by Australian courts is thus justifiable both doctrinally and conceptually. It is therefore disappointing that the legislatures in most Australian jurisdictions have chosen to enact statutory defences that turn upon the claimant's causal contribution for the harm. These will be discussed in the next section.

V. A Statutory Causation Test

A. Overview of the Statutory Defences

Every Australian jurisdiction other than Victoria has enacted statutory defences that have as their central criterion the causal link between the criminal conduct and the harm.[205] Broadly speaking, these provisions are engaged where, at the time of being harmed, the claimant was engaged in conduct that is an indictable or serious offence and that contributed materially to the risk of harm. The evident policy behind these statutory provisions is that persons who sustain injury while committing serious or indictable offences should bear their own losses. However, in recognition that this could operate harshly in individual cases, in four jurisdictions (the Australian Capital Territory, Northern Territory, Queensland and South Australia) courts are given a broad and unstructured discretion to permit a claim where 'the circumstances of the case are exceptional' and the exclusion would operate 'harshly and unjustly'.[206] Despite the variation in titles of the various Acts where these statutory defences reside, I will refer to them compendiously as the 'Civil Liability Acts'.

[204] Sumption, 'Reflections on the Law of Illegality' (n 1) 7.

[205] Civil Law (Wrongs) Act 2002 (ACT), s 94; Civil Liability Act 2002 (NSW), ss 54, 54A; Personal Injuries (Liabilities and Damages) Act 2003 (NT), s 10; Civil Liability Act 2003 (Qld), s 45; Criminal Code Act 1899 (Qld), s 6; Civil Liability Act 1936 (SA), s 43; Civil Liability Act 2002 (Tas), s 6(1); Offenders (Legal Action) Act 2000 (WA), s 5.

[206] Civil Law (Wrongs) Act 2002 (ACT), s 94(2); Personal Injuries (Liabilities and Damages) Act 2003 (NT), s 10(2); Civil Liability Act 2003 (Qld), s 45(2); Civil Liability Act 1936 (SA), s 43(2). In Queensland there is no requirement that the circumstances of the case be exceptional.

While there are jurisdictional differences in the formulation of the defences in the Civil Liability Acts, these Acts are consistent in prescribing three basic preconditions for the operation of the defence. The defence will operate where, on the balance of probabilities (reasonable doubt in South Australia):

(a) the injured person engaged in conduct that constituted a serious or indictable offence; and
(b) the accident or injury occurred 'while' or 'at the time' (in New South Wales: 'or following') that conduct was being engaged in; and
(c) the conduct 'contributed materially' to the risk of injury or risk of the injury.

It appears that the main objective of parliaments in enacting these provisions was to deal with the individual criminal acting alone.[207] Nevertheless, in most jurisdictions the joint illegal enterprise cases have also been swept up in the wide net of the statutory defences. The exception is New South Wales, where the defence does not apply to joint criminal enterprises.[208]

B. The Statutory Defences are Inconsistent with the Correlative Structure of Negligence Liability

The central criterion for the application of the statutory defences is whether the claimant's conduct that constituted an offence contributed materially to the risk of injury. This singular focus on the claimant's illegal conduct is inconsistent with the bipolarity of negligence liability. These defences undermine corrective justice as they depart from the correlative structure of negligence liability pursuant to which the conduct of both parties must be examined relationally. James Goudkamp and John Murphy explain the incompatibility of these statutory defences with a theory of a bilaterally structured tort law as follows: 'These defences centre on the fact that the claimant was injured while engaged in an illegal act. This is a unilateral consideration. It fails to connect the claimant with the defendant.'[209]

It is important to note that corrective justice theory is not intrinsically hostile to legislative reform. Weinrib does not suggest that the state does not have power to legislate in areas of private law, or that it should not do so in order to advance public goals; his argument is only that that part of the private law, which is judge-made

[207] In particular, cases where the claimant was injured while an unlawful entrant on property: J Dietrich, 'Duty of Care under the "Civil Liability Acts' (2005) 13 *Torts Law Journal* 17, 34; J Goudkamp, 'Self-defence and illegality under the Civil Liability Act 2002 (NSW)' (2009) 18 *Torts Law Journal* 61, 71.

[208] Civil Liability Act 2002 (NSW), s 54(2).

[209] J Goudkamp and J Murphy, 'Tort Statutes and Tort Theories' (2015) 131 *Law Quarterly Review* 133, 153. It should be noted that Goudkamp and Murphy are not corrective justice theorists and they are sceptical of its ability to provide a convincing rationale for illegality doctrine, at least in its statutory forms.

rather than legislated, must be goal-free.[210] Thus, the concern is not with whether a given exercise of state power is desirable, but with 'the coherence with which it is integrated into a justificatory ensemble'.[211] Superimposing a one-sided defence onto the existing negligence action that is designed to assess the position of the parties relationally disrupts the coherence of the action, and hence the system for compensating the victims of tort more generally.[212] Beever points out that in deciding whether to implement a political scheme, it is necessary for the legislature to decide whether concerns that support the scheme are sufficient to outweigh the values that the scheme would undermine, including corrective justice.[213] This recognises that a scheme that does not realise corrective justice 'will have a disvalue'.[214] It is arguable that the policy objectives of the statutory defences do not outweigh their 'disvaluing' of corrective justice principles, particularly taking into account the harsh consequences of these defences. Dietrich and Goudkamp have rightly criticised the statutory defences for their wide breadth and the drastic consequences for the seriously injured claimant, whose 'punishment' is out of all proportion to the seriousness of the offence.[215]

Moreover, there is no clear policy rationale for this harsh outcome. These defences were introduced as part of the tort reforms in the early 2000s, which were designed to address perceived concerns about a blow-out in insurance claims and an associated lack of personal responsibility by claimants.[216] Grant Watson has pointed the former concern is peripheral to claims by offenders, as such claims are comparatively small in number.[217] The enactment of the defences was in essence a political reaction to some unpopular (though not legally indefensible) decisions to award damages for injuries suffered as a result of illegal conduct.[218] Dietrich observes that 'populist politics' and 'unthinking sloganeering' that criminals should not be permitted to sue appear to have influenced the drafting process.[219] This highly political process has resulted in broad defences that are insufficiently adapted to securing particular public policy objectives.

[210] Weinrib, *Corrective Justice* (n 190) 6–7. See the discussion in K Barker 'Private law: Key Encounters with public law' in K Barker and D Jensen *Private Law: Key Encounters with Public Law* (Cambridge, Cambridge University Press, 2013) 23.

[211] EJ Weinrib, 'Legal Formalism: On the Immanent Rationality of Law' (1988) 97 *Yale Law Journal* 949, 973. See also EJ Weinrib, *The Idea of Private Law* (n 162) 45–56.

[212] EJ Weinrib, 'Legal Formalism' ibid 973.

[213] Beever, 'Corrective Justice and Personal Responsibility in Tort Law' (2008) 28(3) *Oxford Journal of Legal Studies* 475, 499.

[214] ibid.

[215] Dietrich (n 207) 34. See generally Goudkamp, 'A Revival of the Doctrine of Attainder? The Statutory Illegality Defences to Liability in Tort' (2007) 29(3) *Sydney Law Review* 445.

[216] B McDonald, 'Legislative Intervention in the Law of Negligence: The Common Law, Statutory Interpretation and Tort Reform in Australia' (2005) 27 *Sydney Law Review* 443, 443.

[217] GS Watson, 'Civil claims and civil death: "Offender Damages" and the Civil Liability Act 2002 (NSW)' (2008) 16 *Torts Law Journal* 81, 90.

[218] Goudkamp, 'A Revival of the Doctrine of Attainder?' (n 215) 466 fn 114, 470; Dietrich (n 207) 34.

[219] Dietrich ibid 40. The issue of recovery by criminal claimants was not the subject of the Ipp Review of the Law of Negligence that led to the tort reform legislation: H Luntz, 'The Australian Picture' (2004) 35 *Victoria University of Wellington Law Review* 879, 897. Thus, these provisions were purely the product of political decisions.

A further reason for questioning the justification for these defences is that they impose an additional punishment on the claimant that was not contemplated when the criminal sanctions for the conduct were enacted, potentially interfering with the overall regulatory pattern of the criminal law.[220] It is unlikely the legislatures gave sufficient consideration to this potentially distortive effect when they enacted these politically motivated defences.

The legislature should reconsider whether these defences are fulfilling important public policy objectives. While they are retained, they should be interpreted strictly, in recognition that they derogate from the corrective justice entitlements of the claimant.

VI. Conclusion

The analysis in this chapter has demonstrated that tests that focus on the connection or relationship between the claim and illegality—however formulated—fail to provide satisfactory guidance to the resolution of illegality claims. Connection tests (even the reliance test) require the making of inherently subjective value judgments, and ultimately are a foil for public policy reasoning. Moreover, connection tests disrupt the correlative and relational structure of corrective justice. They introduce 'a one-sidedness inconsistent with the bipolarity of corrective justice'.[221] In the case of the causation test, this results in a distortion of the ordinary principles of causation. It is therefore unfortunate that a causation-oriented statutory defence of illegality has been enacted in most Australian jurisdictions, and the legislatures should reassess whether they are in fact meeting important policy objectives.

The Australian and Canadian courts have been right to reject the connection tests in favour of an approach based on the principle of coherence. I will elaborate on the application of the principle of coherence to illegality claims in Chapters 6–9.

[220] EJ Weinrib, 'Illegality as a Tort Defence' (n 96) 44–46.
[221] Weinrib, *The Idea of Private Law* (n 162) 156.

6

Overview of the Coherence Rationale

I. Introduction

It has been accepted at the highest judicial levels in Australia and Canada that the need to preserve the coherence of the law is the only valid conceptual justification for a doctrine of illegality. In her leading judgment in *Hall v Hebert*, McLachlin J (as she then was) held that a defence of illegality should apply only where it is necessary to preserve the integrity of the legal system.[1] In *Miller v Miller* the High Court of Australia, when deciding a claim for injuries sustained in the course of a joint illegal enterprise, stated that 'the central policy consideration at stake is the coherence of the law'.[2] There is also recognition in England that legal coherence is an underlying rationale of the law of illegality, although it is generally not the only rationale thought to be relevant.[3]

The approach of contemporary courts to claims arising from an illegality has been informed, directly or indirectly, by Weinrib's classic article 'Illegality as a Tort Defence', where Weinrib argued that the preservation of the integrity of the judicial system is the only convincing rationale for a doctrine of illegality.[4] The principles he advanced there were adopted by McLachlin J writing for the majority in *Hall v Hebert*, and have in turn been recognised by courts in Australia and England.[5] In a frequently quoted

[1] *Hall v Hebert* [1993] 2 SCR 159, 176–180 (McLachlin J, La Forest, L'Heureux-Dubé and Iacobucci JJ agreeing).

[2] *Miller v Miller* [2011] HCA 9, (2011) 242 CLR 446 [15], (French CJ, Gummow, Hayne, Crennan, Kiefel and Bell JJ), [108] (Heydon J).

[3] *Gray v Thames Trains Ltd* [2009] UKHL33, [2009] 1 AC 133 [39] (Lord Hoffmann); *Hewison v Meridian Shipping Services Pty Ltd* [2002] EWCA Civ 1821, [2003] ICR 766 [51] (Tuckey LJ), [82] (Ward LJ); *Safeway Stores Ltd v Twigger* [2010] EWCA Civ 1472, [2011] 2 All ER 841 [16] (Longmore J); *Les Laboratoires Servier v Apotex Inc* [2012] EWCA Civ 593, [2013] RPC 21, [67] (Etherton LJ), [92] (Laws LJ) (Kitchin LJ agreeing with both judgments). In *Patel v Mirza* [2016] UKSC 42 Lords Mance, Clarke and Sumption held that legal coherence is the proper basis of illegality doctrine: [192] (Lord Mance), [214] (Lord Clarke), [230]-[232] (Lord Sumption). However, a majority of the Court preferred a broad policy discretion. See also the discussion of the consistency rule in ch 8 as adopted in *Gray* (section III, The Consistency Rule). Other approaches adopted by the UK courts have been discussed in chs 4 and 5.

[4] EJ Weinrib, 'Illegality as a Tort Defence' (1976) 26 *University of Toronto Law Journal* 28.

[5] *Miller v Miller* (n 2) [15] (French CJ, Gummow, Hayne, Crennan, Kiefel and Bell JJ), 483 [108] (Heydon J); See the UK cases cited in n 3.

passage in *Hall v Hebert*, McLachlin J, citing Weinrib's article, explained the coherence rationale of the illegality principle:

> [T]he law must aspire to be a unified institution, the parts of which—contract, tort, the criminal law—must be in essential harmony. For the courts to punish conduct with one hand while rewarding it with the other would be to 'create an intolerable fissure in the law's conceptually seamless web.'[6]

Later in her judgment her Honour confirmed that the 'fundamental rationale' for illegality doctrine is 'the need to maintain internal consistency in the law, in the interest of promoting the integrity of the justice system'.[7]

The need to apply illegality principles so as to preserve legal coherence is a major theme of Weinrib's article on illegality, and the need to preserve legal coherence a major theme of Weinrib's writings in corrective justice more generally (although admittedly his emphasis has been primarily on the need for internal coherence in private law actions). In section III I will explain that the goal of promoting coherence within the legal system is not a policy concern that applies independently of the parties relationship; rather, considerations of legal coherence are relational considerations. For this reason, the objective of promoting coherence within the law is best characterised as a *principle* of coherence rather than a *policy* of coherence.[8]

Weinrib explains in 'Illegality as a Tort Defence' that a principle of illegality comes into play only when it is needed to maintain the integrity of the legal system by preventing an inconsistency arising between the law of torts and the area of law proscribing the conduct.[9] Weinrib identifies two situations where an award of compensation for harm caused by an illegal act could potentially give rise to an inconsistency of this nature: (a) where it would enable the claimant to escape the consequences of the criminal law (as in the sanction-shifting claims); and (b) where it would enable the claimant to profit from the illegal conduct (as in claims for illegal profits and earnings).[10] I will argue that these are not independent categories, but rather are both manifestations of the underlying principle of legal coherence. It is my contention that these two categories can be collapsed into one: namely, that the claim must be rejected where the relevant branches of the law, operating as a whole, have the effect that the claimant has not suffered loss or damage that the law will recognise.

[6] *Hall v Hebert* (n 1) 176 (citation omitted).

[7] ibid 178.

[8] B McLachlin, 'Weaving the Law's Seamless Web: Reflections on the Illegality Defence in Tort Law' in A Dyson, J Goudkamp and F Wilmot-Smith (eds), *Defences in Torts* (Oxford, Hart Publishing, 2015) 214.

[9] Weinrib, 'Illegality as a Tort Defence' (n 4). See also A Beever, *Rediscovering the Law of Negligence* (Oxford, Hart Publishing, 2007) 380.

[10] Weinrib, 'Illegality as a Tort Defence' ibid. Weinrib also includes exemplary damages in category (b).

II. The Principle of Coherence is not Dependent on Corrective Justice for its Validity

I have explained that Weinribian corrective justice proponents view legal coherence as the only legitimate rationale for an illegality defence. I should acknowledge at this point that it is not only corrective justice theorists who take this view. In a highly influential article, 'Recovering Value Transferred under an Illegal Contract', Peter Birks argued that it is the 'principle against self-stultification' that is the legal basis for the application of illegality doctrine in the context of restitutionary claims for the recovery of benefits conferred under an illegal contract.[11] The 'principle against self-stultification' is a reference to the need to ensure 'that the law as stated in one area should not make nonsense of the law as stated in another'.[12] This principle, when expressed in its positive form, reflects the objective of maintaining coherence in the law.[13] Birks' legal coherence approach was adopted by the High Court of Australia in a case subsequent to *Miller v Miller*, which consolidated the coherence rationale in the Australian law of illegality, *Equuscorp Pty Ltd v Haxton*.[14]

James Goudkamp and Lorenz Mayr have pointed out that the legal coherence rationale stands on its own, and that its validity does not depend on whether it can be accommodated within Weinribian corrective justice.[15] This is undoubtedly correct; in an extra-curial piece the Chief Justice of Canada, Beverley McLachlin, has argued persuasively that laws must be coherent in order to be authoritative and intelligible and to provide a sound basis for persons to order their affairs.[16] Her Honour then argues that this norm of coherence:

> 'does not stop with specific subsets of the legal system: it extends to the law as a whole. In this way coherence reaches for the essential unity of the law. … On this view, it is part

[11] P Birks, 'Recovering Value Transferred Under An Illegal Contract' (2000) 1 *Theoretical Inquiries in Law* 155, 160.

[12] ibid.

[13] *Equuscorp Pty Ltd v Haxton* [2012] HCA 7, (2012) 246 CLR 498 [38] (French CJ, Crennan and Kiefel J).

[14] ibid [37]–[38].

[15] J Goudkamp and L Mayr, 'The Doctrine of Illegality and Interference with Chattels' in A Dyson, J Goudkamp and F Wilmot-Smith (eds), *Defences in Torts* (Oxford, Hart Publishing, 2015) 243. James Goudkamp has put forward convincing arguments for a coherence rationale: J Goudkamp, 'A Revival of the Doctrine of Attainder? The Statutory Illegality Defences to Liability in Tort' (2007) 29(3) *Sydney Law Review* 445, 451–55; J Goudkamp, 'The Defence of Joint Illegal Enterprise' (2010) 34 *Melbourne University Law Review* 425, 441–46. However, it appears that, while Goudkamp believes legal coherence has an important role to play in this area (see J Goudkamp, 'A Private Law Hydra' (2015) 6 *The UK Supreme Court Yearbook* 254, 269) he is not convinced that consistency should be the sole rationale for illegality doctrine: Goudkamp and Mayr at 243; J Goudkamp, 'A Long, Hard Look at Gray v Thames Trains Ltd' in PS Davies and J Pita (eds), *Jurisprudence of Lord Hoffmann: A Festschrift in Honour of Lord Leonard Hoffmann* (London, Bloomsbury Publishing, 2015) 54.

[16] McLachlin, 'Weaving the Law's Seamless Web' (n 8) 219.

of a judge's task to seek to develop a coherent system of norms that aim to make sense of different branches of the law. … The obligation extends to reconciling the subset of norms that make up tort law and the subset of norms that make up criminal law, at least where those two subsets of law intersect. The obligation arises … from the requirements of justification and intelligibility'[17]

This explanation of the importance of legal coherence is not dependent on a corrective justice model of negligence law for its validity. Nevertheless, Weinrib's contributions to the illegality debate has informed and shaped the views of courts and theorists alike. The coherence rationale as formulated by Weinrib in his seminal article will have less authority if it cannot be reconciled with his later writings on corrective justice. I will explain in the next section that the principle of coherence is an instantiation of corrective justice principles.

III. Concerns about Legal Coherence are Relational Concerns

In *Hall v Hebert*, McLachlin J indicated that concerns about legal coherence are policy concerns independent of the parties' relationship that operate so as to 'trump' corrective justice.[18] However, Weinrib explains that the principle of coherence applies relationally without invoking an independent policy. This is because it is the whole body of the law—including the criminal, statute and civil law—that must determine the claimant's entitlements against the defendant.[19] Weinrib recognises that the relationship of the parties must be situated within the whole system of law that regulates that relationship:

> [T]he parties to a tort suit are related to each other as legal persons—that is, as parties whose legal relationships are expressive of the systematic coherence of the entire law of obligations. Accordingly, they do not interact juridically apart from the whole ensemble of intertwined legal concepts and principles that governs their participation in the law's systematic nature.[20]

Weinrib endorses the statements by the High Court of Australia in *Sullivan v Moody* that an assessment of a duty of care 'may concern the need to preserve the coherence of other legal principles, or of a statutory scheme which governs certain conduct and relationships'.[21] In *Sullivan v Moody* it had been said that the tort of negligence should not operate so as to 'subvert … other principles of law,

[17] ibid 219–20.

[18] *Hall v Hebert* (n 1) 181–82.

[19] EJ Weinrib, *Corrective Justice* (Oxford, Oxford University Press, 2012) 76.

[20] ibid (footnote omitted).

[21] *Sullivan v Moody* [2001] HCA 59, (2001) 207 CLR 562 [50] (the Court), endorsed in Weinrib ibid 75.

and statutory provisions, which strike a balance of rights and obligations, duties and freedoms'.[22] Similarly, the Supreme Court of Canada in *Cooper v Hobart* held that a duty of care will not be recognised where it would be inconsistent with the statutory framework that created the defendant's powers and duties.[23] Weinrib has commended this aspect of the Court's determination on duty of care for its emphasis on relational reasoning.[24] The decisions of *Sullivan v Moody* and *Cooper v Hobart* were concerned with ensuring that negligence law does not impose obligations on the defendant that conflict with statutory duties or established principles from other areas of the law. However, the same principles apply when one is considering the rights the claimant has. Whether the defendant has infringed a right of the claimant, and the value of that right, must be determined by the entire body of legal principle, including the principles of the criminal law.[25]

The result is that, as Weinrib further explains, the concern about the coherence of the claim within the law as a whole is a relational, not an extra-relational, policy concern. In corrective justice terms, it is the whole body of the law, including the criminal law, which will determine whether the defendant has infringed a right of the claimant that correlated with a duty not to infringe, and whether the claimant is entitled to a remedy to rectify that infringement.[26] Beever makes this same point when discussing illegality doctrine in *Rediscovering the Law of Negligence*.[27] Beever identifies situations where the claim must fail because the combined operation of tort law and criminal law has the result that there is no infringement of a right, or no infringement of a right that has a legal value. (I refer to this as the 'no loss or damage explanation').[28] Beever points out that this conclusion is reached by an analysis of the correlative position of the parties in the context of the whole legal system.[29] He emphasises that this approach does not involve an appeal to external policy but is merely the result of the principles of the two areas of law working in tandem.[30] It 'reflects the interrelatedness of tort law and criminal law' and 'is witness to the fact that the common law is a seamless web'.[31] Beever's insightful analysis in this area has influenced the views of McLachlin CJ. Her Honour in extra-curial writings now recognises that it was wrong to view illegality doctrine when based on the principle of coherence as 'trumping' normal corrective justice entitlements.[32] She is now persuaded to the view that where the principle of

[22] *Sullivan v Moody* ibid [42].
[23] *Cooper v Hobart* [2001] SCC 79, [2001] 3 SCR 537.
[24] Weinrib, *Corrective Justice* (n 19) 66–71.
[25] Beever, *Rediscovering the Law of Negligence* (n 9) 379–83.
[26] Weinrib, *Corrective Justice* (n 19) 77.
[27] Beever, *Rediscovering the Law of Neligence* (n 9) 379–383.
[28] James Goudkamp and Lorenz Mayr have identified support for the no loss or damage explanation in German law: Goudkamp and Mayr (n 15) 236.
[29] Beever, Rediscovering the Law of Negligence (n 9) 379–83.
[30] ibid 383.
[31] ibid 381.
[32] McLachlin, 'Weaving the Law's Seamless Web' (n 8), in particular 220–22.

coherence applies to reject a claim based on an illegality it does so on the basis of the principles of tort and crime acting as a coherent whole.[33]

In essence, then, the coherence approach requires that the claim must fail when, on an assessment of the rights and duties of the parties in the light of the legal system as a whole, an essential requirement for establishing the claim for damages is not met. It is important to emphasise this point; the central question is whether negligence and the governing area of the criminal law intersect so as to negate a requirement of the claim. The statutory purpose explanation (discussed in chapter 7) operates generally[34] to negate duty of care, and thus establishes that there has been no violation of a right of the claimant. The no loss or damage explanation (discussed in chapters 8 and 9) operates to negate the gist damage element of the claim, or to disvalue a specific head of loss, and thus establishes that there has been no violation of a right of the claimant, or that the right that is violated has no value in law.

The general point is that it is the intersection of the *principles* of tort with the *principles* of the area of law proscribing the conduct (usually the criminal law) that negates a requirement for establishing a claim in negligence. It is an important point, and one which the High Court of Australia emphasised in *Miller v Miller*:

> [T]he issue that is presented by observing that a claimant was acting illegally when injured as a result of the defendant's negligence is whether there is some *relevant intersection* between the law that made the claimant's conduct unlawful *and the legal principles that determine whether the claimant should have a cause of action for negligence against the defendant.*[35] (emphasis added)

When the principle of coherence is understood in its correct sense, it can be understood that it does not operate so as to 'trump' the claimant's corrective justice entitlements. To the contrary, it is integral to the conclusion that no such entitlements ever arose.

IV. Categories of Claims Where a Legal Incoherence Might Arise

Weinrib has identified two situations where an award of compensation for harm connected to an illegal act could potentially give rise to an inconsistency in the law: (a) where it would enable the claimant to escape the consequences of the criminal law; and (b) where it would enable the claimant to profit from illegal conduct.[36]

[33] ibid.

[34] Although, as I will discuss in ch 7, there might be circumstances where recognition of a legal loss would be incompatible with the purposes of the statute: see, ch 7, section V, Evaluation of the Statutory Purpose Explanation: Sanction-shifting Claims and Claims for Illegal Profits and Earnings.

[35] *Miller v Miller* (n 2) [16] (French CJ, Gummow, Hayne, Crennan, Kiefel and Bell JJ) [108] (Heydon J).

[36] Weinrib, 'Illegality as a Tort Defence' (n 4). These categories have also been endorsed by Beever: Beever, *Rediscovering the Law of Negligence* (n 9) 380.

Justice McLachlin, in her majority judgment in *Hall v Hebert*, accepted these as the only justifications for the application of a defence of illegality, explaining that 'The idea common to these instances is that the law refuses to give by its right hand what it takes away by its left hand'.[37] The principles from *Hall v Hebert* were applied subsequently by the Supreme Court of Canada in *British Columbia v Zastowny*[38] and by the House of Lords in *Gray v Thames Trains Ltd*.[39]

I will discuss Weinrib's two categories briefly now, while keeping in mind that (as I will explain) these are both examples of the one overarching principle of coherence; further, that they are both manifestations of the principle that a claim should be rejected where the claimant has not suffered loss or damage that is recognisable by the law.

A. Allowing Recovery would Enable the Claimant to Escape the Effects of the Law Proscribing the Conduct

In Chapter 8 I will explain that some sanction-shifting claims must be rejected on the ground that they will permit the claimant to escape the consequences of a sanction imposed by criminal or statutory law. I identify in Chapter 8 two situations where a claim must be rejected on the basis that it would have the effect of deflecting a sanction prescribed by law: (i) a claim to recover a lawfully imposed pecuniary penalty; and (ii) a claim for non-pecuniary losses arising out of a lawfully imposed detention. These claims must be rejected because the effect of the operation of the whole body of the law—including the criminal and regulatory law—is that the claimant has not suffered loss or damage that the law will recognise. This point will be developed further in Chapter 8, with reference to Beever's insightful analysis in this area.

B. Allowing Recovery would Enable the Claimant to Profit from Wrongdoing

A pervasive concern in this area is that claimants will derive a benefit from their illegal act. Ronald Dworkin recognised that it is an underlying principle of the legal system that claimants should not be allowed to benefit from their own wrongdoing.[40] As McLachlin J recognised in *Hall v Hebert*, this 'underlying principle' is best viewed as a particular manifestation of the need to preserve legal coherence.[41] It would create an inconsistency in the law if the profits derived (or expected to be

[37] *Hall v Hebert* (n 1) 169.
[38] *British Columbia v Zastowny* [2008] SCC 4, [2008] 1 SCR 27.
[39] *Gray v Thames Trains Ltd* (n 3) [39] (Lord Hoffmann).
[40] R Dworkin, *Taking Rights Seriously* (London, Duckworth, 1977) 23–28.
[41] *Hall v Hebert* (n 1) 174–76.

derived) from illegal conduct were awarded in a negligence action: 'It would put the courts in the position of saying that the same conduct is both legal, in the sense of being capable of rectification by the court, and illegal'.[42] Beever likewise views instances of wrongful profiting as instances of an incoherence in the law.[43]

That having been said, the potential for a wrongful profiting to occur is limited in torts claims because an award of compensation in tort law is not profit.[44] As Alan Bogg and Tonia Novitz point out, while the principle of no wrongful profiting has 'strong salience' in contract law, it is a 'relatively peripheral' concern in torts.[45] Unlike contract law, where damages are awarded on the expectation measure, damages in tort are awarded to restore the claimant to the pre-tort position. Thus, an award of damages in tort for harm resulting from an illegal act is not 'profit'.[46] It is only in the case of claims for illegal profits or earnings that the line between compensation and profit can become blurred in torts law.

The concern that claimants might use the legal process to enforce their illegal bargains and/or obtain the profits of their illegal conduct does not therefore have the same potency in torts as in contract. Nevertheless, there might be limited situations where the principle of coherence will require a claim to be rejected on the ground that an award of compensation would permit the claimant to obtain or retain the profits of the wrongdoing. Weinrib gives two examples. The first example is an award of exemplary damages to a claimant injured while engaged in an illegal act.[47] The second is an award of illegal profits or earnings.[48] Beever and McLachlin J in *Hall v Hebert* likewise endorse these as situations where recovery would allow the claimant to profit from wrongdoing and thus create an incoherence in the law.[49] In my view, there is a strong basis for arguing that an award of illegal profits or earnings can potentially create a lack of coherence between negligence law and the area of law proscribing the conduct. The same strong argument cannot, however, be made in respect of an award of exemplary damages. I will deal with exemplary damages first.

i. Exemplary Damages

Weinrib argues that an award of exemplary damages to a wrongdoing claimant should not be permitted as this would entitle the claimant to profit from the wrongdoing. A relevant example is where a trespassing claimant is awarded exemplary

[42] ibid 176.

[43] See also Beever, *Rediscovering the Law of Negligence* (n 9) 380.

[44] *Hall v Hebert* (n 1) 174–77; *Hunter Area Health Service v Presland* [2005] NSWCA 33, (2005) 63 NSWLR 22, 40 [94] (Spigelman CJ); Weinrib, 'Illegality as a Tort Defence' (n 4) 40–41.

[45] AL Bogg and T Novitz, 'Race Discrimination and the Doctrine of Illegality' (2013) 129 *Law Quarterly Review* 12, 16.

[46] M McInnes, 'Ex Turpi Causa and Tort—A Canadian Perspective' [1993] *Cambridge Law Journal* 379, 381; Beever, *Rediscovering the Law of Negligence* (n 9) 374; James Goudkamp, 'The illegality defence in the law of negligence after Miller v Miller' (2011) 7(10) *Australian Civil Liability* 130, 131.

[47] Weinrib, 'Illegality as a Tort Defence' (n 4) 41–42.

[48] ibid 42–43.

[49] *Hall v Hebert* (n 1) 174–76, 179–80; McLachlin, 'Weaving the Law's Seamless Web' (n 8) 213; Beever, *Rediscovering the Law of Negligence* (n 9) 380–81.

damages for injuries deliberately inflicted by the occupant.[50] Weinrib's reasoning is that the claimant should be entitled to claim compensatory damages for the injuries so as to ensure the claimant is no worse off as a result of the defendant's negligence, but not exemplary damages as this would confer a windfall on the claimant and enable the claimant to profit from the illegal act.[51] This is also the view of both Beever and McLachlin J (in *Hall v Hebert*), who justify their objections to an award of exemplary damages on the ground that such an award would create an inconsistency in the law.

It is clear that an award of exemplary damages is a windfall to the claimant; as James Goudkamp explains, such an award places the claimant 'in an economically superior position to that which he or she would have occupied but for the defendant's tort'.[52] That much is conceded; however, the principle of legal coherence cannot be used as the justification for denying that windfall. There is no conflict with the criminal law in this situation: it is not as if the claimant is attempting to escape the consequences of a criminal sanction nor (unlike the illegal profits and earnings cases) to obtain the *benefits expected* from the illegal act, such as the income that would have been earned from an illegal activity. An award of exemplary damages is not made to a claimant in order to reward them for that criminal conduct; it is made because the defendant has acted in contumelious and callous disregard of the claimant's rights.[53] If exemplary damages are awarded to a wrongdoing claimant, it is because the wrongfulness of the defendant's conduct in deliberately injuring the claimant has far outstripped the wrongfulness of the claimant's act.

The notion of wrongful profiting should only be considered an acceptable application of illegality doctrine where an award of damages would create an incoherence with the law proscribing the illegal conduct in the sense described in this chapter; that is, where the combined operation of the two areas of law negate an essential requirement of the claim for damages. To use the notion of wrongful profiting to deny the claim in any other way is to use it in a way that undermines corrective justice.

The *real* challenge posed by an award of exemplary damages to corrective justice theory is not that an award of these damages creates a conflict with the criminal law, but rather that it is inconsistent with the *corrective justice structure of negligence law*. Weinrib and Beever argue that exemplary damages are inconsistent with corrective justice as they are directed to punishing the defendant rather than rectifying the wrong.[54] An award of exemplary damages provides a windfall to the claimant 'because they do not represent anything that the claimant has been

[50] The case usually cited in this respect is *Katko v Briney* 183 NW 2d 657 (1971).

[51] Weinrib, 'Illegality as a Tort Defence' (n 4) 41–42.

[52] Goudkamp, 'A Revival of the Doctrine of Attainder?' (n 15) 458–9.

[53] *Lamb v Cotogno* [1987] HCA 47, (1987) 164 CLR 1.

[54] Weinrib, *Corrective Justice* (n 19) 97; Ernest J Weinrib, 'Punishment and Disgorgement as Contract Remedies' (2003) 78 *Chicago-Kent Law Review* 55; Allan Beever, 'The Structure of Aggravated and Exemplary Damages' (2003) 23 *Oxford Journal of Legal Studies* 87; Allan Beever, 'Justice and Punishment in Tort: A Comparative Theoretical Analysis' in Charles Rickett (ed), *Justifying Private Law Remedies* (Oxford, Hart Publishing, 2008) ch 11.

wrongly deprived of'.[55] That is, they go beyond what is necessary in order to rectify the injury to the claimant's right.[56] Thus, the remedies that are available should not include exemplary damages as they are inconsistent with the corrective justice structure of negligence law. The concern here is not, however, about preserving the coherence of the legal system, or preventing a clash with the criminal law; rather, it is about preserving the coherence of the negligence action as a manifestation of corrective justice.

I will argue in Chapter 9 that an award of compensation will only 'wrongfully profit' the claimant in circumstances where the claim is for lost profits or income from hypothetical illegal conduct that, if earned, the claimant would have been required to account for through the application of the legal process. That is not the case in respect of exemplary damages; they would not be liable to forfeiture under criminal legislation nor would they be able to be recovered on civil proceedings.

In summary, an award of exemplary damages should not be made because this remedy is inconsistent with a corrective justice explanation of negligence law, but not on the ground that it creates an incoherence with the criminal law.

ii. Illegal Profits and Earnings

The second situation given by Weinrib of a wrongful profiting is where the claimant seeks an award of damages for being prevented from carrying on an illegal activity. An example would be where a claimant who is incapacitated from pursing an occupation as a bank robber because of injuries negligently inflicted by the defendant claims damages for loss of future earning capacity as a bank robber.[57] While Weinrib does not provide a detailed justification for this preclusion, Beever has put forward an explanation that substantiates the argument that these claims should generally not be permitted. Beever argues that, when the profits or earnings are proscribed by the criminal law, the claimant has not suffered a loss on which the law puts a value.[58] Beever does not, however, explain in detail the principles that should be used to determine whether, and in what circumstances, the loss should be regarded as not having a value in law. I will develop Beever's arguments in Chapter 9, by suggesting that the success of a claim for illegal profits or earnings depends on whether, if the hypothetical illegal activity had been a reality, the claimant would have been notionally required by the legal process to account for those profits or earnings. This is because in those circumstances the claimant has no legal entitlement to the subject matter of the 'loss' representing those profits or earnings.

In summary on this point, I suggest that the policy of the law that a person should not profit from their wrongdoing does not provide an independent justification for

[55] Weinrib, *Corrective Justice* (n 19) 172.
[56] ibid 341.
[57] Weinrib, 'Illegality as a Tort Defence' (n 4) 42–43.
[58] Beever, *Rediscovering the Law of Negligence* (n 9) 382.

a defence of illegality but is a particular manifestation of the relational policy of preserving legal coherence. Where the claim is for illegal profits or earnings this might in some circumstances point to the fact that the claimant has not suffered a loss that has a value in law.

V. The Limited Application of the Coherence Rationale to Personal Injury Claims

The principle of legal coherence has been used as the basis for applying an illegality principle in areas not contemplated by corrective justice theorists (or, for that matter, other commentators in this area). Of relevance to this book is that the coherence rationale has been extended beyond the sanction-shifting claims and claims for illegal profits and earnings to claims for compensation for injuries suffered during the course of an illegal act. In particular, it has been applied to reject claims against an accomplice with whom the claimant was jointly committing the illegal act (the joint illegality cases).

This over-extension of the coherence principle is illustrated by *Miller v Miller.*[59] Briefly, the claimant stole a car so she could get home after a night out in Perth, and allowed the defendant to drive it. The defendant drove the car recklessly and it struck a pole, seriously injuring the claimant. A majority of the Court (Heydon J dissenting on the withdrawal point) held that, had it not been for the fact that the claimant had withdrawn from the joint enterprise by her requests to be let out of the car, the claim would have had to be rejected on the basis that recognition of a duty of care would create an incongruity in the law.

There are two main emphases in the majority judgment in *Miller v Miller*. The first was a narrow principle that a duty of care will not be recognised where it would be incompatible with the purpose of the statute that the claimant contravened (in that case, the offence of unlawful taking and use of a motor vehicle). The second was a more abstract principle that a duty of care will not be recognised where it would create an incongruity in the law. I will explain in Chapter 7 that the evidence regarding statutory purpose in this case was thin and unconvincing, and the majority's purported adherence to statutory purpose dubious.[60] It seems that the incongruity found by the Court on those facts was of the second, more abstract, kind. An important element of the reasoning in *Miller v Miller* was that, by virtue of the governing criminal legislation, the claimant was complicit in, and hence criminally responsible for, the very conduct (the dangerous driving) that caused the harm. This ultimately led the majority to conclude that 'it would evidently be incongruous to decide that the offender who drove the vehicle owed that

[59] *Miller v Miller* (n 2).

[60] See ch 7, Section IV, Evaluation of the Statutory Purpose Explanation: Claims for Harm Sustained in the Course of Committing an Illegal Act.

passenger a duty to drive with reasonable care'.[61] This was because 'To conclude that the driver owed the passenger a duty to take reasonable care when driving would not be consistent with the purpose of the statute proscribing dangerous driving'.[62] The Court referred to no extrinsic materials that could establish that it was part of the purpose of the dangerous driving offence to deprive the claimant of the benefit of the ordinary duty of care.

The reasoning of the majority should be rejected to the extent that it suggests that the existence of a duty of care would be incompatible with the purpose of the criminal statute proscribing dangerous driving *merely by virtue of the fact* that the claimant is found by the criminal law to have been complicit in the conduct that caused the injuries. It would not 'evidently be incongruous' to decide that the claimant is an accomplice to the driver's dangerous driving for the purposes of attributing criminal responsibility and yet recognise that the claimant is nevertheless owed a duty of care by the driver to drive safely. To suggest that such an incongruity exists is to ignore the realities of the parties' relationship, namely that the claimant was a passenger in a motor vehicle driven by the defendant. It involves the application of a fiction that the claimant was responsible for the negligent driving of the vehicle. While this might be true for criminal purposes, it is not true (in the absence of vicarious liability) for negligence purposes. In other words, the fact that the claimant is deemed to have committed the offence of dangerous driving for the purpose of imposing a criminal punishment does not mean that she should be treated *as if she was the driver* for the purpose of determining her claim for compensation in a negligence action.

It is unfortunate then that the English Court of Appeal in *McCracken v Smith* adopted reasoning similar to that in *Miller v Miller* as one of the grounds why a passenger should not be able to recover against a driver in circumstances where the passenger is found to be complicit in the dangerous driving.[63] One of the reasons given by Richards LJ in his leading speech as to why such a claim should be rejected was that:

> '[A]lthough as a matter of fact the negligent act was that of Damian [the driver], Daniel [the passenger] was jointly responsible in law for it and he cannot bring a claim in respect of his own negligent act.'[64]

The application of the legal fiction that the negligent act was that of the claimant in turn manufactures a further fiction, namely that of an incoherence in the law.

In sum, a conclusion that the claimant is criminally complicit in the conduct that gave rise to the losses, yet is able to recover his or her losses in negligence, is not of itself evidence of an incoherence in the law. It is merely the consequence of

[61] *Miller v Miller* (n 2) [93].

[62] ibid [94].

[63] *McCracken v Smith* [2015] EWCA Civ 380.

[64] ibid [47] (Richards LJ, Underhill and Christopher Clarke LJJ agreeing). These statements were only in obiter as the claim by the passenger against the driver was not the subject of an appeal before the Court.

the two areas of law operating harmoniously together and pursuing their different aims. There is no convincing reason why principles of responsibility should operate in *precisely the same way* in the two areas of law as the differences can be justified by reference to the different principles underpinning them. The goal of *coherence* should not be confused with a goal of *sameness*; coherence requires that tort and crime 'fit together', but not that similar concepts or rules must operate identically in the two areas of law.[65] Any differences between the operation of principles of responsibility in criminal law and tort law simply (to adapt the words of Allan Beever from a different context) 'reflect the focus of the former on the defendant's wrongdoing and the latter on the connection between that wrongdoing and the claimant's injuries'.[66]

In conclusion, the Court in *Miller v Miller* was wrong to suggest that the joint illegality cases raise a special risk of incoherence with the criminal law. The only occasion where legal coherence comes into issue in this category of claim is where the recognition of a duty of care would be incompatible with the purpose of the statute proscribing the illegal conduct; in that case, the duty of care must be rejected to preserve the coherence of that statutory scheme.

VI. Other Misappropriations of the Coherence Rationale

In the preceding section it was discussed that at least part of the reasoning in *Miller v Miller* misapplied the principle of coherence. The High Court is not the only court to have done so. In *Hounga v Allen* Lord Hughes suggested (correctly) that an important basis for the law of illegality is that 'the law must act consistently'.[67] However, the consistency principle his Lordship formulated is impermissibly wide. His Lordship framed the principle as being that '[the law] cannot give with one hand what it takes away with another, nor condone when facing right what it condemns when facing left'.[68] This formulation of the consistency principle is elegantly phrased and has considerable intuitive appeal, but is greatly oversimplified, and liable to result in the unjustified denial of claims on the incorrect assumption that this is necessary to prevent a legal incoherence. Indicative of this is Lord Hughes' suggestion that his 'consistency principle' should be used to deny relief in joint criminal enterprise cases, because the law could not consistently condemn the criminal enterprise on the one hand, and give relief on the claim on the other.

[65] cf M Dyson, 'Disentangling and Organising Tort and Crime' in M Dyson (ed), *Unravelling Tort and Crime* (Cambridge, Cambridge University Press, 2014), 13–14.
[66] Beever, 'The Structure of Aggravated and Exemplary Damages' (n 54) 109.
[67] *Hounga v Allen* [2014] UKSC 47, [2014] 1 WLR 2889 [55] (Lord Carnwath agreeing).
[68] ibid.

However, an award of damages to a participant in a joint criminal enterprise cases will usually not result in a legal incoherence, as discussed in the preceding section.

Lord Wilson, who wrote for the majority in *Hounga v Allen*, also appeared to misunderstand the coherence principle as formulated in *Hall v Hebert*, using it to justify what was in fact extra-relational reasoning of public policy. This case involved a claim in the statutory tort of discrimination. The issue before the Court was whether the claim should be defeated by virtue of the fact the claimant was an illegal immigrant and the contract of employment that formed the basis of the discrimination complaint was an illegal contract. The Court held that the claim should be allowed. Lord Wilson (Lady Hale and Lord Kerr agreeing) identified (correctly) the proper rationale of the illegality principle as the need to preserve the integrity of the legal system, but considered (incorrectly) that this gave the court the licence to weigh up public policy considerations underlying the governing area of law.

Lord Wilson cited McLachlin J's judgment in *Hall v Hebert* and the two situations her Honour recognised where legal coherence will be in issue: where a claim would allow a person to evade or obtain a rebate of a penalty prescribed the criminal law; and where it would allow a person to profit from the illegal conduct. Lord Wilson considered, however, that these two situations 'may best be taken as an example of [the coherence principle] rather than as the only conceivable instance of it'.[69] His Lordship recognised that the award of compensation to the claimant in that case would not permit her to evade a criminal penalty, nor would it permit her to profit from her wrongful conduct in entering into the illegal contract. That conclusion should by itself have disposed of the arguments based on legal coherence. Of concern is the fact that his Lordship viewed the policy of preserving the 'integrity' of the legal system as encompassing a range of public policy considerations. For example, his Lordship went on to consider the policy question of the impact of allowing or disallowing the claim on illegal employment contracts, on the basis that these issues were relevant to maintaining the integrity of the legal system.[70] Public policy concerns, which weigh up the broader societal consequences of the claim, should not be admitted as part of a legal coherence analysis. Lord Wilson's approach results in a discrepancy between the legal basis of the principle and its application, a point recognised by James Fisher:

> The majority position in *Hounga* is highly problematic. ... It declares the basis of the [illegality] principle to be the preservation of legal integrity yet adopts a test which focuses on something entirely different: the aspects of public policy each party's position highlights. This creates a gulf between the principle's theoretical basis and the test for its application.[71]

[69] ibid [44].
[70] ibid.
[71] JC Fisher, 'The *Ex Turpi Causa* Principle in *Hounga* and *Servier* (2015) 78 *The Modern Law Review* 854, 869.

This statement succinctly identifies the fundamental objection to the use of the coherence principle to support reasoning of public policy.[72]

In *Patel v Mirza* Lord Toulson asserted that the notion of avoiding an inconsistency in the legal system so as to maintain its integrity can be given a wide or narrow meaning.[73] Like Lord Wilson, Lord Toulson (writing for the majority) preferred a broad interpretation of this concept. His Lordship held that whether a claim based on an illegality is 'contrary to the public interest, because it would be harmful to the integrity of the legal system' depends upon a consideration of competing public policies and other factors that will determine the proportionality of denying relief.[74] This interpretation is inconsistent with McLachlin J's narrow formulation of the coherence principle in *Hall v Hebert*, as explained in this chapter. Lord Toulson has misapplied this principle in order to support a conceptually foreign approach, effectively emptying this principle of meaning.

VII. Does an Exclusive Focus on Legal Coherence Result in an Unjustifiably Narrow Doctrine of Illegality?

It has been argued that if legal coherence is the only recognised rationale of illegality doctrine this will lead to an unacceptably narrow doctrine that would rarely be engaged.[75] The Law Commission of England and Wales (the Commission) noted that illegality doctrine would be 'severely curtail[ed]' if legal coherence was the only legal basis for its application.[76] The particular concern of the Commission was that the doctrine would have no application to personal injury claims.[77] It is, of course, correct to say that claims for personal injury will not usually be denied on the ground of legal coherence—this point was established in section V. The only circumstance where this would occur would be where an award of compensation would undermine or stultify the purpose of the statute against which the

[72] Lord Wilson did allude to the need to ensure adherence to international obligations to pay compensation to victims of human trafficking from the perpetrators. However, no issue of coherence with international obligations arose in that case. As emphasised by Lord Hughes, there had been no factual finding that the claimant was a victim of human trafficking, and the tort of statutory discrimination is not co-extensive with trafficking: (n 67) at [52], [65]. Hence, there was no obligation under international instruments to provide compensation to her as a victim of trafficking.

[73] *Patel v Mirza* (n 3) [93], [101] (Lord Toulson, Lady Hale and Lords Kerr, Wilson and Hodge agreeing).

[74] ibid [101].

[75] PS Davies 'The Illegality Defence and Public Policy' (2009) 125 *Law Quarterly Review* 556; See also G Virgo, 'The Defence of Illegality in Unjust Enrichment' in A Dyson, J Goudkamp and F Wilmot-Smith, *Defences in Unjust Enrichment* (London, Bloomsbury Publishing, 2016) 176, who argues that the principle of coherence must be supplemented by a flexible balancing approach.

[76] The Law Commission, *The Illegality Defence* (Law Comm No 189, 2009) para 7.4.

[77] ibid para 7.11.

claimant has offended. However, the Commission provides no convincing explanation as to why this should matter. As the preceding chapters demonstrate, those in the United Kingdom who support an extended public policy-based doctrine of illegality consistently have failed to put forward an alternative rationale that has secured widespread acceptance and that is capable of achieving stability and predictability in this area. This has left the law in an inferior position in that country, whereby judges have had no choice but to resort to weighing a range of policy and other factors to determine the claim.

Moreover, the negligence action has in-built safeguards to ensure that a personal injury claim will be denied to the extent the wrongdoing claimant has contributed to his or her own harm, or in circumstances where the claimant could not reasonably expect the defendant to comply with normal standards of safe behaviour. The most apparent of these safeguards is contributory negligence, which reduces damages to reflect the extent of the claimant's responsibility for the harm. In some Australian jurisdictions the reduction can be up to 100 per cent.[78] In the United Kingdom, reductions approaching 100 per cent are not unheard of.[79] In some cases, the defence of voluntary assumption of risk will be available.[80] The elements of the negligence action themselves also provide an additional safeguard. In appropriate circumstances the claim will be denied on the basis that there is no duty of care—I will explain in Chapter 10 that a duty of care will not arise in the joint illegal enterprise cases where the nature of the claimant's relationship with the defendant was such that the claimant could not reasonably expect the defendant to exercise the normal standard of care.[81] There will be other cases also where a duty of care will not arise, or where breach or causation cannot be established.[82] Accordingly, whatever the position might be in other areas of private law, in negligence law there are sufficient mechanisms independent of a specific doctrine of

[78] See, eg, Wrongs Act 1958 (Vic), s 63.

[79] J Goudkamp, 'Rethinking Contributory Negligence' in SGA Pitel, JW Neyers, E Chamberlain (eds), *Tort Law: Challenging Orthodoxy* (Oxford, Hart Publishing, 2013), 349. A reduction by 100% is not possible in the United Kingdom: *Pitts v Hunt* [1991] 2 QB 24 (CA); *Anderson v Newham College Further Education* [2002] EWCA Civ 505; [2003] ICR 212. It is the United Kingdom approach that is the most theoretically defensible: Goudkamp, at 344–46.

[80] Though a voluntary assumption of risk is notoriously difficult to establish, some Australian jurisdictions have introduced reforms intended to relax the requirements of the defence: See ch 10, section XIII, Interaction with Defences.

[81] See ch 10 generally.

[82] See, eg, *Vellino v Chief Constable of the Greater Manchester Police* [2001] EWCA Civ 1249, [2002] 1 WLR 218 (police owe no duty of care to a person seeking to evade arrest); *AB v Chief Constable of X Constabulary* [2015] EWHC 13 (QB) (police authority had not breached the duty to provide adequate support to an undercover police officer, and any breach would not have been causative of the psychiatric harm in any event).Where, eg, the claimant is an intruder on property the question of breach must be determined according to the standard of care to be expected of a defendant dealing with the situation of an intruding burglar: *Revill v Newbery* [1996] QB 567 (CA), 577 (Neill LJ, Evans and Millett LJJ agreeing) (though in that case a breach of duty was found due to the use of excessive force). In ch 5 I argued that on principled reasoning of corrective justice there is an argument that the crime of the claimant will constitute an intervening act that will break the chain of causation between the negligence and the harm: see ch 5 text to notes 184–187.

illegality that ensure that the relief given (if any) will properly take into account the illegal conduct of the claimant.

VIII. Conclusion

An important theme of this book is that illegality is a legal doctrine embodying systemic concerns about the coherence of the legal system, not a rule of morality or public policy. Birks has argued that the 'great advantage' of an enquiry into legal coherence is that it 'can be answered analytically' and is divorced from judgments about the morality of the parties.[83] A legal coherence approach 'strips the element of moral condemnation from illegality'[84] and makes questions of turpitude irrelevant: 'The inquiry is constantly an inquiry into consistency and rationality, not into turpitude'.[85]

This chapter has built upon work by Weinrib and Beever in order to answer analytically the question when an award of compensation to a wrongdoing claimant will undermine the coherence of the law. It has been identified that an award of damages to a wrongdoing claimant will only create an incoherence in the law where it would be incompatible with the purpose of the statute or rule against which the claimant offended, or where it would permit the claimant to escape the consequences of a legal sanction or to wrongfully profit from the conduct. These second two categories can be collapsed into one overarching principle: recovery will be denied because the claimed loss or damage was authorised by the law. There are thus two situations where a claim connected to an illegal act must be denied because of the combined operation of the different branches of the law working as a whole: (a) where one of the purposes of the statute infringed by the claimant was to prevent a civil claim (the statutory purpose explanation), and (b) where the loss or damage is one that is authorised by the law proscribing the conduct (the no loss or damage explanation). Where compensation is denied in these circumstances the courts are not 'trumping' corrective justice; rather, principles of corrective justice *demand* an illegality doctrine that denies relief where one of these grounds is established. Moreover, it is not an example of the policies of the criminal law 'trumping' the law of negligence; rather, it is an example of the development of negligence law in a way that, in the words of the Chief Justice of Canada Beverley McLachlin 'consider[s] the principles of both domains as a coherent whole' and that 'respects the principles of each domain'.[86]

[83] Birks (n 11) 158, 168.
[84] ibid 160.
[85] ibid 203. Though it should be noted that Birks does leave open the possibility that gross turpitude might have a role in a rare case, as a long-stop reason for denying the claim: see in particular 199–203.
[86] McLachlin, 'Weaving the Law's Seamless Web' (n 8) 220.

There is a regrettable trend at the highest judicial level in the United Kingdom and Australia to expand legal coherence beyond these two limited circumstances. Some judges (particularly in the United Kingdom) have formulated a very broad consistency principle that would potentially extend to any claim that is founded on illegal conduct. Additionally, recent decisions have purported to rely upon a legal coherence rationale in circumstances where that rationale could have no application. These decisions demonstrate the importance of carefully defining the ambit of the principle of coherence to ensure that it is not misused by judges with a predisposition to reject the claim on public policy grounds. This chapter has begun that process by identifying the broad categories where a claim might fail on the ground of legal coherence; Chapters 7–9 will elaborate on the specific principles that apply to determine whether a particular case falls within one of those categories.

7

Statutory Purpose

I. Introduction

In this chapter I examine the first of the two grounds where a claim connected to the claimant's illegality should be rejected for reasons of legal coherence. This is where it is part of the purpose of the statute proscribing the conduct that the claimant should be deprived of the benefit of a claim in negligence. In *Miller v Miller*, the High Court of Australia held that questions of statutory purpose and legal coherence will determine the success of a claim connected to an illegal act of the claimant.[1] The question in each case must be whether recognition of the claim would be compatible with the purpose of the law imposing the sanction. This approach had been applied previously to cases of unilateral illegality,[2] but was extended in *Miller v Miller* to claims arising from a joint illegal enterprise. In doing so, the Court has sought to revitalise the statutory purpose test, and to establish it as the dominant approach for resolving claims for injuries sustained while engaged in an illegal act. The approach is based on that taken to statutory illegality in other areas of private law, such as contract and property.[3]

The courts in the United Kingdom have also identified statutory purpose (or the purpose of the law that has been infringed more generally) as a relevant consideration, though usually[4] as one of a number of factors to take into account in a multifactorial analysis rather than as the exclusive factor.[5] Recent decisions

[1] *Miller v Miller* [2011] HCA 9, (2011) 242 CLR 446.

[2] *Henwood v Municipal Tramways Trust* [1938] HCA 35, (1938) 60 CLR 438.

[3] *Yango Pastoral Co Pty Ltd v First Chicago Australia Ltd* [1978] HCA 42, (1978) 139 CLR 410; *Nelson v Nelson* [1995] HCA 25, (1995) 184 CLR 538; *Equuscorp Pty Ltd v Haxton* [2012] HCA 7, (2012) 246 CLR 498; *Gnych v Polish Club Ltd* [2015] HCA 23, (2015) 320 ALR 489.

[4] There have been exceptional cases where the claim has been resolved through a process of statutory construction: *R (on the application of Best) v The Chief Land Registrar* [2015] EWCA Civ 17, [2016] QB 2; see in particular the judgment of Arden LJ (McCombe LJ agreeing). Although Sales LJ in that case purported to apply public policy to determine the claim, the substance of his reasons involved a statutory purpose approach.

[5] *Hounga v Allen* [2014] UKSC 47, [2014] 1 WLR 2889 [55] (Lord Hughes, Lord Carnwath agreeing); *Les Laboratories Servier v Apotex Inc* [2012] EWCA Civ 593, [2013] RPC 21 [66] (Etherton LJ, Kitchin LJ agreeing); *Safeway Stores Ltd v Twigger* [2010] EWCA Civ 1472, [2011] 2 All ER 841, [43]–[46] (Pill LJ); *Patel v Mirza* [2014] EWCA Civ 1047, [2015] Ch 271, [62], [65]–[69] (Gloster LJ); (*Patel v Mirza* CA); *Patel v Mirza* [2016] UKSC 42 [101] (Lord Toulson, Lady Hale and Lords Kerr, Wilson and Hodge agreeing).

of the Supreme Court of the United Kingdom have ignored the decision in *Miller v Miller*,[6] and there is no significant support in those cases for applying a statutory construction approach as the sole basis for illegality doctrine.[7] Lord Sumption has recognised that a statutory construction approach will be the correct approach to some cases;[8] however, given the current focus by other members of the Court on flexible policy decision making, it seems unlikely that the statutory purpose explanation will be adopted as the primary explanation for illegality doctrine in the foreseeable future.

Miller v Miller established that a duty of care will not arise where it would subvert the criminal provisions against which the claimant had offended. The Court made clear that this principle is a manifestation of a broader concern about legal coherence and the need to ensure that an award of compensation does not frustrate or undermine the purpose of the statutory scheme governing the conduct.[9] I explained in Chapter 6 that Weinrib has likewise recognised that the relationship between the parties includes their juridical relationship, and hence whether a duty is owed not to violate the rights of the claimant must be assessed in accordance with the whole body of law governing that relationship, including any statute law that governs the conduct of the parties.[10] The effect of this reasoning is that no duty of care can arise at common law where it was part of the purpose of the statute that the defendant did not owe a duty to the claimant to act reasonably. In this way the statutory purpose explanation operates so as to prevent the incoherence in the law that would result if negligence recognised a duty of care in circumstances where this would undermine or stultify the purpose of the statutory scheme.[11] The statutory purpose explanation will therefore (usually)[12] negate the element of duty of care.

[6] *Hounga v Allen* ibid; *Les Laboratoires Servier v Apotex Inc* [2014] UKSC 55, [2015] AC 430; *Bilta (UK) Ltd (in liquidation) v Nazir (No 2)* [2015] UKSC 23, [2016] AC 1; *Patel v Mirza* ibid.

[7] Lords Toulson and Hodge claimed in *Bilta (UK) Ltd (in liquidation) v Nazir (No 2)* to have based their decision in that case on 'statutory policy': ibid [174]. However, their Lordships made no attempt to apply general principles of statutory construction to either the legislation containing the directors' duties or the tax legislation against which *Bilta* offended to identify whether it was a purpose of either piece of legislation to allow a claim against directors for a breach of duty even if the illegal acts of the directors could be attributed to the company. In *Patel v Mirza* the majority recognised that the purpose of the law that has been transgressed is a relevant consideration (ibid [101]), but again made no attempt on the facts to determine whether recognition of the claim would be inconsistent with the legislation regulating insider trading.

[8] *Bilta* ibid [83]. Lord Sumption there recognised that the decision in *Safeway Stores Ltd v Twigger* (n 5) to reject an attempt to shift a statutory penalty onto the individuals responsible for its imposition was correct on the basis that allowing the penalty to be shifted would be inconsistent with the statutory scheme pursuant to which the penalty was imposed. Though *cf* Lord Sumption, 'Reflections on the Law of Illegality' [2012] *Restitution Law Review* 1, 11.

[9] *Miller v Miller* (n 1) [15] (French CJ, Gummow, Hayne, Crennan, Kiefel and Bell JJ), [108] (Heydon J).

[10] EJ Weinrib, *Corrective Justice* (Oxford, Oxford University Press, 2012) 76. See ch 6, section III, Concerns about Legal Coherence are Relational Concerns.

[11] *cf Equuscorp Pty Ltd v Haxton* (n 3) [38] (French CJ, Crennan and Kiefel JJ).

[12] In the sanction-shifting claims and claims for illegal profits and earnings it will instead operate so as to negate loss or damage: see section V, Evaluation of the Statutory Purpose Explanation: Sanction-Shifting Claims and Claims for Illegal Profits and Earnings.

An appeal to the purpose of the statute as a means of resolving claims arising from illegality has significant appeal on first glance: in purporting to base the decision on the purpose of the statute it has an appearance of objectivity; it is consistent with the principles applied in the context of illegal contracts and trusts, and the outcome is that all illegality claims in negligence will be resolved according to the single criterion of legal coherence. Nevertheless, the statutory purpose explanation is unlikely to have a broad application. First, there is the obvious limitation that it will apply only where the conduct is prohibited by statute. Second, even if the offence is a statutory one, it will be rare for a statute to evince a clear purpose to deny a claim for compensation. Accordingly, while the statutory purpose explanation is a conceptually coherent approach, it is likely to be of limited practical relevance in determining the outcomes of particular negligence cases.

The focus of this chapter will be on claims for injuries sustained at the time the claimant was acting illegally. However, I will also consider briefly the implications of this approach for sanction-shifting claims and claims for illegal profits and earnings.

II. Brief Overview of *Miller v Miller*

The appellant (claimant), Danelle Miller, was a 16-year-old girl who stole a car in order to travel home after a night out in Perth. The respondent (defendant), Maurin Miller, who was her mother's cousin (she called him her 'uncle'), insisted on driving the car. Others joined them in the car; in all, there were nine passengers crammed into the car. For a time the respondent drove sensibly, but then he began to speed and run red lights. At that point, the appellant asked him to slow down, and then asked him to stop and let her out. The respondent drove on, and subsequently lost control of the car, which struck a pole. One passenger was killed, and the appellant was rendered a tetraplegic. The respondent was convicted of unlawfully taking and using a motor vehicle pursuant to s 371A of The Criminal Code 1913 (WA); the appellant was never charged with a criminal offence. The appellant sued the respondent for damages and was successful at first instance, though on appeal the Court of Appeal of the Supreme Court of Western Australia rejected the claim.

A majority of the High Court (French CJ, Gummow, Hayne, Crennan, Kiefel and Bell JJ in a joint judgment; Heydon J dissenting only on the issue of withdrawal) allowed the claim on the basis that by her requests to be let out of the car, the appellant had withdrawn from the criminal enterprise. What is significant for present purposes though is that all seven judges unanimously agreed that up to the point in time that the appellant asked to be let out of the car, the respondent did not owe her a duty of care to drive the car carefully for reasons of legal policy. The central policy consideration at stake was identified as the coherence of the law.[13] The Court held that the imposition of liability in tort should not be incongruous with proscription of the appellant's conduct by the criminal law.[14] In reliance on an earlier decision of the Court in *Henwood v Municipal Tramways Trust*[15] where the statutory purpose test had been applied to cases of unilateral illegality, the Court in *Miller v Miller* held that an incongruity would arise between negligence law and the criminal law if the court was to recognise a duty of care in circumstances where it is part of the purpose of the criminal statute to deprive the claimant of the benefit of the ordinary standard of care.[16] Ultimately, the court must determine by reference to the purpose of the legislation whether 'incongruity, contrariety, or lack of coherence' requires the conclusion that a duty of care was not owed.[17] The Court held that this approach provides an answer to criticisms of the illegality doctrine that it is too harsh and undiscriminating in its application, asserting that these objections 'fall away' when it is realised that the relevant principle turns upon a search for statutory purpose and that the outcome is the consequence of the 'proper application of the statute'.[18]

The central statutory provision in *Miller v Miller* was s 371A of the Criminal Code 1913 (WA), which makes it an offence to unlawfully take or use a motor vehicle without the consent of the owner. The majority examined the legislative history behind s 371A and noted that an aggravated form of the offence had been enacted in s 378 in recognition of an association between the theft of a motor vehicle and reckless or dangerous driving. The majority concluded that the offence in s 371A was enacted for the dual purposes of protecting the property interests of vehicle owners, and of promoting general road safety. Their Honours acknowledged that these statutory purposes by themselves did not provide an indication whether a claimant should be deprived the benefit of the normal duty of care.[19] Nevertheless, they held that s 371A had to be read in conjunction with the common purpose provision in s 8(1), which provides that where a further offence is a 'probable consequence' of a common intention by two or more persons to prosecute an unlawful purpose, those persons are deemed to have committed that further offence. The majority acted on the basis that s 8(1) applied so as to render the appellant and respondent jointly complicit in the offence of dangerous driving because this was a probable consequence of the joint unlawful use of the car. The majority held that, when the scheme of the statute was examined as a whole, s 371A proscribed the taking and use of a vehicle illegally in the manner it did because it recognised that when two or more persons form a common intention to effect that unlawful purpose, it will often be a probable consequence that the

[13] *Miller v Miller* (n 1) [15].
[14] ibid [56].
[15] *Henwood v Municipal Tramways Trust* (n 2).
[16] *Miller v Miller* (n 1) [56], [74].
[17] ibid [74].
[18] ibid [98].
[19] ibid [90]; see also [99].

driver will drive recklessly or dangerously.[20] To allow a claim by the appellant for the manner of driving by her criminal accomplice would be inconsistent with this statutory purpose. Accordingly, had it not been for the finding by the majority that the appellant had withdrawn from the criminal enterprise by asking to be let out of the car, the claim would have been rejected on the basis that recognition of a duty of care would be incompatible with the criminal statute that proscribed the unlawful taking and use of the car. In the course of the judgment it was also suggested that it would create an incongruity with the statute proscribing dangerous driving if one co-offender was held to owe a duty of care to another when they were both complicit in that dangerous driving.[21] This aspect of the decision was criticised in Chapter 6.[22]

III. Implications of the Statutory Purpose Explanation

The significance of *Miller v Miller* is that in every case where the claim has a connection with an illegal act, it will be necessary to analyse the purpose of the legislation proscribing that illegal act to determine if an award of compensation would undermine or frustrate that purpose. The decision will not significantly affect unilateral illegality cases as such claims already were determined according to whether there was a legislative intent to deny the claim.[23] The main significance of the decision is for other categories of illegality claims where this approach is novel, including claims arising from a joint illegal enterprise. Following *Miller v Miller*, where the claimant's conduct contravenes a statute, close attention needs to be paid to the scope and purpose of that statute to establish whether a duty of care would be incompatible with that purpose.[24] The central question is, 'can the law of negligence, and the provisions of the [statute], be given congruent operation?'[25]

Following *Miller v Miller*, the statutory purpose explanation will now apply to all claims where the claimant was injured at the time of acting illegally: both where the claimant was acting independently of, and jointly with, the defendant. It will also apply to sanction-shifting claims and claims for illegal profits and earnings. It is therefore important to consider whether the statutory purpose explanation is a convincing explanation for denying negligence claims arising from an illegality. As I will now explain, while the statutory purpose explanation will have a legitimate

[20] ibid [99].

[21] The offences of reckless and dangerous driving were contained in ss 60 and 61 of the Road Traffic Act 1974 (WA).

[22] Ch 6, section V, The Limited Application of the Coherence Rationale to Personal Injury Claims.

[23] *Henwood v Municipal Tramways Trust* (n 2).

[24] *Miller v Miller* (n 1) [74]; see also [56],

[25] *ABN AMRO Bank NV v Bathurst Regional Council* [2014] FCAFC 65, (2014) 224 FCR 1 [717].

role to play in exceptional cases, it is unlikely to provide an explanation that is of general application.

IV. Evaluation of the Statutory Purpose Explanation: Claims for Harm Sustained in the Course of Committing an Illegal Act

The key issue following *Miller v Miller* is whether the purpose of the statute was not just to criminalise the conduct, but also to deprive a person breaching the statute of a right to claim damages on a civil claim. The reality is that it will be rare for the legislature when passing criminal legislation to have contemplated the impact of a breach on a civil claim for compensation. Hence, it is unlikely that the statute will manifest a clear purpose to deny the claim. Accordingly, there are three interrelated objections to the statutory purpose explanation. First, it will often be impossible to discern a clear purpose of the legislation to prevent a civil claim. Second, conclusions regarding statutory purpose are often no more than policy decisions in disguise. Third, it distracts the courts from their true function when assessing claims by one participant in a joint venture against another, which is to focus on the features of the relationship between the parties to determine if the normal standard of care was displaced.

A. Discerning Statutory Purpose can be a Highly Speculative Exercise

The general difficulties that confront a court when attempting to discern the purpose (or purposes) of a statutory enactment are well known. Statutes often have mixed and even inconsistent purposes, and the extent to which they might pursue a particular purpose might be uncertain.[26] Statutes are often the product of compromise, in which case it would be a mistake to attempt to discern the 'supposed purpose' of the legislation.[27] Further, there might be intentional or unintentional gaps in the legislation. The parliament might deliberately refrain from forming or expressing a purpose on some matters because it was not possible to achieve a compromise on them.[28] Alternatively, gaps might be unintentional, because the matter has been overlooked.[29] These deficiencies of a purposive approach

[26] M Gleeson, 'The Meaning of Legislation: Context, Purpose and Respect for Fundamental Rights', Victoria Law Foundation Oration, Melbourne, 31 July 2008, 22.
[27] *Stevens v Kabushiki Kaisha Sony Computer Entertainment* [2005] HCA 58, (2005) 224 CLR 193, [126] (McHugh J).
[28] Gleeson, 'The Meaning of Legislation' (n 26) 22.
[29] ibid.

are particularly significant when a court is seeking to determine whether it was a purpose of the legislation to deny a civil claim. It is widely recognised that it will be unusual for a legislature when enacting criminal legislation to have contemplated what the civil consequences of that enactment should be.[30]

There will therefore usually be a gap in the legislative scheme on this matter. Former Chief Justice of Australia, Murray Gleeson, writing extra-judicially, has recognised that in that situation 'there may be no discernible purpose that is an aid to construction'.[31] In that circumstance, Mitchell McInnes points out that 'talk of adherence to statutory intention … would be artificial'.[32] In the specific context of claims by a claimant in breach of a statute, Weinrib has described any attempt to discern legislative intent on the availability of a civil claim as an 'impossible goal'.[33] Weinrib criticises the statutory purpose explanation on the ground that:

> It sends the court into the *cul de sac* of attempting to ascertain as a matter of statutory construction the legislative intention toward a problem regarding which the legislature did not express, and probably did not have, an intention.[34]

The Chief Justice of Canada, Beverley McLachlin, agrees that a major shortcoming of an approach that devolves on statutory purpose is that the parliament will often not have expressed an intention on the subject. Her Honour is critical of the approach adopted in *Miller v Miller* 'for turning on a potentially elusive search for a legislative intention to negate the duty of care'.[35]

An appeal to the purposes of the statute will thus generally provide no plausible guidance on whether a civil claim in negligence should be refused for a breach of the criminal law. For example, reference to the purpose of a criminal provision imposing a sanction for a property offence would generally provide no explanation as to whether a claimant should be permitted a claim for injuries suffered in the course of making a getaway with stolen property (as occurred in *Joyce v O'Brien*).[36] Such legislation is concerned with the protection of property or possessory rights,[37] not with the question of compensation to a person injured in

[30] *Jackson v Harrison* [1978] HCA 17, (1978) 138 CLR 438, 455 (Mason J); EJ Weinrib, 'Illegality as a Tort Defence' (1976) 26 *University of Toronto Law Journal* 28, 31; B MacDougall '*Ex Turpi Causa*: Should a Defence arise from a Base Cause?' (1991) 55 *Saskatchewan Law Review* 1, 31; RA Prentice, 'Of Tort Reform and Millionaire Muggers: Should an Obscure Equitable Doctrine be Revived to Dent the Litigation Crisis?' (1995) 32 *San Diego Law Review* 53, 89; J Goudkamp, 'The Illegality Defence in the Law of Negligence after Miller v Miller' (2011) 7(10) *Australian Civil Liability* 130, 131.

[31] Gleeson, 'The Meaning of Legislation' (n 26) 22.

[32] M McInnes, 'Advancement, Illegality and Restitution' (1997) 5 *Australian Property Law Journal* 1, 15.

[33] Weinrib, 'Illegality as a Tort Defence' (n 30) 31.

[34] ibid.

[35] Beverley McLachlin, 'Weaving the Law's Seamless Web: Reflections on the Illegality Defence in Tort Law' in Andrew Dyson, James Goudkamp and Fred Wilmot-Smith (eds), *Defences in Torts* (Oxford, Hart Publishing, 2015) 217.

[36] *Joyce v O'Brien* [2014] EWCA Civ 546, [2014] 1 WLR 70.

[37] CR Williams, *Property Offences*, 3rd ed (Sydney, LBC Information Services, 1999) 2; *Miller v Miller* (n 1) [89].

the course of stealing property. Thus, it has never been suggested that it would be inconsistent with the criminal laws relating to criminal trespass and theft or burglary to allow a civil claim by the trespassing thief. Take the example of a burglar of a home who sustains injuries by falling down a defective staircase. Assume further, for the purposes of discussion, that it is possible to conclude that the act of burglary was criminalised not only to protect the occupant's property but also to protect the occupant's well-being and peaceful enjoyment of their property.[38] It is nevertheless still not clear that allowing the claim by the burglar would create an inconsistency with the criminal law. It might perhaps be argued that the occupant's loss of well-being is exacerbated by the need to pay damages to the trespassing burglar; however, it would be difficult to argue convincingly that one of the reasons for the enactment of a burglary offence was to prevent this outcome. Likewise, taking an example from a different area of criminal law, it would be difficult to argue that part of the purpose of a statutory offence of possession of drugs with intent to supply is to prevent a claimant injured in a motor vehicle accident from recovering compensation where the vehicle was being used to carry the drugs (as occurred in *Delaney v Pickett*).[39] There will be exceptions: for example, there was considerable policy background to the enactment of the squatting (criminal trespass) offence considered in *R (on the application of Best) v The Chief Land Registrar* that could be called upon in the decision whether a person should be denied a claim for adverse possession when periods of the occupancy constituted this offence.[40] Presumably, if the claimant was seeking an award of damages for injuries sustained during the period of squatting due to a hidden defect in the property[41] this policy context would assist in determining whether part of the purpose of the statute was to prevent a claim of this kind. However, generally the legislation will provide no guidance on whether it intends privative consequences beyond the imposition of criminal sanctions.

If the central question is identified as whether the law of negligence and the provisions of the statute proscribing the conduct can be given congruent operation,[42] there will not usually be a plausible argument for concluding that a lack of congruence does arise in respect of personal injury claims. This is because, as has been discussed, the negligence claim does not generally frustrate the objectives of the criminal statute (which one might generally assume to be proportional punishment and deterrence). Nevertheless, the majority in *Miller v Miller* considered that the case before it was one where recognition of a duty of care would be incompatible with the purpose of the provision against

[38] As hypothesised in Kit Barker et al in *The Law of Torts in Australia*, 5th edn (Oxford, Oxford University Press, 2012) 623.

[39] *Delaney v Pickett* [2011] EWCA Civ 1532, [2012] 1 WLR 2149.

[40] *R (on the application of Best) v The Chief Land Registrar* (n 4).

[41] Assuming that a duty of care and breach of duty could be established in such a situation, which is probably unlikely given that the owner is out of possession and control of the property.

[42] *ABN AMRO Bank NV v Bathurst Regional Council* (n 25) [717].

which the claimant offended (had the claimant not withdrawn from the criminal enterprise).

It is submitted that the Court's interpretation of the purpose of s 371A is strained and lacks an evidentiary basis. It can be accepted that one of the statutory purposes behind the enactment of the criminal offence was to render the driver liable to an aggravated offence of theft where he or she drives the vehicle recklessly. This recognises the heightened risk that a stolen vehicle will be driven with a lack of responsibility for the safety of the vehicle, its occupants and other road users. That heightened risk is not, however, limited to the situation where a passenger was complicit in the crime of taking and using the vehicle illegally. That same risk also arises where the driver stole the car on his or her own and is the sole occupant of the car. Although the risk might be greater where there are complicit passengers due to the possible added element of encouragement by the passengers for the driver to drive dangerously, an increased risk of dangerous driving applies whenever a vehicle is stolen. The risk is enhanced because the driver is more likely to drive the vehicle without reasonable care because of a lack of incentive to ensure the car is not damaged, for the thrill of flaunting the law, or sometimes in order to evade capture by the police.

Accordingly, the conclusion of the Court that the introduction of aggravated forms of the offence of unlawful use where the car is driven dangerously was directed to the situation where a group of confederates act with a common purpose to steal and use the car is questionable. That same statutory purpose could be said to apply to the situation where a lone thief drives the car dangerously. The majority does not refer to any extrinsic materials that suggest that the Western Australia legislature introduced the aggravated forms of the offence specifically to deal with the situation where two or more persons steal the car in concert; the concern of the legislature might well have been a more general concern to deter theft of cars as all thefts (whether or not jointly committed with others) carry an increased risk of reckless driving. Reliance on s 8(1) (the common purpose provision) does not assist in this respect. That provision was not enacted specifically to deal with the crime of unlawful use of a vehicle; it is a provision of general application to offences prescribed by the Criminal Code. Thus, a clear association would need to be demonstrated between the statutory purpose for enacting the offence and the commission of the offence *jointly* before it could be convincingly argued that one of the purposes was to prevent the ordinary duty of care. In that case there was no evidential foundation on which it could be concluded that part of the purpose of the legislation was that the normal duty to take care when driving did not apply.

In any event, even assuming that the offence of unlawfully taking and using a car was structured in the way that it was in order to deter and punish joint illegal use of a vehicle because of the special risk of reckless and dangerous driving in that situation, it could be argued that the only purpose was to prescribe a higher *criminal* penalty on the parties to the joint crime. It is noted in this respect that in illegal contracts and trusts cases where statutory purpose is the central consideration, the existence of a penalty in the statute is taken to provide an indication that the purpose of the statute is sufficiently met by it.[43]

The analysis of the Court on the points of statutory purpose and incongruity is, I suggest, an example of their Honours succumbing to what Lord Goff described as 'the temptation of elegance': the expression of a solution expressed so eloquently that it seems more credible than it actually is.[44] The reasoning in *Miller v Miller* on coherence has a certain 'neatness' about it and thus has a certain superficial attraction; nevertheless, it is proved on closer examination to be based on questionable reasoning.

It is in fact arguable that the Court decided the case by reference to its own conceptions of the public policy underlying the provisions, rather than on the basis of a purpose that inhered in the statute itself. The majority judgment at one point possibly adverts to the fact that this might be what it is doing.[45] In its subsequent decision in *Gnych v Polish Club Limited* the High Court has emphasised that the only policies that are relevant are those that can be discerned from the scope and purpose of the relevant statute.[46] Justice Gageler observed in that case that:

> It is not the function of the common law to seek to improve on a regulatory scheme by supplementing the statutory sanctions for its breach. If a statute itself does not operate to deny legal operation to an agreement made in breach of one of its prohibitions, or to render that agreement unenforceable by reason of that breach, the coherence of the law is best served by a court respecting and enforcing that legislative choice.[47]

While these comments were made in the context of statutory illegality in contract law, the same sentiments apply to negligence claims. A court that attempts to supplement a statutory scheme by reference to what it considers to be the public policies underlying it will not only be engaging in illegitimate judicial activism; it will also be disrupting the coherence of the law.

For the preceding reasons, a consideration of the purposes of the legislation is unlikely in most cases to shed meaningful light on whether the claim for compensation for personal injury should be permitted. The same can be said of claims for property damage suffered as a result of illegality. An example of such a case might be where the claimant seeks compensation for damage to a vehicle used to

[43] *Yango Pastoral Co Pty Ltd v First Chicago Australia Ltd* (n 3) 428–29 (Mason J), 432–3 (Jacobs J); *Nelson v Nelson* (n 3) 570 (Deane and Gummow JJ), 613–14 (McHugh J); *R (on the application of Best) v The Chief Land Registrar* (n 4) [108] (Arden LJ).

[44] *Henderson v Merrett Syndicates Ltd* [1994] UKHL 5, [1995] AC 145, 186.

[45] *Miller v Miller* (n 1) [102]. The High Court there refers to an argument that the common law might find as a matter of some overarching public policy that a contract is unenforceable even though not expressly or impliedly prohibited by statute. For a recent discussion of the idea that the common law might decide an issue of statutory illegality by reference to public policy, such as the policy that a person should not benefit from their illegal act, see *Gnych v Polish Club Limited* (n 3) [70]–[76] (Gageler J). However, it is not clear whether the majority (in *Gnych*) endorsed this approach, as it emphasises that the question is always one of statutory purpose: at [35] (French CJ, Kiefel, Keane and Nettle JJ).

[46] *Gnych v Polish Club Limited* (n 3) [35].

[47] ibid [73]. Note that Gageler J does take the view that a decision whether the contract is enforceable might be made by reference to common law public policy in some cases.

flee the scene of a crime where the negligence of another driver contributed to the accident. The statutory rules proscribing the relevant crime (for example, theft or burglary) are unlikely to provide meaningful guidance as to whether that property damage should be recoverable from that other driver.

The position might be different in respect of claims for financial loss, particularly those incurred as a result of unlawful conduct contravening a comprehensive regulatory scheme (for example, an insider trading scheme).[48] This is because the policy underlying that scheme, and whether it would be undermined if compensation was awarded, is likely to be expressed more clearly in the terms of the legislation (express or inferred) and extrinsic materials. For example, *Patel v Mirza* concerned a claim of unjust enrichment for recovery of a sum of money paid to the defendant pursuant to an agreement to invest it in shares based on insider information, where that information never eventuated and the money never invested.[49] One of the reasons Gloster LJ in the Court of Appeal gives for permitting recovery was that, as the actual investments made in accordance with the inside information were not made illegal by the governing legislation, there was no reason to believe that it was part of the purpose of the legislation that the antecedent agreement should be struck down as unenforceable and the money paid under it irrecoverable.[50] In fact, it was arguable that to deny the claim would directly conflict with the legislation.[51]

This same reasoning (that the legislation will be sufficiently comprehensive to derive a statutory purpose) cannot, however, be applied to all claims for financial loss. For example, an appeal to the purpose of the statutory offence of obtaining property by deception arguably would not assist in determining whether the liquidators of a company should have a successful claim against an auditor that negligently failed to detect fraud by the director of the company that resulted in a judgment debt against the company.[52]

Moreover, the more remote the connection between the claimant's illegal act and the negligence that resulted in the loss, the less likely it is that the statutory scheme will provide guidance on the question whether the ordinary duty of care was owed.[53] In *ABN AMRO Bank NV v Bathurst Regional Council* the claimant—the purchaser and on-seller of a financial product—commenced proceedings against the credit rating agency (CRA) that rated the product alleging (inter alia) that the CRA had been negligent in providing a good rating. The CRA defended the claim on the basis that the claimant's conduct in on-selling the financial products was in contravention of s 912A of the Corporations Act 2001 (Cth) because the claimant's financial services licence did not permit it to provide financial advice

[48] This is assuming that there is a violation of a right of the claimant where the subject of the claim is pure economic loss.

[49] *Patel v Mirza* CA (n 5).

[50] ibid [69].

[51] ibid.

[52] The facts of *Stone & Rolls Ltd (in Liq) v Moore Stephens (a firm)* [2009] UKHL 39 [2009] AC 1391.

[53] The same principle also applies to claims for physical injury: see the discussion of *Matthews v McCullock of Australia Pty Ltd* [1973] 2 NSWLR 331 in Barker et al (n 38) 622.

and deal in the relevant financial products. The CRA argued that in that circumstance recognition of a duty of care to the claimant would create an incongruity in the law. The Full Court of the Federal Court held that there was no incongruity in the CRA owing the claimant a duty of care as the claimant's conduct in *buying* the notes (the conduct with which the negligence was connected) was not illegal; the illegal conduct was dealing and advising in relation to the notes.[54] Accordingly, the statute did not impact on whether a duty of care arose.

Therefore, with the possible exception of conduct that is the subject of detailed regulation—as to which, see further the discussion of sanction-shifting claims below—it will generally be difficult to make a persuasive case that it is part of the purpose of the statute to deny a civil claim. This is not of itself a problem; the suggestion is not that claims such as those in *ABN AMRO Bank NV v Bathurst Regional Council should* be denied. Rather, the point is simply being made that the statutory purpose explanation is likely to be less helpful in resolving the outcome of a particular case than might be thought following *Miller v Miller*.

B. Appeals to Statutory Purpose can Involve Unarticulated Value and Policy Judgements

A civil claim should be denied only where there is a clear incompatibility between the recognition of a duty of care and the purpose of the legislation proscribing the conduct. However, as discussed in the previous section, an insuperable difficulty with the statutory purpose test is that the legislation will rarely evince a clear intention about the civil consequences that should flow from a breach of its provisions. Other commentators have pointed out that unless the statute in question contains explicit reference to civil liability, an appeal to statutory purpose ultimately involves a value judgment or policy choice as to whether the claim should be permitted:[55] 'It attempts to conceal an instrument of judicial policy in the guise of discerning a legislative intent'.[56] Where the legislature has expressed no intention on the matter, there is a risk that the relevant legislative intention will be 'conjured up by judges to give effect to their own ideas of policy and then "imputed" to the legislature'.[57] This concern was expressed in the context of breach of statutory duty claims, but applies equally to the current context. In commentary on *Miller v Miller* the Chief Justice of Canada, Beverley McLachlin, has highlighted this concern, and clearly views it as a significant drawback of the statutory purpose explanation.[58]

[54] *ABN AMRO Bank NV v Bathurst Regional Council* (n 25) [34]–[36] (the Court).

[55] Barker et al (n 38) 622.

[56] N Thompson, 'The Rights of Parties to Illegal Transactions' (Sydney, Federation Press, 1991) 30; see also 29. See also Prentice (n 30) 90.

[57] *Sovar v Henry Lane Pty Ltd* (1967) 116 CLR 397, 405 (Kitto J) (discussing the breach of statutory duty action).

[58] McLachlin, 'Weaving the Law's Seamless Web' (n 35) 217.

In the context of discussing a claim under a trust, McInnes recognises that often the question whether the parliament intended the forfeiture of a claim will be in genuine doubt. He states: 'In such circumstances, the desirability of achieving what a judge perceives to be the "right" result on the facts of a particular case may well (consciously or subconsciously) colour his or her perception of the proper interpretation of a statutory scheme'.[59] McInnes goes on to point out that, when that occurs, there might well be little substantive difference between the now discredited public conscience test and the statutory purpose explanation. This is because 'Under either test, resolution of the issue will turn largely on the judge's assessment of whether or not, in all the circumstances, it would be appropriate to allow recovery'.[60] It could be argued, consistently with these criticisms, that the invocation of statutory purpose in *Miller v Miller* in fact concealed unarticulated public policy concerns that the consequences of a criminal act would be borne by other citizens via compulsory insurance rather than by the criminal him or herself.[61]

In seeking to identify statutory purpose, a court should not give effect to its own ideas as to the policies underlying the law. In *Miller v Miller*, their Honours appear to adopt the view that a duty of care should not be recognised where it would be contrary to the underlying policies or purposes of the statute even where those policies or purposes are not expressly or necessarily implied by the terms of the statute. The majority was here analogising with that category of illegal contract where the statute does not expressly or impliedly prohibit a contract, but it is nonetheless found to be unenforceable because of the 'policy of the law'.[62] A court should, however, be cautious about inferring policy or purpose where this is not clearly to be derived from the text, structure and context of the Act. When seeking to ascertain the purpose of a statute, the courts should confine themselves to applying ordinary rules of statutory construction that seek to discern the purpose of the statute where the statute itself is silent on the question.[63] In *Lacey v Attorney-General (Qld)* the High Court identified the objective of the process of statutory construction:

> The application of the rules will properly involve the identification of a statutory purpose, which may appear from an express statement in the relevant statute, by inference from its terms and by appropriate reference to extrinsic materials. The purpose of a statute is not something which exists outside the statute. It resides in its text and structure, albeit it may be identified by reference to common law and statutory rules of construction.[64]

[59] McInnes (n 32) 16.

[60] ibid.

[61] This was a concern expressed by Heydon J in the course of argument: Transcript of Proceedings, *Miller v Miller*, High Court of Australia [2010] HCATrans No P25, 4 November 2010, [2840]–[2890].

[62] *Nelson v Nelson* (n 3) 552 (Deane and Gummow JJ); *Equuscorp Pty Ltd v Haxton* (n 3) [23] (French CJ, Crennan and Kiefel JJ). McInnes points out that this approach evokes historical approaches where the courts made decisions based on the spirit, rather than the letter, of the law: McInnes (n 32) 16.

[63] *Yango Pastoral Co Pty Ltd v First Chicago Australia Ltd* (n 3) 413 (Gibbs ACJ), 423 (Mason J).

[64] *Lacey v Attorney-General (Qld)* [2011] HCA 10, (2011) 242 CLR 573 [44].

As this suggests, statutory purpose does not arise independently of the statute. The purpose must be ascertained from the terms of the statute, either expressly or by inference, or from parliamentary materials. A court that gives effect to its own ideas of the policies underlying the statute exceeds its proper judicial function and engages in legislative policy. As Lush J said in *Mills v Baitis* when commenting on *Henwood v Municipal Tramways Trust*, the proper approach to determining if a statute prevents a claim that is connected to an illegality is that 'It is not for the Court to make legislative decrees as to what public policy requires'.[65] Unless there is a clear incompatibility with statutory purpose, the function of the court in the negligence claim is to apply the principles of negligence law to the relationship of the parties to determine what the consequences of the conduct proscribed by the legislation should be.[66]

In summary of the points so far, a major weakness of the statutory purpose explanation is that consideration of the purpose of the statute prohibiting the conduct is unlikely to provide guidance as to whether the statute was intended to have privative consequences beyond criminalising the conduct. The risk is that courts will not closely analyse the statute with reference to supporting extrinsic material to determine if it was clearly part of the purpose of the statute to deny the claim, but will in effect decide the case by reference to what it infers to be the underlying policies of the legislation. James Goudkamp has pointed out that the apparent effortlessness with which the majority in *Miller v Miller* identified that the statutory purpose of the governing offence precluded the recognition of a duty of care could encourage lower courts to take a relaxed approach to determining this issue.[67]

Moreover, in respect of the joint illegality cases in particular, there is a real risk that subsequent courts will not subject the reasoning in *Miller v Miller* to close analysis. The majority emphasised what it saw as an incongruity in recognising a duty of care when the claimant was complicit in the offence of dangerous driving. The risk is that subsequent courts will deny the claim wherever the claimant is found to have been complicit in the act that resulted in the harm to the claimant, without fully analysing the legislative purposes in enacting the relevant offence to determine if recognition of a duty of care would be incompatible with one of those purposes. For example, it has been held that *Miller v Miller* stands for the proposition that it is the 'fact of the complicity in the offence that deprives each party of the benefit of a duty of care'.[68] Thus, despite assertions by the majority in *Miller v Miller* that the effect of the decision was to place joint illegality claims on precisely the same basis as claims arising from a unilateral illegality, the majority's approach does suggest that it will be easier to discern a statutory purpose to deny

[65] *Mills v Baitis* [1968] VR 583, 594.

[66] Weinrib, 'Illegality as a Tort Defence' (n 30) 31.

[67] Goudkamp, 'The Illegality Defence in the Law of Negligence after Miller v Miller' (n 30) 131.

[68] *Quine v Keerasawat* [2014] WADC 150. While this might be explicable on the basis that the court in *Quine* was dealing with the same legislative scheme as in *Miller v Miller*, there was no reference at all to statutory purpose as the governing criterion.

the claim where the parties were jointly engaged in a criminal enterprise. Accordingly, this decision does not necessarily allay the concerns of academic commentators that the rejection of claims arising from joint illegal ventures (but not claims arising from unilateral illegality) is unfair because it confers on the guilty defendant an unjustified advantage over an innocent defendant.[69]

C. Focus on Statutory Purpose Distracts the Court from a Relational Analysis of Duty of Care

The majority in *Miller v Miller* emphasises that it is an analysis of the statute and its purposes that will determine whether a defendant owes a duty of care to a claimant who was in breach of that statute at the time of being injured. However, a single-minded focus on statutory purpose can obscure the proper role of the court. That proper role is not to defer to elusive notions of statutory policy but rather, in the words of Weinrib, 'to determine the relevance of legislative enactments for the application of policies which have been judicially created'.[70] In deciding the case before it, the majority in *Miller v Miller* directed its attention almost exclusively to an analysis of statutory purpose, and in doing so failed to address the fundamental question whether the relationship of the parties gave rise to a liability in negligence on general principles. It simply assumed that a liability would arise if not otherwise prevented by statute.

The Court should have explicitly considered whether the illegal relationship of the parties sufficiently altered that relationship so that it was unreasonable for the claimant to expect that the defendant would exercise reasonable care. I will demonstrate in Chapter 10 that the authorities establish that no duty of care will arise where the nature of the relationship was such that the claimant could not expect the normal standard of care to apply. The proposition that a duty of care might not arise on this basis was endorsed in *Miller v Miller* itself,[71] yet the majority did not address this point. It simply assumed that dangerous driving was a 'probable consequence' of the prosecution of the common purpose to unlawfully take and use the vehicle. There should have been detailed consideration of whether dangerous driving was in fact such a consequence of the agreement to illegally use the car in light of disagreement in the courts below as to the risks involved in the trip.[72] Only Heydon J discusses these issues, but then only in the context of whether there

[69] See, for example, WJ Ford, Tort and Illegality: The *Ex Turpi Causa Defence* in Negligence Law (Part Two) (1977) 11 *Melbourne University Law Review* 164, 176; J Goudkamp, 'The Defence of Joint Illegal Enterprise' (2010) 34 *Melbourne University Law Review* 425, 436.

[70] Weinrib, 'Illegality as a Tort Defence' (n 30) 1.

[71] *Miller v Miller* (n 1) [63]–[64], [108].

[72] The trial judge focused on the purpose of the trip as being transportation home, which (in her view) did not necessarily mean the vehicle would be driven carelessly, whereas the Court of Appeal focused on the risks that were significant and foreseeable from being a passenger in a stolen vehicle. See ch 10, text to nn 153–156.

was a valid withdrawal from the joint enterprise.[73] The Court's blinkered focus on statutory purpose obscured what should have been the most important relational considerations affecting liability, thus undermining corrective justice.

V. Evaluation of the Statutory Purpose Explanation: Sanction-shifting Claims and Claims for Illegal Profits and Earnings

In this section I will discuss the application of the statutory purpose explanation to sanction-shifting claims and claims for illegal profits and earnings. It will be recalled that a sanction-shifting claim involves a claim for compensation for a sanction imposed by the criminal law. A claim of this kind should be defeated where it is the clear purpose of the statute that prescribed the sanction to impose liability for that sanction personally on the claimant and to prevent the claimant deflecting that sanction onto another person whose negligence resulted in its imposition. Again, it will only be in limited situations where such a clear statutory purpose can be inferred from the legislation.

However, there will be cases where it can legitimately be concluded that it was part of the purpose of the statute to prevent the deflection of the penalty. For example, where there is a detailed statutory framework in place that reflects a policy choice to impose criminal or civil penalties on the claimant for infringement of its provisions regardless of fault, an inconsistency in the law would arise if the claimant could recover that penalty from the third party responsible for the infringement. This is the best explanation of the result in *Safeway Stores Ltd v Twigger*.[74] A penalty was imposed on Safeway Stores for unlawful price-fixing conduct engaged in by individual directors and employees in contravention of the Competition Act 1998 (UK). Safeway commenced proceedings in breach of contract, breach of fiduciary duty and negligence against the individuals responsible for the infringement for the amount of the penalty. In the Court of Appeal Pill LJ recognised that it was the purpose of the statutory regime to impose the penalty on the corporation itself rather than on its individual agents as this was the most effective means of achieving deterrence of anti-competitive behaviour.[75] To permit the corporation to recover the penalty from its agents would stultify that statutory purpose.[76] Lord Sumption in *Bilta* endorsed this explanation of *Twigger*.

[73] *Miller v Miller* (n 1) [122]–[124].
[74] *Safeway Stores Ltd v Twigger* (n 5).
[75] ibid [43]–[46].
[76] The same result would apply to a penalty imposed on a corporation under the Competition and Consumer Act 2010 (Cth). There are detailed provisions in in this legislation that determine when a penalty should be imposed on a corporation for the conduct of its agents and employees: see, eg, s 84 of the Act. To allow negligence law to be harnessed to shift responsibility for that penalty onto those individuals would create an incoherence with the statutory code.

His Lordship explained that the Act attributed responsibility for the penalty to the corporation personally, not to those individuals responsible for the infringement, and that to allow the penalty to be recovered from those individuals would create an inconsistency with the statutory scheme.[77] Lord Sumption thereby recognises that where the statute evinces a purpose to impose the penalty on the corporation itself, rather than personally on the individuals who engaged in the anti-competitive behaviour, allowing the corporation to pass its liability onto those individuals through a negligence action would frustrate the carefully designed allocation of responsibilities under the statutory scheme. The negligence claim must be rejected in these circumstances in order to preserve the coherence of the statutory scheme attributing responsibility for the contravention.[78]

Thus, a comprehensive regime that governs the claimant's liability to a penalty might by implication exclude a cause of action based on the negligence that seeks to deflect that penalty.[79] It should be noted, though, that the converse might also be true, and that the legislation might explicitly or implicitly recognise that a cause of action based on negligence is permissible.[80] Ultimately, the legislation must determine the claimant's entitlements. Further, it will only be in the case of detailed statutory schemes that it will usually be possible to identify a clear statutory purpose that liability is to be imposed personally on the claimant and is not to be shifted onto a defendant whose negligence caused to the contravention. In most cases, there will not be such a clear legislative intent, and hence the statutory purpose test will be of limited utility as an explanation why sanction-shifting claims should be rejected. Consider the example of a burglar who is caught and fined because of the negligence of his accomplice.[81] It is not clear that one of the purposes of the statute that criminalises burglary (which would generally be construed as the protection of property, and perhaps peace of mind of property owners)[82] would be undermined if a claim against the negligent accomplice for the amount of the fine was permitted. Rather, it is best to view such claims as impermissible because the fine has been ordered by a criminal court and hence the loss of assets representing the amount of the fine is not one that the law will recognise. This explanation of the sanction-shifting cases (the no loss or damage explanation) is the subject of Chapter 8.

[77] *Bilta (UK) Ltd (in liquidation) v Nazir (No 2)* (n 6) [83]. Lord Neuberger in *Bilta* indicated that he would take 'a great deal of persuading' that the decision in *Twigger* was wrong, but he did not explain his reasons for this: at [31].

[78] Weinrib, *Corrective Justice* (n 10) 75.

[79] This same principle applies to claims in unjust enrichment for overpaid taxes, where the taxing legislation provides a detailed regime for recovery: *Commonwealth of Australia v SCI Operations Pty Ltd* [1998] HCA 20, (1998) 192 CLR 285.

[80] See the interpretation of the former s 251M(1) of the Income Tax Assessment Act 1936 (Cth) in *Markham v Lunt* (1984) 84 ATC 4010; *Pech v Tilgals* (1994) 94 ATC 4206; and *Carmody v Priestley & Morris Perth Pty Ltd* [2005] WASC 120.

[81] This is an example given in Weinrib, 'Illegality as a Tort Defence' (n 30) 51.

[82] Barker et al (n 38) 623.

There is a further issue to be addressed; namely, what should be the effect of the application of the statutory purpose rule where it applies to sanction-shifting claims. In *Miller v Miller* it was held that statutory purpose will, in appropriate cases, prevent a duty of care from arising. However, what effect will it have in the sanction-shifting cases: will it operate to negate a requirement of establishing the claim, or as a defence? My view is that the statutory purpose explanation has the former effect. In essence, when a claim is denied on the ground that a comprehensive statutory regime precludes a claim, the real basis for this conclusion is that the statute has ascribed responsibility for that penalty personally to the claimant and hence, while the amount of the penalty is a factual loss, it is not loss or damage that the law will recognise. Accordingly, it is in fact simply a particular manifestation of the no loss or damage explanation developed in Chapter 8. This approach to the statutory purpose explanation has the advantage that the onus of proof will be the same as for the no loss or damage explanation; that is, the onus will be placed on the claimant to prove a loss of something in which the claimant has a legally recognised interest. It would be unsatisfactory and confusing if illegality doctrine was used as a defence for some claims, but as a basis for negating a requirement of the claim in other cases.

The same analysis applies to claims for illegal profits or earnings. A claim for illegal profits or earnings should be rejected where it is one of the purposes of the statute that renders the conduct unlawful to prevent a claim for income derived from the illegal activity. The problem is that, as Lush J recognised in *Mills v Baitis*, in most cases the statute will provide no indication as to whether it intended to prevent a claim in negligence for the profits or earnings that resulted (or would have resulted) from the illegal conduct.[83]

VI. Statutory Purpose Explanation is Arguably Better Adapted to Other Areas of Private Law Illegality

The statutory purpose explanation is a product of the High Court's recent emphasis on legal coherence. One of the justifications given by the High Court in *Miller v Miller* for the adoption of the statutory purpose explanation was that to achieve legal coherence there must be congruence between the illegality principles applied in the areas of contract and trusts and the principles applied in relation to the tort of negligence.[84] The Court recognised that a statutory purpose test applies in contract and trust law; that is, a claim under a contract or trust unenforceable for illegality will be denied where it would be incompatible with the purpose of the

[83] See, eg, *Mills v Baitis* (n 63).
[84] *Miller v Miller* (n 1) [15].

governing legislation.[85] In order to achieve legal coherence, the Court considered that the same test must be applied in the law of negligence.

In a decision subsequent to *Miller v Miller*, *Equuscorp Pty Ltd v Haxton*, the Court was required to consider a claim for restitution of benefits received under a contract unenforceable for illegality.[86] In a joint judgment, French CJ, Crennan and Kiefel JJ restated the view from *Miller v Miller* that 'the central policy consideration at stake is the coherence of the law'.[87] Their Honours cited with approval the test posed by Peter Birks: 'Would allowing that [restitutionary] cause of action to be maintained make nonsense of the refusal to enforce the contract?'[88] A claim for restitution should be denied where this would frustrate, defeat or be inconsistent with the purpose of the statute that renders the contract unenforceable.[89] A relevant consideration will be that the statutory purpose is protective of the class of persons from whom the claimant seeks recovery.[90] Gummow and Bell JJ wrote a concurring judgment in which they expressed similar views.[91]

The willingness of the Court in *Miller v Miller* to draw on concepts and approaches from other areas of private law is commendable. The different branches of the law of obligations should not be viewed as 'silos' that are incapable of providing guidance on the resolution of claims in other branches.[92] A further reason for welcoming the confluence of approach in contract and negligence claims is that it will remove any potential advantage in bringing a claim in negligence as an alternative to a breach of contract action where the claimant claims for losses sustained as a result of a negligent breach of an illegal contract.[93] Where a concurrent cause of action lies, it is the purpose of the statute that will determine the success of the claim, regardless of whether it is commenced in negligence or for breach of contract.

It is outside the scope of this book to assess the efficacy of the statutory purpose test as a vehicle for resolving claims brought under an illegal contract or trust. An appeal to statutory purpose in this context is amenable to the same criticism identified above: namely, that often the legislature will not have considered

[85] ibid [24]–[27]. The contract and tort cases referred to include *Yango Pastoral Co Pty Ltd v First Chicago Australia Ltd* (n 3), *Fitzgerald v FJ Leonhardt Pty Ltd* [1997] HCA 17, (1997) 189 CLR 215 and *Nelson v Nelson* (n 3).

[86] *Equuscorp Pty Ltd v Haxton* (n 3).

[87] ibid [23].

[88] P Birks, 'Recovering Value Transferred under an Illegal Contract' (2000) 1 *Theoretical Inquiries in Law* 155, 203, cited in *Equuscorp Pty Ltd v Haxton* (n 3) at [37].

[89] *Equuscorp Pty Ltd v Haxton* ibid [38].

[90] ibid [45].

[91] ibid [103]–[104], [111].

[92] See generally J Dietrich, 'What is "Lawyering"? The Challenge of Taxonomy' (2006) 55(3) *Cambridge Law Journal* 549.

[93] A relevant scenario might involve a claim for losses sustained under an illegal contract to engage in insider trading where the negligence of one of the parties has the result that the illegal benefits expected from the insider trading activities are not obtained. While the benefits expected under the illegal contract might not be recoverable on the negligence claim, the claim might include an amount representing the loss of opportunity of investing the money elsewhere.

at all whether a claim should be permitted and therefore any attempt to draw an inference of legislative intent will be highly speculative.[94] An approach based on statutory purpose is, however, perhaps better adapted to the areas of contract and trust than negligence law. This is for two reasons. First, in the area of contract in particular, it will generally be easier to discern a legislative purpose from the reasons why the contract is rendered unenforceable as to whether the defendant was to be protected from a claim. Second, permitting a restitutionary claim under an unenforceable contract can amount to an indirect enforcement of the illegal contract. Applying these two points to *Equuscorp* itself, French CJ, Crennan and Kiefel JJ held that 'The policy was obvious enough. It was to protect members of the public by requiring prior disclosure of information relevant to their investment decisions'.[95] In addition, recognition of a restitutionary claim would have permitted the lender to recover amounts advanced under illegal loan contracts, thus 'mimicking' the enforcement of the loan. The lender 'would have been able to recover by such claims what the statute denied it in respect of the loan agreements';[96] that is, it would have enabled the claimants to recover the benefit they expected from the illegal contract.

However, the only 'obvious' legislative policy in enacting criminal legislation will generally be to criminalise the conduct so as to pursue the goals of the criminal law; any 'underlying' policy beyond that is not likely to be evident from the statute. In addition, a claim for damages in negligence provides compensation to the claimant for their injuries;[97] it does not permit the claimant to obtain the benefit of the wrongdoing, and hence such a claim is less likely to undermine or stultify statutory purpose than a restitutionary claim under an illegal contract (or trust) that seeks to indirectly enforce that contract.

Accordingly, the approach appropriate in other private law contexts is not necessarily one that translates well into—or at least that has a broad practical application in—the law of negligence.

VII. Conclusion

That statutory purpose explanation reflects principles of corrective justice and is justified on the ground of legal coherence. Nevertheless, it will only be in exceptional cases that it will provide a legitimate justification for refusing compensation based on the claimant's illegal conduct. An award of compensation should be denied only where it would clearly be incompatible with the purpose of the statute

[94] McInnes (n 32) 15.
[95] *Equuscorp Pty Ltd v Haxton* (n 3) [22].
[96] ibid [45] (French CJ, Crennan and Kiefel JJ).
[97] *Hall v Hebert* [1993] 2 SCR 159, 172 (McLachlin J, La Forest, L'Heureux-Dubé and Iacobucci JJ agreeing); *Hunter Area Health Service v Presland* [2005] NSWCA 33, (2005) 63 NSWLR 22, 40 [94] (Spigelman CJ).

against which the claimant has offended, but a clear incompatibility will usually be difficult to demonstrate. The weakness of the statutory purpose explanation as a general criterion for resolving these claims is summed up by Robert Prentice:

> In short, the legislative intent approach is appropriate only in the exceedingly rare case where legislative intent clearly establishes that the legislature in passing a statute meant not only to regulate or criminalize conduct but also to deprive violators of their right to recover for injuries inflicted by others. In the remaining cases, the legislative intent approach is ineffectual if not disingenuous.[98]

As this demonstrates, in most cases the court is left to grope around for a basis to infer legislative intent, ultimately applying policy and value judgments to determine the case in a manner that is inconsistent with principled reasoning of corrective justice. Rather than relying on questionable reasoning from statutory policy, the correct approach in the joint illegality cases is to examine the substance of the parties' relationship to ascertain whether the claimant could reasonably expect the defendant to adhere to the normal standard of care. I will return to this argument in Chapter 10. In the next two chapters I will address the second ground on which a claim might be rejected for reasons of legal coherence: the no loss or damage explanation.

[98] Prentice (n 30) 90.

8

No Loss or Damage: Sanction-shifting and Related Claims

I. Introduction

This chapter focuses on the second of the two grounds where a claim for compensation for harm connected to an illegal act should be rejected for reasons of legal coherence. This is where the damage or loss needed to found the claim is not recognised in the law because the area of law proscribing the conduct has mandated that it is damage or loss that the plaintiff must suffer. To put it another way, the argument is that there are certain factual losses incurred or types of damage suffered by the claimant that the law will not recognise because when the principles of the area of law that the claimant has violated are examined, they reveal that the claimant 'is asserting a loss of something to which [the claimant] is not entitled'.[1] My arguments seek to consolidate and develop the insightful principles advanced by Allan Beever in *Rediscovering the Law of Negligence*.[2]

The focus of this chapter will be on claims where the plaintiff is seeking to recover damages for the consequences of the commission of an illegal act. A claim to recover compensation for a sanction imposed by the law (a sanction-shifting claim) is the paradigm case, although the same issues can arise in respect of other heads of loss that do not represent the imposition of a legal sanction (the 'related' claims). I will argue that there are two categories of loss or damage causally related to the commission of an illegal act that the law will not recognise. They are loss or damage that amount to: (i) a pecuniary penalty imposed on the claimant by the criminal or regulatory law; and (ii) non-pecuniary losses resulting from detention. These 'losses' are imposed on the claimant directly through the application of the legal process, and as such they are not losses 'in law'. However, I argue that other losses that are not directly required by the law, such as loss of earning capacity, should be recoverable in full.

[1] B McLachlin, 'Weaving the Law's Seamless Web: Reflections on the Illegality Defence in Tort Law' in A Dyson, J Goudkamp and F Wilmot-Smith (eds), *Defences in Torts* (Oxford, Hart Publishing, 2015) 221.

[2] A Beever, *Rediscovering the Law of Negligence* (Oxford, Hart Publishing, 2007) 379–83.

Analogous issues also arise in respect of claims for illegal profits and earnings, which are discussed in Chapter 9. I will argue there that these claims should be rejected where the legal process would (notionally) apply so as to forfeit those profits or earnings.

II. Background

One of the main contexts in which the claimant's illegality is raised as a bar to the claim is where the defendant's negligence caused or failed to prevent illegal conduct by the claimant, who seeks compensation for losses sustained as a result. Claims of this nature include sanction-shifting claims, where damages are sought for the cost of legal sanctions imposed for the illegal conduct. However, they also include related claims for losses that result from the commission of the illegal act more broadly, and are not the result of the imposition of a sanction. The challenges posed by claims of both kinds are illustrated by the following cases:

— The claimant is a passenger in a train that collides with another train due to the negligence of the defendant rail authority. The claimant suffers only minor physical injuries, but suffers significant psychiatric injury in the form of post-traumatic stress disorder. While under the effects of this disorder, he stabs a man to death. The prosecution accepts a plea to manslaughter on the ground of diminished responsibility and the claimant is ordered to be detained in a psychiatric hospital. The claimant commences proceedings against the defendant for damages representing the consequences of the conviction and detention, namely: (i) loss of earning capacity during and after the period of detention; and (ii) injury to reputation from the conviction. The claimant also claims other losses arising from the crime (but not the conviction and detention), namely: (iii) an indemnity against claims made by the dependents of the deceased man; and (iv) non-pecuniary losses resulting from feelings of guilt and remorse. The House of Lords holds that the claimant is prevented by his own illegality from recovering any of these losses. (*Gray v Thames Trains Ltd* (*Gray*).)[3]

— The claimant, a drug addict and petty criminal, commences proceedings against the defendant prison authority for sexual assaults committed by a prison officer when he was 18 years old. The assaults exacerbated his drug use and subsequent criminal conduct and led to further periods of incarceration. The claimant commences proceedings against the defendant prison authority for damages for loss of earnings during the periods spent in prison subsequent to the assaults. The Supreme Court of Canada rejects the claim. (*British Columbia v Zastowny* (*Zastowny*).)[4]

[3] *Gray* [2009] UKHL33, [2009] 1 AC 1339 (HL).

[4] *Zastowny* [2008] SCC 4, [2008] 1 SCR 27.

— The claimant is seriously injured in a workplace accident caused by the negligence of the defendant employer. He resorts to selling marijuana to support his family when workers' compensation payments are cut off. The claimant is convicted of drug offences and sentenced to a term of imprisonment. He claims damages for future loss of earning capacity. The Court of Appeal of New South Wales by majority (Samuels JA, Handley JA; Kirby P dissenting) holds that the award of loss of earning capacity must be reduced by the amount of the loss that is attributable to the claimant's conviction and imprisonment. (*State Rail Authority of New South Wales v Wiegold* (*Wiegold*).)[5]

There are two distinct approaches taken in the case law to claims of this nature. The first of these is the 'consistency rule' that prevents recovery of compensation for the consequences of a criminal sanction.[6] The second is a broad rule of public policy that prevents recovery of compensation for all losses of which the claimant's illegal act was the 'real' or 'effective' cause.[7] This second 'causation' approach, cannot be justified on the grounds of legal coherence and introduces a doctrinal and theoretical incoherence into the law of negligence. It was rejected in Chapter 5.[8] In this chapter my focus is on the first approach—the consistency rule—which has been justified by the need to preserve the coherence of the legal system. I will argue that the consistency rule does in principle reflect the principle of coherence. I will further argue, however, that the consistency rule is unsatisfactory in its current iteration because it is limited in its application to offences that have a fault element; that is, that involve culpability.

III. The Consistency Rule

A. Overview of the Consistency Rule

I will keep this overview of the consistency rule relatively brief as the development of these principles has been the subject of detailed exposition by James Goudkamp in a series of articles.[9]

[5] *Wiegold* (1991) 25 NSWLR 500 (NSWCA).

[6] ibid; *Zastowny* (n 4); *Gray* (n 3).

[7] *Hunter Area Health Service v Presland* [2005] NSWCA 33, (2005) 63 NSWLR 22 (NSWCA); *Gray* ibid.

[8] Ch 5, section IV, The Causation Test.

[9] See in particular J Goudkamp, 'Can Tort Law be used to Deflect the Impact of Criminal Sanctions? The Role of the Illegality Defence' (2006) 14 *Torts Law Journal* 20; J Goudkamp, 'Self-defence and Illegality under the Civil Liability Act 2002 (NSW)' (2009)18 *Torts Law Journal* 61; J Goudkamp, 'The Defence of Illegality: *Gray v Thames Trains Ltd*' (2009) 17 *Torts Law Journal* 205. Note that Goudkamp has pointed out that a convincing rationale has yet to be articulated for the consistency rule: J Goudkamp, 'A Long, Hard Look at Gray v Thames Trains Ltd' in PS Davies and J Pita (eds), *Jurisprudence of Lord Hoffmann: A Festschrift in Honour of Lord Leonard Hoffmann* (London, Bloomsbury Publishing, 2015) 51–55.

The consistency rule is justified by the courts on the ground it is needed to preserve the coherence of the law. The central argument is that as it is the penal policy of the law that causes the damage it would be inconsistent for the law to require the claimant to be compensated for that damage.[10] There appears to be nearly universal support for a principle that prevents tort law from stultifying a criminal sanction by compensating the offender for the losses flowing from that sanction.[11] The consistency rule has been adopted by courts in Australia,[12] the United Kingdom,[13] Canada[14] and the United States.[15] The rationale given for the consistency rule is that it is required to ensure consistency between the criminal law and tort law. Justice Samuels in *Wiegold*, in a passage approved by the House of Lords in *Gray*,[16] described the rationale for the rule in these terms:

> If the claimant has been convicted and sentenced for a crime, it means that the criminal law has taken him to be responsible for his actions and has imposed an appropriate penalty. He or she should therefore bear the consequences of the punishment, both direct and indirect. If the law of negligence were to say, in effect, that the offender was not responsible for his actions and should be compensated by the tortfeasor, it would set the determination of the criminal court at nought. It would generate the sort of clash between civil and criminal law that is apt to bring the law into disrepute.[17]

In *Gray* Lord Hoffmann provided a similar justification for the consistency rule:

> [Y]ou cannot recover for damage which flows from loss of liberty, a fine or other punishment lawfully imposed upon you in consequence of your own unlawful act. In such a case it is the law which, as a matter of penal policy, causes the damage and it would be inconsistent for the law to require you to be compensated for that damage.[18]

The reasoning in *Gray* was adopted by the English Court of Appeal in *Safeway Stores Ltd v Twigger* to prevent the claimant corporation claiming an indemnity against liability for an infringement of competition legislation from the directors and employees who were responsible for the infringement.[19] In the course of denying the claim, Longmore LJ (Pill and Lloyd LLJ agreeing) described the rationale for the consistency rule in the following terms:

> The rationale of the maxim is the need for the criminal courts and the civil courts to speak with a consistent voice. It would be inconsistent for a claimant to be criminally and

[10] *Gray* (n 3) [29].

[11] Lord Sumption has described this principle as 'obvious': Lord Sumption, 'Reflections on the Law of Illegality' [2012] *Restitution Law Review* 1, 7.

[12] *Wiegold* (n 5).

[13] *Gray* (n 3); *Clunis v Camden and Islington Health Authority* [1998] QB 978 (CA); *Worrall v British Railways Board* [1999] EWCA Civ 1312.

[14] *Hall v Hebert* [1993] 2 SCR 159; *Zastowny* (n 4).

[15] The cases are collected in Ronen Perry, 'The Role of Retributive Justice in the Common Law of Torts: A Descriptive Theory' (2006) *Tennessee Law Review* 177, 215–16. See also the cases discussed in Goudkamp, 'Can Tort Law be used to Deflect the Impact of Criminal Sanctions?' (n 9) 35–36.

[16] *Gray* (n 3) [40] (Lord Hoffmann), [67] (Lord Rodger).

[17] *Wiegold* (n 5) 514 (Handley JA agreeing).

[18] *Gray* (n 3) [29].

[19] *Safeway Stores Ltd v Twigger* [2010] EWCA Civ 1472, [2011] 2 All ER 841.

personally liable (or liable to pay penalties to a regulator such as the OFT) but for the same claimant to say to a civil court that he is not personally answerable for that conduct.[20]

The consistency rule has also been adopted in Canada. In *Hall v Hebert*, McLachlin J held that damages should not be awarded in a civil claim where this would permit an evasion or rebate of a penalty prescribed by the criminal law. Justice McLachlin, who was adopting the views of Weinrib in his 1976 article 'Illegality as a Tort Defence',[21] held that to permit recovery in that situation 'would amount to the law giving with one hand what it takes away with the other'.[22] For the courts to punish the conduct but at the same time 'reward' it would 'create an intolerable fissure in the law's conceptually seamless web'.[23] These views were followed by the Supreme Court of Canada in *Zastowny* to deny compensation for loss of earning capacity resulting from incarcerations for criminal conduct.[24] The Court there held that an award of lost earning capacity would constitute an evasion or partial rebate of a penalty prescribed by the criminal law and that this would 'introduce an inconsistency in the fabric of the law'.[25]

The consistency rule has been applied to pecuniary penalties,[26] and to compensation for loss of earning capacity during a period of incarceration.[27] It has also been applied more broadly to deny compensation for all losses that were caused by the claimant's criminal conviction and detention.[28] Thus, in *Gray*, the consistency rule was applied to deny the claimant recovery for loss of earning capacity after the arrest, non-pecuniary losses resulting from his detention in a psychiatric hospital, and injury to reputation from the conviction.[29] This was because, although the claimant was found to have diminished responsibility, he still did have some responsibility for his crime. Therefore, an inconsistency would arise if he were to be compensated for his loss arising from the imposition of a criminal sentence for a crime for which the criminal law found he was responsible.[30] Lord Brown explained the justification for the consistency rule as being that 'The law cannot at one and the same time incarcerate someone for his criminality and compensate him civilly for the financial consequences'.[31]

There is scant authority on sanction-shifting claims in Australia. The main authority is *State Rail Authority of New South Wales v Wiegold*, where a majority of the New South Wales Court of Appeal held that an award of compensation for loss

[20] ibid [16].
[21] EJ Weinrib, 'Illegality as a Tort Defence' (1976) 26 *University of Toronto Law Journal* 28.
[22] *Hall v Hebert* (n 14) 178; see also 169.
[23] ibid 176, 178.
[24] *Zastowny* (n 4).
[25] ibid [22] (Rothstein J for the Court).
[26] *Colburn v Patmore* (1834) 149 ER 999; *Safeway Stores Ltd v Twigger* (n 19).
[27] *Zastowny* (n 4).
[28] *Gray* (n 3). See also *Wiegold* (n 5).
[29] *Gray* (n 3) [50] (Lord Hoffmann, Lords Phillip and Lord Scott agreeing), [82] (Lord Rodger), [101]–[102] (Lord Brown).
[30] ibid [50] (Lord Hoffmann).
[31] ibid [93].

of earning capacity resulting from injuries negligently inflicted by the defendant could not include the loss of earning capacity that was the result of the claimant's conviction and detention for growing marijuana.[32] The majority reached this conclusion on the ground of legal causation, holding that it was not appropriate (as a matter of public policy) to extend the liability of the defendant to the consequences of the claimant's criminal act.[33] Thus, the main Australian authority supports the consistency rule, albeit viewed it as a question of legal (scope of liability) causation. There have been Australian cases where taxpayers have been successful in recovering the amount of a fine or other penalty payable for which the taxpayer became liable as a result of the negligence of a tax accountant.[34] However, the sanction-shifting aspect of the claim was not raised in argument, and further, the tax legislation at the time recognised a statutory cause of action to recover these amounts, which was thought to be indicative of a statutory policy that such penalties were to be borne by the defaulting tax agent.[35] The tax penalty provisions in the income tax legislation have since been substantially amended,[36] thus those cases are perhaps best confined to the particular taxation regime that was in place at the time.

The High Court of Australia has not specifically addressed sanction-shifting claims. However, in *Miller v Miller* the Court stated that the central policy consideration at stake where the claimant claims damages resulting from his or her illegal conduct is legal coherence.[37] Their Honours referred to the judgment of McLachlin J in *Hall v Hebert* with apparent approval.[38] Accordingly, it seems likely that the Court would adopt the consistency rule should a suitable case arise. In the next section, I will therefore turn to examine whether there is a convincing rationale for the consistency rule. I will conclude that there is no convincing rationale for the consistency rule *in its current formulation*, which is linked to the need to ensure that the civil claim does not undermine the finding by a criminal court of criminal responsibility. I then turn to formulate an alternative explanation why certain categories of loss or damage should be irrecoverable.

B. Is there a Convincing Rationale for a Consistency Rule Tied to the Claimant's Culpability?

The usual rationale put forward for the consistency rule is that an award of compensation for the consequences of a criminal act should not be made where the

[32] *Wiegold* (n 5).
[33] ibid 511–16 (Samuels JA; Handley JA agreeing).
[34] *Markham* v *Lunt* (1984) 84 ATC 4010; *Pech v Tilgals* (1994) 94 ATC 4206; *Carmody v Priestley & Morris Perth Pty Ltd* [2005] WASC 120.
[35] See the discussion of the former s 251M(1) of the Income Tax Assessment Act 1936 (Cth) in *Markham* v *Lunt* ibid 4017 (Pidgeon J).
[36] CCH *Tax Agents Manual: Commentary*, 'Client issues' [9080] 'Penalty Safe Harbours' (accessed 18 August 2014).
[37] *Miller v Miller* [2011] HCA 9, (2011) 242 CLR 446 [15].
[38] ibid.

criminal courts have found that the claimant was criminally responsible for that act.[39] The rule is one of public[40] or judicial[41] policy invoked where the claimant 'retain[s] a degree of moral and legal responsibility for the commission of the offence'.[42] The argument is that a finding of civil responsibility on the part of the defendant would undermine a finding of criminal responsibility on the part of the claimant by the criminal courts. The courts are not clear about precisely why an award of compensation would create an inconsistency with a finding of criminal responsibility. Academic commentators have suggested that the relevant concern is that a successful claim would undermine principles of autonomy and free will that provide the justification for criminal punishments.[43] Lorne Neudorf, in the course of commenting on *Zastowny*, articulates this as the underlying policy concern:

> [S]hifting sanctions is tantamount to passing criminal blameworthiness from the offender to others, which would attack the law's view of individual autonomy and personal responsibility and ultimately erode the justification for criminal law and the imposition of punishment.[44]

There is a strong argument that there is no conflict between a finding of criminal responsibility of the claimant for the illegal conduct and a finding of civil responsibility of the defendant for the harm resulting from that conduct. This argument is based on the divergent operation of principles of responsibility in the two areas of law. Principles of criminal responsibility are developed for the purposes of determining whether the claimant should be punished and the form that punishment should take. They are designed to draw a 'clear dividing line' between conduct for which the offender is criminally responsible and conduct for which no responsibility should be attributed.[45] However, principles of responsibility in tort law perform the different function of attempting to strike a fair balance between the conflicting rights and interests of the parties by providing a normative framework for compensation.[46] Any differences between the operation of principles of

[39] *Wiegold* (n 5) 514 (Samuels JA; Handley JA agreeing); *Clunis and Islington Health Authority* (n 13) 990; *Zastowny* (n 4) [30] (Rothstein J for the Court); *Gray* (n 3) [69] (Lord Rodger), [93] (Lord Brown). In *Gray* Lords Phillips, Rodger and Brown expressly reserved judgment on whether the rule would apply where no, or limited, criminal responsibility is found: at [15] (Lords Phillips), [83] (Lord Rodger), [103] (Lord Brown).

[40] *Gray* (n 3) [7] (Lord Phillips), [24], [29] (Lord Hoffmann).

[41] *Zastowny* (n 4) [23], [30] (Rothstein J for the Court); *H.L. v Attorney General of Canada* [2005] SCR 401, [143] (Fish J).

[42] *Clunis and Islington Health Authority* (n 13) 990 (Beldam LJ for the court).

[43] See Goudkamp, 'Can Tort law be used to Deflect the Impact of Criminal Sanctions?' (n 9) 40–43. Though in a more recent article Goudkamp discusses two potential rationales for the consistency rule—goal consistency and pronoucement consistency—but does not find either rationale to be a convincing justification for the consistency rule: James Goudkamp, 'A Long, Hard Look at Gray v Thames Trains Ltd' (n 9) 51–4.

[44] Lorne Neudorf, 'Case Comment on British Columbia v Zastowny: Shifting Sanctions and Personal Responsibility' (2010) 73 *Saskatchewan Law Review* 131, 132.

[45] *Corr v IBC Vehicles Ltd* [2008] UKHL 13, [2008] AC 884 [16] (Lord Bingham).

[46] *cf Ashley v Chief Constable of Sussex Police* [2008] UKHL 25, [2008] AC 962 [18] (Lord Scott), [76] (Lord Carswell).

responsibility in criminal law and tort law simply (as Beever has said) 'reflect the focus of the former on the defendant's wrongdoing and the latter on the connection between that wrongdoing and the claimant's injuries'.[47] The different purposes of the two areas of law not only justify, but *require*, different conditions of responsibility.[48]

Accordingly, an incoherence in the law will not arise *merely because* a claimant was found by a criminal court to be criminally responsible for the conduct that gave rise to the harm, and yet on a civil claim was able to successfully establish that the defendant was, wholly or partly, responsible for the harm that results. The Court of Appeal in *Gray* recognised that the fact that the claimant was found to retain some criminal responsibility for the killing did not mean that he should automatically be assumed solely responsible for the harm that resulted from that act for the purpose of negligence law.[49] The principles of criminal responsibility (such as the *M'Naughten* test of insanity) are too 'blunt an instrument' to be useful in negligence law as a means of allocating responsibility for harm between the parties.[50] In negligence, the fact that the claimant is criminally responsible for the conduct that was the most direct and immediate cause of the harm does not automatically sever the causal responsibility of the defendant and deem the claimant's conduct to be the sole cause of the harm.[51] Negligence law recognises that *both* the claimant and defendant might have causally contributed to the harm, and deals with the respective causal contributions of the parties through the mechanism of contributory negligence.[52]

What emerges from this discussion is that, due to the divergent functions of principles of responsibility in tort law and criminal law, no actual incoherence (conflict) arises between them where compensation is awarded for the consequences of the conduct *merely because* of the finding that the claimant was criminally responsible for that conduct. The finding of criminal responsibility does not negate the civil responsibility of the defendant for the harm—mediated primarily through the mechanism of causation—and hence, does not as such affect the legal relationship of the parties to the interaction that resulted in the harm. Courts should thus resist 'the temptation … to import a meretricious symmetry'[53] between the principles of responsibility in tort and criminal law.

[47] A Beever, 'The Structure of Aggravated and Exemplary Damages' (2003) 23 *Oxford Journal of Legal Studies* 87, 109.

[48] *cf* RA Duff, 'Torts, Crimes and Vindication: Whose Wrong Is It?' in M Dyson (ed), *Unravelling Tort and Crime* (Cambridge, Cambridge University Press, 2014) 147.

[49] *Gray* [2008] EWCA Civ 713, (2009) 1 AC 1339 (*Gray* CA).

[50] ibid [48] (the Court), citing *Corr v IBC Vehicles Ltd* (n 45) (Lord Bingham).

[51] That is, it does not amount to a *novus actus interveniens*. In *Gray* both the Court of Appeal and the House of Lords acted on the basis that the crime of manslaughter did not amount to an intervening act that severed the chain of causation between the negligence and the harm: *Gray* CA ibid [39]–[46] (the Court); *Gray* (n 3) [28]–[29], [45]–[46] (Lord Hoffmann); see also Lord Brown at [94]–[98].

[52] See, eg, *Reeves v Commissioners of Police for the Metropolis* [1999] UKHL 35, [2000] 1 AC 360.

[53] *Attorney General (NSW) v Perpetual Trustee Co Ltd* [1952] HCA 2, (1952) 85 CLR 237, 285 (Kitto J).

Accordingly, if sanction-shifting claims are to be denied, it should not be on the basis of a consistency rule that seeks to reinforce principles of criminal responsibility and punishments imposed by the criminal law. Rather, the claim should be defeated only where negligence law and the area of law proscribing the conduct intersect with the result that the loss or damage suffered is not one that the law will recognise. I will develop this point in the next section. The no loss or damage explanation admittedly will give rise to many of the same outcomes as the consistency rule in individual cases. Nevertheless, due to the different focal points of these two approaches (the former on the intersection of principles of tort and crime; the latter on criminal responsibility) there will be divergent outcomes in some cases, as will be demonstrated.

IV. A Corrective Justice Perspective

A. Introduction

In the previous section I set out my objections to the consistency rule. Hence, it is initially disconcerting to realise that Weinrib advocated for this rule in 'Illegality as a Tort Defence'. Weinrib there argues that a claimant should not be permitted to use tort law to stultify or undermine a criminal sanction. Weinrib explained his reasoning as follows:

> Criminal law provides a mechanism whereby punishment is consequential upon the authoritative ascription of criminal responsibility. The effect of the private action, however, is to deflect the punishment on to other shoulders while leaving the ascription of responsibility in place. The approach of *Colburn v Patmore* [where the court denied a claim by the claimant for an indemnity for a criminal fine] was to prevent this fissure by denying that the punishment could be dissociated from the person adjudged responsible.[54]

Weinrib gives the example of two burglars who break into a house, and burglar A negligently fails to deactivate the alarm system, resulting in both burglars being captured, convicted and sentenced to pay a fine. Weinrib argues that burglar B has no claim in negligence against burglar A to recover the amount of the fine. Burglar B has violated the criminal law and 'conviction and sentencing by a criminal court is the law's method of ascribing to burglar B the responsibility for his action'.[55] Accordingly, burglar B should not be 'able to utilize tort law's mechanism of shifting losses in order to avoid the very consequences which criminal law has imposed upon him for his intentionally culpable conduct'.[56] On initial consideration this

[54] Weinrib, 'Illegality as a Tort Defence' (n 21) 53.
[55] ibid.
[56] ibid 51.

appears to contradict Weinrib's later works on corrective justice. The central thesis of corrective justice is that the focus must be on the relationship and interactions of the parties to the dispute to the exclusion of concerns external to that relationship, such as whether the claim would undermine the goals of the criminal law.[57] Why, when consideration of other external policy concerns is impermissible, is it permissible to promote a goal of ensuring that criminal punishments are not undermined? In *The Idea of Private Law*, Weinrib refers to his earlier article and gives no indication that he resiles from the views expressed there,[58] suggesting that he sees no contradiction in his position. However, he is yet to provide a detailed explanation of the relationship between corrective justice and illegality doctrine. To reconcile his approach to illegality doctrine with his corrective justice model of tort law, it is necessary to have regard to Beever's enlightening discussion of this area in *Rediscovering the Law of Negligence*.[59]

B. Overview of the No Loss or Damage Explanation

Beever agrees with Weinrib that a doctrine of illegality is needed in order to maintain the integrity of the legal system, rejecting the suggestion that the doctrine is based on public policy considerations in contradiction of corrective justice theory.[60] Beever provides two distinct though related propositions as to why some claims must be defeated by reason that they are connected to an illegal act of the claimant. Both propositions are based on the principle of coherence, and the recognition that loss or damage cannot be claimed where the criminal or regulatory law has mandated that loss or damage. The first proposition is that there can be no violation of a right where the law has authorised that violation (the no violation of a right proposition). The second proposition is that a head of loss will have no legal value where the law has authorised that loss (the no legal value proposition). (I have referred to both propositions compendiously throughout the book as the 'no loss or damage explanation.') As I will explain in this section, both propositions have an application to the kinds of claims currently under consideration, although it is the second of these which will have the broader application (and hence, the broader appeal).

i. Proposition One: No Violation of a Right (No Damage)

The first rationale advanced by Beever for a doctrine of illegality is that there can be no violation of a right where the law has authorised that violation. Beever

[57] Weinrib, 'Punishment and Disgorgement as Contract Remedies' (2003) 78 *Chicago-Kent Law Review* 55; Weinrib, *Corrective Justice* (Oxford University Press, 2012) 97, 171.

[58] Ernest J Weinrib, *The Idea of Private Law*, (Cambridge Mass., Harvard University Press, 1995)169 fn 53.

[59] Beever, *Rediscovering the Law of Negligence* (n 2), 379–83.

[60] ibid 381.

argues that this is the basis for denying relief in the sanction-shifting claims. To illustrate this approach he gives a similar example to Weinrib's burglar scenario:

> Imagine that the claimant is a 'professional' burglar who hires the defendant as a lookout man. However, due to the negligence of the defendant, the claimant is apprehended by the police, convicted and subjected to a fine or term of imprisonment.[61]

Beever argues that the fine is not recoverable because the loss of the assets representing the fine imposed by the criminal law 'is not a violation of the claimant's rights to those assets'.[62] While property law confers in the claimant a right as against the defendant to those assets, criminal law dictates the payment of the fine, and thus dictates that there is no violation of the property rights in respect of the amount of the fine.

Beever argues similarly that the hapless burglar cannot recover compensation for his jail term. Beever again justifies this conclusion on the basis that there is no violation of a right. In particular, there is no violation of the right to freedom of movement where the jailing is in accordance with the due application of the criminal process. In that circumstance, 'though the defendant created an unreasonable risk of loss to the claimant, the loss actually suffered by the claimant was suffered through no violation of the claimant's rights'.[63]

Support for approaching the sanction-shifting claims as instances where there is no violation of the relevant right because that violation was one that was authorised by the law might be derived from Weinrib's discussion of *Colburn v Patmore*[64] in 'Illegality as a Tort Defence'.[65] The claimant was a newspaper publisher who was convicted of criminal libel and sentenced to pay a fine. The claimant sought an indemnity from the defendant editor who was responsible for the publication of the libel. Weinrib argues that the Court was correct to deny the claimant a right to recover the fine because what was essential in the case was 'that the claimant has been duly convicted *and that that conviction forms the damage element of his tort*' (emphasis added).[66] Weinrib seems to be suggesting that because the imposition of the fine resulted from a conviction, there was no normative 'damage'. I will argue below that this approach operates so as to negate the threshold requirement of proof of damage that is legally recognisable (that is, negates 'gist damage').[67]

A conclusion that a claim should be rejected on the ground that there is no violation of a right is not, as Beever observes, an example of tort law deferring to the policies of the criminal law; rather, it is the outcome of the combined operation of the principles of the two domains.[68] When the requirements of the negligence

61 ibid.
62 ibid 383.
63 ibid.
64 *Colburn v Patmore* (n 26).
65 Weinrib, 'Illegality as a Tort Defence' (n 21) 51–52.
66 ibid 52.
67 See text to nn 78–85.
68 Beever, *Rediscovering the Law of Negligence* (n 2) 381.

claim are considered in conjunction with the principles of the criminal law, the resulting conclusion is that there is no infringement of the right. Moreover, this approach does not involve an appeal to external policy considerations;[69] it is not an example of policy 'trumping' corrective justice. Rather, it is (to quote Weinrib) the outcome of the operation of 'the whole ensemble of intertwined legal concepts and principles that governs [the parties] participation in the law's systematic nature.'[70]

This first proposition provides a convincing explanation for a subset of sanction-shifting cases, in particular the penalty cases. However, for reasons that I will discuss below, it is the second proposition (the no legal value proposition) that will have the broadest application to the typical sanction-shifting claim that reaches the court.

ii. Proposition Two: No Legal Value (No Loss)

The second rationale advanced by Beever for a doctrine of illegality is that the law does not recognise some factual losses as having a legal value. Beever explains this proposition as follows:

> The reason the claimant cannot recover when the defence of illegality applies is that the claimant must assert a loss of something to which she is not entitled in law. Hence, the claimant cannot succeed, because she cannot establish in law that she suffered loss. … [W]hen the defence of illegality applies, the claimant does possess a right held as against the defendant. Accordingly, even when the defence applies, the claimant's right is relevant to the relationship between the parties and the defendant did owe the claimant a duty of care. The reason the claimant cannot recover is not that she possessed no primary right, nor that the right was not violated by the defendant, but that *in law* the violation of the right had no *value*. In consequence, the defendant need not compensate the claimant because, in the eyes of the law and in the eyes of corrective justice, she suffered no loss.[71]

The no legal value proposition is distinct from the no violation of a right proposition. The argument is not that there is no violation of a right, but rather that when valuing the right that has been violated the law must disregard certain factual losses as not having a value in the law.[72] Beever explains that while corrective justice demands that the value of the claimant's loss be given by the defendant, corrective justice does not value the amount of that loss. To illustrate these principles, Beever gives an example of a situation where the defendant negligently causes the destruction of the claimant's heroin stash. Even though this amounts to a violation of the claimant's property rights in the heroin, and causes a factual loss, 'Because the possession of heroin is illegal, in the eyes of the law the loss of the heroin is no loss to the claimant'.[73] Thus, damages are awarded for the value of the right.

[69] ibid 383.
[70] Weinrib, *Corrective Justice* (n 57) 76.
[71] Beever, *Rediscovering the Law of Negligence* (n 2) 381–82.
[72] ibid 382–83.
[73] ibid 382.

However, no damages can be awarded if the law does not place a value on the right because of the operation of criminal law principles. Beever applies the same approach to claims for illegal earnings. A bank robber who is injured in a car accident cannot recover for loss of earning capacity as a result of being incapacitated from robbing banks as that loss is not one that has a legal value.[74]

Unlike the no violation of a right proposition which focuses on whether liability has been established, the no legal value proposition focuses on a specific head of claimed loss. It recognises that the loss claimed will not have a value in the law where the claimant is asserting a loss of something to which the claimant is not entitled by virtue of the operation of the area of law proscribing the conduct. Beever explains that the no legal value proposition will prevent claims for illegal profits and earnings, because the claimant has no legal entitlement to those profits or earnings, and hence in law the loss of them has no legal value. Beever does not discuss the application of this proposition to sanction-shifting claims; however, I submit that it does have an application to these claims as well. I will explain this further below.[75] For now it is sufficient to make the point that in extra-curial writings the Chief Justice of Canada, Beverley McLachlin, has endorsed Beever's no legal value proposition. Her Honour regards this proposition as providing the explanation why the illegality defence is applied both to claims for illegal profits and earnings and to sanction-shifting claims, stating that:

> In these two situations, the principles of the criminal law are relevant to the tort law analysis because they tell us that the claimant is asserting a loss of something to which she is not entitled. Since the criminal law holds that she has no legally recognised interest in the profit of her illegal conduct, she cannot therefore establish a loss in tort. Similarly, a claimant has no legally recognised interest in evading or lessening the penalty prescribed by the criminal law and, as such, cannot establish a loss in tort.[76]

Importantly, her Honour agrees with Beever that this analysis does not involve the criminal law or the principle of coherence overriding the claimant's corrective justice entitlements:

> [I]t is not that tort law's objective of providing redress for wrongs is made secondary to the goal of coherence, but rather that by a taking a coherent view of the different branches of the law it becomes clear that the law does not accord the violation of the claimant's right any legal value. In this way, respecting the principle of coherence leads to the interrelation of tort and criminal law, while maintaining the integrity of each. It does not disrupt the correlative relationship between the claimant and the defendant inherent in a corrective justice model of tort law.[77]

Thus, Beever's analysis is compatible with a corrective justice conception of tort liability. However, the great advantage of Beever's analysis is that it is equally

[74] ibid.
[75] See section V, Loss or Damage that is Irrecoverable.
[76] McLachlin, 'Weaving the Law's Seamless Web' (n 1) 221 (footnotes omitted).
[77] ibid 221–22.

compatible with conventional loss-based conceptions of tort liability. The no loss or damage explanation is thus likely to have broad appeal to jurists and theorists regardless of their views about the conceptual foundation of tort law. I will expand on these points now.

C. The No Loss or Damage Explanation is Compatible with a Loss-based Model of Negligence Law

In this section I will demonstrate that Beever's two propositions (which together make up the no loss or damage explanation) are consistent with the conventional view that the primary objective of tort law is to provide compensation for loss.

The no violation of a right proposition corresponds to the threshold requirement in negligence for the claimant to establish a legally recognisable form of damage.[78] It will be recalled[79] that Weinrib explained that the Court in *Colburn v Patmore* was correct to deny the claimant a right to recover a fine imposed for criminal libel because 'the claimant has been duly convicted and that … conviction forms the damage element of his tort'.[80] This is an apparent reference to the requirement of threshold damage in a negligence action, or what might be called 'gist damage'. This is a term coined by Jane Stapleton,[81] and refers to the well-established principle that damage is the 'gist' of a negligence action.

The requirement of gist damage is typically associated with a loss-based approach to negligence, but Donal Nolan explains that it is equally compatible with a rights-based theory of negligence law. Nolan argues that the requirement of damage in a negligence action is simply one element of the characterisation of the rights that are protected against negligent interference.[82] He explains that the rights protected by negligence are rights not to suffer damage of a particular kind and hence there cannot be a violation of a right without there being damage of that kind.[83] Importantly for the present context, Nolan further recognises that 'damage' is a normative concept and is not to be equated with a factual loss.[84] Other theorists writing outside of a rights framework have also taken this view.[85] Thus, applying Nolan's theory to the present context, the question is not simply whether the claimant has suffered a *factual detriment* but rather whether the law recognises the detriment as 'damage'. Where the damage is one that was mandated

[78] As to this threshold requirement see *Harriton v Stephens* [2006] HCA 15, (2006) 226 CLR 52. See also D Nolan, 'Damage in the English Law of Negligence' (2013) 4(3) *Journal of European Tort Law* 259, 263–64.

[79] See text to notes 64–67 above.

[80] Weinrib, 'Illegality as a Tort Defence' (n 21) 52.

[81] J Stapleton, 'The Gist of Negligence: Part 1' (1998) 104 *Law Quarterly Review* 213, 213.

[82] Nolan (n 78) 268.

[83] ibid.

[84] ibid 266–67.

[85] K Amirthalingham, 'The Changing Face of the Gist of Negligence' in Jason W Neyers, E Chamberlain and SGA Pitel (eds), *Emerging Issues in Tort Law* (Oxford, Hart Publishing, 2007) 483.

by the area of law proscribing the conduct (such as a statutory penalty) it is not, in law, damage. This analysis conforms to Weinrib's justification of the decision in *Colburn v Patmore* to reject the claim for damages for the fine: because the imposition of the fine resulted from a conviction, the plaintiff was unable to establish the 'damage' element of the claim. Hence, there is no violation of a right because no damage was suffered of a kind that the law will recognise.

The second (no legal value) proposition has an even stronger fit with conventional loss-based theories of tort law. Unlike the first proposition, the focus of the no legal value proposition is not on whether the cause of action is established, but rather on whether a particular head of loss is recoverable on an established cause of action.[86] Beever's argument in essence is that, where a claimant is asserting an interest in something to which there is no legal entitlement, while there is a factual loss, there is no loss to the claimant capable of valuation for the purposes of a damages award. Andrew Tettenborn (who is not a corrective justice theorist) similarly views 'loss' as being a normative, not a factual, concept.[87] Tettenborn has rejected the idea that a 'loss' is an 'objectively observable juridical phenomenon', instead preferring the view that, like questions of legal causation, a determination of whether a loss has been suffered involves normative and evaluative elements as well as factual ones.[88]

Accordingly, the concept that some factual losses or 'damage' are not recognisable in the law is one that is not unfamiliar to a loss-based model of tort law. There is case law in Australia supporting the view that loss or damage is a normative concept, and that there are some factual detriments that the law will not recognise.[89] Notably, the Supreme Court of the United Kingdom also appears amenable to an argument that a particular loss that is caused by a criminal act is not a loss that the law will recognise, and that hence the claim connected to illegal conduct must fail on that basis. In *Bilta (UK) Ltd (in liquidation) v Nazir (No 2)* (*Bilta*) the Supreme Court addressed an argument whether a corporation that was caused by its directors to be involved in a carousel VAT fraud leaving it with a large VAT liability and no means of paying it, had suffered a 'recognisable form of loss'.[90] I will discuss this aspect of the case further in Chapter 9;[91] the point for present purposes is that three members of the Court (Lord Sumption, Lord Toulson and Lord Hodge) accepted that it will be a valid issue in illegality claims whether the claimant has suffered a claimable loss.[92]

[86] Nolan explains that the distinction is 'between the damage necessary to establish a cause of action, and the harms in respect of which recovery is permitted once the cause of action has been established': Nolan (n 78) 262.

[87] A Tettenborn, 'What is a Loss?' in JW Neyers, E Chamberlain and SGA Pitel (eds), *Emerging Issues in Tort Law* (Oxford, Hart Publishing, 2007) ch 17.

[88] ibid 456–57.

[89] *Hunter Area Health Service v Presland* (n 7); *Mills v Baitis* [1968] VR 583.

[90] *Bilta (UK) Ltd (in liquidation) v Nazir (No 2)* [2015] UKSC 23, [2016] AC 1 [178] (Lord Toulson and Lord Hodge).

[91] See ch 9 text to nn 41–50.

[92] *Bilta* (n 90) [96] (Lord Sumption), [176]–[178] (Lord Toulson and Lord Hodge).

The appeal of the no loss or damage explanation to illegality claims and its application to a loss-based model of tort law is also apparent to commentators. Goudkamp is generally sceptical of the ability of corrective justice theory to explain illegality doctrine,[93] but accepts the explanatory power of a no loss or damage analysis for actions for interference with chattels.[94] In a paper co-written with Lorenz Mayr, Goudkamp argues that where a claimant has no entitlement to something as a matter of law, its loss will not be actionable on the basis either that gist damage or a particular head of loss cannot be established.[95] These authors have identified support for this approach in decisions of the German courts.[96]

Accordingly, the cogency of a no loss or damage explanation is not dependent on the acceptance of a rights-based conception of tort law or, for that matter, on a particular conception about the rights basis underlying tort law. This explanation reveals that, whatever one's views about the conceptual foundation of the law of torts, the principle of coherence demands denial of compensation to a wrongdoing plaintiff where the loss or damage is one that the law does not recognise.

It is sometimes argued (for example, in the context of wrongful life claims) that a decision that damage is not a legally recognisable form of damage is a decision of policy, made because the courts consider the claim unpalatable to the community.[97] Those commentators might direct the same accusation to the argument developed here that certain losses or damage that arise from illegal conduct are not recognisable in the law. That is, it might be argued that a decision that loss or damage is not actionable is in fact a policy choice, made because the law considers the claim by the criminal claimant distasteful. However, no reasoning of public policy is involved in the current context. This is because a conclusion that the loss or damage is not legally recognisable is one that is made by the application of the *principles* of tort and criminal law working in combination to establish that the loss or damage is one that is authorised by law, and that is therefore not actionable.[98] That is, this conclusion is justified by reference to the whole body of the law working as a whole—in particular tort law and criminal law working in tandem. It is a particular application of the relational policy of legal coherence, and does not involve an appeal to extra-relational policy choices,[99] whatever might be the case in other unrelated contexts. In the next section I will elaborate on the specific circumstances where tort law and criminal law principles combine so as to negate the element of loss or damage.

[93] J Goudkamp and J Murphy, 'Tort Statutes and Tort Theories' (2015) 131 *Law Quarterly Review* 133.

[94] J Goudkamp and L Mayr, 'The Doctrine of Illegality and Interference with Chattels' in A Dyson, J Goudkamp and F Wilmot-Smith (eds), *Defences in Torts* (Hart Publishing, Oxford, 2015) 236–37. The authors rely in part upon Beever's analysis as well as decisions of the German courts.

[95] ibid.

[96] ibid 236.

[97] M Beazley, 'Damage' in C Sappideen and P Vines (eds), *Fleming's The Law of Torts*, 10th edn (Sydney, Lawbook Co, 2011) 194, 225. See also C Witting, 'Tort Law, Policy and the High Court of Australia' (2007) 31 *Melbourne University Law Review* 569, 583–89.

[98] Beever, *Rediscovering the Law of Negligence* (n 2) 381.

[99] ibid.

V. Loss or Damage that is Irrecoverable

In this section I examine in detail the circumstances where the no loss or damage explanation will operate to prevent a claim connected to illegal conduct. I will demonstrate that there are two kinds of loss or damage that are irrecoverable on the ground that they are not recognisable under the law. They are: pecuniary penalties; and non-pecuniary losses arising from detention. I discuss these in turn below, and in doing so develop further my arguments regarding the no loss or damage explanation. In section VI, I will then explain that other forms of loss or damage, such as economic losses resulting from detention, should be recoverable.

A. Pecuniary Penalties

I have referred to the burglar example used by Beever and Weinrib to illustrate the point that legal fines are not actionable damage in a negligence claim. I agree with this conclusion, on the ground that there has been no violation of a right, as no gist damage has been established. This is because the combined operation of the criminal law and negligence law dictates that the claimant has not suffered *legally relevant* damage. The claimant has been required, through the application of the processes of the criminal (or statutory) law, to pay the fine, and hence the factual loss (the expenditure of money to pay the fine) was one that was authorised by the law. In that circumstance, it would create an incoherence in the law if that loss—which has been prescribed by the criminal law—was recoverable in negligence law. The application of illegality doctrine in this context respects the principles of both criminal and tort law.[100]

Beever's no violation of a right proposition provides a convincing explanation for a case such as the burglar example, where the only right on which the claimant relies is the right to the assets that represent the penalty. However, not all claims to recover a penalty will fall within that category. There will potentially be cases where a violation of a right (and thus gist damage) can be established, and the issue is whether the amount of a penalty that is causally linked to that rights violation is recoverable as a particular head of loss. This point can be illustrated by assuming that Mr Gray [in *Gray*] committed a minor assault while suffering the effects of post-traumatic stress disorder, and was fined by the criminal justice system. Assuming that the fine is causally linked to the initial violation of the right to bodily integrity, gist damage will be established. In that circumstance, the issue becomes (it is submitted) one of the valuation of the infringed right, rather than whether a right has been infringed. That is, it will be necessary to call upon Beever's no legal value proposition to resolve a claim of this kind. The rationale for denial

[100] McLachlin, 'Weaving the Law's Seamless Web' (n 1) 220.

of recovery of the fine in this hypothetical situation becomes that there is no loss that has a legal value. There is a violation of a right (the violation of the right to bodily integrity by the negligent operation of the train network); however, the loss of the assets representing the fine is not a loss on which the law will place a value. This is because it is a loss that the criminal law *demands* the claimant must suffer.

It is important to acknowledge at this point that Beever does not apply the no legal value proposition to sanction-shifting claims, preferring instead to analyse these cases exclusively as instances where there is no violation of a right. Beever would likely argue that the assault is an act that intervenes between the negligence and the loss (the penalty), and hence there is no causal link between them. I will return to these arguments below,[101] and will explain that that is not the basis on which the courts have acted. In any event, for present purposes it will be assumed that a causal link does exist between the initial rights violation and the penalty incurred. It is my contention that the no legal value proposition provides a plausible explanation as to why certain heads of sanction-shifting losses that are causally linked to a rights violation should be irrecoverable. The argument in effect is that, where it is the criminal law that has caused the loss through the operation of its penal function, there is no legally recognisable loss for the purposes of an award of damages. To award damages for a loss of this kind would create an incoherence in the law. This also appears to be the view of the Chief Justice of Canada. In her recent paper on the illegality defence in negligence law, McLachlin CJ relies upon Beever's no legal value proposition to argue that claims to recover damages for the amount of a penalty imposed by the criminal law should be rejected. Her Honour explains that 'a claimant has no legally recognised interest in evading or lessening the penalty prescribed by the criminal law and, as such, she cannot establish a loss in tort'.[102]

The principles expressed here can be easily accommodated within a loss-based model of negligence law. The law has ordered the claimant to forfeit a sum of money to the Crown. Accordingly, while there is a factual loss to the claimant in the sense of a subtraction from assets, it is not loss or damage that is recognisable by law as it came about through statutory authority. Thus, as discussed in the preceding section the validity of the no loss or damage explanation is not conditional upon acceptance of a corrective justice model of negligence law. This explanation is based upon the fundamental legal norm of coherence, and the need to respect the principles of both tort and criminal law.

I will return to the topic of pecuniary penalties in section VIII, where I will explain that these same principles apply even where liability to the penalty is strict. From the perspective of legal coherence it is the ascription of responsibility that is crucial, not whether there was fault or turpitude by the claimant. However, to summarise the main points so far, where the only right on which the claimant relies is the right to the assets that represent the penalty, the no violation of a right

[101] See text to nn 105–107 below.

[102] McLachlin, 'Weaving the Law's Seamless Web' (n 1) 221

proposition provides the rationale for refusing compensation for the amount of the penalty. However, where the penalty is causally linked to an earlier rights violation, the rationale for refusing compensation for the penalty is to be found in Beever's second proposition, the no legal value proposition. As I will explain next, it is the no legal value proposition that also provides the rationale for denying recovery of non-pecuniary losses arising from detention that are causally linked to an earlier rights violation.

B. Non-pecuniary Losses Resulting from Detention

In his article 'Illegality as a Tort Defence', Weinrib focused on the question of recovery of pecuniary penalties, with reference in particular to *Colburn v Patmore.*[103] However, the consistency rule has not been confined to pecuniary penalties; it has been applied also to prevent claims for non-pecuniary loss and loss of earning capacity resulting from the claimant's detention. It is not clear that Weinrib would agree that losses resulting from non-pecuniary forms of punishment, such as imprisonment, should automatically be irrecoverable by the application of the consistency rule; this is not something he explicitly discusses. However, Beever does discuss these claims, arguing that if the hypothetical burglar is imprisoned because of the negligence of his accomplice, he cannot recover compensation for his jail term. (It is not clear whether Beever is referring only to non-pecuniary losses or also to pecuniary losses arising from the jail term.) Beever justifies this conclusion on the basis of the no violation of a right proposition. In particular, his argument is that there is no violation of the right to freedom of movement where the jailing is in accordance with the due application of criminal process.[104]

This convinces as an explanation why a criminal should not be permitted to shift the consequences of his punishment on to a negligent accomplice. However, this analysis arguably does not provide an adequate explanation of whether there should be recovery in a typical case, of which *Gray*, *Wiegold* and *Zastowny* are exemplars, where there is a violation of the claimant's right to bodily integrity and the losses sought to be recovered were caused by the violation of that right. That is, the claim to damages is not based on the violation of the claimant's right to freedom of movement, but on the earlier violation of the claimant's right to bodily safety. Thus, while Beever's no violation of a right proposition explains the hypothetical scenario with which he was dealing, it arguably does not suffice as an explanation for the other kinds of sanction-shifting claims that have come before the courts.

In *Gray*, the defendants created an unreasonable risk of injury from a train crash, and thus violated the claimant's right to bodily safety. Further, the members

[103] *Colburn v Patmore* (n 26).
[104] Beever, *Rediscovering the Law of Negligence* (n 2) 383.

of the House of Lords (like the Court of Appeal below) acted on the basis that the manslaughter was not a *novus actus interveniens*.[105] Accordingly, the losses sought by the claimant relating to his conviction and detention for the crime were found to be causally connected to the defendant's negligence. This case (and others such as *Wiegold* and *Zastowny*) cannot be explained on the basis that there is *no* violation of the claimant's rights *at all*. Beever would likely argue that the courts in *Gray should* have found that the manslaughter was a *novus actus*, and that the claims for losses resulting from conviction and detention were irrecoverable for a lack of causation. I explained in Chapter 5 that the application of principled reasoning of corrective justice arguably would bring about this result.[106] However, the courts in *Gray* acted on the basis that there was no *novus actus* and, as I also explained in Chapter 5, the current legal principles governing intervening acts provides some support for this approach.[107]

Accordingly, if such claims are to be excluded another basis for doing so must be found. In respect of a claim for non-pecuniary losses resulting from detention, corrective justice theorists might argue that there has been no violation of a *relevant* right. To explain this, one might point to the explanation of the nature of general damages (non-pecuniary damages) provided by Robert Stevens. According to Stevens, an award of general damages substitutes for the violation of the right.[108] Where the right in question is the right to freedom of movement, general damages 'substitute for' the loss of that freedom. Where a claimant is sentenced to a term of imprisonment by a criminal court, the law authorises the loss of that freedom and hence (as Beever might argue) there is no violation of *that* right. Accordingly, it might be argued that it would be contrary to corrective justice principles to award general damages for the imprisonment, as general damages substitute for a right. The argument would be that, in this circumstance, the *relevant* right has not been violated.

However, there is a simpler explanation that does not depend on a technical analysis of rights violations. The non-pecuniary losses arising from the detention are causally linked to the violation of the right to bodily integrity. It seems that in that situation, there is a good argument for approaching the matter as one of the *valuation of the right to bodily integrity*. That is, to the extent that the losses claimed for the personal injuries sustained in the accident are non-pecuniary losses arising from detention, these losses do not have a legal value because the restriction on the freedom of movement (and hence the non-pecuniary losses flowing from the restriction) is authorised by the law. Putting it more simply, when the courts assess the value of the injury to the right to bodily integrity, it should disregard

[105] *Gray* CA (n 49) [39]–[46]; *Gray* (n 3) [28]–[29], [45]–[46] (Lord Hoffmann). See also Lord Brown at [94]–[98].

[106] See Ch 5, text to nn 184–187.

[107] See Ch 5, text to nn 177–83.

[108] R Stevens, *Torts and Rights* (Oxford, Oxford University Press, 2007) 60. This view appears to have been endorsed by Weinrib: Weinrib, *Corrective Justice* (n 57) 95.

non-pecuniary losses resulting from the detention because these were authorised by the law. This is a straightforward application of the no legal value proposition. This approach has the advantage of being able to be accommodated within both rights-based and loss-based conceptions of negligence law. From the latter perspective, the onus is on the claimant to establish that the head of loss that is being claimed has a value that the law will recognise. This will not be possible where the claimant is claiming damages for an interest (freedom of movement) to which the claimant was not legally entitled.

There is authority in the case law for this approach. The Australian case of *Hunter Area Health Service v Presland* (*Presland*) recognises that where the detention is authorised by law, the law will not place a value on the loss of freedom that results.[109] The court will not therefore award damages for non-pecuniary losses arising from a period of lawfully imposed detention. The claimant in *Presland* commenced proceedings against a psychiatric hospital for negligently discharging him where he was a risk to himself and to others, and where six hours after he was discharged he killed his brother's fiancée. The claimant was acquitted of the murder by reason of insanity, but was ordered pursuant to mental health legislation to be detained in a psychiatric hospital under a strict detention order. He claimed, inter alia, non-pecuniary damages for the deprivation of his liberty and for his mental anguish and sense of guilt and alienation from his family, and damages for loss of earnings during the period of incarceration. The majority of the Court of Appeal of New South Wales (Sheller and Santow JJA; Spigelman CJ dissenting) rejected the claim on a number of grounds, namely that a duty of care was not owed, that the defendant's scope of liability did not extend to preventing losses arising from the killing, and on the ground of public policy.

It is outside the scope of this book to discuss whether a hospital owes a duty of care to a mentally ill patient to exercise a statutory power under mental health legislation to compulsorily detain the patient. That question would need to be determined in light of the statutory powers of detention and the principles laid down in subsequent cases such as *Stuart v Kirkland-Veenstra*[110] and *Hunter and New England Local Health District v McKenna*.[111] The crucial issue will be whether a common law duty of care would be consistent with the mental health legislation providing the juridical framework for the relationship of the parties.[112]

[109] *Hunter Area Health Service v Presland* (n 7). *Contra Meah v McCreamer* [1985] 1 All ER 367 (QB). For potent criticisms of *Meah v McCreamer* see EK Banakas, 'Tort Damages and the Decline of Fault Liability: Plato Overruled, But Full Marks to Aristotle!' [1985] *Cambridge Law Journal* 195, 197.

[110] *Stuart v Kirkland-Veenstra* [2009] HCA 15, (2009) 237 CLR 215.

[111] *Hunter and New England Local Health District v McKenna* [2014] HCA 44, (2014) 253 CLR 270.

[112] ibid. For general academic commentary on the issues raised by cases such as *Presland* see I Freckelton, 'Liability of Psychiatrists for Failure to Certify: Presland v Hunter Area Health Service and Dr Nazarian [2003] NSWSC 754' (2003) 10(2) *Psychiatry, Psychology and Law* 397; K Peterson, 'Where is the Line to be Drawn? Medical Negligence and Insanity in Hunter Area Health Service v Presland' (2006) 28 *Sydney Law Review* 181; A Stickley, 'Tort Law' (2014) 34 *Qld Lawyer* 23; I Freckelton, 'Legal Liability for Psychiatrists' Decisions about Involuntary Inpatient Status for Mental Health Patients' (2014) 22 *Journal of Law and Medicine* 280; R Scott, 'Liability for Health Services for Not Involuntarily Detaining and Treating a Mentally Ill Person' (2015) 22(1) *Psychiatry, Psychology and the Law* 1.

What is relevant about *Presland* for present purposes is that all judges (including Spigelman CJ, who would have allowed recovery of the other losses) agreed that the claimant should not recover non-pecuniary damages for his loss of liberty during the period of remand, detention in a psychiatric hospital and conditional release. While the claimant was acquitted and held not criminally responsible for the murder, his remand, detention and conditional release were authorised by statute. Thus, in the course of his reasons for rejecting the claim, Sheller JA observes:

> [T]he detention and treatment of the claimant was that prescribed by law as the consequence of the unlawful killing of [the victim]. Yet, the damages here awarded are similar to those which would be awarded, as general damages, if the claimant had been unlawfully detained.[113]

In other words, the claimant cannot be compensated for a lawful detention as if it was unlawful; hence, the claimant cannot recover non-pecuniary losses resulting from the authorised restrictions on the claimant's liberty. Santow JA also recognised that such damages 'represent the lawful conduct of the authorities'.[114] Spigelman CJ, who would have allowed the claimant to recover other losses such as loss of earning capacity,[115] agreed with the other judges that an award of non-pecuniary damages should not be made for loss of liberty or for the traumatic experiences suffered by the claimant while detained and while on conditional release. His Honour observed that: 'All of these were matters which arose from the lawful conduct of the authorities'.[116]

Accordingly, all members of the Court in *Presland* emphasised that the non-pecuniary losses sought were for a loss of freedom that was lawfully authorised. I would extrapolate on that reasoning to conclude that, where a restriction on liberty was authorised by the law, non-pecuniary damages will not be recoverable for that loss of liberty because the law does not place a value on that loss. This is a straightforward application of the no legal value proposition. Moreover, this explanation is one that can be accommodated straightforwardly within a loss-based model of negligence law.

VI. Loss or Damage that is Recoverable

In the preceding section I argued that a claimant should be denied damages for a lawfully imposed pecuniary penalty or for non-pecuniary losses resulting from a lawfully imposed detention because in those two categories of claim the claimant is asserting a loss of something to which the law does not recognise an entitlement.

113 *Hunter Area Health Service v Presland* (n 7) [298].
114 ibid [383].
115 It should be noted, however, that only the award of non-pecuniary losses was being challenged: ibid [101].
116 ibid [100].

In this section, I argue that other losses that are causally related to the illegal conduct, but which do not directly result from a court order imposing a particular legal sanction on the claimant, should be recoverable in full. They are: claims for loss of earning capacity; and non-pecuniary losses for feelings of guilt and remorse and for injury to reputation. I will address these in turn, and will also say a few words at the end of this section about claims for an indemnity against civil liability.

A. Loss of Earning Capacity

I argued in the last section that non-pecuniary losses resulting from a period of authorised detention are irrecoverable. An award of non-pecuniary damages substitutes for the right—in this case the right to freedom; thus where the law authorises the loss of that freedom there is no violation of the relevant right. An alternative (and arguably more important) explanation was also given; namely, that the law does not place a value on those losses because the restriction on the freedom of movement (and hence the non-pecuniary losses flowing from the restriction) is authorised by the law.

A different analysis applies to damages for loss of earning capacity. Such damages do not *substitute* for a right; these are *consequential* on the violation of a right.[117] An award of damages for loss of earning capacity is the monetary measure of the worth of the use to which the claimant was putting, or was likely to put, his or her right to bodily integrity (that is, the past and future use of the right).[118] Accordingly, where, by the application of ordinary causation principles, the loss of earning capacity is consequential upon a violation of the claimant's right to bodily integrity that loss will be recoverable. The same result is reached when the alternative no legal value proposition is applied. Unlike an economic loss representing a fine, or non-pecuniary losses claimed for a loss of freedom, the loss of earning capacity is not the *direct subject of a court order* but only arises indirectly from that order. In other words, the loss of earning capacity does not directly arise from the imposition of an order for detention and (unlike a penalty or loss of freedom) is not *mandated* by the criminal court. Hence, the claimant is not seeking to assert a loss of something (earning capacity) to which the claimant is not entitled.

The same conclusion is possible on a loss-based view of negligence law. Damages for loss of earning capacity are merely consequential on a detention order, not an integral part of that order. They are therefore not authorised by the law in the same direct sense as an order to pay a penalty of a fixed amount, or an order for loss of liberty. I accept that this view will be controversial. Furthermore, I acknowledge the point made by Rothstein J (for the Court) in *Zastowny* that

[117] Stevens (n 108) 59, 75; Weinrib, *Corrective Justice* (n 57) 95–96.
[118] Weinrib, *Corrective Justice* ibid 52.

one of the 'natural consequences' of imprisonment is usually wage loss, as the claimant becomes unavailable to earn an income.[119] However, the wage loss is only the *consequential* result of the order of imprisonment; it is not the direct subject of the order. Whether there is a loss of earning capacity, and the extent of that loss, is purely fortuitous and will depend on the circumstances of the particular prisoner; some prisoners might not have had an ability to earn income before the imprisonment, and the extent to which they were utilising that capacity will vary from prisoner to prisoner. Accordingly, while the sentence of imprisonment directly imposes on the claimant the punishment of the loss of liberty (and thus the loss of liberty is directly authorised by the law), the sentence does not include a forfeiture of a certain amount of earnings to the Crown (contrast also an order for a pecuniary penalty). The economic loss representing loss of earning capacity is thus recognisable in law. On this view, the claimant is entitled to a full award of past and future earning capacity with no reduction made for the effects of the criminal punishment on the ability to earn income. In a case such as *Gray*, the result would be that the claimant could successfully recover the difference between his earning capacity at the time of the train collision and his earning capacity after his conviction and imprisonment.

To be clear, my argument is that the claimant should be permitted to recover for the *full* earning capacity that is lost because the claimant has been convicted and imprisoned for the crime. This includes the loss of ability to earn income during the period of detention. This is because the loss of income is *consequential* on the prison sentence, and is not the *direct subject* of the sentence. That is, the court order is that the claimant's liberty is to be restricted for a certain period of time, but not that the claimant must therefore forego $X in income during that time (contrast again statutory penalties). Loss of earning capacity following release from prison should also be paid in full, including loss that is causally connected to the conviction and detention. For example, the claimant should be able to recover for the fact that he or she can obtain only low-paid employment as a result of the conviction and jail term. This conclusion follows from the fact that, if the conviction and detention are not intervening acts—and authorities such as *Gray* would suggest that they are not—then these are events that are causally connected to the defendant's negligence and the loss of earning capacity that flows from them should be recoverable.

This approach (non-pecuniary losses irrecoverable; loss of earning capacity recoverable) corresponds with the result in the Court of Appeal in *Gray*. That Court held that non-pecuniary losses are 'inextricably bound up and linked with' the conviction and detention, but that loss of earning capacity is not so inextricably linked.[120] For the reasons given in Chapter 5, I do not support the 'inextricable link' test as a basis for applying illegality doctrine: that test does not respect the

[119] Zastowny (n 4) [22]; See also *Gray* [(n 5) [79] (Lord Rodger).
[120] *Gray* CA (n 49) [28] (the Court); see also [27].

bipolarity of negligence law, it is inherently subjective, and it appears to be based partly on policy considerations of whether the courts should appear to condone the criminal conduct.[121] Nevertheless, the Court of Appeal's approach is of value in highlighting that non-pecuniary losses are more integrally connected to the conviction and detention than pecuniary losses.

I have conceded that the conclusion that the convicted claimant should be permitted to recover loss of earning capacity in full will be controversial. The Supreme Court of Canada in *Zastowny* held that allowing recovery for loss of earning capacity would provide the claimant with a 'rebate' on the criminal punishment.[122] The Court (of which McLachlin CJ was a member) relied on a passage from *Hall v Hebert* that cites Weinrib's article.[123] However, I submit that reliance on Weinrib's article to support this argument was misplaced. Weinrib's focus in that article was on pecuniary penalties, to which the rebate argument would have considerable force. The effect of a successful cause of action would be to permit recovery of a loss of assets that the law has mandated. In that circumstance, 'the laws' condemnation of what is unlawful would be partial and inconsistent.[124] Likewise, it could be argued that to allow a claim for non-pecuniary losses resulting from detention would amount to a rebate. The law has mandated that the claimant must suffer the loss of amenity and mental suffering that is a concomitant of detention and thus, those losses are not something the claimant should be able to deflect, even if only in monetary terms. However, a claim for loss of earning capacity is different. This loss is not directly authorised by the law, thus no issue of a 'rebate' arises. The claimant serves his or her time in prison (and bears the responsibility for the resulting loss of amenity and mental suffering), but is entitled to recover for that part of his or her consequential financial losses for which the defendant is causally responsible. The claimant does not in that circumstance receive a rebate, or make a 'profit' from his illegal act; rather, as Spigelman CJ noted in *Presland*, 'Insofar as money can do so, he [the claimant] comes out square'.[125]

Compensation for loss of earning capacity is therefore not an evasion or rebate of the claimant's criminal punishment, because the criminal punishment is a term of confinement, and an award of loss of earning capacity resulting from negligently inflicted physical injuries does not (unlike an award of non-pecuniary damages) compensate for the confinement or seek to undo the time spent in confinement.[126] The claimant has served his or term of imprisonment, and should not be punished further by being denied recovery of the pecuniary losses resulting from the negligently inflicted injuries.[127] In *Wiegold*, Kirby P points out that the claimant is duly

[121] Ch 5, section III, The Inextricable Link (Sufficient Connection) Test.
[122] *Zastowny* (n 4).
[123] ibid [3], citing *Hall v Hebert* (n 14) 176.
[124] *Les Laboratoires Servier v Apotex Inc* [2012] EWCA Civ 593, [2013] RPC 21 [93] (Laws LJ).
[125] *Hunter Area Health Service v Presland* (n 7) [94] (Spigelman CJ).
[126] *X v M (RD)* [2004] BCSC 1273, [245] (Cohen J) (revd on appeal): *Zastowny* (n 4).
[127] K Roach, 'Blaming the Victim: Canadian Law, Causation and Residential Schools' (2014) 64 *University of Toronto Law Journal* 566, 582–83.

punished for the illegal conduct by serving the term of imprisonment, and that it is justifiable to take the view that he or she should not be 'punished twice by then being denied the economic consequences which otherwise flowed from the injuries done to [the claimant] by the negligence of the defendant'.[128]

In essence, then, my argument is that the principle of coherence requires a rule that damages cannot be recovered for the subject of the legal sanction itself, but does not require a rule that damages cannot be recovered for the indirect consequences of the sanction. The claimant's entitlement to an award of damages for loss of earning capacity for the period of detention and following should be assessed according to ordinary principles of causation, remoteness and contributory negligence. In this respect I agree with the stance of the Court of Appeal in *Gray* that, in respect of claims for loss of earning capacity, 'the ends of justice are … sufficiently served by the principles of foreseeability, causation and contributory negligence without the need for a further principle of public policy in such a case'.[129]

In conclusion on this point, I do not view a principle that would permit the claimant to recover his or her loss of earning capacity as stultifying the criminal law. The claimant is punished (and forced to suffer the mental consequences of that punishment) but to the extent the defendant is causally responsible for the financial losses suffered by the claimant, the defendant is required to pay.[130] This is an example of the separate spheres of operation of the two areas of law (ie, tort and criminal law each fulfilling their divergent functions).

B. Other Non-pecuniary Damages

General damages for feelings of guilt and remorse for the killing and for injury to reputation—at least to the extent that the latter are attributable to commission of the crime rather than the conviction and detention—are straightforward. These are not causally related to the legal sanction, and as such are not attempts to evade or lessen the sanction. Lord Hoffmann in *Gray* recognised that the consistency rule had no application to these losses, but nonetheless refused recovery of them on the basis of a broader rule of public policy that a claimant cannot recover losses that were caused by the claimant's own criminal conduct.[131] I have rejected the public policy causation rule in Chapter 5; it is inimical to ordinary principles of causation and to the correlativity of negligence law.[132] These losses should be recoverable in full.

[128] *Wiegold* (n 5) 505. The same point was made by Finch CJBC (dissenting) in the British Columbia Court of Appeal decision in the *Zastowny* litigation: *X v M (RD)* [2006] BCCA 221, [57].

[129] *Gray* CA (n 49) [49] (the Court).

[130] *cf* M Dyson, 'Challenging the Orthodoxy of Crime's Precedence over Tort: Suspending a Tort Claim Where a Crime May Exist' in SGA Pitel, JW Neyers, E Chamberlain (eds), *Tort Law: Challenging Orthodoxy* (Oxford, Hart Publishing, 2013) 125–26.

[131] *Gray* (n 3) [54]–[55].

[132] Ch 5, section IV, The Causation Test.

A different position potentially applies where the claim is for injury to reputation caused by the conviction and prison sentence, which appeared to be the claim in *Gray*. Lord Hoffmann held that this injury was not compensable as it fell within the consistency rule.[133] I do not agree that the principle of coherence requires the rejection of these claims. In essence, my argument has been that the principle of coherence requires that the claimant cannot recover the legal sanction itself, but does not require that the claimant cannot recover for the indirect consequences of the sanction. Injury to reputation arguably is not an integral part of the sanction, but rather the consequence of the sanction. In that circumstance rejection, of a claim for non-pecuniary losses for injury to reputation is not required in order to preserve the coherence of the legal system. The law should recognise that a claimant has an entitlement to recover damages for the injury to reputation caused by the defendant's negligence.

C. Claims to be Indemnified for a Third Party Civil Liability

It is necessary to make some general observations about claims for an indemnity against third-party civil liabilities. The courts have generally rejected such claims, though for differing reasons. In *Gray*, the claimant sought an indemnity against liability in damages to his victim's dependents. Lord Hoffmann viewed this claim as falling outside of the consistency rule because it was not the consequence of a sentence of a criminal court. Lord Hoffmann instead denied recovery for this head of loss based on the causation test.[134] Lord Rodger agreed, but thought also that these claims should be denied on consistency grounds—namely that a person is not entitled to be indemnified for the consequences of criminal acts for which that person has been found responsible.[135]

Beever does not discuss this type of claim. There is a good reason for this: there is no need to apply illegality doctrine to these claims. The law of torts recognises that where a loss has been suffered there might be more than one person responsible for that loss, in which case the loss is to be apportioned among the wrongdoers. The right of a wrongdoer to claim a contribution (or indemnity where 100 per cent contribution is sought) against a concurrent wrongdoer is governed by detailed statutory rules.[136] A claim for damages against a concurrent wrongdoer should be determined in accordance with the principles developed under these statutory rules for apportioning responsibility between wrongdoers whose wrongs

[133] *Gray* (n 3) [50].

[134] ibid [50].

[135] ibid [84]–[86]. See also *Meah v McCreamer (No 2)* [1986] 1 All ER 943.

[136] *Patel v Mirza* [2016] UKSC 42 [244] (Lord Sumption, Lord Clarke agreeing). For a comprehensive discussion of the rules governing contribution between tortfeasors and the statutory proportionate liability provisions, see generally K Barker et al, *The Law of Torts in Australia*, 5th edn (Oxford, Oxford University Press, 2012) ch 18; J Murphy, 'Joint Liability and Contribution' in MA Jones (ed), *Clerk & Lindsell on Torts*, 21st edn (London, Sweet & Maxwell Thomson Reuters, 2014) ch 4.

have combined to cause the claimant harm. When determining claims for contribution or an indemnity, however, courts must be vigilant against attempts by claimants to use a claim for compensatory damages to avoid their proportion of legal responsibility for the harm done to the third-party victims. The claimant should be indemnified only to the extent to which the defendant is legally responsible for the victim's injuries, and should be denied a claim to the extent to which the claimant's own conduct contributed to the third-party victim's losses.

Gray can be used to illustrate the operation of contribution principles in this context. In that case there was recognition that the dependants of the claimant's manslaughter victim would potentially have had a claim against the defendant (Thames Trains Ltd) in negligence (remembering that the commission of the crime was not treated as a *novus actus interveniens*).[137] Lord Brown specifically makes the point that in that circumstance Thames Trains Ltd should 'surely not' be granted an indemnity from the claimant Mr Gray in respect of liability found to be owed to the victim's dependants.[138] This is a recognition that Mr Gray would potentially be entitled to seek contribution from Thames Trains Ltd for part of any judgment against him in favour of the dependants. For example, if Mr Gray was 70 per cent responsible for the dependants' losses and Thames Trains Ltd were 30 per cent responsible for those losses, contribution principles require only that Mr Gray be required to bear the 70 per cent legal responsibility attributed to him. Thus, while the court was correct to reject the claim by Mr Gray for a full indemnity, it should have recognised that Mr Gray would be entitled to a partial indemnity reflecting the contribution made by Thames Trains Ltd to the dependents' losses. This is because it is only the 70 per cent proportion of liability the law has apportioned to the claimant that should be irrecoverable. This conclusion can be reached without reliance on illegality doctrine. The coherence of the law in respect of such claims is maintained by the rules relating to contribution and apportionment. These will ensure that each wrongdoer will bear that proportion of the loss that reflects their responsibility for the harm.

It would also be convenient at this point to make a few observations regarding the case of *Stone & Rolls Ltd (in liq) v Moore Stephens (a firm)*.[139] That case involved a claim by a corporation against its auditors for an indemnity against a judgment debt. The sole director and shareholder of the claimant corporation (S&R) used it as a vehicle for defrauding banks. The banks successfully sued the claimant and director in deceit and obtained judgment in the amount of US$94 million. The liquidators of the claimant corporation commenced proceedings against the corporation's auditors on behalf of the creditors, claiming that the auditors were negligent in detecting that the fraudulent activities had taken place and that, had they not been negligent, the fraud would have been detected earlier and the claimant's liability not as great. A majority of the Court (Lords Phillip, Walker

[137] *Gray* (n 3) [28]–[29], [46] (Lord Hoffmann) [94]–[96] (Lord Brown).
[138] ibid [94].
[139] *Stone & Rolls Ltd (in liq) v Moore Stephens (a firm)* [2009] UKHL 39, [2009] AC 1391.

and Brown; Lords Scott and Mance dissenting) upheld an application to strike out the proceedings on the ground that the claimant's illegality prevented the claim. It is difficult to establish a reliable statement of principle from the case due to the diversity of reasoning adopted in the five separate judgments. The decision comprised a confusing mix of views on the scope of the auditors' duty to creditors, as well as the principles that will determine attribution of director illegality to a corporation, with these two separate questions not always kept distinct.[140] This led to divergent views in *Bilta* about whether the case was concerned primarily with the scope of the auditors' duties or whether it was a case about attribution.[141] It was suggested in *Bilta* that *Stone & Rolls* should be confined to its own special facts.[142]

Fortunately, when the proper basis of illegality doctrine is understood to be the principle of coherence, it becomes apparent that the illegality issue was a red herring in *Stone & Rolls*. There was no issue of legal coherence in that case. Allowing recovery would not have created a statutory inconsistency. Nor would it have permitted the claimant to shift responsibility for a legal sanction onto the defendants, or to recover for a loss that was not legally recognisable.[143] It is true that the claimant was seeking to deflect its civil liabilities to its third-party victims on to the auditors. However, the rules of contribution recognise that where a judgment has been made against the defendant in tort that defendant can claim contribution from a concurrent wrongdoer. There is thus much to be said for the view of Lord Mance that the central issue in *Stone & Rolls* was not the application of illegality doctrine, but rather whether the scope of the auditor's liability extends to the protection of the interests of creditors in the circumstance where the company is insolvent.[144]

In conclusion on the question of claims for an indemnity, the responsibility of concurrent wrongdoers for the losses of a third-party victim should be left to the operation of the statutory rules relating to contribution and apportionment. Illegality doctrine is not required to preserve the coherence of the law in this area. To the contrary, if illegality doctrine was applied, it would disrupt the carefully designed statutory schemes that allocate responsibility between concurrent wrongdoers.

[140] *Bilta* (n 90) [81] (Lord Sumption), [142], [152]–[153] (Lord Toulson and Lord Hodge).

[141] Lord Toulson and Lord Hodge saw it as being primarily about the scope of auditors' duties to creditors ([152]), as did Lord Mance: at [46]. Lord Sumption saw it primarily as a case about attribution: at [80].

[142] ibid [23], [30] (Lord Neuberger, Lord Clarke and Lord Carnwath agreeing), [154] (Lord Toulson and Lord Hodge), *cf* [80]–[81] (Lord Sumption).

[143] S&R was not seeking to recover the proceeds of its fraud, but rather the additional losses it sustained due to the auditor's negligent failure to detect the fraud.

[144] Lord Mance expressed that view in *Stone & Rolls* itself, and reiterated it in *Bilta: Stone & Rolls* (n 139) [265]; *Bilta* (n 90) [46]. A majority of the Court in *Stone & Rolls* (Lord Mance and Lord Scott dissenting) held that a duty of care would not be owed. For a recent Canadian case where auditors were found to owe a duty of care to the liquidators on behalf of innocent shareholders for the losses they suffered as a result of the fraud perpetrated by the creators of the corporation, see *Livent Inc (Receiver of) v Deloitte &Touche* (2014) ONSC 2176.

VII. Culpability of the Claimant Is Irrelevant

In section III I discussed that the consistency rule is generally linked to the criminal culpability of the claimant. Where there is no element of culpability—for example, because the claimant was of unsound mind at the time of the offence, or it was an offence of strict liability—it is generally thought that there is no basis for the application of the consistency rule. Although Lord Hoffmann in *Gray* would not have inquired into the criminal culpability of the claimant, indicating that the sentence must be assumed to reflect the claimant's responsibility for the crime, the other judgments left open whether the rule would apply where no, or limited, criminal responsibility is found.[145] In *Safeway Stores Ltd v Twigger*, the English Court of Appeal recognised that the weight of authority suggests that a doctrine of illegality should be applied only where the crime or other illegal act involved a mental element.[146] In that case, the Court held that the consistency rule would apply to a penalty imposed as a result of an infringement that was committed intentionally or negligently, but left open its application to an offence of strict liability where there might not have been any fault on the part of the claimant.[147] The view that there is no justification for the consistency rule in the absence of culpability is also one that is broadly endorsed by academic commentators.[148]

However, the illegal character of the act becomes irrelevant once attention is properly focused on whether the claim will create an incoherence in the law. This is because the potential for a dissonance in the law if the claimant is permitted to deflect a legal sanction is the same regardless of whether the illegal act imports a fault element or is one of strict liability. James Fisher has expressed this proposition in the following terms: 'Acting inconsistently in the face of a minor wrong is no less an example of judicial inconsistency than acting inconsistently in the face of a grave wrong'.[149] This proposition is a reflection of what Birks termed the 'non-judgmental' nature of the principle of coherence, and its concern with 'consistency and rationality' rather than moral condemnation or turpitude.[150]

[145] *Gray* (n 3) [41] (Lord Hoffmann) [15] (Lords Phillips), [83] (Lord Rodgers), [103] (Lord Brown).

[146] *Safeway Stores Ltd v Twigger* (n 19) [17] (Longmore LJ, Lloyd and Pill LJJ agreeing).

[147] ibid [18] (Longmore LJ, Lloyd LJ agreeing), [51]–[52] (Pill LJ).

[148] Goudkamp, 'Can Tort Law be used to Deflect the Impact of Criminal Sanctions?' (n 9) 45–46; PJ Yap, 'Rethinking the Illegality Defence in Tort Law' (2010) 18 *Tort Law Review* 52, 52–53, 56; G Virgo, 'We Do This in the Criminal Law and That in the Law of Tort: A New Fusion Debate' in SGA Pitel, JW Neyers, E Chamberlain (eds), *Tort Law: Challenging Orthodoxy* (Oxford, Hart Publishing, 2013) 109–10. See also JR Spencer, 'Civil Liability for Crimes' in M Dyson (ed), *Unravelling Tort and Crime* (Cambridge, Cambridge University Press, 2014) 317–18.

[149] JC Fisher, 'The *Ex Turpi Causa* Principle in *Hounga* and *Servier*' (2015) 78 *The Modern Law Review* 854, 863.

[150] P Birks, 'Recovering Value Transferred Under An Illegal Contract' (2000) 1 *Theoretical Inquiries in Law* 155, 203.

Where the statute in question reflects a clear policy choice to impose criminal or civil penalties on the claimant for infringement of its provisions regardless of fault, an inconsistency in the law will arise if the claimant can deflect that penalty. An example is provided by the criminal and civil penalties that a court can impose on a corporation for a contravention of a provision in the Australian Consumer Law (ACL) prohibiting false representations and misleading conduct.[151] The liability of corporations under these provisions is strict; it is irrelevant whether the corporation intended to mislead or deceive consumers,[152] and mistake of law is not a defence.[153] Further, a criminal and/or civil pecuniary penalty can be imposed for the purposes of general deterrence, even in the absence of fault by the corporation.[154] There are also comprehensive provisions dealing with attribution of the conduct and accessorial liability that determine when civil and criminal liability should be imposed on the corporation,[155] as well as provisions that determine when a defence is available to the corporation on the ground the contravention was due to the act or default of another person.[156] The coherence of this comprehensive statutory scheme for allocation of responsibility for penalties would be disrupted if the corporation was able to successfully shift the amount of the penalty on to the individuals responsible for the infringement, in circumstances where the statutory scheme has assigned responsibility to the corporation even in the absence of corporate culpability. The explanation for refusing to permit the corporation to deflect the sanction is based on the purpose of the statute or on the basis that there is no loss (both explanations seem to be applicable); either way the rejection of the claim is necessary in order to preserve the coherence of the legal system.

This demonstrates that the risk of legal incoherence is not limited to illegal acts that involve a mental element. The character of the illegal act is not what is relevant; what is relevant is that an incoherence in the law can arise where the claimant seeks to recover compensation for a sanction for which legal responsibility has been attributed to the claimant. This was the view of Lord Hoffmann in *Gray*, who considered that the court should not enquire as to the moral culpability or blameworthiness of the claimant, but should act based on the attribution of responsibility made by the criminal law.[157] This approach is also supported by the seminal case of *Colburn v Patmore*. Weinrib observed that the court in that case 'impliedly regarded strict liability offences and *mens rea* offences as being relatively undifferentiated, from the standpoint of the ascription of personal responsibility'.[158]

[151] Competition and Consumer Act 2010 (Cth) Sch 2, Part 2-1, Part 3-1.

[152] *Parkdale Custom Built Furniture Pty Ltd v Puxu Pty Ltd* [1982] HCA 44, (1982) 149 CLR 191, 198 (Gibbs CJ).

[153] A reasonable mistake of fact is a defence under s 207 of the *ACL* but a mistake of law is not.

[154] See, eg, *Singtel Optus Pty Ltd v ACCC* [2012] FCAFC 20.

[155] See, eg, Australian Consumer Law, ss 139B and 139C.

[156] Australian Consumer Law, s 208.

[157] *Gray* (n 3) [41].

[158] Weinrib, 'Illegality as a Tort Defence' (n 21) 52.

Weinrib explains that claims to deflect a penalty imposed for a strict liability offence do cause an incoherence in the law:

> Criminal law provides a mechanism whereby punishment is consequential upon the authoritative ascription of criminal responsibility. The effect of the private action, however, is to deflect the punishment on to other shoulders while leaving the ascription of responsibility in place. The approach of *Colburn v Patmore* was to prevent this fissure by denying that the punishment could be disassociated from the person adjudged responsible.[159]

This eloquent explanation highlights that the crucial factor is the *legal ascription of liability*. Some academic commentators have interpreted the relevant passages in Weinrib as suggesting that an action to deflect a strict liability sanction on to the blameworthy actor should be permitted.[160] As I understand these passages, however, Weinrib's objection was to the enactment of strict liability offences, not to the result in *Colburn v Patmore*. He acknowledged that shifting a strict liability sanction on to the defendant was an understandable reaction of the courts to a strict liability offence, but recognises that it does create an inconsistency in the law and hence does not amount to 'a satisfactory general position' or 'completely coherent' response.[161] This is why he refers to the decision in *Colburn v Patmore* to refuse to allow the claimant to deflect a strict liability sanction as one that prevented a 'fissure' in the law.[162]

Accordingly, attempts to recover damages for a strict liability sanction should not be permitted where this would create an incoherence with the statutory scheme imposing the sanction. The decision of the Supreme Court of the United Kingdom in *Les Laboratoires Servier v Apotex Inc* provides some support for this view.[163] Lord Sumption, who wrote for the majority, held in that case that a defence of illegality should be confined to acts of turpitude (in essence, criminal and quasi-criminal conduct) and should not extend to strict liability offences, at least where the claimant was not aware of the illegality.[164] Nevertheless, Lord Sumption acknowledged that different principles might apply to sanction-shifting actions in recognition that these cases fall to be decided by reference to the consistency rule. His Lordship apparently endorsed Lord Hoffmann's observation that, in the context of sanction shifting claims attracting the operation of the consistency rule, a court should not enquire into the criminal culpability of the claimant as it should be assumed that the sentence was what the criminal court regarded as appropriate to reflect the personal responsibility of the claimant.[165]

159 ibid 53.

160 Goudkamp, 'Can Tort Law be used to Deflect the Impact of Criminal Sanctions?' (n 9) 45–46; Yap 'Rethinking the Illegality Defence in Tort Law' (n 148) 56.

161 Weinrib, 'Illegality as a Tort Defence' (n 21) 53–54.

162 ibid.

163 *Les Laboratoires Servier v Apotex Inc* [2014] UKSC 55, [2013] RPC 21.

164 ibid [29] (Lord Sumption, Lords Neuberger and Clarke agreeing).

165 ibid, citing *Gray* (n 3) [41] (Lord Hoffmann).

The refusal to allow recovery of a sanction imposed for contravention of a strict (or even absolute) liability offence might cause injustice in some cases;[166] however, the solution should be provided by the legislators and not by judicial application of an illegality doctrine. The law of negligence should not be called upon to redress the deficiencies of a regulatory scheme; rather, the onus rests with the legislature to ensure that there are appropriate defences to a contravention. It is worth noting in this respect that, unless the offence is found to be one of absolute liability, a defence of honest and reasonable mistake of fact is potentially available for a statutory offence that otherwise does not contain a mental element.[167]

The discussion so far has focused on pecuniary penalties, which is the main context in which the debate about the need for culpability has arisen. However, the same argument applies to other legal sanctions, such as a detention order. A conclusion that the detention was authorised by law should prevent a claim for non-pecuniary damages arising from the detention, regardless of whether the claimant is criminally responsible. I would reject the suggestion by Lord Phillips in *Gray* (Lord Rodger and Lord Brown agreeing on this point) that a distinction should be drawn between detention in a mental hospital where no criminal responsibility has been found and detention for a crime.[168] Lord Phillips suggests that there is an argument that recovery should be permitted in the former case, but not in the latter. This approach accords notions of criminal responsibility an unjustifiably central role in the negligence claim. Whether or not the claimant is criminally responsible for the act is irrelevant; it is the lawfulness of the detention that prevents an award of non-pecuniary damages. Thus, the Court in *Hunter Area Health Service v Presland* denied recovery of non-pecuniary damages for mental suffering and loss of liberty during the period of remand and detention in a mental hospital, at least partly on the basis that suffering and loss of liberty was authorised by the law.[169] The lack of criminal responsibility was in that case, and should be in others, an irrelevant consideration.

VIII. Corporate Responsibility

It will be convenient at this point to explain more fully the application of the principles from the preceding section to cases where a corporation is seeking to shift responsibility for a penalty onto those persons working for it whose actions led to

[166] See, for example, the facts of *Osman v J Ralph Moss Ltd* [1970] 1 Lloyd's Reports 313 (motorist fined for driving without insurance due to the negligence of an insurance broker); *United Project Consultants Pty Ltd v Leong Kwok Om* [2005] SLR 214 (trading corporation fined for incorrect tax returns prepared by accountant).

[167] For a discussion of the common law and statutory forms of this defence in Australia, refer to S Bronitt and B McSherry, *Principles of Criminal Law*, 3rd edn (Sydney, Lawbook Co, 2010) 218–24.

[168] *Gray* (n 3) [15] (Lord Phillips), [83] (Lord Rodger), [103] (Lord Brown).

[169] See text to nn 109–116 above.

the imposition of the penalty. There is a debate in the United Kingdom regarding whether a corporation will be prevented from recovering a penalty from those persons only where it is found to be directly or primarily liable for the penalty, or whether it will also be prevented from doing so where it is vicariously liable for the penalty. Specifically, the issue is whether the principles discussed in this chapter which prevent the shifting of responsibility for a penalty onto the individuals responsible for the infringement will not apply where the corporation was not *primarily* liable for the penalty but only vicariously liable through the conduct of the individual. This issue was left open in *Les Laboratoires Servier v Apotex Inc v Servier*.[170]

The issue is one that arises because of the different effects of principles of attribution (on the one hand) and principles of vicarious liability (on the other). Illegal acts committed by those agents who are the directing mind and will of the corporation (such as directors) are directly attributable to the corporation; that is, the illegal act *itself* is attributed to the corporation.[171] However, where the corporation is vicariously liable for an illegal act the corporation is held responsible for that act, but the act itself is not deemed to have been committed by the corporation.[172] This distinction is important for the UK law of illegality, which following *Servier* requires turpitude or culpability on the part of the claimant.[173] On this approach, corporate responsibility will need to be established by attribution to the corporation of the *mens rea* (guilty state of mind) of its directing mind and will.[174] Rules of vicarious liability will not be sufficient to establish corporate responsibility, as they do not have the effect of attributing the guilty state of mind of the employees to the corporation.[175] As Lord Sumption pointed out in *Bilta (UK) Ltd (in liquidation) v Nazir (No 2)* (*Bilta*), if vicarious liability is sufficient to assign the illegality to the corporation then the question of attribution of knowledge of wrongdoing (ie attribution of culpability) to the corporation becomes irrelevant.[176] Lord Sumption was able to derive from *Stone & Rolls Ltd (in liq) v Moore Stephens (a firm)* the proposition that the illegality defence does not apply where the corporation is only responsible for the illegal conduct through the application of vicarious liability principles.[177] The other members of the Court disagreed that *Stone & Rolls* established this proposition,[178] though Lord Neuberger (Lord Clarke and Lord Carnwath agreeing) could see its attraction.[179]

170 *Les Laboratoires Servier v Apotex Inc* (n 163) [29].
171 *Bilta* (n 90) [70] (Lord Sumption), [186], [203], [205] (Lord Toulson and Lord Hodge).
172 ibid.
173 *Les Laboratoires Servier v Apotex Inc* (n 163). Lord Sumption again reiterated the need to prove culpability of the claimant in *Bilta* (n 90) [70], [102].
174 *Bilta* ibid [70].
175 ibid; see also [186] (Lord Toulson and Lord Hodge); William Day, 'Attributing Illegalities' (2015) 74 *Cambridge Law Journal* 409, 411.
176 ibid [80].
177 ibid.
178 ibid [29] (Lord Neuberger, Lord Clarke and Lord Carnwath agreeing), [48]–[50] (Lord Mance).
179 ibid [29].

However, the other members of the court were of the view that whether the acts or state of mind of the agents are to be attributed to the corporation will depend upon the specific context in which the claim has arisen.[180]

The debate about the principles that should govern the attribution of an illegal act of an agent to the corporation has encompassed the case of *Safeway Stores Ltd v Twigger*, which involved a sanction-shifting claim and which is thus particularly relevant to the principles under consideration in this chapter.[181] Safeway Stores commenced proceedings in breach of contract, breach of fiduciary duty and negligence against a number of directors and senior employees who had engaged in anti-competitive activity and caused the corporation to be liable to a penalty under the Competition Act 1998 (UK). The Court of Appeal applied the consistency rule to strike out Safeway's claim, holding that it would be inconsistent for the law to allow the corporation to evade a statutory penalty for which it was personally liable under the Act.[182] The court emphasised that the liability of the corporation was personal not vicarious; 'personal' in the sense that the Act imposed the penalty directly—and exclusively—on the corporation.[183] The court in *Twigger* thus emphasised that its decision was based on the assignment of liability for the penalty to the corporation in the statute itself. Despite this, the case has prompted the debate whether illegality doctrine will apply only where the corporation is personally liable for the conduct of the agents because those agents were the directing minds and will of the corporation, or whether vicarious liability will suffice to attract the operation of the doctrine.

This debate overlooks the fact that in the case of statutory penalties these questions do not come into the matter. This is because the sole criterion for resolving the penalty cases is whether the legislation ascribes responsibility for the penalty personally to the corporation. If it does, it will create an incoherence with the statutory scheme to permit responsibility for that penalty to be shifted onto the corporation's agents via a negligence action. The Court in *Twigger* was correct to reject the claim on the basis that the Act imposed the penalty personally on the corporation, and not on the individuals responsible for the infringement. Lord Justice Pill in the Court of Appeal recognises that it was the purpose of the statutory code to impose the penalty on the corporation itself rather than on its individual agents because deterrence of anti-competitive behaviour would be achieved only if the corporation itself bears the responsibilities to comply with the Act and meets the consequences for non-compliance.[184] To allow the corporation to shift responsibility for the consequences of non-compliance onto its agents would

[180] ibid [40]–[44] (Lord Mance), [202]–[209] (Lord Toulson and Lord Hodge).
[181] *Safeway Stores Ltd v Twigger* (n 19).
[182] ibid [23]–[29] (Longmore LJ), [35]–[38] (Loyd LJ), [51]–[52] (Pill LJ).
[183] ibid [20]–[29] (Longmore LJ), [37] (Lloyd LJ), [46] (Pill LJ).
[184] ibid [44].

frustrate that statutory purpose.[185] Lord Sumption recognised in *Bilta* that this was the true basis on which the decision in *Twigger* could be justified. His Lordship explained that the Act attributed responsibility for the penalty to the corporation personally, not to those individuals responsible for the infringement, and that therefore to allow the penalty to be recovered from those individuals would be inconsistent with the Act.[186] This is a straightforward application of the statutory purpose approach (see generally, Chapter 7); in this context the statute operates so as to negate the loss element of the negligence action. That is, the effect of the statutory code is that the claimant has no legally recognised interest in the subject matter of the loss.

In *Bilta* Lord Toulson and Lord Hodge were critical of the reasoning in *Twigger* on the ground that there is no reason in public policy (or in the law of agency) why a corporation should not be able to hold its employees and other agents to account for their breach of contractual and fiduciary duties.[187] Lord Mance was also sympathetic to this view.[188] However, Lord Toulson and Lord Hodge did recognise that the result in *Twigger* might be defensible on the ground that the policy of the Act would be undermined if the corporation was able to pass its liability onto its agents.[189] This is a promising acknowledgement that ultimately it is the statutory ascription of responsibility for the penalty that must determine the corporation's ability to recover the amount of that penalty from its agents.[190]

This analysis of *Twigger* obviates the need to consider difficult questions about whether the corporation's liability was direct or vicarious, and whether the illegal acts and state of mind of the agents are attributed to the corporation so as to prevent the corporation claiming against those agents for a breach of their contractual and fiduciary duties. The question becomes quite simple once it is understood that the determining factor is the coherence with the statutory scheme. Issues about culpability, attribution and vicarious liability fall away: the only criterion is whether the legislation assigns personal responsibility for the penalty to the corporation. If it does, it would create a statutory inconsistency for the corporation to shift responsibility for the penalty onto the individuals responsible for the infringement through the mechanism of a negligence action. This is because of the policy choice expressed in the legislation that the penalty must be borne by the corporation directly.

185 The same result would apply to a penalty imposed on a corporation under the Competition and Consumer Act 2010 (Cth) (which contains anti-competitive provisions). There are detailed provisions in the Act (see, eg, s 84) which determine when a penalty should be imposed on a corporation for the conduct of its agents and employees. To allow negligence law to be harnessed to shift responsibility for that penalty onto those individuals would create an incoherence with the statutory code.

186 *Bilta* (n 90) [83]. Lord Neuberger in *Bilta* indicated that he would take 'a great deal of persuading' that the decision in *Twigger* was wrong, but he did not explain his reasons for this: at [31].

187 ibid [159]–[160]. Their Honours were persuaded in this regard by an article by Peter Watts: P Watts, 'Illegality and Agency Law: Authorising Illegal Action' (2011) 3 *Journal of Business Law* 213.

188 ibid [52].

189 ibid [162], [164]

190 ibid [162].

IX. Conclusion

Weinrib has recognised that the legal relationship of the parties to a negligence claim reflects the 'systematic coherence' of the entire body of law.[191] The consequence of this for the current context is that a claim must be rejected where the effect of the various branches of the law operating in combination is that the claimant has not suffered loss or damage that is legally recognisable. This will be the case where the claimant is attempting to use negligence law to shift a sanction imposed personally on the claimant onto the third party responsible for the imposition of the penalty, and where the claimant is seeking to recover non-pecuniary damages for a period of lawfully imposed detention. The focus of this chapter has been on sanction-shifting and related claims for the consequences of an illegal act. In Chapter 9 the focus shifts to claims for illegal profits and earnings. The principles formulated in respect of these claims will again build upon Beever's important work in this area.

[191] Weinrib, *Corrective Justice* (n 57) 76.

9

No Loss or Damage: Illegal Profits and Earnings

I. Introduction

This chapter focuses on claims for lost profits or earnings where the defendant's negligence prevented the claimant from pursuing an illegal activity from which those profits or earnings would have been derived. The issue in this context is whether illegality doctrine applies to disallow a particular head of loss.[1] In its simplest form, the issue is whether a person who is incapacitated from pursing a criminal occupation through the negligence of the defendant can claim damages for the loss of the future earnings that would have been derived from that criminal occupation.[2] The problem, however, is broader than illegal earnings, and will arise wherever a claimant is seeking to recover profits that were expected to be earned from an illegal activity. Courts have generally refused to permit such claims on public policy grounds.[3]

In this chapter I will apply the no loss or damage explanation, as formulated by Allan Beever, and as developed in Chapter 8, to these claims. That aspect of the no loss or damage explanation that is particularly relevant to this category of claim is the proposition that in some circumstances the loss in question is not recognised as having a legal value because the claimant has no legal entitlement to the subject matter of the loss (the no legal value proposition). In reliance on this proposition I will argue that a claim for illegal profits or earnings should be rejected where another area of law would notionally apply to forfeit those benefits, such that the loss claimed is not one in which the claimant has a legally recognisable interest. This outcome is not dependent on public policy, but instead is the result of the different domains of the legal system operating as a coherent whole.

[1] *Hall v Hebert* [1993] 2 SCR 159, 174 (McLachlin J, La Forest, L'Heureux-Dubé and Iacobucci JJ agreeing).

[2] The hypothetical example given by Weinrib and Beever involves the lost earnings of a bank robber: EJ Weinrib, 'Illegality as a Tort Defence' (1976) 26 *University of Toronto Law Journal* 28, 442–43; A Beever, *Rediscovering the Law of Negligence* (Oxford, Hart Publishing, 2007) 380.

[3] *Sami v Roads Corporation* [2008] VSC 377; *Meadows v Ferguson* [1961] VR 594; *Burns v Edman* [1970] 2 QB 541; *Hewison v Meridian Shipping Services Pty Ltd* [2002] EWCA Civ 1821, [2003] ICR 766 (CA).

II. The No Legal Value Proposition

Weinribian corrective justice theorists have argued that claims for illegal profits and earnings must be rejected, as they would enable claimants to profit from their wrong.[4] Ernest Weinrib does not provide a detailed justification for denying recovery of these losses. Allan Beever does, explaining that the underlying reason why a criminal cannot recover for loss resulting from an inability to pursue a criminal activity is that the loss does not have a legal value. This is an application of the no legal value proposition, as explained in Chapter 8.[5] This proposition establishes that a particular head of loss will not have a value in law where the claimant is asserting a legal interest in something to which the claimant is not entitled by virtue of the operation of the criminal law. Beever explains the application of this proposition to claims in negligence for illegal profits and earnings as follows:

> The question is whether the claimant suffered a loss of something over which he had a legally recognised interest. ... This is ... why a claimant personally injured and unable to continue a 'career' in bank robbing cannot recover loss of earnings as a bank robber. The claimant did possess a right as against the defendant in relation to the injury—bodily integrity—and hence the defendant owed the claimant a duty of care. But, as a matter of law, the claimant is entitled to no earnings from bank robbing. Hence, in the eyes of the law, the loss of that 'career' was no loss at all.[6]

More generally, Beever explains that claims for illegal earnings should not be permitted because 'the [criminal] law states that the claimant is not entitled to enjoy the subject matter of the loss'.[7] This outcome is achieved because of the combined workings of the criminal and tort law and the need to ensure coherence in the law. It is not brought about because of an external policy consideration that the claimant must not profit from wrongdoing.[8]

The Chief Justice of Canada, Beverley McLachlin, has endorsed the no legal value proposition as the true basis for application of illegality doctrine to claims for illegal profits and earnings. In *Hall v Hebert*, her Honour explained that claims for illegal profits and earnings must not be allowed as they would enable the claimant to derive the benefit of the (hypothetical) illegal conduct, and thus create a dissonance with the criminal law.[9] In subsequent extra-curial writings, her Honour argues, in reliance on Beever, that the reason for this is that where the claim is for profits from an illegal act, 'the claimant is asserting a loss of something

[4] Weinrib, 'Illegality as a Tort Defence' (n 2) 42; *Hall v Hebert* (n 1) 174–75; Beever (n 2) 379–83.
[5] Ch 8, section IV, A Corrective Justice Perspective.
[6] Beever (n 2) 382.
[7] ibid 512.
[8] ibid 381.
[9] *Hall v Hebert* (n 1) 174–76, 179–80

to which she is not entitled'.[10] Her Honour further explains that the effect of this approach is that the claimant has not established a 'loss' that is claimable in tort: 'Since the criminal law holds that [the claimant] has no legally recognised interest in the profit of her illegal conduct, she cannot therefore establish a loss in tort'.[11] Chief Justice McLachlin confirms that this approach does not involve the policies of the criminal law or the principle of coherence trumping the law of torts; rather, it is the consequence of the criminal law and tort law operating in tandem so as to negate an essential requirement for establishing an entitlement to damages:

> [I]t is not that tort law's objective of providing redress for wrongs is made secondary to the goal of coherence, but rather that by a taking a coherent view of the different branches of the law it becomes clear that the law does not accord the violation of the claimant's right any legal value. In this way, respecting the principle of coherence leads to the interrelation of tort and criminal law, while maintaining the integrity of each. It does not disrupt the correlative relationship between the claimant and the defendant inherent in a corrective justice model of tort law.[12]

Like McLachlin CJ, I find Beever's arguments persuasive, and would apply them to this category of claim. I will argue that a loss representing lost profits or earnings from a hypothetical illegal activity will have no legal value where another branch of the law would notionally have applied so as to require the forfeiture of those profits or earnings to the State or to the defendant. In framing the principle in this way I am not intending to formulate a different principle to that laid down by Beever, but merely to identify more precisely the circumstances where his no legal value proposition will apply to claims of this kind.

Before elaborating on this proposition in sections II and III below, it is worth noting at this point that there are indications that the Supreme Court of the United Kingdom is amenable to an argument that a particular loss that has a relation to an illegal act is not a loss that is legally recognisable. In *Bilta (UK) Ltd (in liquidation) v Nazir (No 2)* (*Bilta*) an issue arose whether the claimant corporation was seeking to recover the proceeds of a fraud, and if so, whether the claim should be precluded on the ground that it had not suffered a 'recognisable form of loss'.[13] Although the issue was only briefly discussed and was not the subject of full argument, it was adverted to by three members of the Court, who apparently saw it as a legitimate enquiry.[14] I will discuss this aspect of the case further below.[15]

[10] B McLachlin, 'Weaving the Law's Seamless Web: Reflections on the Illegality Defence in Tort Law' in A Dyson, J Goudkamp and F Wilmot-Smith (eds), *Defences in Torts* (Oxford, Hart Publishing, 2015) 221.

[11] ibid.

[12] ibid 221–22.

[13] *Bilta (UK) Ltd (in liquidation) v Nazir (No 2)* (*Bilta*) [2015] UKSC 23, [2016] AC 1 [178] (Lords Toulson and Hodge).

[14] ibid [96] (Lord Sumption), [178] (Lords Toulson and Hodge).

[15] See text to nn 41–50.

III. Relevance of the Proceeds of Crime Legislation

It might be argued that common law principles can play only a limited role in this area due to the operation of proceeds of crime legislation.[16] Thus, the argument would continue, there would be little point to a civil action to recover profits or earnings acquired illegally if they are liable to forfeiture anyway. However, the ability or willingness of the State agencies responsible for enforcing that legislation to commence an action to forfeit profits or earnings acquired illegally will be dependent on their resources and whether the matter falls within their priority areas. The Law Commission of England and Wales has pointed out that these agencies will usually not have sufficient resources to institute forfeiture proceedings in every case in which a benefit has been obtained through criminal conduct.[17] Moreover, the profits or earnings that are sought will not necessarily be derived from a criminal occupation, and thus will not be liable to forfeiture under the statutory schemes.[18] These statutory forfeiture regimes do not supersede the need for illegality doctrine, and common law actions to recover the proceeds of wrongful conduct will continue.[19] The question, however, arises as to the interaction between the common law action and the proceeds of crime legislation where there is an overlap.

In *R (on the application of Best) v The Chief Land Registrar* Sales LJ was of the view that the application of illegality doctrine is separate to statutory forfeiture schemes, and that the former should not be used in a way which attempts to 'short-circuit' the statutory scheme.[20] Lord Justice Sales was there dealing with a claim for adverse possession in circumstances where part of the period of occupation constituted a criminal act of trespass. His Honour considered that the Proceeds of Crime Act 2002 (UK) could have no bearing on whether the illegality doctrine operated to preclude the claimant's adverse possession claim. The proceeds of crime legislation was a separate regime, with its own distinct concepts, procedures and safeguards, and it should not be imported into the legislative scheme regulating possessory title.[21]

Contrary to the view of Sales LJ, I submit that the proceeds of crime legislation cannot be put to one side and ignored in the question whether illegality doctrine

[16] See, eg, Confiscation Act 1997 (Vic); Proceeds of Crime Act 2002 (UK).

[17] The Law Commission of England and Wales, *The Illegality Defence* (Law Comm, No 189, 1989) (Law Comm No 189) para A.16.

[18] If the applicable legislation was the Proceeds of Crime Act 2002 (UK), it would be necessary (s 6) to establish that the profits or earnings were derived from a 'criminal lifestyle'. Not all of the claims currently under consideration would fall into that category; see, eg, the facts of *Les Laboratoires Servier v Apotex Inc* [2014] UKSC 55, [2015] AC 430, involving a cross-undertaking as to damages following discharge of an interim injunction.

[19] Law Comm No 189 (n 17) para 2.33.

[20] *R (on the application of Best) v The Chief Land Registrar* [2015] EWCA Civ 17, [2016] QB 23 [95] (McCombe LJ agreeing).

[21] ibid. However, Lord Neuberger in *Patel v Mirza* [2016] UKSC 42 [185] stated in dicta that an order by the court arguably should not run counter to the provisions of the proceeds of crime legislation or to any step which was being contemplated under that legislation by the relevant authorities.

applies. This is because it would create an incoherence in the law if negligence law was to award lost profits or earnings as damages, yet the legal system (through the application of proceeds of crime legislation, or another piece of legislation) has identified those as benefits that cannot be lawfully obtained or retained. A claim for lost profits or earnings should be rejected where the claimant would be required to account for those benefits to the State. In the case of the hypothetical bank robber (for example), this would depend on whether the income, if earned, would have been liable to forfeiture under proceeds of crime legislation. It would create a legal inconsistency if one branch of the law has identified that income as income that cannot be lawfully obtained or retained, and yet another branch of the law makes an award of damages representing that income. A negligence action in that circumstance would undermine the coherence of the criminal law (interpreting that broadly to include statutory forfeiture schemes applying to criminal conduct).

If the benefit in question does not meet the criteria in place for forfeiture to the State, no issue of legal coherence arises, and the claim should proceed. In this respect it is noted that Sales LJ in *R (on the application of Best) v The Chief Land Registrar* thought it unlikely in any event that, if the claim for adverse possession was successful, the claimant could be found to have obtained the property through criminal conduct for the purpose of the proceeds of crime legislation. This was because the acts of adverse possession the claimant needed to rely upon were not criminal acts, but other acts of assertion of possession, such as maintaining the property and the boundary fence.[22] Thus, no question of coherence with the proceeds of crime legislation arose on those facts.

This proposed refinement of Beever's theory that focuses on the application of the statutory forfeiture schemes to the loss claimed (where applicable) might not be of any practical importance in the hypothetical bank robber situation, as I will explain below,[23] but can be important in other cases. This approach might be criticised on the ground that it will require a 'trial within a trial' on the question whether the forfeiture statutes notionally would apply to confiscate the profits or earnings. However, this did not cause considerable difficulties in *R (on the application of Best) v The Chief Land Registrar*, where Sales LJ felt competent to express an opinion on the likely application of the proceeds of crime legislation to the property in question in the case before him.

IV. Statement of the No Legal Value Proposition

I explained in the preceding section that a claim for illegal profits or earnings must be rejected where the claimant would notionally be required to account to the State for those benefits. It is necessary, however, to add one further refinement

[22] ibid [94].
[23] See the discussion below of Burns v Edman (n 3), text to nn 24–27.

to this principle as it applies to claims of this kind. This is that the same principle will apply where it is the civil law that notionally requires the claimant to account for those profits or earnings to the defendant. Thus, in the same way that a loss does not have a legal value where the relevant statutory forfeiture scheme would notionally apply to require the claimant to account to the State for the profit or earnings, that loss will not have a legal value where the civil legal process would notionally apply to require the claimant to account to the defendant for the lost profit or earnings had the illegal conduct taken place.

In sum then, the relevant proposition is that a loss of profits or earnings is not a loss that has a legal value where another branch of the law would notionally apply to require the claimant to account for the profit or earnings, either to the State or to the defendant, because the claimant is asserting an entitlement to something in which the claimant has no legally recognised interest. The statement of the principle in this form is not intended to depart from Beever's no legal value proposition, but merely to emphasise that the focus must be on liability to forfeiture. It is only where, had the illegal conduct taken place, another area of the law would have intervened to ensure that the claimant could not retain those profits or earnings that it can be argued that the claimant has no legal entitlement to claim an interest in those lost amounts. If the claimant would have been entitled to retain them, he or she does have a legally recognised interest in obtaining compensation for their loss.

V. Application of the No Legal Value Proposition to the Case Law

A. Illegal Earnings

A straightforward case to test the application of the principles identified so far is the English case of *Burns v Edman*.[24] The claimant's husband was killed in a motor vehicle accident caused by the defendant's negligence, and the claimant commenced proceedings in negligence for loss of financial support. The evidence was that the husband earned his income from robberies and had never earned income from a lawful occupation. Mr Justice Crichton applied a defence of illegality to reject the claim. His Honour rejected an argument that the deceased might have taken up a lawful occupation in the future, dismissing this possibility as 'entirely speculative'.[25]

Mr Justice Crichton's decision was correct, assuming that, had the deceased notionally earned income from robberies, he would have been liable to forfeit that

[24] *Burns v Edman* (n 3).
[25] ibid, 546.

income to the Crown under proceeds of crime legislation.[26] If the deceased could not have lawfully retained that income if earned, an inconsistency in the fabric of the law would be created if the dependants could recover that income as damages. In that circumstance, the effect of the notional operation of the criminal law (through the operation of the statutory forfeiture scheme) is that the loss of that future income is not one that has a value in the law. Justice Crichton in fact accepted an argument of the counsel for the defendant that there was no *legal injury* resulting to the dependants, and as such, they had not suffered an injury which was claimable on a wrongful death action. This supports the notion that in these cases recovery is denied because there is no loss.[27]

A less straightforward case is *Hewison v Meridian Shipping Services Pty Ltd.*[28] The claimant, a merchant seaman, was injured through the negligence of his employer and commenced proceedings for future loss of earning capacity. The employer defended the claim for this head of damages on the ground that it was founded on an illegality of the claimant. The claimant had deliberately concealed from the employer that he was an epileptic, a condition that would have made him ineligible for work as a seafarer. In deliberately concealing this condition, he committed a criminal offence of obtaining a pecuniary advantage by deception. A majority of the English Court of Appeal (Clarke LJ and Tuckey LJ; Ward LJ dissenting) rejected his claim for future loss of earning capacity on the ground that, in order to continue to work as a seafarer, the claimant would have had to continue committing that criminal offence. A defence of illegality applied because the claim for loss of earning capacity was based centrally or substantially (not collaterally or insignificantly) on an illegal act.[29]

In Chapter 5 I pointed out that the 'close connection' test is inconsistent with corrective justice due to its one-sided focus on the claimant's illegal conduct. Further, it is inherently subjective, and leads to uncertainty of application in particular cases.[30] The correct resolution of a case such as *Hewison* should not depend on the application of a connection test, but rather on whether, if the claimant had earned the income, he would have been notionally liable to account for it to the through the legal process. That is unlikely. The forfeiture legislation would not have applied to these earnings—Ward LJ pointed out in his dissenting judgment that the income earned was not the proceeds of a crime, in the sense of earnings from an unlawful occupation, but was the income from a lawful occupation.[31] Nor is it likely that the claimant would notionally have been required to account to the defendant for the earnings in civil proceedings. The defendant employer would

[26] If the case were to arise today, this would require proof that the claimant would have been liable to be convicted of a crime and derived the income claimed from a 'criminal lifestyle': Proceeds of Crime Act 2002 (UK), s 6.

[27] *Burns v Edman* (n 3) 546.

[28] *Hewison v Meridian Shipping Services Pty Ltd* (n 3).

[29] ibid [45] (Clarke LJ), [52] (Tuckey LJ).

[30] See Ch 5, section III, The Inextricable Link (Sufficient Connection) Test.

[31] *Hewison v Meridian Shipping Services Pty Ltd* (n 3) [88] (Ward LJ).

not have had a good claim in restitution to recover the income payments on the ground of mistake as the defence of the provision of good consideration would apply.[32] Nor would the defendant have suffered a loss for the purposes of bringing a claim in deceit; the employer would have had to employ someone else to do the job, and hence, could not claim the payments made as a loss. Consequently, no legal incoherence would have been created had the claim been permitted.

B. Illegal Profits

These principles are not confined to claims for illegal earnings, but apply also to claims for illegal profits more generally. The decision of the English Court of Appeal in *Les Laboratoires Servier v Apotex Inc* is relevant in this context, although it involved a claim for a patent infringement rather than a claim in negligence.[33] Servier was the holder of a patent on pharmaceutical products enforceable in the United Kingdom and obtained an interim injunction against Apotex selling infringing products there. Servier gave the normal undertaking as to damages. The patent was subsequently held to be invalid and the injunction discharged. Apotex sought compensation pursuant to the undertaking for damages for the profits lost because of its inability to sell the products in the United Kingdom. Servier defended the claim on the basis that the defence of illegality applied because the products Apotex would have sold would have been manufactured in Canada in breach of a valid patent granted and enforceable there.

The Court of Appeal held that the illegality defence did not defeat Apotex's claim on the damages undertaking because this would not be a 'just and proportionate response' to the illegality involved.[34] Lord Justice Etherton (who wrote the leading judgment) took into account a range of considerations, such as that Apotex honestly and reasonably believed that the Canadian patent was invalid and thus the infringement was low on the scale of culpability.[35] This discretionary approach (which was discussed in Chapter 4)[36] was rejected by the Supreme Court of the United Kingdom on appeal.[37] I am not here concerned with the actual grounds for these decisions. The point relevant for present purposes is that, putting to one side questions of extra-territoriality for the moment, both courts were right to reject the defence of illegality. This is because of a concession by Counsel for Apotex that there should be deducted from any damages awarded an amount equal to

[32] *Barclays Bank Ltd v WJ Simms Son & Cooke (Southern) Ltd* [1980] QB 677, 695 (Lord Goff); *Australia & New Zealand Banking Group Ltd v Westpac Banking Corp* [1998] HCA 17, (1988) 164 CLR 662, 673; *David Securities Pty Ltd v Commonwealth Bank of Australia* [1992] HCA 48, (1992) 175 CLR 353; 379–80 (Mason CJ, Deane, Toohey, Gaudron and McHugh JJ).

[33] *Les Laboratoires Servier v Apotex Inc* [2012] EWCA Civ 593, [2013] RPC 21 (*Servier* CA).

[34] ibid [82] (Etherton LJ, Laws LJ and Kitchin LJ agreeing.

[35] ibid.

[36] See ch 4, section IX, A Structured Discretion.

[37] *Les Laboratoires Servier v Apotex Inc* (n 18).

that which a Canadian court would have ordered it to pay for infringement of the Canadian patent had the manufacture and export of the products occurred. This concession was correctly made because to the extent the legal process in Canada would have applied to 'forfeit' the profits made from the notional illegal conduct (the manufacture and export of the products), the loss representing that profit does not have a legal value. Nevertheless, Apotex was entitled to recover the profits from sale of the products in the United Kingdom to the extent those profits exceeded the amount of profits that it would notionally have been required to account for in Canada. This is because, as Counsel for Apotex argued, 'All that would be notionally actionable, and actionable only in Canada, would be Apotex's manufacture and export in Canada in breach of the Canadian Patent'.[38]

The account of Apotex's assumed Canadian profits removed any potential for legal incoherence. In rejecting the defence, and allowing the assessment of profits to occur, Etherton LJ in the Court of Appeal expressly recognised that this concession meant that damages would be reduced to the extent that Apotex would notionally have been required to account to Servier in Canada for profits made had it gone ahead with the manufacture and export of the products, and that that deduction would remove any inconsistency with Canadian law.[39]

This case does raise difficult questions regarding whether courts should seek to promote consistency with the law of an international jurisdiction. It is a large enough task for a court to ensure coherence within the legal system in which that court is operating, without it also being required to ensure consistency with the laws of overseas jurisdictions. However, due to a concession by the Apotex Group of companies (including the Canadian and United Kingdom companies) that it should be treated as one entity, it seems conceptually correct to assess the rights of the Apotex Group on the basis of both legal systems to which its conduct was subject. This is because both legal systems comprised the juridical framework for the legal relationship of the parties.[40]

There might sometimes be a threshold question in a particular case regarding whether the loss claimed is in fact the 'profits' of illegal conduct. In *Bilta (UK) Ltd (in liquidation) v Nazir (No 2)* an issue arose whether the claimant corporation was seeking to recover the proceeds of a fraud.[41] The directors of Bilta caused it to be involved in a carousel VAT fraud, resulting in a liability to the tax and customs authority (HMRC) in excess of £38 million. Bilta could not meet this liability as the funds from the sale of goods to UK purchasers, together with the VAT charged on them, had been paid on by Bilta's directors to another company, Jetivia. Bilta was wound up by HMRC and the liquidators commenced proceedings against, inter alia, Bilta's directors for breach of fiduciary duty. The claim against the directors was that they breached their fiduciary duties to Bilta by causing it to conduct

[38] *Servier* CA (n 33) [35].
[39] ibid [88].
[40] EJ Weinrib, *Corrective Justice* (Oxford, Oxford University Press, 2012) 76.
[41] *Bilta (UK) Ltd (in liquidation) v Nazir (No 2)* (n 13).

its business in a manner calculated to prevent it from meeting its obligation to the HMRC to account for VAT. More specifically, the basis of the breach of duty alleged was that the directors had caused the proceeds of the sales to UK purchasers and the VAT charged on them to be paid out to Jetivia, making those funds unavailable to pay the HMRC. The defendants sought to strike out the claim in part on the ground that Bilta was prevented from recovering losses caused by its own illegal actions in committing the fraud.

The case turned primarily on the question of whether knowledge of illegality by director-shareholders was to be attributed to the corporation. On this question the Court held, for various reasons, that the illegality could not be attributed to the corporation, and hence the claim against the directors was permitted to proceed.[42] One of the arguments raised before the Court was that Bilta had suffered no loss because the assets from the sale of the goods represented 'the fruits of the fraud'. Lord Sumption explained the argument as follows: 'The … argument is that Bilta has suffered no loss because they had not been deprived of any assets that they had legitimately acquired.'[43] Reliance for this proposition was placed on a statement in obiter by Lord Phillips in *Stone & Rolls Ltd (in Liq) v Moore Stephens (a firm)* that 'if a person starts with nothing and never legitimately acquires anything, he cannot realistically be said to have suffered any loss'.[44] Lord Sumption in *Bilta* said that it is 'a difficult question' whether the payment out to Jetivia of funds 'which may represent the fruits of the fraud is truly a loss'.[45] His Honour declined to address that question on the ground that it had not been the subject of full argument before the court.[46] However, Lord Toulson and Lord Hodge did address the argument, albeit briefly. Their Honours rejected the argument that Bilta had not suffered a legally recognisable loss:

> A company's profit and loss account and its balance sheet may be positive or negative. When the directors caused Bilta to incur VAT liabilities, and simultaneously caused it to misapply money which should have been paid to HMRC, leaving the company with large liabilities and no means of paying them, the directors caused it to suffer a recognisable form of loss.[47]

This approach identifies the relevant loss as the liability to HMRC for the VAT, rather than loss of the profits from the sale of the goods. It is submitted that Lord Toulson and Lord Hodge were correct to characterise the loss in this manner, and to conclude that it is a 'recognisable form of loss'. Bilta was not seeking to recover

[42] For academic commentary on this aspect of the case see S Griffin, 'Attribution Rules and Issues Around the Illegality Defence' (2015) *Company Law Newsletter* 1; I Fletcher, 'Fraudulent Trading, Ex Turpi Causa, and the Directors' Duties: the Supreme Court Rulings in Bilta (UK) Ltd (in Liquidation) v Nazir (No 2)' (2016) 29 *Insolvency Intelligence* 12.

[43] *Bilta* (n 13) [96].

[44] *Stone & Rolls Ltd (in Liq) v Moore Stephens (a firm)* [2009] UKHL 39 [2009] AC 1391 [5] (Lord Walker agreeing at [171]).

[45] *Bilta* (n 13) [96].

[46] ibid.

[47] ibid [178].

profits earned from illegal sales of the goods to UK purchasers. If it had been seeking to recover profits from illegal sales, then it might have been prevented from doing so on the basis that it had no legally recognised interest in the profits of its illegal conduct (assuming that those profits would be liable to forfeiture to the Crown). In that circumstance (if its claim had been for the profits), Bilta would genuinely be seeking recovery of the 'fruits of the fraud', and the principle of coherence would operate to prevent the claim. Likewise, if Bilta commenced conversion proceedings against the directors or Jetivia to recover damages for the assets that were paid away, such a claim would have to fail. Because the assets were acquired as a result of illegal activities (and would presumably be liable to forfeiture) those assets would be valued in the law as having no value.[48] However, Bilta was not claiming profits or assets to which it had no legal entitlement. Rather, it was seeking to recover as damages the debt it incurred as a result of an alleged conspiracy to defraud and injure it by depriving it of the money needed to pay its VAT liabilities. Bilta's claim was thus correctly focused on the injury that was caused to it by this conspiracy which left it without the means of meeting its liabilities and thereby rendering it insolvent. As Lord Mance observed in *Stone & Rolls*, to cause a company to suffer a deficit that renders it insolvent is to cause it loss.[49] *Bilta* is not a case where the claimant is asserting an interest to which it is not legally entitled; the law does recognise that Bilta has an interest in recovering funds that were misapplied so as to enable it to meet its obligations to HMRC. It is true that Bilta will indirectly benefit if the claim is upheld in that it will be able to discharge its liabilities to the HMRC; however, the real beneficiary in this circumstance would be the HMRC rather than Bilta itself, which is insolvent.[50]

VI. Application of the Statutory Purpose Explanation

An alternative ground on which a claim for illegal profits or earnings should be rejected will be where it is one of the purposes of the statute that renders the conduct illegal to prevent a claim for income derived from the illegal activity.[51] However, a statute will rarely evidence such an intention. Ordinarily, the only penalty applied by the statute will be a criminal penalty, and there will be no

[48] Beever (n 2) 382; J Goudkamp and L Mayr, 'The Doctrine of Illegality and Interference with Chattels' in A Dyson, J Goudkamp and F Wilmot-Smith (eds), *Defences in Torts* (Oxford, Hart Publishing, 2015) 236–37.

[49] *Stone & Rolls* (n 44) [231]. Lord Toulson and Lord Hodge in *Bilta* endorsed this view: (n 13) [176].

[50] Contrast Mummery LJ in the Court of Appeal in *Stone & Rolls: Stone & Rolls Ltd (in Liquidation) v Moore Stephens (a firm)* [2008] EWCA Civ 644, [2008] 3 WLR 1146 [116], [119].

[51] See Ch 7 generally for a discussion of the statutory purpose explanation.

indication from the statute whether it was intended to have privative consequences beyond this. Thus, in *Mills v Baitis* the claimant, injured in a motor vehicle accident caused by the defendant's negligence, claimed damages for loss of earnings due to an inability to carry on a business as an automotive engineer.[52] That business was conducted from premises situated within a residential zone in breach of the planning scheme. The legislation provided a penalty for contravention of the provisions of the planning scheme. The Full Court of the Supreme Court of Victoria held that the illegality of the claimant did not prevent a claim for damages, correctly identifying the central issue as being whether the loss of earning capacity was to be treated as a loss of a kind that was recognised by law.[53] Justice Gowans (Winneke CJ agreeing) held that the sole intention of the Act was to impose a penalty on the claimant, and that it could not be inferred that it was part of the purpose of the Act to disentitle a person breaching its terms from recovering compensation for personal injuries.[54] Further, the Court emphasised that the income was derived from a lawful occupation and not an unlawful one.[55] Accordingly, the loss to the claimant was one that the law would recognise; further, the claim did not offend the governing statute. In that circumstance, an award of compensation would not create an incoherence in the law, and the Victorian court was correct to award compensation for loss of earning capacity.

VII. Onus of Proof

I have explained that particular heads of loss are irrecoverable where that loss does not have a legal value. As the onus is always on the claimant to establish a loss that is compensable, the effect of these principles is that the onus will be on the claimant in each case to plead and prove that he or she has suffered a loss that the law will recognise. James Goudkamp and Lorenz Mayr argue that this would be an absurd result; it would waste time and resources as most cases do not involve illegal behaviour by the claimant.[56] It does not, however, seem unduly onerous to require a claimant to plead and establish a loss in those limited categories of case where the illegality principle would potentially come into play. In any event, any inconvenience to claimants could be overcome by placing an evidential onus on the defendant to plead and prove that the factual loss as pleaded by the claimant is not a loss recognised by the law. This would be a departure from normal rules regarding the burden of proof. However, it might well be a justified departure in

[52] *Mills v Baitis* [1968] VR 583.
[53] ibid 588–89 (Gowans J, Winnke CJ agreeing), 594 (Lush J).
[54] ibid 590–1, 594.
[55] ibid 591.
[56] Goudkamp and Mayr (n 48) 236.

this limited category of case. It is worth noting that the High Court of Australia has shown a willingness to adopt this bifurcated approach to onus of proof in other illegality contexts.[57]

VIII. Conclusion

A claim for lost profits or earnings that would have been derived from illegal conduct had it not been for the defendant's negligence will be defeated where the claimant has not suffered a loss that has a legal value. This will be the case where the claimant would notionally have been required to account for those profits or earnings to the State or to the defendant had that illegal conduct actually taken place. This is not an example of the law subordinating negligence principles to the policies of other areas of law, but rather an example of the legal system operating as a unified institution to prevent the claim.

[57] *Gala v Preston* [1991] HCA 18, (1991) 172 CLR 243, 254 (concerned with whether a duty of care was owed in the context of a joint illegal enterprise).

10

A Relational Explanation: Joint Illegal Enterprise Cases

I. Introduction

In Chapter 7 I examined the application of the statutory purpose explanation to claims arising from an illegality, including claims arising out of a joint illegal enterprise. I concluded that, while this explanation is consistent with corrective justice reasoning, it is unlikely to provide a test of general application for the resolution of illegality claims. In this chapter, I advance an alternative 'relational' basis for resolving illegality claims that arise out of injuries sustained while the parties were engaged in a joint illegal enterprise.

I will argue that the substance of the reasoning underlying authorities from Australia and the United Kingdom on joint illegal enterprises is that the claim should be denied where, due to the features of the relationship between the parties (including their illegal relationship), the claimant could not reasonably expect the defendant to exercise the ordinary standard of care. The main focus will be on Australian authorities as the principle is more developed in this jurisdiction. Presently the courts in the United Kingdom are straightjacketed by the authority of *Gray v Thames Trains Ltd*[1] into applying a causation analysis to resolve claims arising out of a joint illegality. However, prior to *Gray* the standard of care approach was the leading approach to these claims,[2] and it would seem that, if the shackles of *Gray* were removed, the United Kingdom courts would prefer to revert to this approach.[3]

It is a well-established principle, originating from the decision of the High Court of Australia in *Insurance Commissioner v Joyce*, that a claim in negligence must be rejected where the nature of the relationship between the claimant and

[1] *Gray v Thames Trains Ltd* [2009] UKHL33, [2009] 1 AC 1339.

[2] *Ashton v Turner* [1981] QB 137; *Pitts v Hunt* [1991] 2 QB 24 (CA).

[3] *Joyce v O'Brien* [2014] EWCA Civ 546, [2014] 1 WLR 70 [25]–[26], 28 (Elias LJ, Rafferty and Ryder LJJ agreeing); *McCracken v Smith* [2015] EWCA Civ 380 [46] (Richards LJ, Underhill and Christopher Clarke LJJ agreeing).

defendant is such that the claimant could not reasonably expect the defendant to adhere to the normal standard of care (the *Joyce* principle).[4] To date, in Australia this principle has been applied primarily to claims by passengers against drivers known to be drunk. However, there is an emerging trend for it to be applied in a broader range of contexts, one of which is the joint illegality cases. I will demonstrate that the factors and circumstances that are relevant to determining the application of the *Joyce* principle are likewise relevant to resolving claims involving a joint illegal enterprise, and provide guidance as to how such a principle would be further developed and applied to claims of this kind. I explain that through a process of analogical reasoning—a means of development of the law that conforms to a corrective justice viewpoint[5]—a new explanation for the joint illegality cases emerges.

I explain that the *Joyce* principle is consistent with a corrective justice (relational) view of negligence law. Although Weinrib and Beever would argue that the concerns underlying the *Joyce* principle are relevant to setting the *standard of care* rather than defining the scope of the *duty of care*, from a practical perspective either approach will give rise to the same outcomes. The cases addressed in this chapter do not raise issues of legal coherence in the sense in which I have used that term in the preceding chapters, namely coherence between different branches of the law. Instead, the concern about legal coherence in the present context is a concern with the internal cohesion of the negligence analysis and the need to ensure that the obligations of the defendant fairly reflect the nature of the relationship between the parties. The preservation of the internal coherence of private law actions is of fundamental importance to corrective justice theory.[6]

The principles I identify are not based specifically on the claimant's criminality, nor limited to claims arising out of the joint commission of a crime. They will apply in all cases where the nature of the relationship between the parties is such that the claimant could not reasonably expect the defendant to act in a different (safer) manner. Accordingly, it would be incorrect to characterise these principles as giving rise to an illegality principle or 'defence'. The outcome is one that arises out of the relationship of the parties. As I will explain in the next section, the fact that the claimant was in an illegal relationship with the defendant can never *by itself* provide an explanation for refusing compensation. Even though the principle developed here is not an illegality doctrine as such, it is relevant to include it in this book. The courts in Australia and the United Kingdom are regularly called upon to resolve claims arising out of joint illegal enterprise cases, and it would be a significant gap in this book if the correct basis for resolving these cases was not covered.

[4] *Insurance Commissioner v Joyce* [1948] HCA 17, (1948) 77 CLR 39.

[5] EJ Weinrib, *Corrective Justice* (Oxford, Oxford University Press, 2012) 72–79; A Beever, *Rediscovering the Law of Negligence* (Oxford, Hart Publishing, 2007) 509–10.

[6] It was the main objective of Weinrib's breakthrough treatise on corrective justice: EJ Weinrib, *The Idea of Private Law* (Harvard, Harvard University Press, 1995).

II. The Illegal Relationship Between the Parties Will not *of Itself* Negate Duty of Care

A relational approach to negligence requires a consideration of the *whole* of the relationship between the parties. *All* aspects of the relations between the parties must be considered, and no one particular characterisation of the relationship should be isolated as being determinative. This is a point that has been emphasised by the High Court of Australia, in the context of the principles that are relevant to ascertaining the existence and content of a duty of care.[7] Applied to the current context, the fact that one characterisation of the relationship between the parties involved an illegal activity should not of itself negate liability. Cases of joint illegality commonly arise out of the relationship of driver and passenger, and there is no justification for disregarding this aspect of the relationship and focusing only on the parties' illegality. As McLachlin J stated in *Hall v Hebert*, there is no a priori reason why a duty of care cannot subsist between criminals.[8]

This discussion so far is sufficient to dispose of earlier suggestions by members of the High Court that liability should never arise where the parties were engaged jointly in an illegal act and the claimant sustained injuries because of the manner of the performance of that illegal act. That approach, often attributed to *Smith v Jenkins*[9] (a case involving the joint unlawful taking and use of a motor vehicle), is inconsistent with a relational approach to negligence liability in that it focuses only on that aspect of the relationship that involved the joint illegal enterprise of the parties and ignores other aspects of their relationship.[10] The majority in *Miller v Miller* correctly observed that the reasoning in *Smith v Jenkins* is flawed to the extent that, for reasons of policy, it assigned a single characterisation to the relationship of the parties (namely that of participants in a joint criminal enterprise) and ignored the driver–passenger aspect of the relationship.[11]

That is not, however, to suggest that the existence of a joint illegal enterprise between the parties is irrelevant. The whole relationship of the parties must be considered, including the joint participation in an illegal act, to determine the claimant's entitlements on a negligence action.[12] The issue is how, and in what circumstances, the illegality will transform the relationship into one where liability should not be imposed. As I will explain below, the authorities suggest that this will be where the nature of the relationship was such that the claimant could not reasonably expect the defendant to act sensibly. To understand the relevant principles,

[7] *Miller v Miller* [2011] HCA 9, (2011) 242 CLR 446 [46], [64]. See also *Graham Barclay Oysters Pty Ltd v Ryan* [2002] HCA 54, (2002) 211 CLR 540 [145] (Gummow and Hayne JJ).

[8] *Hall v Hebert* [1993] 2 SCR 159, 176, 184.

[9] *Smith v Jenkins* [1970] HCA 2, (1970) 119 CLR 397.

[10] *Miller v Miller* (n 7) [41].

[11] ibid [46].

[12] ibid [47].

it will first be necessary to canvass the leading authorities on joint illegal enterprises and the now discredited standard of care approach, as these authorities form an important background to the development of the principles in the remainder of the chapter.

III. Background: The Standard of Care Approach

A. Development of the Standard of Care Approach

In a series of decisions prior to *Miller v Miller*, the High Court held that the true explanation for the denial of liability in joint illegality cases is that the nature and character of the joint illegal venture makes it inappropriate or impossible to set a standard of care.[13] For convenience I will label this approach the 'standard of care approach', although it is important to keep in mind that the effect of this principle was to negate a duty of care on the basis that it was not possible to define the content of the duty, rather than a denial of a remedy for a breach of duty.[14] Although I reject the standard of care approach, I will discuss the relevant Australian High Court authorities, as they form the foundation for a new relational explanation of the joint illegal enterprise cases.

The standard of care approach for the joint illegality cases was first adopted in *Progress and Properties Ltd v Craft* by Jacobs J (Stephen, Mason, and Murphy JJ agreeing).[15] The claimant Craft was employed on a building site when he allowed himself to be carried on a hoist in contravention of building regulations. The claimant suffered injuries when he fell from the hoist due to the negligence of the operator. Justice Jacobs recognises that in appropriate cases a joint illegal activity can operate to extinguish or modify the duty of care otherwise owed. This will be the case where the criminal act is of such a kind that the court is not prepared to hear evidence for the purpose of establishing a standard of care between the joint participants to the crime.[16] His Honour gave the much (over)used example from *National Coal Board v England*[17] that a court would not hear evidence for the purpose of setting a standard of care owed by a safe-blower to a criminal accomplice.[18] However, Jacobs J held that the case before him was not a case where a court would decline to determine a standard of care. The same standard of care applied to the operation of the hoist regardless of whether it was legal to ride on the hoist platform, and as such, the court would not be required to embark on an

[13] *Progress and Properties Ltd v Craft* [1976] HCA 59, (1976) 135 CLR 651; *Jackson v Harrison* [1978] HCA 17, (1978) 138 CLR 438; *Gala v Preston* [1991] HCA 18, (1991) 172 CLR 243.

[14] *Jackson v Harrison* ibid 457 (Jacobs J).

[15] *Progress and Properties Ltd v Craft* (n 13).

[16] ibid 668.

[17] *National Coal Board v England* [1954] AC 403, 429.

[18] *Progress and Properties Ltd v Craft* (n 13) 668.

inquiry as to the reasonableness of the operator having regard to the joint illegal purpose.[19]

The standard of care approach was further adopted and developed by a majority of the High Court (Barwick CJ dissenting) two years later in *Jackson v Harrison*.[20] The claimant was injured while a passenger in a car driven by the defendant, whom the claimant knew to be disqualified from driving. Justice Jacobs (Aickin J agreeing) adhered to the views he expressed in *Progress and Properties Ltd v Craft* and held that a duty of care will be denied if a court is unable properly to establish the content of the duty (the standard of care). His Honour held that on the facts of the case before him, the disqualification of the driver, as known to the passenger, had no bearing whatsoever on the standard of care reasonably to be expected of the driver, and hence allowed the claim.[21] Justice Mason, like Jacobs J, preferred an approach based on whether a court could give content to the duty of care. His Honour proposed that the claim 'must fail when the character of the enterprise in which the parties are engaged is such that it is impossible for the court to determine the standard of care which is appropriate to be observed'.[22] In that case, the normal duty of care of driver and passenger was owed as the illegal act (driving while disqualified) did not affect the standard of care that could reasonably be expected of the driver. The evidence was that the parties contemplated the vehicle would be driven carefully, and there was no evidence that the driver lacked the experience or ability to do so.[23]

In *Gala v Preston*, a majority of the High Court again adopted this approach from *Progress and Properties Ltd v Craft* and *Jackson v Harrison*.[24] In a joint judgment, Mason CJ, Deane, Gaudron and McHugh JJ held that a duty of care will not arise where it is not 'appropriate or feasible' to set a standard of care (and therefore the content of the duty of care could not be identified).[25] On the facts of the case before them, it was held that a duty of care was not owed. In that case, a group of intoxicated friends (that included the claimant and defendant) stole a car to take a trip to another town, in what the claimant conceded was to be something of a joy ride. While the claimant was asleep, the defendant (who was driving the car) crashed it into a tree, injuring the claimant. The plurality held that no duty of care was owed. Due to the nature and character of the enterprise of the parties (the joint drinking binge and the joyride in the stolen vehicle), the claimant could not expect the defendant to exercise the standard of care ordinarily owed by a driver to a passenger.[26] Moreover, to seek to define a more limited duty of care owed by one drunken thief of a car to another would involve a process of 'weighing and

[19] ibid 668–69.
[20] *Jackson v Harrison* (n 13).
[21] ibid 461.
[22] ibid 456.
[23] ibid.
[24] *Gala v Preston* (n 13).
[25] ibid 253.
[26] ibid 254.

adjusting of the conflicting demands of the joint criminal activity and the safety of the participants in which it would be neither appropriate nor feasible for the courts to engage'.[27]

The principles formulated in these cases were followed and applied by lower courts in Australia[28] and also by the English Court of Appeal in *Pitts v Hunt*;[29] however, they were rejected by the Supreme Court of Canada in *Hall v Hebert*.[30]

B. The Standard of Care Approach Is not an Appropriate Explanation of the Joint Illegality Cases

The standard of care approach was rejected in *Miller v Miller* in favour of the statutory purpose explanation.[31] The High Court was correct to reject the standard of care approach. This approach is ultimately a guise for the application of judicial policy,[32] and hence is not a plausible or coherent basis for resolving claims arising from a joint illegal enterprise. It is based on a fiction that it will be impossible to set a standard of care to be observed by the defendant when the real reason for rejecting the claim is policy. In *Miller v Miller* the majority recognises that it is possible to set a standard of care even between joint participants to a crime: 'Setting a norm of behaviour as between criminals may be difficult, but it is not impossible'.[33] It has been pointed out elsewhere that a standard of care can even be set for safe-breakers based on statutory or regulatory standards that govern the safe use of explosives when used for legal purposes.[34] Beever illustrates the same point by referring to a different hypothetical example; namely, a situation in which two parties are conducting a murder when one is accidentally shot by the other. Beever argues:

> In determining the standard of care here, a court need not formulate a standard of care for murderers. Instead, the court could inquire into the precautions usually imposed on those handling firearms.[35]

The real reason why the courts declined to set a standard of care in a case such as *Gala v Preston* was not that the courts *could not* set a standard, but because they *would not* do so as a matter of policy. As Dawson J observed in that case, the

[27] ibid 255.

[28] *Fabre v Arenales* (1992) 27 NSWLR 437 (NSWCA); *Italiano v Barbaro* (1993) 40 FCR 303 (FCFCA); *Kickett v State Government Insurance Commission* (1997) 26 MVR 321 (FC WA).

[29] *Pitts v Hunt* (n 2) 49–51 (Balcombe LJ), 57–60 (Dillon LJ). See also *Ashton v Turner* (n 2).

[30] *Hall v Hebert* (n 8) 182–83.

[31] *Miller v Miller* (n 7) [56], [108].

[32] *Jackson v Harrison* (n 13) 463 (Murphy J).

[33] *Miller v MIller* (n 7) [54].

[34] *Jackson v Harrison* (n 13) 463 (Murphy J). See also *Gala v Preston* (n 13) 269 (Brennan J); *Italiano v Barbaro* n 28) 309 (Black CJ and Beazley J), 330 (Neaves, Burchett and Whitlam JJ); R Glofcheski, 'Claimant's Illegality as a Bar to Recovery of Personal Injury Damages' (1999) 19(6) *Legal Studies* 6, 11–12.

[35] Beever, *Rediscovering the Law of Negligence* (n 5) 377.

'impossibility' of setting a standard of care exhibited 'an unwillingness rather than an incapacity to do so'.[36] The claim that it was impossible to set a standard of care was in fact a cloak for a policy decision to deny claims that were closely related to serious illegality.[37]

The public policy basis of the standard of care approach is most clear from the judgments of Jacobs J in *Progress and Properties Ltd v Craft* and *Jackson v Harrison*, where his Honour states that the court will 'decline to permit the establishment of an appropriate standard of care' where it could only do so by having regard to the joint illegal activity.[38] This led Elias LJ in *Joyce v O'Brien* to observe that the judgment of Jacobs J in *Progress* 'suggests not so much that the court could not undertake that task [fix a standard of care] but that as a matter of policy it should not do so'.[39] Likewise, the majority in *Miller v Miller* identified these cases as resting on a policy judgment that the courts *should not* regulate the activities of wrongdoers by setting a standard of care.[40]

The High Court in *Miller v Miller* was correct to reject the standard of care approach to the extent that it was used as a foil for policy decisions. To refuse to set a standard of care is a form of judicial abdication.[41] This approach also suffers from the pragmatic problems of policy-based reasoning canvassed in Chapter 4. It confers an undefined discretion on the court to decline to hear evidence on the content of the duty of care where it considers that is the appropriate course of action due to the seriousness of the crime, resulting in uncertainty and the introduction of an undesirable subjective element into the law. Any appearance of greater objectivity than other policy approaches is purely illusory.[42] Rick Glofcheski has argued that the standard of care approach is 'nothing more than a disguised version of the "public conscience" test, the court having to determine which cases of criminal conduct are sufficiently unsavoury as to warrant the court's condemnation'.[43]

For these reasons, the standard of care approach does not represent a plausible basis for the denial of a claim in the joint illegal enterprise cases. This does not mean, however, that the reasoning underpinning these cases should be completely jettisoned.[44] That underlying reasoning is still valid to the extent that it can be divorced from a policy-based conclusion that it was not *appropriate* to set a standard of care. Corrective justice requires a court to set a standard of care that is appropriate and fair for the relationship of the parties, and thus the known risks

[36] *Gala v Preston* (n 13) 275–76.

[37] Glofcheski (n 34) 11–14.

[38] *Jackson v Harrison* (n 13) 457–58. See also *Progress and Properties Ltd v Craft* (n 13) 668.

[39] *Joyce v O'Brien* (n 3) [12]. See also JP Swanton, 'Claimant a Wrongdoer: Joint Complicity in an Illegal Enterprise as a Defence to Negligence' (1981) 9 *Sydney Law Review* 304, 320–22.

[40] *Miller v Miller* (n 7) [70]. See also *Jackson v Harrison* (n 13) 463 (Murphy J).

[41] Glofcheski (n 34) 30, 13.

[42] Swanton (n 39), 322; see also 326.

[43] Glofcheski (n 34) 12; see also 13–14.

[44] It is worth noting that the reasoning in *Gala* is not invalidated merely because of the reliance in the reasoning on the now outmoded notion of proximity: *Miller v Miller* (n 7) [60]; *Imbree v McNeilly* [2008] HCA 40, (2008) 236 CLR 510, [46]–[47] (Gummow, Hayne and Kiefel JJ).

involved in the illegal enterprise will be relevant to determining that standard of care.[45] I will discuss this point further below, but before doing so it is necessary to explain the *Joyce* principle in more depth.

IV. The Relationship Between the Parties Is such that the Claimant Cannot Expect the Defendant to Act Carefully (the *Joyce* Principle)

There is significant authority in Australia for the principle that a claim in negligence must be rejected where the nature of the relationship of the parties is such that the claimant could not reasonably expect the defendant to act with ordinary care and competence. This principle finds its provenance in *Insurance Commissioner v Joyce* in the context of a claim by a passenger against a driver known to be drunk.[46] In the course of rejecting the claim on the grounds of contributory negligence and voluntary assumption of risk, Latham CJ said:

> In the case of the drunken driver, all standards of care are ignored. The drunken driver cannot even be expected to act sensibly. The other person simply 'chances it'. Accordingly, the case may be described as involving a dispensation from all standards of care, so that … there was no breach of duty by the defendant.[47]

In his dissenting judgment, Dixon J formulated a similar principle, holding that there will be cases where the relationship of the parties will require modification of the applicable standard of care:

> [T]he principle applied to the case of the drunken driver's passenger is that the care he may expect corresponds with the relation he establishes. If he knowingly accepts the voluntary services of a driver affected by drink, he cannot complain of improper driving caused by his condition, because it involved no breach of duty.[48]

This case establishes the principle that the relationship between a drunk driver and passenger might be such that the passenger could not reasonably expect the defendant to exercise the ordinary standard of care and hence, there would be no breach of duty. This principle was endorsed by the High Court on subsequent occasions.[49] In *Imbree v McNeilly*, Gummow, Hayne and Kiefel JJ expressly endorsed the reasoning underlying *Joyce*:

> The conclusion that a defendant owed the claimant *no* duty of care is open in a case like *Joyce* if, as Latham CJ said, 'In the case of the drunken driver, *all* standards of care are

[45] Beever, *Rediscovering the Law of Negligence*, (n 5) 377.
[46] *Insurance Commissioner v Joyce* (n 4).
[47] ibid 46.
[48] ibid 57.
[49] *Roggenkamp v Bennett* [1950] HCA 23, (1950) 80 CLR 292; *Cook v Cook* [1986] HCA 73, (1986) 162 CLR 549; *Joslyn v Berryman* [2003] HCA 34, (2003) 214 CLR 552 [29] (McHugh J).

> ignored [because the] drunken driver cannot even be expected to act sensibly' (emphasis added). And as indicated earlier in these reasons, it is that same idea which would underpin a conclusion that the claimant voluntarily assumed the risk of being driven by a drunken driver.[50]

However, in *Imbree* the High Court rejected the notion that a driver could owe variable standards of care to different persons. Hence, as can be seen from the passage quoted, their Honours held that the reasoning underpinning *Joyce* is relevant to the assessment of the existence and scope of duty of care, rather than the standard of care owed by the defendant. The majority in *Miller v Miller* subsequently confirmed the continued availability of the *Joyce* principle, as being relevant to assessing the existence and scope of a duty of care.[51] This has led to its invocation in cases following *Miller v Miller*, which have applied the *Joyce* principle in addition to the statutory purpose explanation, in assessing the existence of a duty of care.[52] Given the inability of the statutory purpose explanation to provide a practical criterion for the resolution of these cases, it is likely there will be growing reliance on the *Joyce* principle in future cases.

The *Joyce* principle (either in its 'no breach' or 'no duty' form) has been widely accepted as relevant to cases involving inebriated drivers.[53] However, there is no principled reason why it should be so confined,[54] and it has been invoked in other contexts. For example, it has been recognised that in an appropriate case, there might be an argument that the claimant could not expect the normal standard of care to apply because of the age and inexperience of the driver.[55] It has also been recognised as potentially applicable to other contexts, such as whether an owner of a car owed a duty to the driver to warn of the defective condition of the car.[56]

In the specific context of joint illegality, there appears to be a growing recognition by courts that it is this principle—whether the claimant could expect the defendant to act carefully—that underpins previous decisions of the High Court, in particular the joint judgment in *Gala v Preston*. In their joint judgment in that case, Mason CJ, Deane, Gaudron and McHugh JJ stated:

> [E]ach of the parties to the enterprise must be taken to have appreciated that he would be encountering serious risks in travelling in the stolen vehicle when it was being driven

[50] *Imbree v McNeilly* (n 44) [82] (footnote omitted). Gleeson CJ also contemplated that there might be situations where a duty of care will not be owed to a passenger who permits a driver to take control of a motor vehicle who is clearly not competent to do so: at [7].

[51] *Miller v Miller* (n 7) [63]–[64].

[52] See *Green v Nominal Defendant* [2012] NSWDC 37, in particular [13]–[24] (Sidis DCJ) (appealed on other grounds: [2013] NSWCA 219); *Harmer v Hare* [2011] NSWCA 229, (2011) 59 MVR 1, 52–53 [201] (Whealy JA, Beazley JA and Sackville AJA agreeing); *Stafford v Carrigy-Ryan* [2013] ACTSC 99, [72] (Sidis AJ) (appealed on other grounds: [2014] ACTCA 27).

[53] *Avram v Gusaroski* [2006] WASCA 16, (2006) 31 WAR 400, 403 [5] (Pullin JA, Malcolm CJ agreeing); *Green v Nominal Defendant* ibid, in particular [13]–[24]; *Stafford v Carrigy-Ryan* ibid.

[54] *Miller v Miller* [2008] WADC 46, [105] (Schoombee DCJ) (*Miller v Miller* WADC).

[55] *Zanner v Zanner* [2010] NSWCA 343, (2010) 79 NSWLR 702 [44]–[49] (Tobias JA, Allsop P and Young JA agreeing).

[56] *Harmer v Hare* (n 52) [197]–[207] (Whealy JA, Beazley JA and Sackville AJA agreeing).

> by persons who had been drinking heavily and when it could well be the subject of a report to the police leading possibly to their pursuit and/or their arrest. *In the special and exceptional circumstances that prevailed the participants could not have had any reasonable basis for expecting that a driver of the vehicle would drive it according to ordinary standards of competence and care.*[57] (emphasis added)

Later in the judgment, their Honours stated that to conclude on the facts of the case that the defendant 'should have observed the ordinary standard of care to be expected of a competent driver would be to disregard the actual relationship between the parties as we have described it'.[58] Accordingly, the underlying reasoning of the joint judgment in *Gala v Preston*—or what has been described as the 'penultimate finding' of that judgment[59]—was that the claim should be denied where (considering the relationship of the parties and the risks appreciated by the claimant from involvement in the joint enterprise) there was no reasonable basis for expecting that the defendant would act with ordinary care. It is this 'penultimate finding' that has been applied in cases following *Gala v Preston*. In *Fabre v Arenales* the claimant was injured in an accident that occurred while the parties were being pursued by the police and fleeing the scene of a crime.[60] Mahoney JA in his leading judgment concluded that no duty of care was owed on the basis that, in the circumstances, the claimant could not expect from the defendant any more care than he in fact took in the circumstances.[61] His Honour apparently considered that this was the critical consideration following *Gala v Preston*. Likewise, the Court of Appeal in *Miller v Miller* placed considerable emphasis on whether the claimant could reasonably expect the defendant to act with care; again, this was seen as the critical consideration following *Gala v Preston*.[62]

In the High Court in *Miller v Miller*, the majority referred to the *Joyce* principle with approval, but gave no indication as to its applicability to the joint illegality cases, preferring instead to focus on considerations relating to statutory purpose.[63] The majority did, however, acknowledge that what 'lies beneath the conclusions reached in both *Smith v Jenkins* and *Gala v Preston* [is that the] joint criminal venture to which reference was made in those cases was a venture in which reckless or dangerous driving was a probable … incident of the venture'.[64] This recognition, that the inherently hazardous nature of the illegal enterprise underpinned the negation of liability in those cases, is at least consistent with a principle that

[57] *Gala v Preston* (n 13) 254.
[58] ibid 255.
[59] *Miller v Miller* [2009] WASCA 199, (2009) 54 MVR 367 WASCA, [6] (McLure JA) (*Miller v Miller* WASCA).
[60] *Fabre v Arenales* (n 28).
[61] ibid 453.
[62] *Miller v Miller* WASCA (n 59) [79]–[81] (Buss JA), [152]–[153] (Newnes JA). See also *Brown v Harding* [2008] NSWCA 51, [40]; *Kickett v State Government Insurance Commission* (n 28) 324 (Kennedy J, Scott J agreeing).
[63] *Miller v Miller* (n 7) [64]–[65].
[64] ibid [92].

focuses on the risks inherent in the venture with a view to determining whether the claimant could expect the defendant to exercise reasonable care.

It is also possible to find support in Mason J's judgment in *Jackson v Harrison* for the proposition that the reasoning underpinning the High Court decisions on joint illegality was whether, in the circumstances of the case, the claimant could reasonably expect the defendant to act with care. The tenor of the judgment of Mason J is that these cases will turn on the difficulties of defining the content of the duty of care due to the inherently hazardous nature of the activity. Justice Mason stated that the explanation for the denial of relief to a participant in a joint illegal enterprise for injury sustained 'is related not to the illegal character of the activity but rather to the character and incidents of the enterprise and to the hazards which are necessarily inherent in its execution'.[65] The focus of Mason J's judgment was on whether the relevant illegal enterprise increased the hazards of the activity to which the duty of care was directed and was of such a character as to materially alter the ordinary duty obligation.[66]

V. Support for the *Joyce* Principle in the United Kingdom

Courts in the United Kingdom appear receptive to a principle that would resolve joint illegality claims through duty of care and a consideration whether the claimant could expect reasonable care to be exercised in the circumstances.[67] In *Joyce v O'Brien* Elias LJ (who wrote the leading judgment) reviewed the Australian High Court authorities on joint illegal enterprises and identified the underlying rationale as being that 'the joint criminal illegality affects the standard of care which the claimant is reasonably entitled to expect from his partner in crime'.[68] Similarly, his Honour had earlier observed that the case of *Progress and Properties Ltd v Craft* marked a significant shift from *Smith v Jenkins* in that a duty of care will only be extinguished 'where the character of the activity is such that the claimant cannot expect the defendant to comply with the normal standard of the duty of care'.[69] Elias LJ unfortunately felt constrained by authority to force these principles into a causation analysis;[70] he was bound by the prior decision of the Court of Appeal in *Delaney v Pickett* where Lord Hoffmann's causation test from *Gray v Thames Trains Ltd* was applied to a joint illegal enterprise.[71] Elias LJ made a valiant attempt

65 *Jackson v Harrison* (n 13) 455.
66 See *Preston v Gala* [1990] 1 Qd R 170, 178 (Williams J, Connolly J agreeing) (*Preston v Gala* QCA).
67 Though see *Nettleship v Weston* [1971] 2 QB 691.
68 *Joyce v O'Brien* (n 3) [28].
69 ibid [12].
70 ibid [25]–[26].
71 *Delaney v Pickett* [2011] EWCA Civ 1532, [2012] 1 WLR 2149.

to frame the relevant principle as an amalgam of the causation and standard of care approaches, in a way that retained the substance of the former while paying heed to the latter. His Honour formulated the principle as follows:

> [W]here the character of the joint criminal enterprise is such that it is foreseeable that a party or parties may be subject to unusual or increased risks of harm as a consequence of the activities of the parties in pursuance of their criminal objectives, and the risk materialises, the injury can properly be said to be caused by the criminal act of the claimant even if it results from the negligent or intentional act of another party to the illegal enterprise.[72]

It is clear, however, that he had he been free to decide the correct approach, Elias LJ would directly have approached the case according to whether the claimant could reasonably expect the normal standard of care in the circumstances. In this respect he obviously viewed the reasoning of the earlier Court of Appeal decision in *Pitts v Hunt* (which had adopted the standard of care approach) to the causation approach.[73] In the subsequent Court of Appeal decision in *McCracken v Smith* Richards LJ (who wrote the leading judgment) expressed 'considerable sympathy' for this position, and indicated that the Court of Appeal in *Delaney v Pickett* (of which he was a member) may have acted too precipitately in seizing on the causation test as the basis for resolving the joint illegal enterprise cases.[74] Richards LJ considered, though, that it was too late to try to backtrack and that the court was bound to apply the principles formulated by Elias LJ in *Joyce v O'Brien* to the joint illegal enterprise in that case.[75] However, it seems apparent that the English Court of Appeal is poised to resolve joint illegal enterprise cases through the mechanism of duty of care, should the Supreme Court of the United Kingdom give them the green light to do so.[76]

VI. The *Joyce* Principle should be Adopted as the Basis for Resolving Joint Illegality Cases

I submit that the underlying rationale of the Australian authorities was identified correctly by Elias LJ in *Joyce v O'Brien*; namely that a duty of care will not be owed by one participant in an illegal enterprise to another participant where 'the

[72] *Joyce v O'Brien* (n 3) [29].
[73] ibid [28].
[74] *McCracken v Smith* (n 3) [46].
[75] ibid.
[76] There is no significant support in Canada for approaching joint illegal ventures as a question of the expected standard of care. Justice Sopinka in his dissenting judgment in *Hall v Hebert* would have rejected the claim, inter alia, on the basis that the claimant could not in the circumstances have expected the defendant to act with reasonable care (*Hall v Hebert* (n 8) 193–94); however, this was not adopted by a majority of the court. Canadian courts prefer to approach analogous cases

character of the activity is such that the claimant cannot expect the defendant to comply with the normal standard of the duty of care'.[77] The law in both jurisdictions should develop in accordance with this reasoning. It should now be recognised that the true explanation for refusing a claim is that, taking into account the totality of the relationship of the parties, the claimant could not expect the defendant to exercise reasonable care. (Fortunately, due to the serendipitous confluence of names of the two leadings cases in Australia and the United Kingdom, the *Joyce* principle is appropriate terminology for both jurisdictions to describe these principles.)

The development of the law in this respect will be assisted by the principles derived from cases dealing with claims against intoxicated (and inexperienced) drivers in which the *Joyce* principle has been invoked, in recognition that similar considerations will arise. Although the joint judgment in *Gala v Preston* did not cite *Insurance Commissioner v Joyce*, the similarity of this principle and that laid down in the former case is striking and it is submitted that the principles developed in the cases following *Insurance Commissioner v Joyce* can be used by analogy to develop criteria for the resolution of the joint illegality cases. The trial judge in *Miller v Miller* (Schoombee DCJ) drew considerably upon these cases,[78] recognising that the factors relevant to determining the success of the *Joyce* principle in the case of an inebriated driver are similar to the factors relevant to assessing a duty of care in a case concerning a joint illegal enterprise consisting of the illegal use of a car.[79]

Ultimately, the question will be whether the risks inherent in the execution of the joint venture sufficiently altered the circumstances of the relationship between the parties to make it unreasonable for the claimant to expect the defendant to adhere to the normal standard of care.[80] Before exploring in further detail the particular application of this principle to the joint illegality cases, it is necessary to address an argument commonly made that the courts should always use the mechanism of contributory negligence to resolve cases involving joint illegality in preference to a blunt 'no duty' or 'no breach' defence. I will discuss this point in the next two sections, and will conclude that the *Joyce* principle—at least in its 'no breach' form—is required to maintain the coherence of the negligence action.

(involving drunk drivers and willing passengers) as a matter of voluntary assumption of risk. The Canadian courts will reject the claim where it is possible to imply from the parties' conduct an agreement that the claimant will not hold the defendant legally responsible if injury should result. In essence the claimant, knowing of the virtually certain risk of harm, 'bargains away' the right to sue: see, eg, *Dubé v Labar* [1986] 1 SCR 649 (SCC), 658 [6].

[77] *Joyce v O'Brien* (n 3) [12].

[78] In particular, the decision of the Full Court of the Supreme Court of Western Australia in *Avram v Gusaroski* (n 53).

[79] *Miller v Miller* WADC (n 54) [96]–[107] (Schoombe DCJ).

[80] S Ginsbourg and BJ Newton, '*Gala v Preston*: The Defence of Illegality to an Action in Negligence' (1992) 18(2) *Monash University Law Review* 243, 246.

VII. Is an 'All or Nothing' Approach Ever Appropriate?

In *Avram v Gusaroski*, Murray AJA said that the notion of a complete defence arising from the application of the *Joyce* principle is 'less attractive conceptually' than using the mechanism of contributory negligence to evaluate the respective responsibility of the parties for the harm.[81] His Honour described an approach that apportions responsibility as more 'socially appropriate' than a complete 'all or nothing' approach.[82] Others have also argued (in different contexts) that an apportionment using the mechanism of contributory negligence is more appropriate than a blunt 'no duty' or 'no breach' approach.[83] Joachim Dietrich has referred to the all or nothing nature of such an approach as extreme, harsh and unjust, and stated that 'justice demands the flexibility of apportionment remedies'.[84]

In the specific context of claims arising out of a joint illegal enterprise, the predominant academic view is also that the claimant's illegal conduct should be treated as a matter of comparative fault.[85] Thus, Margaret Fordham states that there is:

> no clear reason for linking the destruction of the claim with the danger of the activity—especially since the defence of contributory negligence already provides for the apportionment of damages to take account of the danger to which a claimant in a joint illegal enterprise case has exposed himself.[86]

Likewise, James Goudkamp prefers to treat the dangerousness of the parties' enterprise as a matter for apportionment for contributory negligence, describing this as 'a much more subtle and sophisticated way of taking stock of unjustified risk-taking' than a defence.[87] There is also judicial support for approaching the matter as one of comparative fault. In *Hall v Hebert*, McLachlin J (writing for the majority) preferred a contributory negligence approach over a 'no duty' approach to resolve the joint illegality cases.[88]

While there is considerable force in these arguments, a countervailing argument is that the *Joyce* principle is required in order to maintain the internal cohesion of

[81] *Avram v Gusaroski* (n 53) [67] (Murray AJA, Malcolm CJ agreeing).

[82] ibid.

[83] J Allen, 'Variable Standards of Care in Negligence' (2009) 17 *Tort Law Review* 5, 9.

[84] J Dietrich, 'The Decline of Contributory Negligence and Apportionment: Choosing the Black or White of All-Or-Nothing over Many Shades of Grey?' (2003) 11 *Torts Law Journal* 1, 2. See also J Dietrich, 'Duty of Care under the "Civil Liability Acts"' (2005) 13 *Torts Law Journal* 17, 25.

[85] M Fordham, 'Stop I Want to Get out!—The Joint Illegal Enterprise which Ceased to Be' (2012) *Singapore Journal of Legal Studies* 165, 173; PJ Yap 'Rethinking the Illegality Defence in Tort Law' (2010) 18 *Tort Law Review* 52; Glofcheski (n 34) 6; J Goudkamp, 'The Defence of Joint Illegal Enterprise' (2010) 34 *Melbourne University Law Review* 42.

[86] Fordham, 'Stop I Want to Get Out!' ibid 173.

[87] Goudkamp, 'The Defence of Joint Illegal Enterprise' (n 85) 438.

[88] *Hall v Hebert* (n 8).

the negligence action. Counsel for the appellant (Brett Walker QC) in the High Court in *Miller v Miller* pithily stated the argument as follows:

> The justification is that the whole body of the law should not contain contradictory elements. In the tort of negligence, a contradiction would arise if the act of which the claimant complains is the very thing which the claimant intended should occur as part of the joint criminal enterprise ...[89]

I submit that the claimant's claim should be rejected where it would undermine the internal cohesion of negligence law in the manner described. Questions of internal cohesion will arise where the execution of the joint venture, as contemplated by the parties, necessarily involves the defendant acting in a manner that would fall below the standard of care ordinarily expected for that activity. In that circumstance, the claimant could not reasonably expect the defendant to execute the enterprise and at the same time execute the ordinary standard of care. In the words of Black CJ and Beazley J in *Italiano v Barbaro*, that aspect of the relationship between the parties that comprised the joint commission of a crime might involve 'conflicting demands of the joint criminal activity and the safety of the participants'.[90] The imposition on the defendant of the ordinary standard of care in that circumstance would impose an obligation that is incompatible with the actual expectations of the parties.

A closely related argument is that the *Joyce* principle—at least in its 'no breach' form—is required in order to maintain the coherence of the negligence action as a manifestation of corrective justice. It is to that point that I will now turn.

VIII. Corrective Justice Requires an Examination into the Standard of Care that could Reasonably be Expected

The *Joyce* principle embodies a relational approach to negligence liability. Where the features of the parties' relationship necessarily affect the degree of care that could reasonably be expected of the defendant, the normal standard of care must be displaced in order to preserve the equality of the parties to the interaction.[91] In the context of discussing the modification of the standard of care of children when playing, Beever points out that the relationship between the parties 'affects the normative character of their interaction' so that the claimant cannot expect the defendant to comply with the ordinary adult standard.[92] It would 'privilege the position of the claimant to insist upon the application of the ordinary adult

[89] *Miller v Miller* (n 7) 449 (during argument B W Walker QC).
[90] *Italiano v Barbaro* (n 28) 310.
[91] Beever, *Rediscovering the Law of Negligence* (n 5) 87–96.
[92] ibid 90.

standard' when it was clear to the claimant that the defendant was a child and this was the basis of their interaction.[93] This is an instance of a more general proposition advanced by Beever that the ordinary standard of care will not apply where the nature of the relationship between the parties would make it unfair as between them to apply the ordinary reasonable person standard.[94]

Applying this proposition to illegality claims, Beever recognises that there will be situations where the illegal relationship between the parties will require an examination into whether the normal standard of care could reasonably be expected.[95] It is important to note, however, that he views these situations as requiring *adjustment of the standard of care*, rather than as matters relevant to the assessment of *duty of care*.[96] Beever's argument is that there will be circumstances where the features of the relationship between the parties (such as the commission of a joint illegal act) requires a court to adjust the standard of care in order to preserve equality between the parties and do justice as between them.[97] This will (Beever says) be the case, for example, where one car thief knows the other will driver carelessly and yet nevertheless chooses to ride with the driver in that knowledge. In that case, the standard of care the claimant 'could rightly expect of the defendant was that of a careless driver'.[98]

Beever approaches these issues through the medium of standard of care rather than duty of care because he sees the former as playing the central role in mediating between the interests of the parties.[99] In order to fulfil this role, the standard of care must be adjusted where the characteristics of the parties affect the normative character of the relationship between them:[100] 'the point of the standard of care … is to do justice between the actual parties.'[101] Thus, he argues that McLachlin J's judgment in *Hall v Hebert* (where it was held that illegality must operate as a defence rather than a negation of the element of a claim), while understandable in the legal environment in which her Honour was operating, 'does not do justice to the fact that courts must set the standard of care with reference to the relationship between the parties'.[102]

To my knowledge, Weinrib has not addressed issues relating to the modification of the standard of care in great depth; however, it seems he also views the

[93] ibid. See also 376–67.

[94] ibid 90, 359–60.

[95] ibid 376–77.

[96] ibid 359–60, 375–77.

[97] ibid 375–77. See also A Beever, *Forgotten Justice: The Forms of Justice in the History of Legal and Political Theory* (Oxford, Oxford University Press, 2013) 257–59.

[98] Beever, *Rediscovering the Law of Negligence* ibid 376.

[99] ibid Ch 3; See also Beever, *Forgotten Justice* (n 97) 257–59.

[100] Beever, *Rediscovering the Law of Negligence* (n 5) 87–96. See also Beever, *Forgotten Justice* ibid 261.

[101] Beever, *Rediscovering the Law of Negligence* ibid 360.

[102] ibid 376. For a comprehensive examination of the divergent views taken in Australia and Canada to the proper role of duty of care at the time that the cases of *Gala v Preston* and *Hall v Hebert* were decided, see Rande W Kostal, 'Currents in the Counter-reformation: Illegality and Duty of Care in Canada and Australia' (1995) *Tort Law Review* 100.

standard of care as being relational in nature. For example, Weinrib indicates that the question whether a child is liable for the harm negligently inflicted on another must be mediated through the mechanism of standard of care, indicating that an adjusted objective standard applies in that situation.[103] It seems likely, therefore, that he would likewise view the illegal relationship of the parties as requiring an examination into whether there needs to be an adjustment of the standard of care.

The relational approach to standard of care is grounded in the judgment of Dixon J in *Insurance Commissioner v Joyce*, who considered that a claimant is 'to be entitled only to that standard of duty or of care which arises from the relation that he has established'.[104] Where the parties are jointly committing a crime, the claimant is entitled only to that standard of care that arises from the relations established with the defendant, and thus that standard might need to be 'adjusted to the exigencies' of the crime.[105] This might sometimes give rise to difficulties in determining the content of the attenuated standard of care.[106] However, as discussed above,[107] such difficulties can be overstated. The High Court in *Miller v Miller* acknowledged that 'Setting a norm of behaviour as between criminals may be difficult, but it is not impossible'.[108] Moreover, as my discussion progresses it will become clear that I take a restrictive view as to when the relationship between the parties requires displacement of the ordinary standard of care. A conclusion that the ordinary standard of care does not apply should be made only in exceptional cases, such as the drunken joyriding cases, where in effect *no* degree of care is required; that is, where the demands of the criminal enterprise outweigh *any* concern for the safety of the participants. In that situation, the driver in effect cannot be expected to exercise *any* level of care for the safety of the participants, because such an expectation would conflict with the execution of the enterprise. In that circumstance, there is no need to determine a standard of care, as none could reasonably be expected. If, contrary to this view, it was thought necessary to determine a standard of care, the standard would be that of the defendant intent on executing the demands of an inherently dangerous joint criminal enterprise; for example, a driver intent on driving recklessly so as to engage in a joyride or to evade police. Although it is possible in other contexts for an attenuated standard of care to be breached,[109] in this particular context in effect no degree of care is owed—and hence the principles as formulated effectively involve an 'all or nothing' approach.

[103] Weinrib, *The Idea of Private Law*, (n 6) 183 fn 22.
[104] *Insurance Commissioner v Joyce* (n 4) 56.
[105] *cf Cook v Cook* (n 49) 383 (Mason CJ, Wilson, Deane and Dawson JJ).
[106] Dietrich, 'The decline of contributory negligence and apportionment' (n 84) 16.
[107] See text to notes 31–43.
[108] *Miller v Miller* (n 7) [54].
[109] In *Cook v Cook* (n 49) the defendant was held to have breached the standard of care that could reasonably be expected of an unqualified and inexperienced driver.

The implication of the corrective justice account of the relational nature of standard of care is that the High Court has taken a wrong turn in suggesting that relational factors that impact on the expected degree of care must now be assessed according to whether a duty of care was owed, rather than through the application of variable standards of care.[110] Whether this is correct cannot be answered satisfactorily within the confines of this book. In any event, the same relational factors are relevant on either approach. Thus, the reasoning in the cases discussed above remains valid, albeit from a corrective justice perspective; the concerns underlying *Joyce* are relevant to the question of standard of care rather than (as they are currently being treated in the case law) to duty of care.

Moreover, while the conceptually superior approach might be to mediate the features of the parties' relationship that affect the level of care to be expected through the element of standard of care, consideration of those features as part of the duty element is at least broadly consistent with the relational focus and correlative structure of corrective justice. In his chapter 'The Disintegration of Duty' in *Corrective Justice*, Weinrib welcomes the emphasis on the relational nature of the considerations taken into account by the Supreme Court of Canada in *Cooper v Hobart* to the determination of duty of care.[111] Weinrib appears to acknowledge that other relational factors (in addition to reasonable foreseeability) will be relevant to the assessment of duty of care, provided that they are relevant to the inquiry 'into the risks by reference to which the defendant's action is characterised as negligent'.[112] It is submitted that the *Joyce* principle, even when applied as a question of duty, does pursue that central inquiry. That inquiry is whether the claimant (as a participant in the joint venture) was a member of a class of persons who was *wrongfully* put at risk by the defendant's negligence. The focus is on the features of the parties' relationship rather than on external policy considerations, and reflects the need for the justifications for imposing a duty on the defendant to be the same as those that establish the claimant's right.

To summarise so far, my argument is that there will be some relationships based on a joint illegal activity that require a conclusion that, while the defendant's behaviour potentially was wrongful towards others, it was not wrongful *towards the claimant*. This will be because the claimant, through participation in the joint illegal enterprise, knew that the negligent conduct would be an incident of the execution of that enterprise. On this view, the claimant is not a member of the class of persons *wrongfully* put at risk: while others might be, the claimant as a criminal accomplice is not.[113] Conceptually, these relational factors should be addressed when setting the standard of care. However, the current 'no duty'

[110] Beever's work pre-dates *Imbree*; nevertheless, it is clear from his discussion of modified standards of care that he would consider it to be wrongly decided.

[111] Weinrib, *Corrective Justice* (n 5) 66–69, discussing *Cooper v Hobart* [2001] SCC 79, [2001] 3 SCR 537.

[112] Weinrib, *Corrective Justice* ibid 69.

[113] ibid 49; Weinrib, *The Idea of Private Law* (n 6) 160.

approach is consistent with the bipolar structure of negligence law and hence is consistent with the central tenets of corrective justice theory.

IX. The Requirements for the Establishment of the *Joyce* Principle

There was disagreement in the lower courts in *Miller v Miller* regarding whether an objective or subjective approach is appropriate; that is, is the question one of the subjective expectations of the claimant as to whether the defendant would act reasonably, or the objective expectations of the reasonable person in the circumstances? The claimant, a 16-year-old girl, stole a car to take herself and her sister home after a night out. The defendant (whom she called her 'uncle') insisted on driving the car. He did so recklessly, and the claimant was seriously injured in the resulting crash. At first instance, Schoombee DCJ focused on the risks that were understood and accepted by the claimant and her subjective expectations about the manner in which the defendant would control the car.[114] The Court of Appeal criticised this approach, however, and held that the test is an objective one: whether the claimant ought reasonably to have appreciated or foreseen the risks.[115] On my view, the test contains both subjective and objective elements. The subjective element relates to the claimant's knowledge of the risks, and the objective element to whether the claimant could, based on that knowledge of the risks, reasonably expect the defendant to act safely. This requires further explanation.

The *Joyce* principle requires actual subjective knowledge or appreciation by the claimant of the defendant's condition that makes the defendant incapable of acting safely.[116] In *Imbree v McNeilly*, Gummow, Hayne and Kiefel JJ considered the *Joyce* principle to share the same underpinnings as the defence of voluntary assumption of risk, which requires actual knowledge of the risks.[117] The focus should thus be on whether the claimant had *actual* knowledge and understanding that the defendant will act carelessly; not whether this is something that the hypothetical reasonable claimant *should have known or understood*.[118] This is also consistent with Beever's approach.[119] However, unlike voluntary assumption of

[114] *Miller v Miller* WADC (n 54) [96]–[107]. Her Honour relied on statements to this effect by Pullin JA in *Avram v Gusaroski* (n 53) [14] (Malcolm CJ agreeing).

[115] *Miller v Miller* WASCA (n 59) [79]–[81] (Buss JA), [152]–[153] (Newnes JA).

[116] *Avram v Gusaroski* (n 53) [14] (Pullin JA), 413 [75] (Murray AJA, Malcolm CJ agreeing with both); *Wok v O'Keefe* [2006] WADC 159, [20] (Muller DCJ); *Harmer v Hare* (n 52) 53–54 [205] (Whealy JA, Beazley and Sackville AJA agreeing); *Stafford v Carrigy-Ryan* (n 52) [77] (Sidis AJ). See further K Hogg, 'Guest Passengers: A Drunk Driver's Defences' (1994) 2 *Torts Law Journal* 37, 45–47.

[117] *Imbree v McNeilly* (n 44) [77].

[118] *Avram v Gusaroski* (n 53) [14] (Pullin JA), [75] (Murray AJA, Malcolm CJ agreeing with both); *Miller v Miller* WADC (n 54) [73], [97] (Schoombee DCJ).

[119] Beever, *Rediscovering the Law of Negligence* (n 5) 360, 376.

risk, it is not necessary to show that the claimant knew the exact extent of the carelessness that would be exercised and consented to it, but merely that the claimant contemplated that careless behaviour would be a feature of the joint venture.[120] Knowledge or awareness of this fact can be established directly from the claimant's own evidence, from witness evidence, as well as by inference from that evidence and the surrounding facts and circumstances: that is, inferred from the objective facts known to the claimant.[121]

An objective element is also involved by virtue of the fact that the focus—again, unlike the defence of voluntary assumption of risk—is not on whether the claimant consented to bear that risk, but whether the claimant could in those circumstances reasonably expect the defendant to exercise the ordinary standard of care. This by its nature imports an objective determination by the court: whether the claimant in those circumstances *could* (reasonably) expect the defendant to act sensibly based on the known risks, not whether the claimant *did* expect the defendant to act sensibly. This approach conforms to the *Gala v Preston* formulation and Beever's approach.[122]

The implication of these principles for the joint illegality cases is that it will be necessary to examine the evidence to determine the claimant's knowledge, actual or inferred, as to the purpose and scope of the joint venture and evaluate the degree of care the claimant could reasonably expect the defendant to exercise in that circumstance. As I will discuss in the next section, this requires an examination of the steps that the parties contemplated would be taken in the execution of the criminal purpose. The claim should not be permitted where the defendant's performance of the venture as contemplated by the parties carried an inherent risk that the defendant would act in a manner that is incompatible with an obligation to act carefully.

X. Application of the *Joyce* Principle to Joint Illegal Enterprise Cases

A. Nature, Purpose and Scope of the Joint Enterprise

The nature, purpose and scope of the joint criminal venture must be incompatible with a reasonable expectation that the normal standard of care would be exercised. More particularly, the evidence must be examined to ascertain whether one of the

[120] *Miller v Miller* WADC (n 54) (Schoombee DCJ).

[121] *Howard v Hamilton* (1996) 16 WAR 292, 308 (Murray AJA). Where the risk should have been apparent, a court might not credit the evidence of the claimant that he or she had no knowledge of that risk: Mark Lunney, 'Personal Responsibility and the "New" Volenti' (2005) 13 *Tort Law Review* 76, 80.

[122] *Gala v Preston* (n 13) 254; Beever, *Rediscovering the Law of Negligence* (n 5) 360. See also *Zanner v Zanner* (n 55) [46] (Tobias JA, Allsop P and Young JA agreeing).

key features of the joint enterprise, or one of the steps to be taken in its execution, necessarily or inevitably involved the risk of the kind that materialised. It would be unreasonable to impose an obligation on the defendant to act in a manner that is inconsistent with the parties' expectations. In other words, the *Joyce* principle will apply where the demands of the joint criminal activity inherently conflict with the safety of the participants.[123]

A review of the authorities indicates that the *Joyce* principle, though regularly invoked, is rarely successful in claims against intoxicated and/or underage and inexperienced drivers.[124] This has led Goudkamp to query whether there is a valid basis for applying the principle in the joint illegality cases, but not in other cases that do not involve joint illegality but where questions might also legitimately arise about the claimant's knowledge of the defendant's inability to exercise the ordinary standard of care.[125] My argument is that the relationship of the parties in the joint illegality cases will (sometimes) involve an additional element not present in the cases involving drunk or inexperienced drivers: namely, the understanding of the parties that the illegal venture is to be conducted in a particular (dangerous) manner to successfully effect the commission of the crime.[126] There can be no reasonable basis for expecting that the defendant will act carefully if the venture between the parties necessarily requires that the defendant will not act carefully. The relationship of a passenger to a drunk or inexperienced driver does not, however, necessarily possess these features. A passenger in a car driven by an inexperienced driver might reasonably expect that the driver will drive more cautiously in order to compensate for the lack of experience and formal qualifications,[127] and (if the driver is unqualified) to escape the attention of the police. Further, unless the parties have agreed to embark on a dangerous venture (such as a joyride or a street race), reckless or dangerous driving is not an inherent feature (an 'objective') of the trip. Thus, a drive undertaken for normal purposes (such as to drive to a particular destination) is not undertaken for the purpose of driving in an unsafe manner. Similar considerations apply to a passenger in a car driven by a drunk driver. Unless the parties have set out together on a wild drunken joyride, where the pursuit of the venture necessarily requires that the defendant drive in an unsafe manner, the purpose of the trip can be effected without negligence and the *Joyce* principle will have no application.

Accordingly, the relevant enquiry is whether it is necessary for the defendant to act in an unsafe manner in order to perform his or her part in the venture undertaken by the parties. It is the incompatibility of an expectation that reasonable

[123] *Italiano v Barbaro* (n 28) 310 (Black CJ and Beazley J).

[124] See, eg, *Avram v Gusaroski* (n 53); *Wok v O'O'Keefe* (n 116); *Zanner v Zanner* (n 55); *Green v Nominal Defendant* (n 52); *Stafford v Carrigy-Ryan* (n 52).

[125] Goudkamp, 'The Defence of Joint Illegal Enterprise' (n 85) 438.

[126] Thus, it has been suggested that the joint illegal use of a vehicle can transform the relationship between the parties into one in which the ordinary duty of care is displaced: *Brown v Harding* (n 62) [40]; *Stafford v Carrigy-Ryan* (n 52) [79].

[127] *Cook v Cook* (n 49) 87 (Mason, Wilson, Deane and Dawson JJ).

care and skill will be exercised with the expectation that the defendant will execute the joint illegal enterprise as planned that distinguishes these cases from other relationships in which the principle has sought to be invoked, such as passenger–drunk driver relationships. The justification for denial of liability is based on the fact that 'a contradiction would arise if the act of which the claimant complains is the very thing which the claimant intended should occur as part of the joint criminal enterprise'.[128]

B. Time at Which the Claimant's Knowledge of the Risks Is to be Assessed

The authorities suggest that the question whether the claimant understood that he or she was agreeing to involvement in an activity that gave rise to an increased risk of harm is a matter to be assessed at the time when the claimant first enters into the activity. In the case of a motor vehicle accident, this will be when the claimant first decided to accept a lift with the defendant.[129] The *Joyce* principle does not apply to defeat the claim if the claimant only became aware of the risks once the vehicle was moving, even if the claimant did not ask to be let out of the vehicle.[130]

However, what if the claimant does ask to be let out of the vehicle once the driving turns careless? The courts have generally rejected the relevance of a withdrawal on the basis that claimants cannot avoid responsibility by voluntarily placing themselves in a situation of risk and then claim to have withdrawn from that situation at the point when the risk eventuated.[131] Given, however, that the basis for the negation of liability is the claimant's agreement to participate in a risky joint venture, it seems correct that a withdrawal from that venture should preclude the operation of the *Joyce* principle. The focus should be on the nature of the relationship of the parties at the time the alleged act of negligence occurred.[132] If the claimant had withdrawn from the joint illegal enterprise and could no longer be said to 'want' the defendant to act in the manner that carries the inherent risk of harm, then the normal duty (standard) of care is resurrected at that point.[133]

[128] *Miller v Miller* (n 7) 449 (during argument B W Walker QC).

[129] *Avram v Gusaroski* (n 53) [19] (Pullin JA, Malcolm CJ agreeing); *Miller v Miller* WADC (n 54) [97] (Schoombee DCJ); *Miller v Miller* WASCA (n 59) [79] (Buss JA), [154] (Newnes JA).

[130] *Avram v Gusaroski* ibid; *Miller v Miller* WADC ibid.

[131] See, example, *Stafford v Carrigy-Ryan* (n 52) [87]; *Miller v Miller* WASCA (n 59) [90] (Buss JA).

[132] *cf Italiano v Barbaro* (n 28) 311 (Black CJ and Beazley J).

[133] This approach to withdrawal is broadly analogous with the *locus poenitentiae* principle applied in restitution and trusts claims that a party to an illegal agreement can withdraw from that agreement and recover benefits conferred under it: *Patel v Mirza* [2014] EWCA Civ 1047 (CA).

XI. Joint Illegal Relations that Displace the Normal Standard of Care

In this section I will provide examples of claims that are likely to fall within the *Joyce* principle. It must be kept in mind that the application of the principle to the facts of a particular case will ultimately depend on the evidence as to the scope and character of the joint criminal venture and, consequently, the risks known to the claimant. In my discussion, I will focus on the leading cases in this area, rather than some of the more outlandish hypothetical examples given in the authorities. 'Old chestnuts', such as the safe-breaker example, are rarely of assistance in deciding on the facts of an individual case whether an illegality principle should apply.[134] I will also focus on personal injury cases, as these represent the cases that have come before the courts. It has been suggested that a *Joyce* principle would have no application to financial crimes.[135] This should not be assumed, however, as the principles I have formulated are not limited to *dangerous* joint illegal enterprises that create a risk of *physical* injury, but would apply wherever the risk of harm was inherent in the execution of that joint enterprise. The precise application to financial crimes cases would need to be determined in the light of the facts of a suitable case.

The *Joyce* principle provides an explanation for the refusal of compensation in cases where a stolen motor vehicle is driven recklessly for the purposes of a joy ride (as in *Pitts v Hunt*)[136] or where a vehicle is used for an illegal road race (as in *Bondarenko v Sommers*).[137] It also explains cases where a getaway vehicle is driven recklessly to escape from the scene of a crime (as in *Joyce v O'Brien*),[138] including where the police are in pursuit (as in *Fabre v Arenales*).[139]

A. The Joyriding Cases

The *Joyce* principle has a potential application in cases where the parties have embarked on a joyride. Parties contemplating a joyride can be taken to have contemplated that the vehicle will be driven at high speed in contravention of the road rules for the 'thrill' of it.[140] They intend that reckless driving will be a key feature of the trip. Accordingly, the pursuit of that purpose will necessarily adversely affect the manner in which the defendant drives the vehicle so that the risk of negligent

[134] ibid [75] (Gloster LJ).
[135] Fordham, 'Stop I Want to Get Out!' (n 85) 173 fn 52.
[136] *Pitts v Hunt* (n 2).
[137] *Bondarenko v Sommers* (1968) 68 SR (NSW) 269.
[138] *Joyce v O'Brien* (n 3).
[139] *Fabre v Arenales* (n 28).
[140] *Miller v Miller* WADC (n 54) [85] (Schoombee DCJ).

driving is inherent to the execution of the joint criminal purpose. In those circumstances, the claimant cannot reasonably expect the vehicle to be driven safely, and it would be unfair, between them, to apply the normal standard of care. The vehicle might or not be stolen; that is not the crucial question. The question is whether in all the circumstances the claimant understood that the vehicle would be driven dangerously and yet decided to participate in the dangerous venture.

The English case of *Pitts v Hunt*—not involving a stolen vehicle—arguably provides the strongest example of a case where the claim should be denied because of the clear evidence that the claimant had been encouraging dangerous driving as part of a joyride.[141] The claimant, a teenager, was a pillion passenger on a motorcycle ridden by the 16-year-old defendant, whom the claimant knew to be unlicensed and uninsured. Both claimant and defendant had been drinking and the claimant had been encouraging the driver to drive in a 'reckless, irresponsible and idiotic way'.[142] The motorcycle collided with a car, killing the defendant, and leaving the claimant with permanent disabilities. The very essence of the joint venture in *Pitts v Hunt* was the reckless driving. In that circumstance, it was not reasonable to expect that the defendant would drive safely; in fact, the claimant was encouraging him not to do so. In those circumstances, the English Court of Appeal was correct to conclude that the ordinary standard of care was displaced; the claimant could not, in effect, expect any degree of care to be exercised for his safety.[143]

In another English Court of Appeal case, *McCracken v Smith*, the claimant was injured when the trials bike on which he was a passenger collided with a minibus. The trials bike was stolen, but this had occurred at an indeterminate point in time before the accident, and there was no suggestion that this factor contributed to the accident. A trials bike is designed for off-road competition, and is not intended to be ridden on a road or to have a pillion passenger. The driver of the bike was a 16-year-old boy who did not have a driving licence, and who prior to the accident was driving the bike dangerously in a cycling lane. The claimant was successful in a negligence claim against both the driver of the bike and the driver of the minibus. Keith J at first instance rejected an argument that the claim against the driver of the bike was barred for illegality, and apportioned liability between the driver of the bike and the driver of the minibus on the ground they were both negligent.[144] The driver of the minibus appealed, inter alia, on the ground that the trial judge was wrong to reject the illegality defence. The main judgment in the Court of Appeal was delivered by Richards LJ who held that illegality doctrine applied to prevent a claim against the driver of the bike. The claimant was a participant in a joint illegal enterprise to drive the bike dangerously, and this participation was the cause of his injuries.[145] (These findings were in obiter only, as the driver of the bike had not appealed.) However, the driver of the minibus was liable for his

141 *Pitts v Hunt* (n 2).
142 ibid 36 (Beldam LJ).
143 ibid 49–51 (Balcombe LJ), 57–60 (Dillon LJ).
144 *McCracken v Smith* [2013] EWHC 3620 (QB) (*McCracken v Smith* EWHC).
145 *McCracken v Smith* (n 3) [20]–[24] (Richards LJ, Underhill and Christopher Clarke LJJ agreeing).

contribution to the accident. His Honour applied a causation analysis to reach this conclusion, though recognised that the answer would been easier if the court had been at liberty to adopt a duty-of-care analysis. The dangerous driving of the bike clearly did not impact on the nature of the duty or standard of care reasonably to be expected of the minibus driver, and hence the normal duty of care owed by a driver to another road user would apply.[146]

The decision in *McCracken v Smith* in respect of the minibus driver was clearly correct; there were no special features of the relationship between the claimant and this driver that would modify the normal expectation that the driver would drive competently. (I will address below the argument that this creates an anomaly whereby the criminally complicit driver is provided with a defence, but not an 'innocent' third-party driver.)[147] The decision that the illegality doctrine applied to the driver of the bike requires further analysis. The trial judge (Keith J) in rejecting the application of illegality doctrine emphasised that the claimant had not been encouraging the driver of the bike to drive the bike dangerously; he had just been going along for the ride.[148] The case is therefore not as strong as *Pitts v Hunt* in that the element of encouragement to drive recklessly was not present. However, it seems that there was sufficient evidence to support the conclusion of the Court of Appeal that the claimant was a party to the enterprise to drive the bike dangerously, and that he could not in those circumstances expect the driver to exercise the normal standard of care owed to a passenger. The factors relied upon by Richards LJ in the Court of Appeal to reach this conclusion were that the claimant: knew that trials bikes are not suitable for pillion passengers or being ridden on a road; knew that the driver did not have a valid licence; knew that trials bikes had previously been ridden on the road in a dangerous manner, and must have expected that this would happen when he was picked up; and had not taken a couple of opportunities to get off the bike despite the fact that it was being driven dangerously.[149] In those circumstance Richards LJ concluded that the claimant was not just getting a lift; he was going along for a ride with 'whatever that entailed' and what it 'entailed' was the very kind of dangerous driving that in fact occurred.[150] Moreover, although there was no evidence that the claimant had given express encouragement to drive dangerously, the inference could be drawn that he gave implied encouragement by getting on the bike and remaining on it in the identified circumstances.[151] There is thus considerable weight to Richard LJ's conclusion that it was 'the common purpose from the outset' that the ride would be a joyride, the essence of which was that the bike would be ridden dangerously.[152] In those circumstances the claimant could not reasonably expect the driver to drive safely.

[146] ibid [50].
[147] See text to nn 176–83.
[148] *McCracken v Smith* EWHC (n 144), see [50] in particular.
[149] *McCracken v Smith* (n 3) [20]–[24].
[150] ibid [20].
[151] ibid [20]–[24].
[152] ibid [31].

There is no basis for application of the *Joyce* principle where reckless driving is not one of the contemplated purposes of the joint enterprise.[153] The facts of *Miller v Miller* arguably support a conclusion that the execution of the joint venture in that case did not inherently involve reckless driving. The trial judge, Schoombee DCJ, found that the purpose of the joint illegal use of the vehicle was not to engage in a joyride, but to take the participants home.[154] Judge Schoombee observes (correctly) that the mere fact the parties were driving in a stolen car should not by itself be taken as justifying a conclusion that the claimant must have understood that reckless driving would be a key feature of the trip home, at least in the absence of evidence that the parties were about to embark on a joyride.[155] While the claimant must be taken to have understood that there was the possibility of a police pursuit (and thus a risk the driver would act recklessly in that event), this was not the risk that actually materialised. In the absence of a pursuit, the claimant could reasonably expect that the driver would exercise the ordinary standard of care while taking herself and the other passengers home.

In the Court of Appeal in *Miller v Miller*, Buss and Newnes JJA point out that there were other factors (in addition to the unlawful use of the car) that affected whether the claimant could reasonably expect the defendant would drive safely, including the knowledge that the defendant had been drinking and the gross overloading of the car.[156] Nevertheless, there was arguably too much emphasis in the Court of Appeal on the risks that could be foreseen by the claimant, rather than whether it was contemplated by the parties that reckless driving would be an element of the trip home. It is arguable that the Court of Appeal failed to give due weight to the relationship between the claimant and defendant (the claimant called the defendant her 'uncle') and the claimant's evidence that she trusted the defendant to look after her and her sister. It also failed to give due weight to the claimant's requests to be let out of the car once the driving became reckless; this is evidence that the claimant had not contemplated when agreeing to drive home with the defendant that the trip would be in the nature of the a wild joy ride. Further, there was an over-reliance in the judgments of the Court of Appeal on the fact that the defendant did not hold a valid driver's licence; the absence of a formal qualification does not mean that the defendant was incapable of driving the car safely. There is much to be said for the view that Schoombee DCJ's judgment correctly weighted the various features of the parties' relationship that made it reasonable for the claimant to expect that the normal standard of care would be exercised by the defendant in operating the vehicle.

Even if the parties did intend that a joyride (and hence reckless driving) would be a feature of the illegal use of the vehicle, if the accident that actually occurred is unrelated to the joyride, there will be no basis for applying the *Joyce* principle.

153 ibid.
154 *Miller v Miller* WADC (n 54) [86].
155 ibid [98]. See also *Brown v Harding* (n 62) [40].
156 *Miller v Miller* WASCA (n 59) [78] (Buss JA), [150]–[151] (Newnes JA).

In *Gala v Preston* (the facts are given earlier),[157] the High Court characterises the illegal enterprise as a 'spontaneously planned "joyride" or adventure', which was 'of its nature, fraught with serious risks' due to the heavy consumption of alcohol by the parties and the possibility that the theft could be reported to police, leading to the pursuit and arrest of the parties.[158] In those circumstances, the participants 'could not have had any reasonable basis for expecting that a driver of the vehicle would drive it according to ordinary standards of competence and care'.[159] However, that statement needs further examination with reference to the finding of the Full Court of the Supreme Court of Queensland that the circumstances of the case did not displace the ordinary standard of care. Justice Williams (Connolly J agreeing) in the Full Court allowed the claim on the basis that, at the material time, the claimant could reasonably expect that the driver would drive carefully; the accident occurred some hours after, and some distance from where, the vehicle was stolen, and they were not attempting to evade police at the time. In those circumstances, Williams J considered that the claimant could expect the ordinary standard of care to be exercised.[160] Likewise, McPherson J held that the risk that eventuated was not one that was an inherent risk of participation in the joint venture: 'The accident that occurred was not a foreseeable consequence of the illegal enterprise or a hazard incidental to or inherent in its execution'.[161]

This demonstrates that there must be a sufficient relationship between the risk of reckless driving agreed to as part of a decision to embark on a joyride, and the accident that actually occurred. In some cases, it might be possible to divide the criminal enterprise (and hence the relationship of the parties) into stages: one stage involving a joyride where the ordinary standard of care would not apply, and another stage merely involving the illegal use of the vehicle as a means of transportation when the claimant could reasonably expect the defendant to drive safely. Thus, if in *Gala v Preston* the joyriding activity had ceased by the time of the accident and the parties were simply using the vehicle to take a trip 'up north' (the conclusion of the Full Court), there is no unfairness to the parties in applying the ordinary standard of care as between them.

B. Illegal Road-racing

The same principles would apply where the claimant is injured while a participant in an illegal road race, as in *Bondarenko v Sommers*.[162] If a similar case were to arise today, it would presumably not be difficult to establish that the nature of the

[157] See text to nn 25–27.
[158] *Gala v Preston* (n 13) 254.
[159] ibid.
[160] *Preston v Gala* (n 66) 179.
[161] ibid 172.
[162] *Bondarenko v Sommers* (n 137).

enterprise (to conduct a high speed road race) was such that the vehicles would be driven in a manner that necessarily (and adversely) affected the care that would be exercised by the driver. Thus, Jacobs JA stated that the parties had engaged in an 'extremely dangerous kind of race'.[163] In *Jackson v Harrison*, Mason J refers to the case (of *Bondarenko v Sommers*) as one where relief was correctly refused on the basis that it 'entail[ed] an agreement to drive the car recklessly'.[164] In those circumstances, the claimant could not reasonably expect the defendant to act with competence and care, and it would be unfair, as between the parties, to apply the ordinary standard of care.

C. Fleeing the Scene of a Crime

Another type of case that attracts the operation of the *Joyce* principle is where the parties are fleeing the scene of a crime in circumstances where they contemplated that a speedy getaway would be required. In *Joyce v O'Brien*, the claimant sustained injuries when he fell from a van that was fleeing the scene of a theft.[165] The claimant and defendant had stolen a set of ladders from the front garden of a house, which they put into the back of the van. The claimant rode in the back with the ladders, while the defendant drove the van at high speed along side streets. The doors of the van could not close as the ladders were too long, so the claimant was holding onto the ladders while at the same time also trying to hang onto the door or roof with his other hand while the open door was flapping. The claimant was unable to stabilise himself when the defendant took a couple of sharp turns at high speed, and he fell from the van, suffering a serious head injury. The defendant subsequently pleaded guilty to dangerous driving. The trial judge (Cooke J) found from the available evidence (mainly witness statements) that the parties were both participating in a criminal enterprise that had two elements: the theft of the ladders; and the unlawful removal of them in a van. His Honour further found that 'speed was of the essence of the getaway and the claimant's actions were an essential part of the joint enterprise'.[166] The only means of making the speedy getaway, where there was no time to properly secure the ladder by rope, was for the claimant to engage in a dangerous attempt to secure the ladders in the way that he did.[167]

[163] ibid 279.

[164] *Jackson v Harrison* (n 13) 456. Although the claimant might not have voluntarily accepted the risk of the very act of negligence that occurred (see Jacobs JA in *Bondarenko v Sommers* (n 137) at 279–80), it should not be difficult to persuade a court that reckless driving would be an inherent risk of engaging in a high-speed road race.

[165] *Joyce v O'Brien* (n 3).

[166] *Joyce v O'Brien* [2012] EWHC 1324 (QB) [37] (*Joyce v O'Brien* EWHC).

[167] ibid [46].

On appeal, Elias LJ (Rafferty and Ryder LJJ agreeing) agreed that there was an 'abundance of evidence' that a key feature of the joint enterprise was the plan to quickly leave the scene so as to avoid detection of the theft.[168] Counsel for the claimant conceded this point, and conceded also that a degree of careless driving was 'inevitably envisaged' by the claimant.[169] Elias LJ rejected an argument by the claimant that the reckless driving fell outside the scope of the joint enterprise, noting that there 'is no sensible basis for asserting that the very act which naturally arises in a quick getaway, namely driving too fast for the nature of the road, takes the case outside the scope of the joint enterprise'.[170] There was sufficient evidence that, to the claimant's knowledge, one of the steps involved in the execution of the joint venture was that the defendant would drive in a manner and at a speed that did not give sufficiently careful consideration to the safety of the claimant in the back of the van. While bound by the authority of *Gray v Thames Trains Ltd*[171] to apply these principles through a test of causation, Elias LJ's analysis in substance embodies the *Joyce* principle.

The case of *Fabre v Arenales* provides direct authority for the application of the *Joyce* principle to the getaway cases.[172] This case involved an accident that occurred while the claimant and defendant were attempting to flee the scene of a crime (an attempted robbery); there were also the added elements that they were in a stolen car and the police were in pursuit. The claimant knew of the presence of the police car before setting off, and was attempting (with the defendant) to escape apprehension. The New South Wales Court of Appeal (Mahoney JA; Priestley and Sheller JJA agreeing) held that the crucial question following *Gala v Preston* is whether the claimant could reasonably expect the defendant to act in a different (safer) manner. Justice Mahoney concluded on the facts that the claimant 'could not expect from him [the defendant] any more care than in fact he took' because 'What happened, namely, the car striking the pillar box and the wall, was the kind of thing apt to happen in such a venture'.[173] While the claimant might not have consented to the precise manoeuvres undertaken by the defendant, she was a party to the escape and the driving by the defendant (driving fast, cutting corners) was of a kind that was to be expected as part of an escape.[174] The circumstances of the getaway sufficiently altered the relationship of the parties from merely that of driver–passenger such that the claimant could not reasonably expect the defendant to adhere to the normal standards of competence and care expected of a driver.[175]

[168] *Joyce v O'Brien* (n 3) [43]–[44].
[169] ibid.
[170] ibid [46].
[171] *Gray v Thames Trains Ltd* (n 1).
[172] *Fabre v Arenales* (n 28).
[173] ibid 453.
[174] ibid.
[175] A further example is provided by *Ashton v Turner* (n 2) (parties fleeing the scene of a burglary).

XII. Does the *Joyce* Principle Give an Unjustified Advantage to a Criminal Accomplice?

One criticism of any rule that precludes recovery by a claimant against a criminal accomplice is that it gives a complicit defendant an unjustified advantage over a non-complicit defendant.[176] For example, should a stolen car be involved in an accident that was caused by the negligence of a third-party driver, or by a driver who was unaware that the car was stolen, that non-complicit driver will be required to compensate the claimant for injuries sustained. This is said to give rise to the anomalous result that the 'innocent' driver is denied a defence that is available to the claimant's criminal confederate. 'Justice hardly seems served by a rule which penalizes a defendant for his innocence but not for his guilt'.[177] This 'anomalous result' has now arisen in the English Court of Appeal case in *McCracken v Smith*.[178] In that case it was held that a participant in a joint enterprise to drive a motorbike dangerously was prevented from bringing a claim against the driver of the bike, but could bring a claim against the driver of another vehicle whose negligence contributed to the accident.[179] Lord Justice Richards (Underhill and Christopher Clarke LJJ agreeing) recognised that this result is the inevitable consequence of approaching these claims as a question of duty of care:

> If the duty of care analysis formerly applied in the joint enterprise cases had any application here, it would tell decisively against the *ex turpi causa* defence succeeding. It is clear that the dangerous driving of the bike had no effect whatsoever on [the third party driver's] duty of care or on the standard of care reasonably to be expected of him.[180]

As this recognises, the result that the third party is liable but not the criminal accomplice simply arises from the relationship of the parties and the fact that negligence principles are designed 'to do justice between the actual parties [to the relationship]'.[181]

Moreover, it needs to be kept in mind that these principles are not directed specifically to provide a defence to that class of person who is a criminal accomplice. This is because the application of the *Joyce* principle is not dependent on the claimant's participation in a *criminal* enterprise (though this might well be the

[176] *Jackson v Harrison* (n 13) 453 (Mason J); Bruce Macdougall '*Ex Turpi Causa*: Should a Defence arise from a Base Cause?' (1991) 55 *Saskatchewan Law Review* 1, 25–28; RA Prentice, 'Of Tort Reform and Millionaire Muggers: Should an Obscure Equitable Doctrine be Revived to Dent the Litigation Crisis?' (1995) 32 *San Diego Law Review* 53, 91–92.

[177] WJ Ford, 'Tort and Illegality: The *Ex Turpi Causa* Defence in Negligence Law (Part Two)' (1977) 11 *Melbourne University Law Review* 164, 176. See also Goudkamp, 'The Defence of Joint Illegal Enterprise' (n 85) 436.

[178] *McCracken v Smith* (n 3).

[179] ibid [52]–[53].

[180] ibid [50].

[181] Beever, *Rediscovering the Law of Negligence* (n 5) 360.

main context in which they would apply). The *Joyce* principle will apply wherever the evidence demonstrates that the parties have jointly embarked on a venture (whether of a criminal nature or not) that is inherently hazardous and therefore carries an increased risk of injury which materialises. The fact that the parties are engaged in criminal conduct at the time of the injury might well form the evidential basis for the application of these principles. However, the character of the conduct as criminal is, in principle, irrelevant. Accordingly, the *Joyce* principle should not be characterised as an 'illegality principle'. In this respect, Beever has observed that the concerns that underlie the *Joyce* principle 'have nothing to do with illegality'.[182]

Justice Sopinka makes the same point in his dissenting judgment in *Hall v Hebert*:

> Criminal conduct can be the basis for negating a duty of care not because it is criminal but because it can be inferred from the conduct itself, apart from its criminal character, that no reasonable expectation of care existed on the part of the person injured.[183]

XIII. Interaction with Defences

It is worth briefly making the point that, assuming the claimant can establish a prima facie case, an apportionment of damages will be made for contributory negligence. The difference between a 'defence' based on the *Joyce* principle and contributory negligence principles was explained by Pullin JA in *Avram v Gusaroski*.[184] His Honour points out that the application of the *Joyce* principle depends on the claimant's subjective knowledge of the risks, whereas contributory negligence is based on objective knowledge of the risks: that is, the risks that a reasonable person in the defendant's position should have known.[185] This explains why it is possible for the defendant to fail to establish the *Joyce* principle yet succeed in establishing that there was contributory negligence. Based on previous authorities, a claimant injured in the course of participating in the joint commission of a crime can expect to recover no more than about 50 per cent of his or her damages.[186]

It is also possible that in some cases, a defence of voluntary assumption of risk will apply. At common law, this defence is rarely successfully invoked due to the

[182] ibid 377.

[183] *Hall v Hebert* (n 8) 193.

[184] *Avram v Gusaroski* (n 53).

[185] ibid [25]–[28]. See also *Wok v O'Keefe* (n 116) [24] (Muller DCJ). In most states, the objective nature of the standard of care is enacted in legislation: Civil Liability Act 2002 (NSW), s 5R(2); Civil Liability Act 2003 (Qld), s 23(2); Civil Liability Act 2002 (Tas), s 23(2); Wrongs Act 1958 (Vic), s 62(2); Civil Liability Act 2002 (WA), s 5K(2).

[186] *Gala v Preston* (n 13) (60%); *Miller v Miller* WADC (n 54) (50%; figure agreed by the parties at trial); *Ashton v Turner* (n 2) (50%); *Joyce v O'Brien* EWHC (n 166) (50%); *McCracken v Smith* (n 3) (50% plus an additional 15% for failure to wear a helmet).

strict requirements placed on its application.[187] It applies only if the claimant freely and voluntarily, with full knowledge of the nature and extent of the risk, assumed both the physical and legal risk of the harm.[188] The *Joyce* principle will be easier to establish because, as mentioned, it will be necessary to show only that the claimant knew that the execution of the joint venture would involve some degree of careless behaviour and enhanced risk; it is not necessary to show that the claimant knew and consented to the *exact extent* of the carelessness that would be exercised. Thus, in *Joyce v O'Brien* Elias LJ rejected an argument that the claim should be permitted because, while a degree of careless driving was inevitably envisaged by the claimant, he did not contemplate that the defendant would drive in as reckless a manner as he did. This was rejected because the careless driving was of a kind that was within the scope of the joint venture.[189] The claimant's argument, if accepted, would have been sufficient, however, to preclude the defence of voluntary assumption of risk.[190]

Legislative reform in Australia has sought to make it easier to establish the defence of voluntary assumption of risk by creating a presumption that the claimant was aware of 'obvious risks', with some jurisdictions providing that it is sufficient to show that the claimant was aware of the type or kind of risk, even if not aware of the precise extent of the risk.[191] Nevertheless, even in those jurisdictions, there is still a requirement to establish that the claimant fully assumed the risk of injury and consented to absolve the defendant from legal responsibility, which will be an issue where the claimant was intoxicated.[192] Further, the defence has no application at all to motor accidents in the important jurisdiction of New South Wales,[193] and its application to drivers known to be drunk has been curtailed in some jurisdictions.[194] Accordingly, the *Joyce* principle is likely to have a more general application than *volenti*.

In any event, of course, these statutory defences become relevant only where a duty of care is otherwise found to arise. Thus, an important anterior question in all joint illegality cases should be whether the *Joyce* principle precludes a duty of care.

[187] The narrow application of the defence has been noted in: *Joslyn v Berryman* (n 49) [26]–[27] (McHugh J); *Imbree v McNeilly* (n 44) [79] (Gummow, Hayne and Kiefel JJ). See also J Goudkamp, 'Defences to Negligence' in C Sappideen and P Vines (eds), *Fleming's The Law of Torts*, 10th ed (Sydney, Lawbook Co, 2011) 335; N Katter, 'Negligence and Intoxication; Has Civil Liability Reform Gone Too Far?' (2006) 11(2) *Deakin Law Review* 161, 171

[188] *Imbree v McNeilly* ibid [81] (Gummow, Hayne and Kiefel JJ).

[189] *Joyce v O'Brien* (n 3) [44]–[46].

[190] While statutory provisions in each Australian jurisdiction deem a claimant to be aware of 'obvious risks', these are unlikely to affect this analysis as the full extent of the reckless driving might not be construed as an 'obvious' risk.

[191] Civil Liability Act 2002 (NSW), s 5G(2); Civil Liability Act 2003 (Qld), s 14(2); Civil Liability Act 1936 (SA), s 37(2); Civil Liability Act 2002 (Tas), s 16(2); Civil Liability Act 2002 (WA), s 5N(2).

[192] This has led Mark Lunney to question the utility of these reforms: M Lunney, 'Personal Responsibility and the "New" Volenti' (n 121) 87.

[193] Motor Accidents Act 1998 (NSW), s 76; Motor Accidents Compensation Act 1999 (NSW), s 140. The defence has also been abolished in respect of motor vehicle accidents in the United Kingdom: see Road Traffic Act 1998 (UK), s 149(3).

[194] Civil Liability Act 2003 (QLD), s 48(5); Civil Liability Act 1936 (SA), s 47(6).

XIV. Conclusion

Corrective justice requires an enquiry into the standard of care that the claimant could reasonably expect the defendant to exercise in the circumstances of their particular relationship. The *Joyce* principle, in the form developed in this chapter, facilitates this enquiry and provides the necessary analytical framework for determining circumstances when one participant to an illegal enterprise will not be required to compensate another participant for injuries suffered in the commission of the enterprise. The relational principle developed in this chapter is consistent with corrective justice and is required to preserve the coherence of the law; in this situation the internal coherence of the negligence action.

11

Conclusion

Lord Justice Etherton in *Les Laboratoires Servier v Apotex Inc* observed that the jurisprudence surrounding claims connected to illegal conduct 'has been an evolving one, but its evolution has not followed a consistent pattern'.[1] This area is characterised by contradictory principles and case law, and there remains considerable uncertainty about the correct basis of illegality doctrine.[2] These statements apply with the most force to English law, where the courts consistently have failed to identify a single overarching test to resolve claims connected with illegal conduct, relying instead on a variety of unstable and subjective public policy tests. It has been suggested that achieving certainty in this area after centuries of confusion is not possible.[3] Peter Birks was less pessimistic about the ability of private law to move toward an intelligible theory of illegality, remarking that '[t]he one great advantage of the common law is that, where it falls into trouble, it is never more than one great case away from pulling itself together'.[4] Birks recognised that the only rational basis for a doctrine of illegality is the principle of coherence, or (expressed negatively), the principle against 'self-stultification'.[5]

While the decision of the Australian High Court in *Miller v Miller* might not be that 'one great case' referred to by Birks, it does move Australian law away from public policy confusion and down a more principled path based on the need to preserve the coherence of the legal system.[6] There is also an emerging recognition in the Australian courts of the need to use relational rather than public policy reasoning to resolve claims for harm sustained during the commission of a joint illegal enterprise. These developments indicate that the Australian common law is gradually evolving in a manner consistent with corrective justice and the principle of coherence. The existing state of the common law is not, however, entirely satisfactory or certain and in this book I have sought to redress the gaps and deficiencies in this area. I have explained the scope and limits of the statutory purpose explanation, as well as the principles that should govern sanction-shifting claims and claims for illegal profits and earnings—areas which to date have not been

[1] [2012] EWCA Civ 593, [63].

[2] ibid. See also Lord Sumption, 'Reflections on the Law of Illegality' [2012] *Restitution Law Review* 1, 12.

[3] N Strauss, '*Ex Turpi Causa Oritur Actio?*' (2016) 132 *Law Quarterly Review* 236, 257.

[4] P Birks, 'Recovering Value Transferred Under An Illegal Contract' (2000) 1 *Theoretical Inquiries in Law* 155, 158.

[5] See generally ibid.

[6] *Miller v Miller* [2011] HCA 9, (2011) 242 CLR 446.

the subject of significant judicial consideration by Australian courts. I have also developed the relational principles that should determine the joint illegality cases, building upon principles advanced in analogous contexts such as claims by a passenger against a driver known to be drunk.

I have established that the only sound conceptual basis for an illegality principle is legal coherence. Other (non-coherence) policy criteria put forward for resolving these claims are inconsistent with principles of corrective justice and with established legal principles applying to all other categories of claimants. Robert Prentice has observed that a valid doctrine should have a strong theoretical underpinning and an articulated rationale that allows for clarity and consistency of application.[7] The various public policy approaches formulated in this area are inconsistent with the correlative structure of negligence liability and thus lack a strong theoretical justification. Moreover, public policy reasoning is unstable and leads to inconsistent and unpredictable decision-making. These defects of public policy reasoning apply to tests that are explicitly based on public policy considerations, such as that proposed by the majorities in *Hounga v Allen and Patel v Mirza*,[8] as well as to public policy tests that purport to have a doctrinal foundation. Lord Hoffman's causation test appears on first glance to have a sound basis in principles of causation, but on closer examination is revealed as being inconsistent with established principle, and with the bipolarity of negligence liability. It is also highly subjective in nature, as are related connection tests, such as the inextricable link test. Likewise, the standard of care approach previously adopted by the High Court of Australia in the context of claims arising from the commission of a joint illegal enterprise has been shown to be lacking a sound doctrinal and conceptual foundation. This approach distorts ordinary principles of duty and standard of care in pursuit of a policy of refusing to regulate the rights of parties jointly engaged in an offence of a serious nature.

Conversely, I have demonstrated that legal coherence provides a sound theoretical underpinning for a doctrine of illegality. It is a fundamental legal value that the legal system should function as a unified, coherent institution and an award of compensation to the wrongdoing claimant should be rejected where it would disrupt this coherence. Concerns about legal coherence are relational, not extra-relational concerns, and are concerns of corrective justice. The relationship between the parties includes their legal relationship and their rights and duties are to be determined by the whole body of law that governs that relationship.

I have formulated principles that clarify the ambit of the coherence rationale and that ensure that it will be applied in a consistent, predictable manner (Prentice's second criterion for sound legal doctrine). I have argued that legal coherence provides a reason for rejecting a claim connected to an illegality where the various branches of the law, working in combination, would operate so as to negate a

[7] RA Prentice, 'Of Tort Reform and Millionaire Muggers: Should an Obscure Equitable Doctrine be Revived to Dent the Litigation Crisis?' (1995) 32 *San Diego Law Review* 53, 88.

[8] *Hounga v Allen* [2014] UKSC 47, [2014] 1 WLR 2889; *Patel v Mirza* [2016] UKSC 42

requirement of establishing the claim. I have argued further that this will occur in two circumstances: (a) where an element of the claim would be incompatible with the purpose of the statute proscribing the conduct (the statutory purpose explanation); and (b) where the loss or damage claimed is authorised by the law and hence is not a legally recognisable form of loss or damage (the no loss or damage explanation).

The first ground—the statutory purpose explanation—was adopted by the High Court of Australia in *Miller v Miller* as the key criterion for resolving claims for injuries sustained while the claimant was engaged in illegal conduct, although I have demonstrated that it also has a potential application to sanction-shifting claims and claims for illegal profits and earnings.[9] The statutory purpose explanation is consistent with a coherence rationale: the rights and duties of the parties to a particular interaction must be determined in accordance with the statutory law governing that interaction.[10] However, this explanation is unlikely to become an important justification for the denial of liability as it will only be in exceptional cases where a clear purpose can be identified in the legislation to deny a civil claim. In the absence of a clear purpose, there is a risk that judges will make decisions based on their own predispositions as to whether the circumstances warrant relief.

The second ground—the no loss or damage explanation—has relevance to the sanction-shifting claims and claims for illegal profits and earnings, and develops ideas advanced by Beever in *Rediscovering the Law of Negligence*.[11] In respect of the sanction-shifting claims I have argued that some claims to recover compensation for a legal sanction should be rejected on the basis that, where that sanction was imposed personally on the claimant by the criminal or statutory law, the loss or damage suffered by the claimant is not one that the law will recognise. In corrective justice terms, where the loss or damage was authorised by the law there will be no violation of a right, or the legal value of the right that is violated will not encompass the factual loss mandated by the law. This reasoning will apply in order to disallow claims for: (i) a pecuniary penalty imposed on the claimant by the criminal and regulatory law; and (ii) non-pecuniary losses resulting from an order for detention. The legal system has directly authorised those losses and, accordingly, the claimant is unable to claim a legally recognised interest in the subject matter of those losses. This conclusion is not based on a finding of criminal culpability of the claimant, but rather on the legal ascription of responsibility to the claimant for those losses. The no loss or damage explanation is not a convincing explanation for denying claims for loss of earning capacity resulting from the conviction and detention of the claimant. This economic loss arises only indirectly from the application of the legal process and, unlike non-pecuniary losses arising from detention and pecuniary penalties, is not directly authorised by the law. I have argued that claims for loss of earning capacity should be permitted. I have

[9] Miller v Miller (n 6).
[10] EJ Weinrib, *Corrective Justice* (Oxford, Oxford University Press, 2012), 175–76.
[11] A Beever, *Rediscovering the Law of Negligence* (Oxford, Hart Publishing, 2007).

also argued that not all claims for illegal profits and earnings should be rejected. The central question in these claims will be whether the criminal or civil legal process would notionally have applied so as to 'forfeit' those profits to the State or to the defendant. It is only if this condition is met that it can be argued that the claimant has no legally recognised interest in the subject matter of the loss.

There is one other circumstance where the claimant's illegal conduct will impact on the availability of a claim. This is where the claimant is injured in the course of the commission of a joint illegal venture with the defendant, and the negligent behaviour that caused the harm was inherent in the execution of the venture as contemplated by the parties. Corrective justice requires that the claim must fail where the nature of the relationship between the parties is such that the claimant could not reasonably expect the defendant to exercise the ordinary standard of care. However, this outcome arises from the relationship between the parties, and is not based on the claimant's illegality per se.

As already mentioned, the current state of the common law of Australia in this area is evolving in a manner consistent with corrective justice. The intervention of the legislature in this area is therefore disappointing and unwelcome. The statutory provisions superimpose on the negligence action a defence that focuses one-sidedly on the claimant's illegal conduct, disrupting the coherence of the system in place to compensate victims for negligently inflicted injuries. These statutory defences disvalue corrective justice, and, in the absence of countervailing policy considerations, it must be questioned whether they have a legitimate role to play within a coherent system of compensation. They should be repealed, leaving the common law free to continue evolving in a coherent, principled manner.

If the views expressed in this book are accepted, a principle of illegality will have a clear—though narrow—sphere of operation. This conclusion would be confronting to those who would instinctively have reservations about permitting a claim by a wrongdoing claimant, in particular where the wrongdoing was of a very serious nature. However, it must be kept in mind that the elements of the negligence action are designed to mediate the interests of the wrongdoing claimant and defendant and ensure that compensation is recoverable only where the defendant acted *unreasonably* in violating the claimant's right. In this respect, the position of the parties to a joint illegal enterprise must be mediated through principles that determine whether the claimant could reasonably expect the defendant to adhere to the normal standard of care. In addition, even if the claim succeeds, it is likely that there will be a very substantial reduction for contributory negligence, perhaps near to 100 per cent.[12] The defence of voluntary assumption of risk might also be available on some facts. Accordingly, whatever the position might be in other areas of private law, in negligence law there are sufficient mechanisms independent of a

[12] In some Australian jurisdictions the reduction can be 100%: see, eg, Civil Liability Act 2002 (NSW), s 5S.

specific doctrine of illegality that ensure that the relief given (if any) will properly reflect the illegal conduct of the claimant.

It is also important to keep in mind the warning by Santow JA that 'an instinctive recoil [to claims arising from an illegality] is no substitute for the objective application of tort principle'.[13] To paraphrase Prentice, when initial feelings of discomfort subside and are replaced with reasoned legal analysis, it becomes clear that illegality doctrine should not be utilised to deny compensation merely because of a lack of sympathy with the claimant.[14] Judges should put aside any feelings of personal distaste about the claim, and focus exclusively on principled reasoning and the coherence of the claim within the whole body of law governing the parties' relationship. This is the only conceptually sound and coherent way forward for resolving illegality claims in negligence.

[13] *Hunter Area Health Service v Presland* (2005) 63 NSWLR 22, 105 [312], paraphrasing McHugh J in *Cole v South Tweed Heads Rugby League Football Club Ltd* (2004) 217 CLR 469, 485 [46].

[14] Prentice (n 7) 53.

INDEX

www.ingramcontent.com/pod-product-compliance
Ingram Content Group UK Ltd.
Pitfield, Milton Keynes, MK11 3LW, UK
UKHW021908150926
475560UK00003B/252

9 781509 906666